ANTHROPOLOGICAL PAPERS

MUSEUM OF ANTHROPOLOGY, UNIVERSITY OF MICHIGAN

NO. 49

THE MOCCASIN BLUFF SITE AND THE WOODLAND CULTURES OF SOUTHWESTERN MICHIGAN

BY

ROBERT LOUIS BETTAREL AND HALE G. SMITH

ANN ARBOR

THE UNIVERSITY OF MICHIGAN, 1973

ISBN (print): 978-0-932206-47-3
ISBN (ebook): 978-1-951519-21-6

Browse all of our books at
sites.lsa.umich.edu/archaeology-books.

Order our books from the University of Michigan
Press at www.press.umich.edu.

For permissions, questions, or manuscript queries, contact Museum publications by email at umma-pubs@umich.edu or visit the Museum website at lsa.umich.edu/ummaa.

PREFACE

This study is the result of the continuing interest and encouragement of Dr. James B. Griffin, Director of the Museum of Anthropology, The University of Michigan. His long-time interest in the prehistory of the Eastern United States and his continued support for research in the archaeology of the Upper Great Lakes lie behind this work. Dr. Griffin's interest in Moccasin Bluff stimulated the excavation of the site in 1948 under the direction of Hale G. Smith, and Griffin's continuing support and encouragement led to this report of those excavations. Hale Smith's name has been added as co-author in recognition of his contribution to this study.

In addition to Dr. Griffin I wish to acknowledge the aid and assistance of Mr. Volney H. Jones, Dr. Edwin N. Wilmsen, Dr. Joseph G. Jorgensen, and Dr. Noel J. Hicks, all members of my doctoral committee.

I also wish to express my thanks to the following people for aid and assistance in various parts of this study: Mr. William L. Laubernds for assistance in compiling the data used in Table 20, to Wilma Koschik, Suzanne Harris, and Mr. Fel Brunett for aid in plant identification, to Susan Greenberg for assistance in preparing some of the illustrations, to Dr. Henry van der Schalie for aid in identifying the Mollusca remains, and to Mr. William Adams for identifying some of the faunal remains.

The following local archaeologists also deserve mention for their assistance during the excavations: Mr. John C. Birdsell of South Bend, Indiana, whose large collection from the area was donated to the Museum of Anthropology, The University of Michigan; Mr. Amos Green, Robert Merrill, Harvey Franz, Mr. W. M. Cunningham, and Mr. Horner, all of Berrien County, Michigan.

Regular members of the crew who assisted Hale G. Smith in the excavations were Robert F. Gray, A. K. Guthe, and Henry R. Brett, who took the excellent photos of the excavation.

The Rackham School of Graduate Studies at The University of Michigan also assisted by providing funds for the project. In 1948 a grant from the Horace H. Rackham School of Graduate Studies Project 210 was awarded to Dr. Griffin to carry out the excavations at the Moccasin Bluff site with the assistance of Dr. Albert C. Spaulding, and in 1965 the author received a Rackham dissertation research grant to aid in the preparation of this report.

In addition I wish to thank Syracuse University for granting me leave in the year 1971-72 and Memorial University of Newfoundland for granting me a Postdoctoral fellowship for the same period. Part of the time spent on leave and on the fellowship allowed me to revise selected sections of the original work.

Special recognition should be given to Mr. Eli Lilly of Indianapolis who has been interested in the cultural affiliations of the Moccasin Bluff site for some thirty-five years. He has provided a generous subvention for the support of this publication.

Finally, I wish to call attention to the constant aid and support of Mr. George Stuber of the staff of the Museum of Anthropology. Mr. Stuber's heroic efforts in providing much excellent photographic work can be clearly seen in this volume. His constant aid, help, and good humor in innumerable other areas of this work, although less noticeable, were of equal importance. His stability, around which much of the detailed work of preparing a manuscript of this sort rests, provided the foundation for the work as a whole.

To the above mentioned people and to my very good friend, Mary Ellen Ragland, who helped edit the original manuscript, to my typist, Mrs. Helen Mysyk, and to Barbara Z. Bluestone, publications editor at the Museum of Anthropology, who did an outstanding piece of editing, must go most of the credit for any merit this work may have. Any shortcomings or deficiencies are strictly my own.

TABLE OF CONTENTS

LIST OF TABLES

LIST OF FIGURES

INTRODUCTION

THE Michigan area has recently been the focal point of several research programs designed to clarify some of the problems in the prehistory of the Upper Great Lakes. As a result of these programs a number of papers have appeared dealing with various aspects of the area's prehistory. Prehistoric plant and animal exploitation was outlined by Yarnell (1964) and Cleland (1966). The Middle Woodland cultures of western Michigan were examined by Flanders (1965). The Late Woodland period of southeastern Michigan was described by Fitting (1965) and McPherron (1967) reported on the Late Woodland period from the Mackinac area. A notable gap remains in the unreported Late Woodland cultures of western and southwestern Michigan. This report is an attempt to collect the currently available data and present an account of the late prehistoric groups in southwestern Michigan.

The core of material used in the study is the archaeological data from the Moccasin Bluff site, Berrien County, Michigan. This site was excavated in 1948 by a University of Michigan, Museum of Anthropology expedition. The site itself represents a large and important village of the Late Woodland period, with evidence of Early and Middle Woodland occupations. The site and its material were first identified by J. B. Griffin (1946: Fig. 7) as the McCartney focus. In the late 1940's it appeared that the site might be endangered by highway construction activities and a salvage operation was planned by Museum of Anthropology personnel. It was during this time, in the fall of 1947, that John C. Birdsell of South Bend, Indiana, donated a large collection from the site to the Museum. The following summer, during 1948, the Museum sent a field party to excavate the site.

A secondary interest of this study is to examine the subsistence base of the prehistoric societies and to investigate the nature of the relationship between the human population and other species in the eco-system. A complete description of these relationships is certainly not possible at this time but this study attempts to lay the foundation for an understanding of the prehistoric human ecology in this area.

It is with these general ideas and purposes in mind that the following study was undertaken.

I

THE SETTING

LYING in Berrien County, Michigan, just north of Buchanan, along the banks of the St. Joseph River, Moccasin Bluff occupies one of the more attractive locations in the state. The settlement was located on the west terrace of the river at an elevation of about 640 feet above sea level. The terrace here is about 15 feet above the river. At one time it apparently extended out to the bank of the river; but in 1870 it was cut back for passage of the railroad, and in 1933 it was cut back still farther to lay the bed for the Red Bud Trail Highway. Both of these construction projects seem to have removed significant portions of the site. The terrace at this point along the river forms a half circle with a radius of about 2000 feet, ringed on the north, west, and south by a semi-circular group of bluffs (see Fig. 1 and Pl. 1-3). These bluffs are known as Moccasin's Bluffs, named after a historic Potawatomi chief, Coggamoccasin (Macousin), whose village occupied the terrace around 1828. The bluffs, part of the Valparaiso morainic system, rise rapidly to stand nearly 140 feet above the terrace. The terrace itself is fairly level except for a slight 100-foot-wide, muck-filled depression—possibly an ancient channel of the river—which runs along the base of the bluffs. On the bluffs to the south of the site, ground water seeps out from many places and collects in the depression at their base where it forms a small marsh before draining off into the St. Joseph River.

The river at this point is rather broad and shallow with two small islands in its center. Local tradition records this as the spot where two fords crossed the river during the period of early settlement. The shallow, rocky bottom and the rapidly flowing water provide what may once have been an ideal setting for the spawning of sturgeon.

The region is characterized by a number of topographic features which form long ridges or belts that have a general northeast-southwest orientation. These are the moraines left by the Michigan lobe of the Wisconsin glaciation. More or less smooth

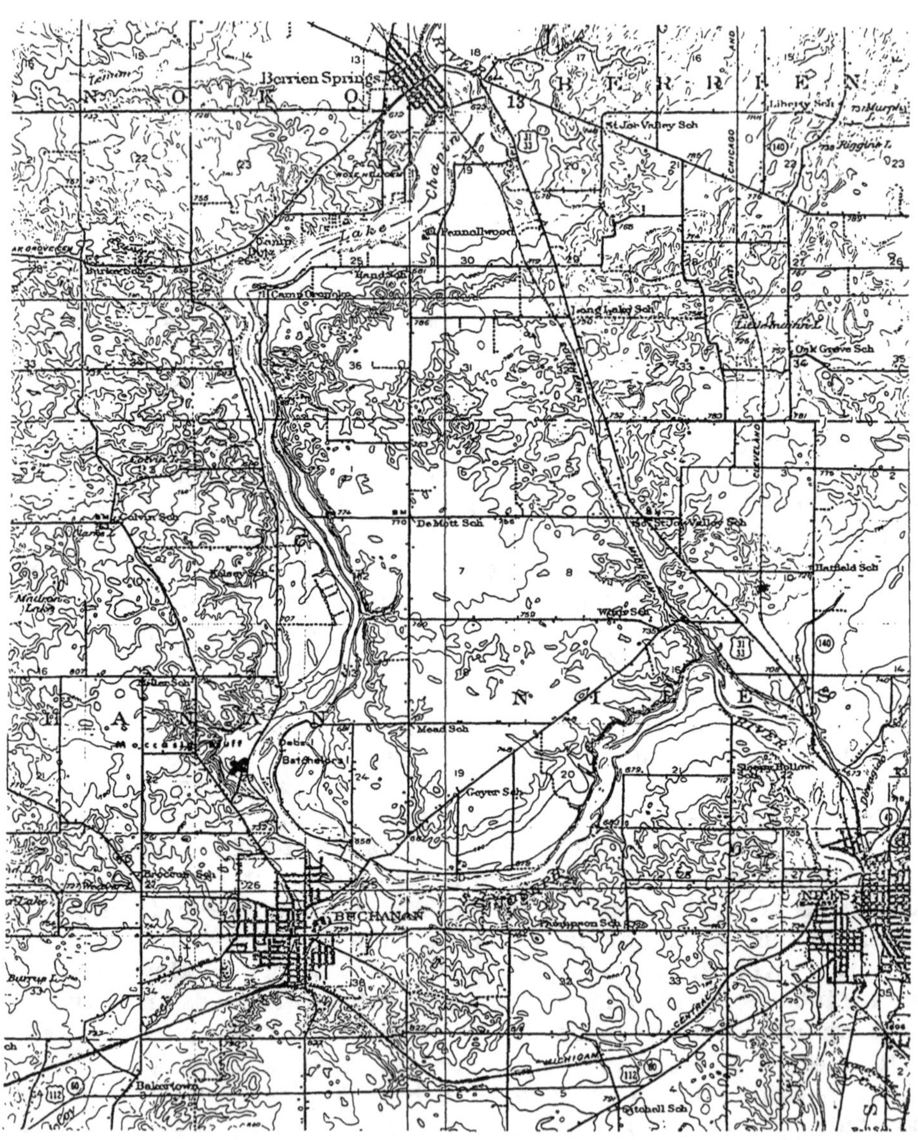

FIG. 1. Moccasin Bluff and Vicinity (U.S.G.S., Niles, Mich. Quad.).

belts between these moraines represent the outwash plains formed at the glacial front. A sand dune ridge runs along the Lake Michigan shore, reaching a width of almost a mile below Stevensville and narrowing toward the south and to the north at the mouth of the St. Joseph River.

Berrien County may be divided into four physiographic divisions which run roughly parallel to the shore of Lake Michigan. These divisions were first recorded by Veatch and Partridge:

> The most westerly division consists of a belt of sand dunes which have been heaped up on a discontinuous narrow low-lying plain bordering Lake Michigan. A remnant of this low-lying plain without the covering of sand dunes may be seen in the vicinity of the Grand Mere Lakes near Stevensville, and extensions of it, also without the covering of dunes, run inland up the Paw Paw and St. Joseph river valleys. The lowest plain bordering Lake Michigan is only 10 or 15 feet above the lake while the dunes occupying it may rise to a height of more than 200 feet.
>
> The second division is a nearly level plain at an elevation of about 40 to 80 feet above the level of Lake Michigan. In general, it lies back of the dunes, although at some points it reaches the lake and terminates as lake shore bluffs. Its width varies from six to eight miles except that it is considerably wider southeast of Benton Harbor where the terrace plains of the St. Joseph River valley merge with the broader lake shore plain. The plain is apparently the bed of an old glacial lake and consists of a floor of glacial clay, or till, which is partly exposed and partly covered with sand of varying thickness resulting in a complex association of wet and dry soils. Terrace plains, or benches of sand and gravel, presumably of the same physiographic age as the broader lake shore plain, extend inland up the valleys of the St. Joseph and Paw Paw rivers.
>
> The third division consists of broad swells, inconspicuous smooth ridges, and detached high plains lying at slightly higher levels than the second physiographic division. This land is from 80 to 120 feet above Lake Michigan and possibly represents a stage of a lake during the Glacial period, since the original inequalities and constructional features common to till plains and terminal moraines are absent, apparently having been smoothed off by wave action and obscured by deposition.
>
> The fourth major division is the plateau-like highland which occupies most of the southeastern and eastern parts of the county. In places, it is marked by a bold front facing the lake shore plain on the west. Its elevation ranges from 120 to a little more than 300 feet. above Lake Michigan. The area is of varied topography, including some broken land where deep basins and sharp slopes predominate, extensive smooth plains, and plains diversified by lakes, swamps, potholes and stream valleys. The surface features are of glacial origin and comprise till plains, terminal moraines and outwash plains. (1934:6-7).

Moccasin Bluff lies in the heart of the plateau highland division. In acreage this division ranks first. It also contains the best land for aboriginal agriculture, level sand and gravel plains with fertile, well-drained loams and sandy loams. These soils are easily worked with primitive technology and the sand, which gains heat rapidly, gives a warmth to the soil that is moderated by the presence of clay. Moisture is well proportioned: The porosity of the sand prevents the crops from drowning; the depth of the soil and the clay keep the soil from drying out.

Much of the area is well-drained by numerous creeks and streams that empty directly into Lake Michigan or that flow into the St. Joseph River, which winds its way along and through the various moraines, past St. Joseph, Michigan, and finally into Lake Michigan. The river itself is often tightly confined by the moraines and lacks extensive bottomlands until it is well past the site at Berrien Springs, where a small alluvial plain borders the river until it reaches the lake. Along the borders of the streams and the numerous small lakes that dot the area is much swamp and marsh land containing many of the resources exploited by the aboriginal peoples.

The Prehistoric and early Historic vegetation of the area is shown in Figure 2. The area was a mosaic of plant associations containing oak-hickory, beech-maple, and oak-pine woodlands, prairies or oak openings, swamps and marshes and, along the Lake Michigan shore, stands of hemlocks and white pines. The oak-hickory stands contained species such as red oak, white oak, black oak, hickory, and variable occurrences of sugar maple, beech, elm, cherry, occasional black walnut, butternut, tulip poplar, and other more southern species. The beech-maple stands included, in addition to sugar maple and beech, elm, ash, basswood, variable proportions of oaks, hickories, and black cherry. The slopes of the bluffs surrounding the site are today covered with poplar, basswood, ash, butternut, sycamore, walnut, hard maple, and cherry.

The climate of the area is somewhat milder than much of the surrounding region due to the modifying effect of Lake Michigan. Most of the county has an average growing season of 180 days per year, with the last spring frost expected somewhere around May 1, and the first frost of the fall about October 20. On the average, the area receives about 34 inches of rainfall per year, distributed evenly throughout the year. The prevailing winds are from the southwest; occasional winds come from the northwest. Due to the favorable climate and adequate rainfall, the area is today noted for its orchards and truck farming. Apples, peaches,

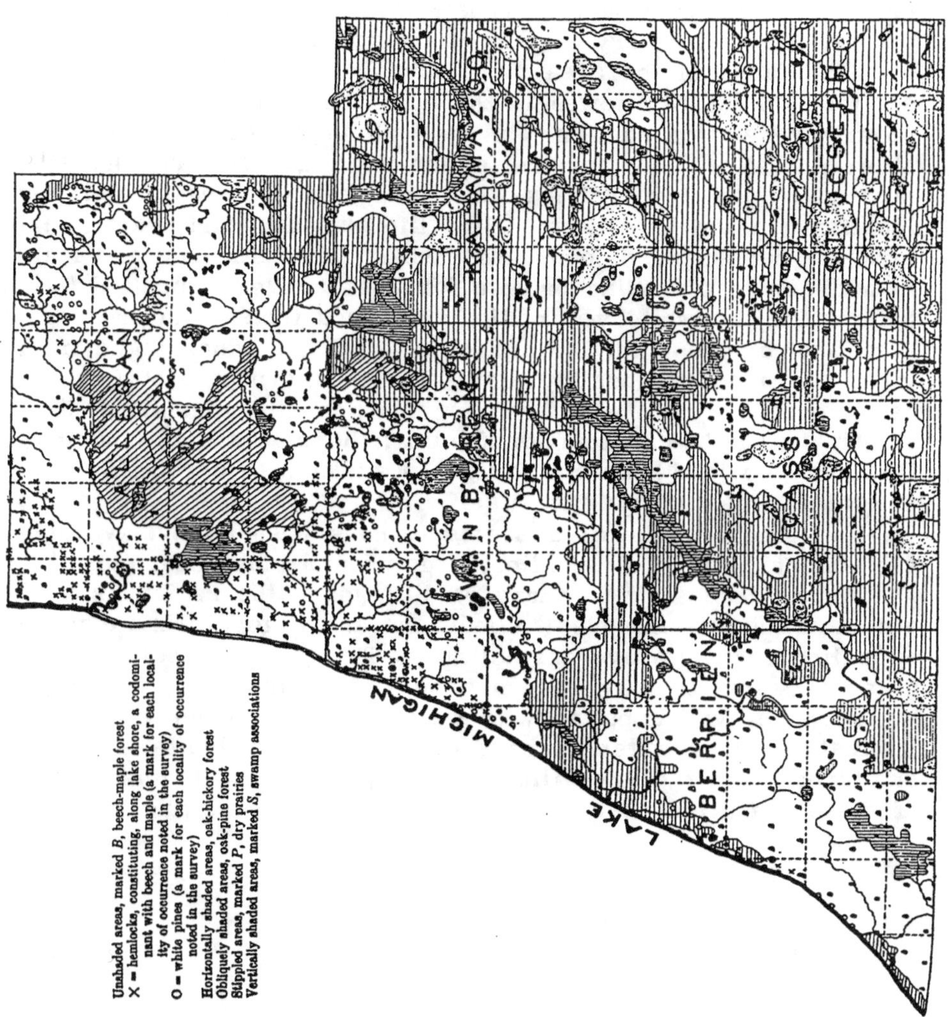

FIG. 2. Aboriginal vegetation of southwestern Michigan (From Kenoyer, 1934).

cherries, and pears are the principal fruit crops; 75 percent of the state's bearing grape vines are found in Berrien and neighboring Van Buren County. The truck farms produce cucumbers, onions, melons, celery, cabbage, and tomatoes.

The fauna of the area must have been abundant. Deer and elk found plentiful browse in the numerous edges created by the mosaic vegetation patterns, as well as in the edges of the prairies, streams, lakes, and marshes of the region. Elk must have been favored by the dry prairies which supplied grasses as well as locations in which to herd. Bird life was abundant, particularly turkeys, passenger pigeons, and ducks. The streams and marshes, in addition to providing browse for deer and elk, supplied the habitat for the white water lily, a favored food of the natives, and also for numerous turtles and other wild life which together provided a varied and healthy diet. The southern part of Lake Michigan provided a favorable area for sturgeon that preferred its relatively shallow bottom for feeding; the rivers emptying into the lake provided spawning areas in addition to certain favorable spawning areas in the lake itself.

In summary, the area seems to have been highly favorable for settlement. Plentiful supplies of game and plant life, plus the resources necessary to carry on life, made the region as a whole very attractive. Good soil conditions and a good climate made it appealing for primitive agriculture. The terrace itself, located at what seems to have been a good site on the river for spawning sturgeon, is well supplied with water from the river itself and from the ground water seepage on the southern bluffs and is sheltered from the prevailing winds by the bluffs themselves. All of these conditions help to create an attractive setting.

FIG. 3. Mid-Western United States showing counties (Map by American Map Co., Inc., N.Y.).

FIG. 4. The Upper Great Lakes Region showing the location of some of the sites mentioned in the text. (Map by Erwin Raisz, Landforms of the United States) 1. Schultz, 2. Bowmanville, 3. Plum Island, 4. Summerville, 5. Norton, 6. Spoonville, 7. Brooks, 8. Mallon, 9. Juntunen, 10. Brems, 11. Spring Creek, 12. Oak Forest, 13. Oakwood, 14. Gentlemen Farm, 15. Robinson Reserve, 16. Zimmerman, 17. Fisher, 18. Huber, 19. Anker, 20. Ada, 21. Dumaw Creek, 22. Griesmer, 23. Fifield, 24. Moccasin Bluff.

II

THE EXCAVATIONS

EXCAVATIONS were begun in the area of the site which yielded the greatest amount of surface material. This area was located just west of the road and had nothing to distinguish it from the rest of the site except for the greater amount of pottery and other artifacts which could be collected there. A grid system was laid out over the site and excavation was begun in five foot squares (see Table 1 for areas of excavated trenches). The trench was extended square by square in directions dictated by the nature of the material found in the previously excavated units. Because of

TABLE 1

AREA OF EXCAVATED TRENCHES

Trench	Area (sq. ft.)	% of total area excavated	Correction factor*
A	1900	32.33	÷ 1.90
B	630	10.72	x 1.59
C	525	8.93	x 1.90
D	155	2.63	x 6.45
E	360	6.12	x 2.77
F	650	11.06	x 1.54
G	75	1.27	x 13.33
H	412.5	7.02	x 2.42
K	125	2.12	x 8.00
L	62.5	1.06	x 16.00
M	500	8.50	x 2.00
N	260.5	4.43	x 3.84
O	200	3.40	x 5.00
Total	5855.5		

*This is a figure which is used to either divide or multiply the artifact totals from each trench to correct for the size differences between the trenches and to make the artifact totals from the various trenches comparable. The standard unit is arbitrarily fixed at 1000 square feet and all artifact totals can be adjusted to this standard 1000 square foot unit for comparative purposes.

this procedure, the trenches developed their somewhat irregular outlines (see Fig. 5).

It was decided to remove the top 10 inches of each square as a unit since this zone had been disturbed by plowing. Below this plow zone the levels were removed in four-inch deep units until sterile soil was reached. This procedure was followed, except in a few special instances, throughout the entire course of the excavation.

Trench A was begun and was followed by trenches B, C, and D in the area of high artifact concentration. When it became apparent that a large number of pits and features were located in this area, it was decided that a large area would be opened as a unit in order to obtain a clearer picture of the association among the features and possibly to locate evidence for structures which may have been present. This large area developed into a somewhat irregular 35 by 40 foot rectangle also called trench A (see Fig. 5).

To the west of trench A a long narrow two and one-half foot wide trench was extended from trench D into the main excavation area. This trench was designed to connect trench D to this main area. A similar two foot wide excavation, called trench E, was dug, extending some 350 feet to the south from trench B.

Trenches F, G, H, and K were laid out in a partly wooded area around the southern end of trench E. Their purpose was to test the possibility of a Middle Woodland occupation in this area of the site and to sample this area for further Late Woodland material. These trenches did not yield great amounts of Middle Woodland material, but they did add to the sample of later materials. In an effort to further explore the possible Middle Woodland occupation, an additional series of trenches was laid out farther to the south in an area believed to have had some Middle Woodland surface material; the same area was rumored to have had a small mound. These two and one-half foot wide excavations, known as trench M and trench N, proved to be largely unproductive. No pits or features were encountered and only a few potsherds and other artifacts were found. The mound was not visible at the time of excavation; presumably it had been leveled by agricultural activities and previous explorations.

Several other minor excavations known as test pits A, B, C, and D and trenches O and L were scattered over the site and proved to be of as little significance as size. In fact, a direct relationship generally exists between the size of an excavation unit and its contribution to producing useful material for interpretation. Trenches A and C, being the largest excavation units in

MOCCASIN BLUFF SITE
BERRIEN COUNTY, MICHIGAN
Plan of excavations
Scale in feet
0 20 40 60 80 100
LEGEND
Fence
Building
Telephone or power lines
COUNTY ROAD
Trench A
Trench B
Trench C
Trench D
Trench E
Trench F
Trench G
Trench H
Trench K
Trench L
Trench M
Trench N
Trench O
Test pit A
Test pit B
Test pit C
Test pit D
W1500
W1400
W1300
W1200
W1100
W1000
W 900
W 800
W 700
N 1800
N1700
N1600
N1500
N1400
N1300
N1200
N1100
N1000
N900
N800
N700
N600
N500
N400
A.L.B.

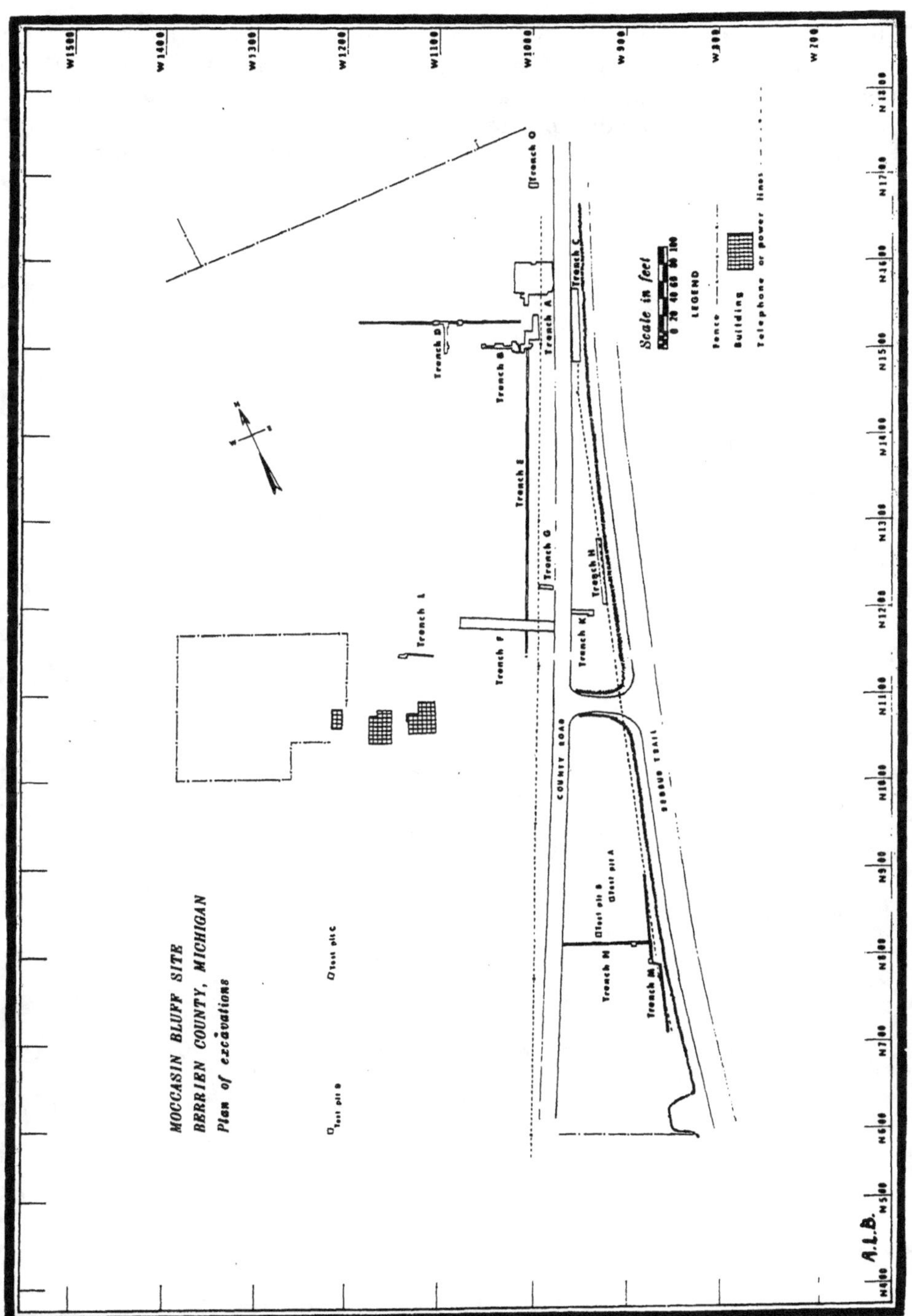

FIG. 5.

size, were also the most important units for producing material. One can clearly see how the archaeological concepts of the late 1940's influenced the layout and design of the excavations. The emphasis was on producing as much material as possible, and the excavation plan clearly was designed to achieve that result.

III

PITS AND FEATURES

ONE of the most impressive aspects of the Moccasin Bluff site is the large number of pits that were uncovered in the course of the excavations (see Figs. 6-8 and Tables 3 and 4). These pits were impressive for both their density and their number. It is interesting that the greatest concentration of pits in trenches A and C is also the area of the greatest concentration of pottery. One wonders what the camp must have looked like during the period of the occupation. Was the ground potmarked with holes left unfilled after use or was the landscape more carefully tended?

The nature of the pits presents several interesting problems which cannot be fully resolved with the present data but which are nevertheless worth mentioning. The first problem results from the nature of the stratigraphy at the site. It was difficult to locate the tops of the pits in the Genesee silt loam because the fill of the pits and the surrounding soil were not easily distinguishable. In many cases a number of different pits were found to intersect and the individual pits could not be distinguished from one another. Therefore, in the upper levels of the pits, material from the intersecting pits and from outside of the pit proper could be mixed. The pits were more easily differentiated when they penetrated the yellow sand below the Genesee silt loam. The drawings of the distribution of pits within the trench generally include pits that penetrated the yellow sand and were easily distinguishable. It is remarkable that at this level the outline of many of the pits was an almost perfect circle (see Pl. 7).

Other aspects of the distribution of the pits are their clustering and intersection (see Figs. 7 and 8). Usually pits of similar type are found in small clusters, some intersecting one another. The significance of this clustering is not clear from the data at hand, but some hint is given from Binford's work at Hatchery Creek (Binford, et al. 1966). His work indicates that at Hatchery Creek the clustering may have chronological significance, that the different clusters may represent functionally specialized areas

MOCCASIN BLUFF SITE
BERRIEN COUNTY, MICHIGAN
TRENCH A
Distribution of pits
W1020
W1010
W1000
N15|00
N15|10
N15|20
N15|30
Hearth over pit
LEGEND
Dimension of pit unknown
Previous excavation
Scale in feet
0 1 2 3 4 5
R.L.B.

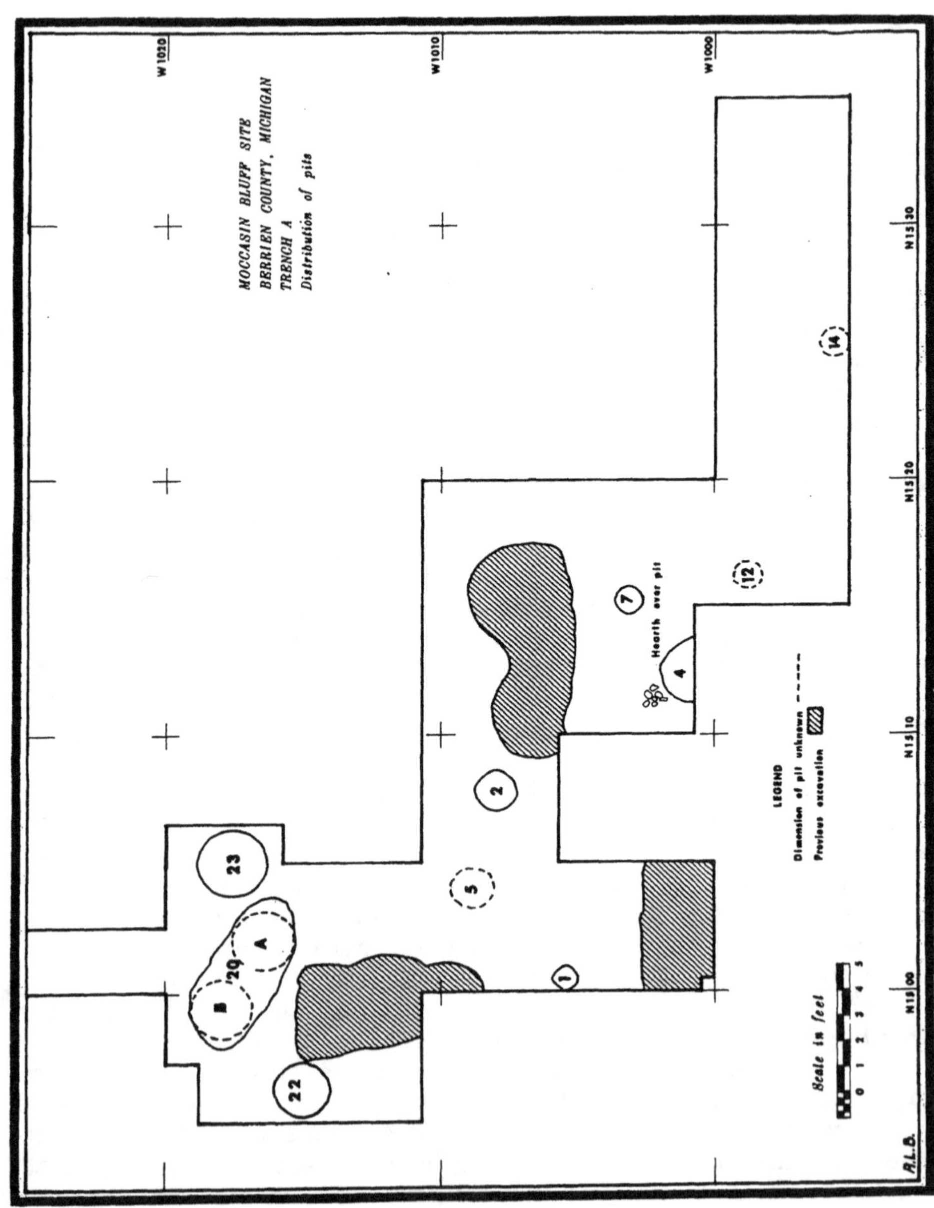

FIG. 6.

MOCCASIN BLUFF SITE
BERRIEN COUNTY, MICHIGAN
TRENCH A
Distribution of pits
Scale in feet
LEGEND
Dimension of pit unknown
Previous excavation
Telephone post
Pit 12 below pit 3
R.L.B.

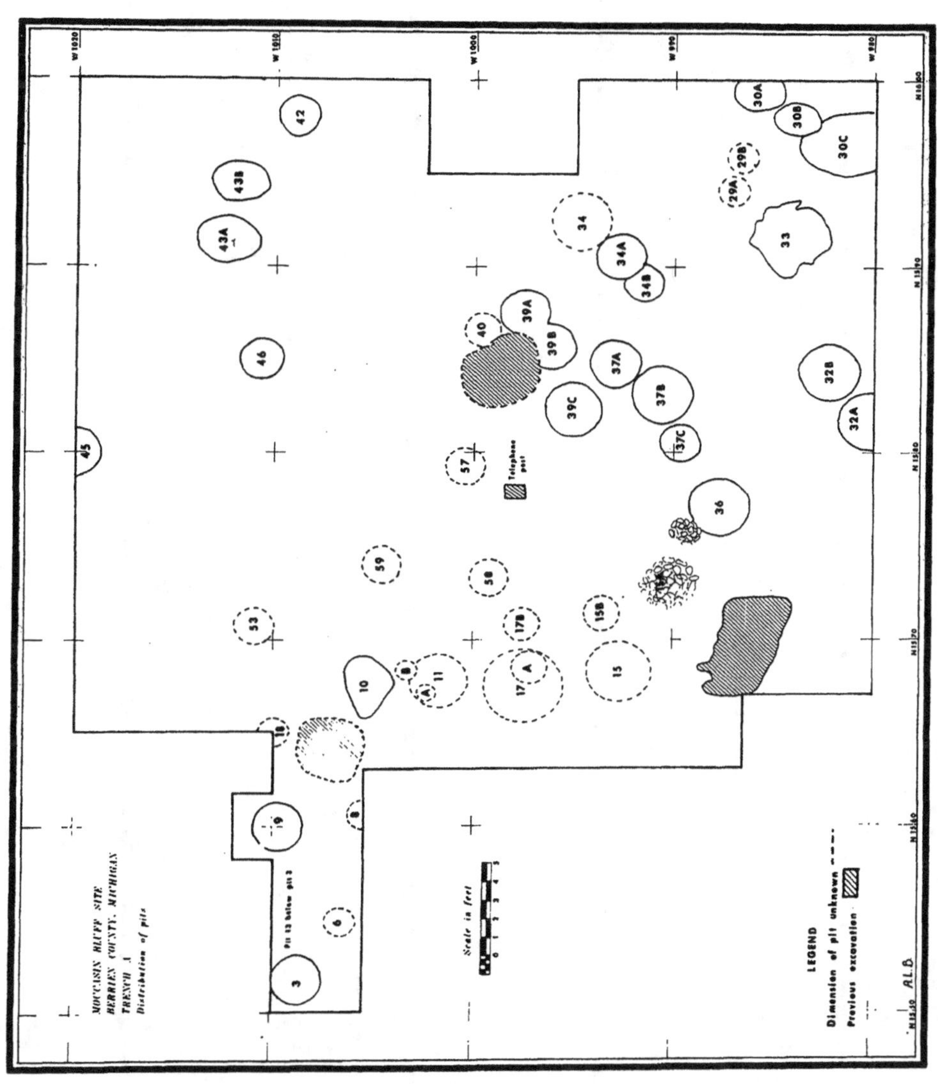

FIG. 7.

MOCCASIN BLUFF SITE
BERRIEN COUNTY, MICHIGAN
TRENCH F
Distribution of pits

MOCCASIN BLUFF SITE
BERRIEN COUNTY, MICHIGAN
TRENCH C
Distribution of pits
Scale in feet

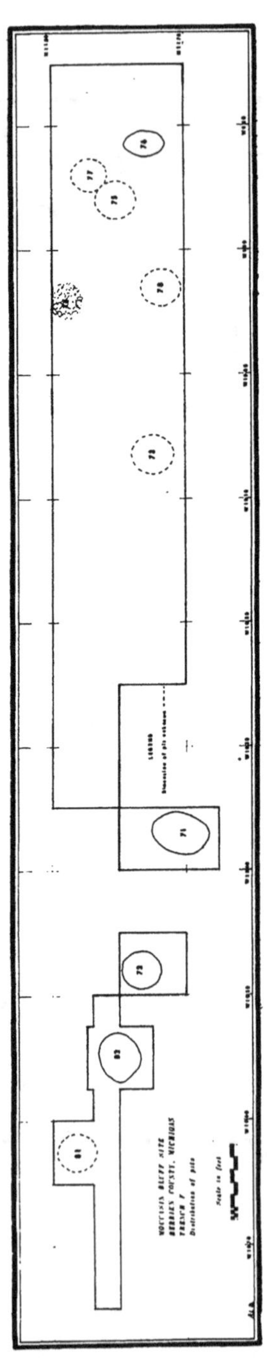

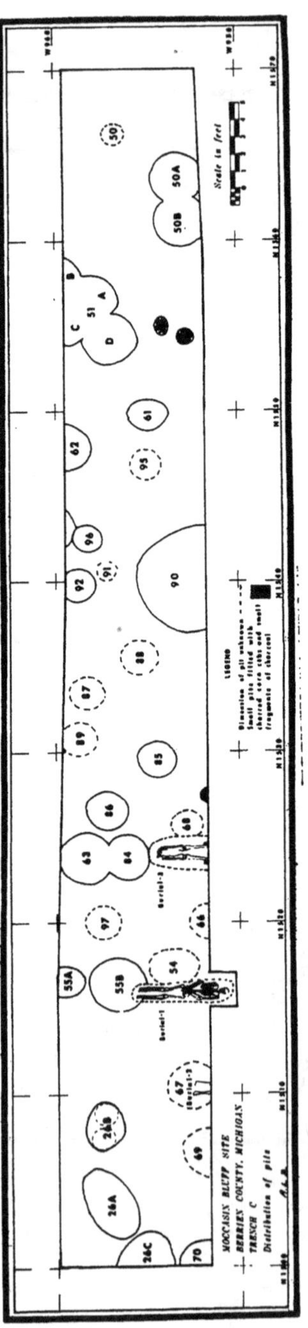

FIG. 8.

within the site at different periods of time: for example, at one occupation, roasting pits may have clustered in one area of the site, whereas during another occupation at a different period of time, the roasting pits may have been located in another part of the camp. An alternative, and perhaps complementary, explanation might be that the clustering of roasting pits in different areas of the site was related to the social divisions or groupings within the camp: the pits of one social or family group, for instance, might have formed one cluster while the pits of another group might have formed a separate cluster. Integrating the dimension of time with this possible social difference, the situation becomes even more complex. Again, it is unfortunate that we do not have a complete plan of the camp to help solve some of these problems and yield a clearer understanding of life at this settlement.

The apparent large quantities of refuse in some of the pits (4, 14, 15, 17, 20, 51, 88, 92) and the relative absence of material in most of the others (see Appen. 5) also raises some questions. Although the primary data are fragmentary and incomplete, some differences in the pit contents are in evidence. Among those pits with large amounts of material, some (e.g., 4, 14, 17, 20, 51, 88 and 92) contain large amounts of faunal refuse and artifacts, while others (e.g., pit 15), in addition to being exceptionally large, contain a large number of artifacts and apparently little faunal material.

The rationale for the apparent concentration of artifactual material in pit 15 remains unclear. Several factors might have produced a concentration of faunal material in some of the pits. One possibility is that, because some subsistence activities were concentrated—such as the sturgeon spawn in the spring or the historically-recorded deer drives in the fall—large amounts of refuse would accumulate and be disposed of by burial in special pits dug for the purpose or in exhausted storage pits. If this were the case, such pits would yield a concentration of different species. The data in Appendix 5, however, suggest that this is not the case because sturgeon and deer are found in practically all the pits containing faunal material. In addition, pits with large amounts of faunal material also contain a variety of species. These findings indicate that the concentration of subsistence activities does not account for the variation of artifactual material in the pits.

Another possibility is that the concentration of material may represent refuse accumulated after a social event, such as a feast or a ceremony. The variety of species in the pits may support this alternative. Also suggestive of this possibility is the presence of dog remains in these pits. Ethnographic accounts from the Eastern Woodlands point to the eating and sacrifice of dogs on ceremonial occasions.

Future excavations at similar sites should attempt to document more fully similarities and differences among pits and to test for functional, chronological, and social factors in their variation.

DWELLINGS

The concentration and density of the pits indicates that the dwellings, either actual structures or spatial areas in the camp reserved for particular families, might possibly have been located elsewhere. Cleland's analysis of some of the faunal material from the site led him to postulate that the site was occupied continuously throughout the entire year (Cleland, 1966). If his conclusion is accepted, then the residents most certainly required shelters during the winter months, if not throughout the entire year. Spring, summer, and fall have a fair amount of rainfall against which we might expect the people to have been sheltered. No traces of such shelters were discovered during the course of the excavations.

The greater density of pits in trench C indicates that the major occupation area of the site was probably located next to the river and that the excavations in trench A only explored the western boundary of the site. Apparently the major portion of the site had been destroyed in cutting back the old river bank for the construction of the railroad and later for the construction of the Red Bud Trail Highway.

PIT VARIETIES

The data suggest that at least four varieties of pits are present at the site. The first group is listed as pits. These were dug by the inhabitants and are traditionally referred to as storage pits. What was being stored in them at the Moccasin Bluff site, if, indeed, anything at all was stored in them, is not clear from the information presently available. After their original purpose had been served, some of these pits were re-used as trash pits to dispose of garbage and trash, while others seem simply to have been refilled. Precise information on the structure of these pits is not available, but some idea of the variation can be seen in the drawings in Figures 9-14 and in Appendices 2-5 (see Pl. 7, 8).

The next class of pits is referred to as fire pits. These pits appear to be structurally similar to the previous group, except for the presence of a perimeter of burned or oxidized reddish-

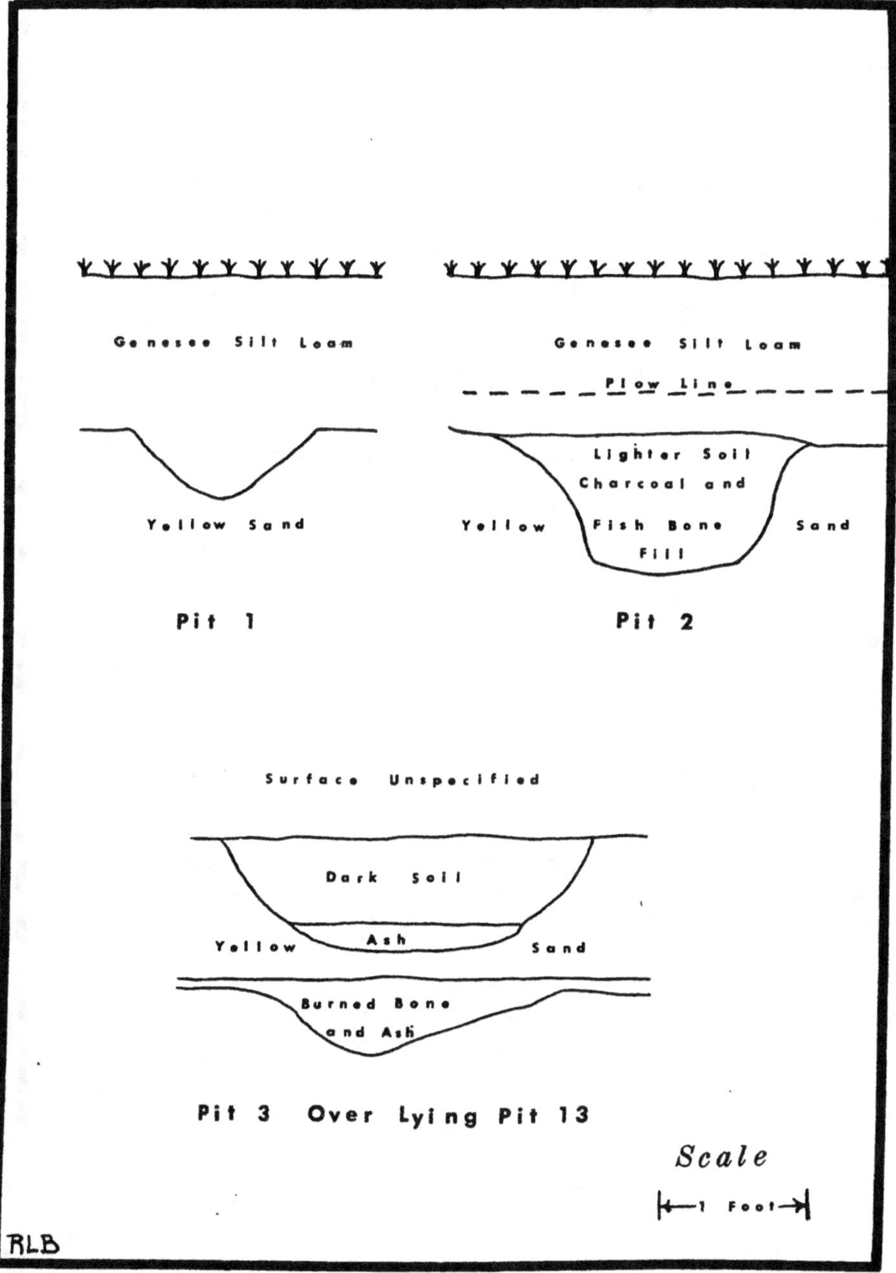

FIG. 9. Profiles of pit 1, pit 2, and pit 3 overlying pit 13.

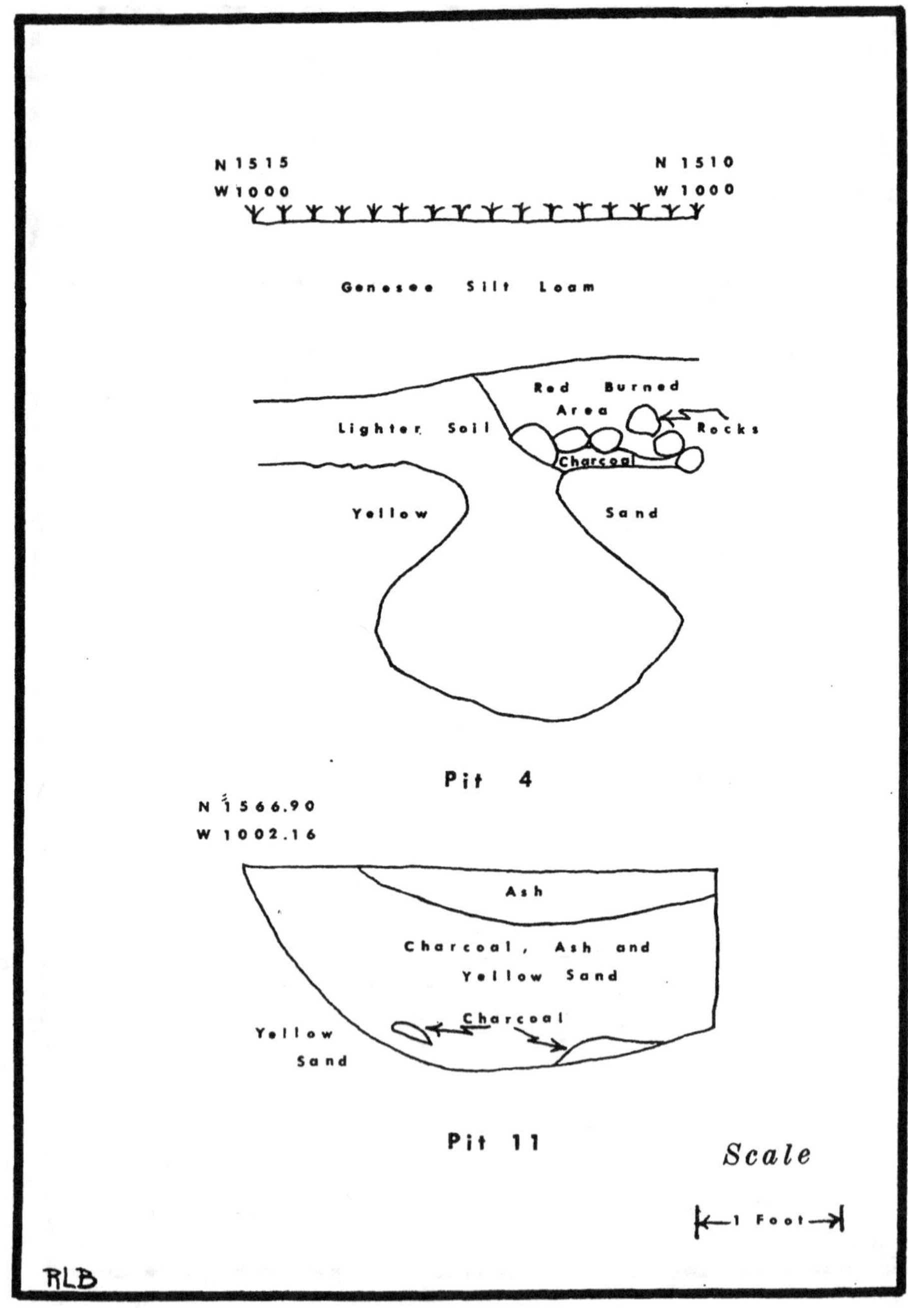

FIG. 10. Profiles of pit 4 and pit 11.

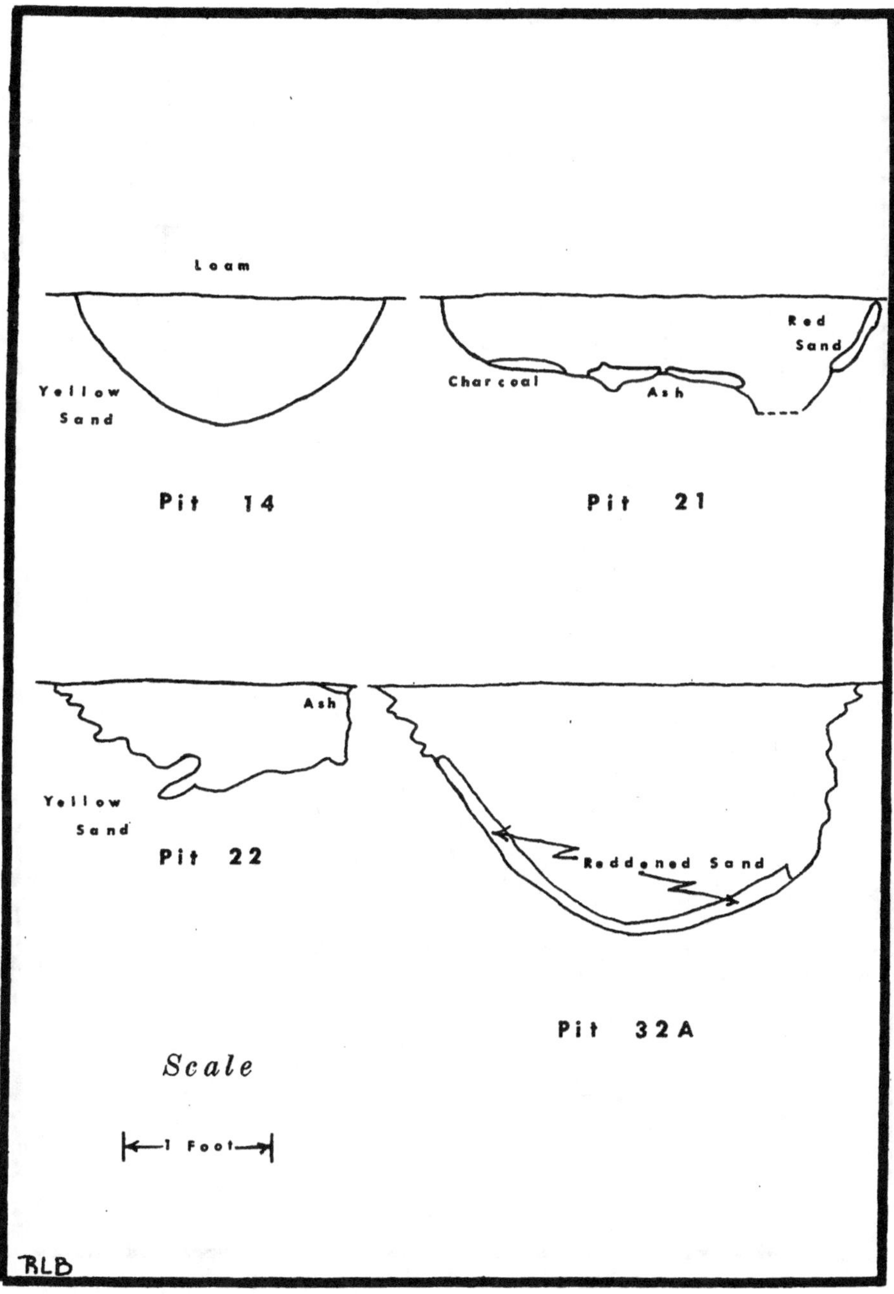

FIG. 11. Profiles of pit 14, pit 21, pit 22, and pit 32A.

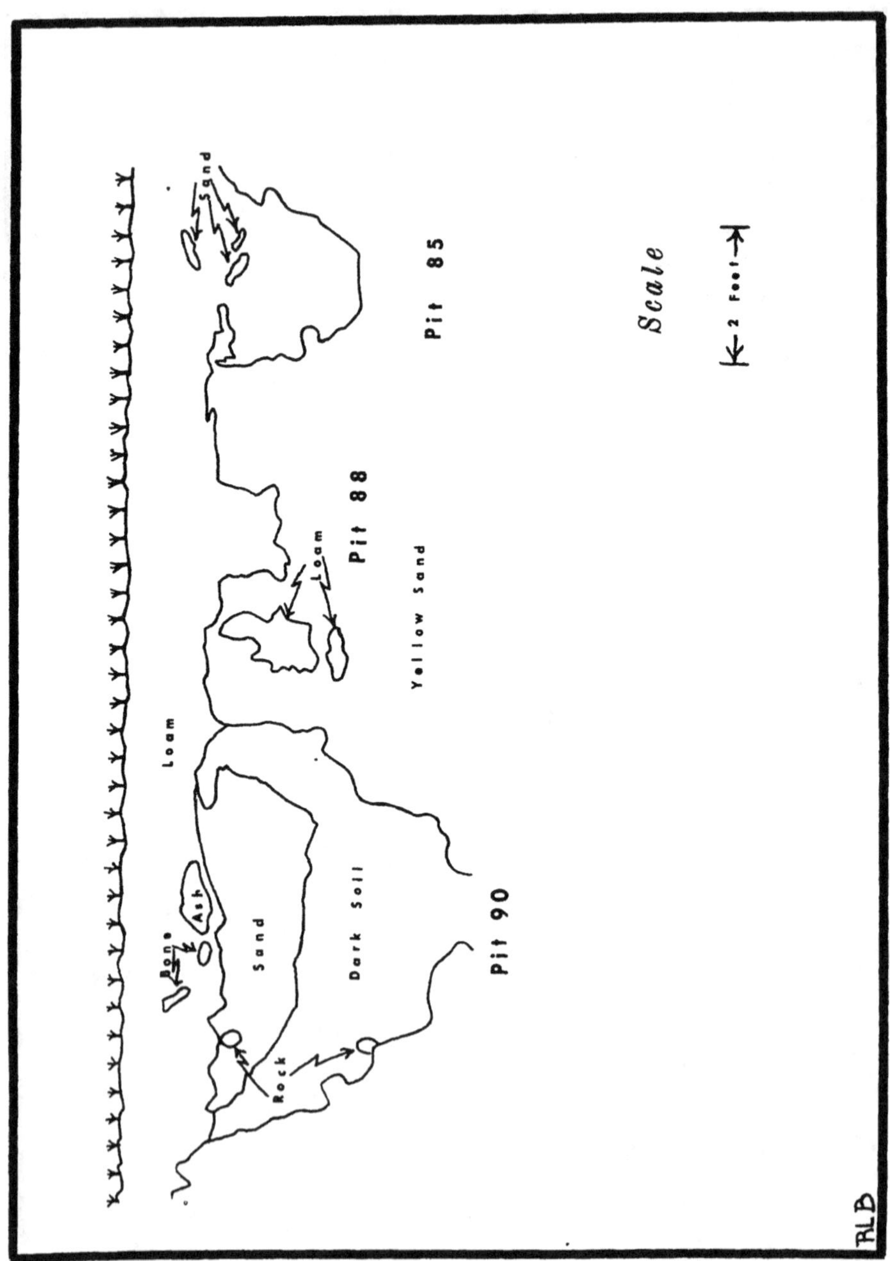

FIG. 12. Profiles of pit 66 and pit 32A.

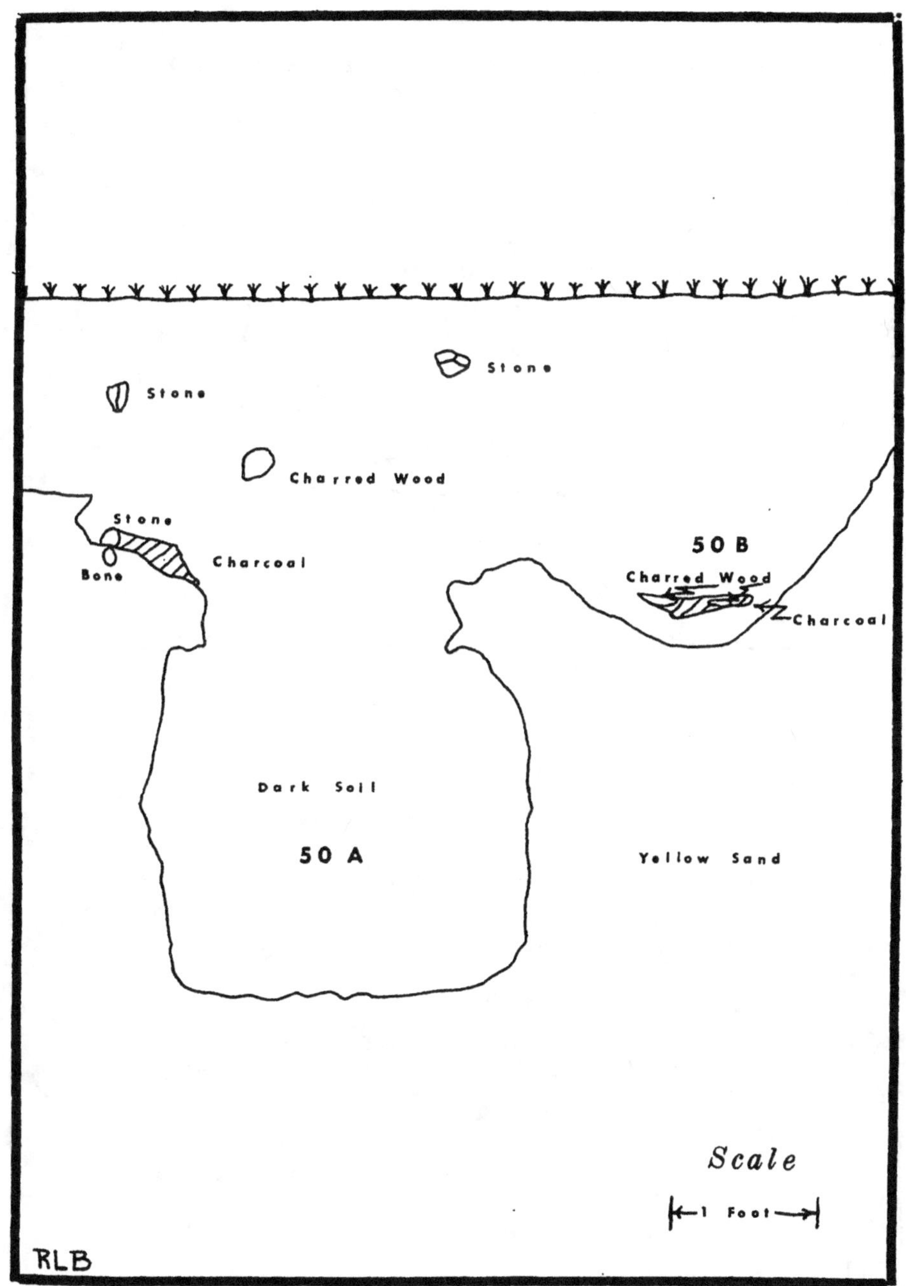

FIG. 13. Profiles of pit 50A and pit 50B.

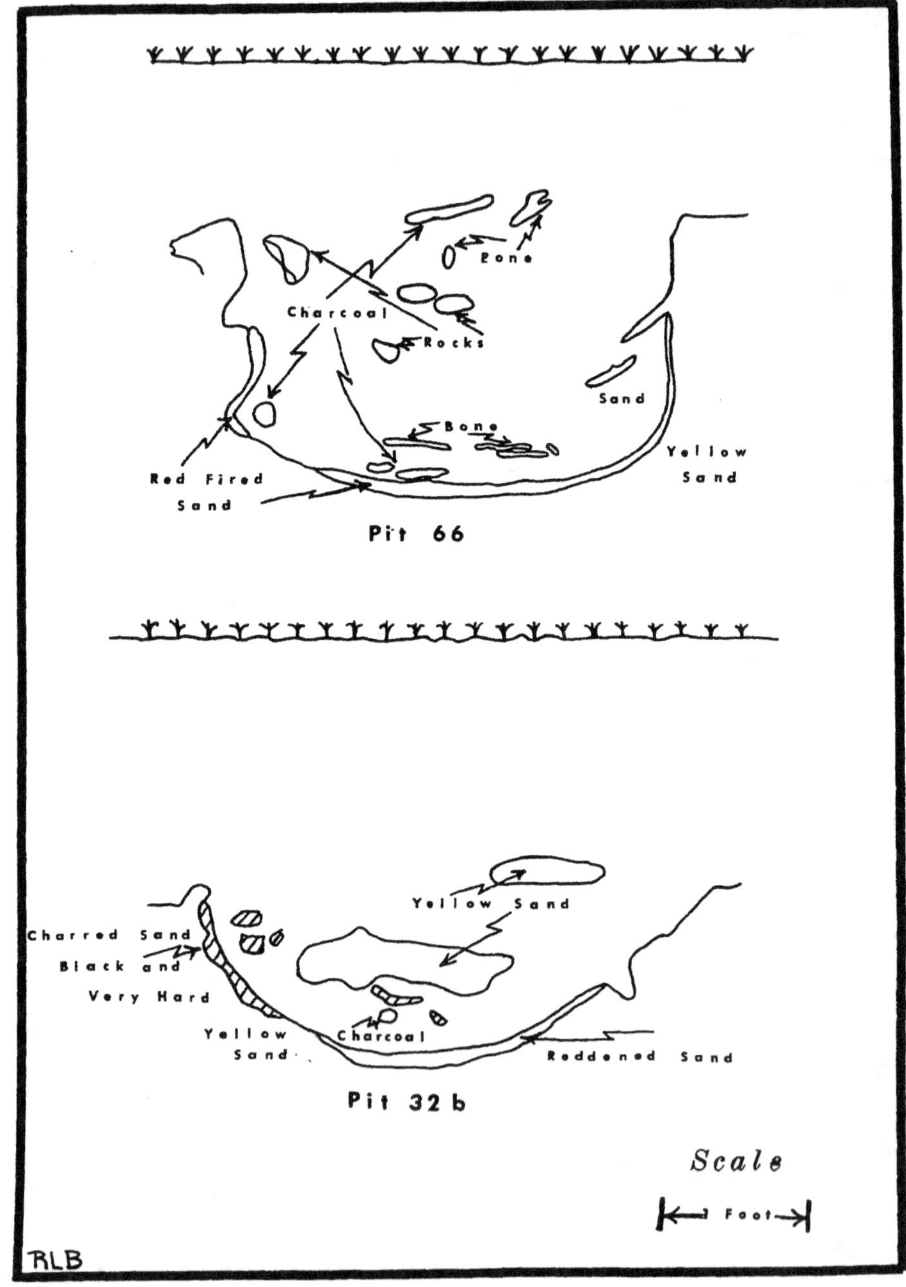

FIG. 14. Profiles of pit 90, pit 88, and pit 85.

sand which is assumed to have resulted from heat or fire within the pit. What function these pits may have had is still an open question. Binford has suggested that they represent earth ovens (Binford, et al., 1966:70, 75). This is an attractive suggestion; but what was baked in the pits, how was it baked, and why was it baked rather than prepared in some other way? The answers to these questions are not obvious from the data at hand. In the section on adaptation and subsistence, however, it is suggested that one function of these pits may have been to bake the white water lily, *Nymphaea tuberosa*. After their use as ovens some of the fire pits (e.g., pit 51) were re-used as trash pits (see Pl. 9).

The third category of pits is called hearths. The hearth has three attributes: the first and primary attribute is the shallow depth of the pit (see Table 2); the second attribute may be the presence of an area of oxidized sand or soil associated with the pit; and the last is the presence of a concentration of fire-cracked rocks in the pit. In some cases there is a concentration of

TABLE 2

SUMMARY OF PIT MEASUREMENTS

	Depth (ft.)	Diameter (ft.)
Pits		
Number 62		
Total of measurements	82.44	81.23
Number measured	56	31
Mean	1.47	2.62
Fire Pits		
Number 17		
Total of measurements	24.73	34.06
Number measured	17	13
Mean	1.45	2.62
Hearths		
Number 19		
Total of measurements	10.09	18.35
Number measured	15.0	7.0
Mean	0.67	2.62

charcoal in the pit. These features need not always be present in any one pit. In some cases, only one or two attributes are present; in other cases, all of them are. The only attribute common to all of the hearths is their shallow depth (see Pl. 10).

The final class of pits includes several small, shallow holes, approximately six inches in diameter, filled with charred corn and corn cobs. These features occurred only in trench C. Binford has suggested that similar pits at Hatchery Creek represent smudge pits, used for the tanning of hides (Binford, et al., 1966). This interpretation could be supported by the character and nature of the pits at the Moccasin Bluff site. Densmore (1929) also describes similar pits used for hide smoking by the Chippewa.

Since the attributes selected for the pit classification above were not systematically recorded by the excavators, the absence of an attribute in association with a pit simply indicates that its presence could not be positively determined. Therefore, the classification of many of the pits is not completely accurate. Some pits which may have been fire pits may be grouped with the simple pits because they lacked a recognized oxidized sand perimeter or because this oxidized sand perimeter may not have been recorded on the notes. Several different methods of ordering the pits for chronological, stylistic, and functional analysis were tried, but none proved very satisfactory. The data that could be assembled on the pits is presented in the following tables. (See Appendices 1-7 for complete information.)

DISTRIBUTION OF PITS

Looking at the corrected distribution of pits (Table 4), we see that the greatest density of pits occurs in trench C. Fire pits are also concentrated in trench C while hearths have their greatest concentration in trenches D and F. The significance of these distributions is not clear from the data at hand, but they probably reflect chronological and/or functional differences at the site.

BURIALS

Three burials were discovered in the course of the excavation. All were uncovered in trench C. Burial 1 was an extended burial of an adult. It was fully excavated. Burial 2 consisted of two femurs, with the tibia and foot bones not present. The upper torso was presumably under the road and therefore not excavated. The entire lower body of burial 3 was excavated; the upper body presumably was also under the road and not excavated. Burials 2 and 3 were not completely excavated. The remains of these individuals were not available for analysis (see Pl. 11).

TABLE 3

DISTRIBUTION OF PITS BY TRENCH

Trench	A	B	C	D	E	F	H	N	O	Total
Type of Pit										
Pit	37	3	16	1	1	1	1	0	2	62
Fire pit	4	1	10	0	1	0	0	1	0	17
Hearth	5	0	3	2	1	8	0	0	0	19
Total	46	4	29	3	3	9	1	1	2	98*

*Totals do not agree with number of designated pits since some numbers do not refer to pits and some pits having one number represent two features, i.e., pit 9 represents a hearth and a pit. See Appendix 1 for complete listing.

TABLE 4

DISTRIBUTION OF PITS BY TRENCH
(trenches adjusted to uniform size)

Trench	A	B	C	D	E	F	H	N	O	Total
Type of Pit										
Pit	20	5	30	6	3	2	2	0	10	78
Fire pit	2	2	19	0	3	0	0	4	0	30
Hearth	3	0	6	13	3	12	0	0	0	37
Total	25	7	55	19	9	14	2	4	10	145*

*Totals do not agree with number of designated pits since some numbers do not refer to pits and some pits having one number represent two features, i.e., pit 9 represents a hearth and a pit. See Appendix 1 for complete listing.

IV

THE CHIPPED STONE INDUSTRY

THE University of Michigan excavations at Moccasin Bluff recovered a large variety of chipped stone material of which 1,484 pieces were analyzed in this study. The vast majority of this material was manufactured from locally derived chert, much of which was deposited by glacial action. The bed of the St. Joseph River may also be an abundant source of nodules as raw material for the knappers.

For purposes of classification eight varieties of stone were recognized and described. A ninth miscellaneous class contains the remaining varieties of stone, many of which are represented by only one object.

STONE VARIETIES

Type A is a pale brown, Munsell color 10YR 7/2 to yellow-brown 10YR 5/6 opaque chert with a slightly glossy surface. Part of the cortex when present appears as a strong brown 7.5YR 5/6 glossy coating. The stone is rarely banded but does have a faint mottling of light gray 7.5YR 7/0 material, which in some examples blends into the dark strong-brown shadings.

Type B is a very pale brown 10YR 8/4 to 7/4 colored opaque chert with a dull surface. It is rarely banded but does show some mottling of a lighter gray 10YR 7/1 material. The coloring is remarkably uniform and consistent in the examples studied.

Type C is a smooth surface, glossy, opaque chert with a purple tint. It is uniformly mottled ranging from a light gray 5YR 8/1 to 7/1 to purple. In some examples the purple cast is much lighter than in others.

Type D appears to be a smooth, shiny surface, good quality chert which can almost be classified as a flint. In its finest form it is a gray to gray-brown 10YR 6/1 to 6/2 in color, but is often combined with large inclusions of much poorer quality stone resembling type B. It is rarely banded or mottled but fades from one coloring to the other. When held in front of a light source the edges of the pieces are translucent.

Type E is a coarse, rough, opaque chert of a reddish-brown 2.5YR 5/2 to 4/2, purple coloring. It is mottled with a lighter gray to cream material. The texture is coarse and rough, almost like granite.

Type F is a smooth surface, glossy, light gray 7.5YR 7/0 opaque chert. It is often banded or mottled with dark gray 7.5YR 5/0 material. This seems to fall into the range of variation of what has been called Eastport Chert (see Binford and Papworth, 1963).

Type G is a translucent, white, chert-like stone very uniform in coloring except where the cortex—a coarse, white, weathered material—is visible.

Type H is a glossy surface, cream-colored 10YR 8/2 to 8/3, good quality, opaque chert. It is uniform in color, showing little banding or mottling. Inclusions are not visible.

Group M is a miscellaneous group containing all varieties which do not fall into any of the above categories.

DISTRIBUTION OF TYPES OF FLINT AMONG ARTIFACT TYPES

The association between artifacts and varieties of stone is not very strong in the majority of cases (see Table 5). Two examples, however, do seem worthy of notice. The first is the association between the small triangular points and varieties A, B, and C stone. These all seem to be locally derived and may simply reflect the greater availability of these types of stone. The second association may be of greater cultural significance. This is the association of ovate-shaped blades with variety G stone. Although the source of this stone is not known, it may be non-local. It is of somewhat better quality than the rest of the stone. Blades or knives made of this variety of stone have been reported from the Dumaw Creek site (Quimby, 1966*a*:28-30).

MANUFACTURING TECHNIQUES

Although a detailed examination of manufacturing techniques was not undertaken, some general comments on methods of production of lithic tools are possible from a superficial examination of the collected material. The descriptions offered here probably refer to the Late Woodland occupation at the site since this is the best represented component in the entire collection.

TABLE 5

DISTRIBUTION OF STONE VARIETY BY ARTIFACT

Stone Varieties	A	B	C	D	E	F	G	H	Misc.
Small triangular points	16	20	12	5	5	5	3	5	33
Scrapers, thumb nail	1	1	1					1	4
Scrapers, other			1	1					4
Scrapers, hafted						1			2
Small stemmed points									3
Large stemmed points									4
Expanding stem points		1	1						2
Side and corner notched points									
A				1				2	1
B									2
C		2						1	3
D								1	1
E									2
F									2
Dustin-like		1							1
Blades or blanks									5
Ovate-shaped blades						1	2		0
Drills	2	1					2		1

The most striking feature of the collection is the extent to which small-sized pebbles, perhaps obtained from the river bed, were utilized as the raw material for the manufacture of tools. The size of the original nodule could often be estimated by the presence of weathered cortex on two or more sides of a bifacially flaked piece. The diameter of some of the nodules was estimated to be as low as 1.5 cm.

At least two types of blanks must have been produced: a thin blank from which the natives manufactured many of the triangular points and a thicker blank from which they worked such heavier wood-working tools as the small, thick, steep-edge pieces. Evidence for the steps in the manufacturing process were noticeably absent in the collections. Only four cores were recognized. The small number of cores and the relative lack of flakes resulting from manufacturing activities suggest that most of the rough chipping and processing operations may have been carried out in a different locality (see Table 6). However, if small-sized nodules were widely used at the site for the manufacture of most of the tools, the number of cores and waste flakes would have been very small and manufacturing activities may have been carried out locally. The author's suspicion is that different nodules were used to produce different tool types, but larger samples and an intensive study would be required to test this possibility. Most certainly the ovate blades and the larger drills were made from a different source of raw material and with a different manufacturing technique than the small, thick, steep-edge pieces and thumb-nail scrapers. Future work on this problem might prove rewarding and highly productive.

TABLE 6

SUMMARY OF CHIPPED STONE

		N	%
Primary flakes		122	8.0
Block flakes		235	15.5
Simple flakes		724	47.6
Utilized and/or retouched flakes		54	3.5
Flakes of bifacial retouch		34	2.2
Blades		6	0.4
Scrapers		23	1.5
Points and bifacial tools		143	9.4
small triangular	104		
small stemmed	3		
large stemmed	4		
expanding stemmed	2		
small side and corner notched	18		
Dustin-like	2		
large blade or knife	7		
ovates	3		
Drills		6	0.4
Gravers		6	0.4
Small, thick, steep-edge pieces		53	3.5
Miscellaneous		5	0.3
Fragments of bifacial tools		104	6.8
Cores		4	0.3
	Totals	1519	99.8

One noteworthy feature is the almost complete absence of bipolar techniques reported from many of the sites to the north of the Moccasin Bluff site. Only one example of the bipolar technique was identified in the analysis (see Fig. 17).

FLAKES

Six classes of flakes were recognized in this study: primary flakes, block flakes, simple flakes, utilized and/or retouched flakes, flakes or bifacial retouch, and blades.

Primary flakes have been defined in the literature by White (1963:5), Binford and Quimby (1963:287), and Fitting (1968:24). These flakes are the result of the rough trimming of the nodule and in all cases are characterized by the presence of weathered cortex on the exterior surface of the flake.

Block flakes have been reported by White (1963:13-14), Fitting (Fitting, DeVisscher, and Wahla, 1966:24), and many other writers. They are blocky, triangular, or prismatic in cross-section and of irregular form. At the Moccasin Bluff site most of these flakes were the result of further trimming of the nodule after the removal of the primary flakes. There appears to have been no break in the process of manufacture between the production of the primary flakes and the block flakes. The flint knapper simply continued to modify the nodule to the desired shape; his working rhythm probably did not change and neither did his technique. In fact, the removal of the cortex does not even seem to have been a goal of the knapper; in a number of the finished pieces, large areas of the original cortex are still in place. The primary goal was the production of the tool, or more specifically, of the working edge, and as long as presence of the cortex in no way interfered with the function of the tool, no effort was made to remove it (indeed, there was no need to do so). A small percentage of the block flakes show evidence of having been in fire or in contact with fire or great heat. Some of these flakes might have resulted from heat fracture.

Simple flakes are flat, generally smaller-sized flakes which result from the finer trimming of the tools. Some of them may have been produced in the initial trimming of the nodules to prepare striking platforms, but the great majority seem to have been produced in the final stages of manufacture.

Utilized and/or retouched flakes (Fig. 15) are generally simple flakes which have been modified by retouch or by use. They did not appear to have any uniform shape. Based on the shape of working edge, these flakes were classified into four types. Concave flakes are those on which the retouch or use resulted in the formation of a concave working edge. Convex flakes are those on which the working edge is predominately convex in form. Those flakes classified as complex contain two or more different types of working edges. They may be concave and convex or convex and straight, or perhaps a combination of all three. The last class represents those flakes which have a predominately straight working edge. This is by far the largest class of utilized flakes in the collection. In all classes of utilized flake the angle of the working edge of these flakes is rather acute compared to the group of tools classified as scrapers. Scrapers are generally thicker and have a less acute working edge than the utilized flakes.

TABLE 7

SUMMARY OF THE FREQUENCY OF UTILIZED FLAKE BY CLASS

	Concave	Convex	Complex	Straight	Total
Frequency	10	12	6	25	53

Flakes of bifacial retouch resemble simple flakes in general size and shape. They differ from them in at least two primary ways. The exterior side of the flake resembles the retouch seen on the exterior surface of a typical bifacially flaked tool while the interior of the flake represents the typical pattern seen on most flakes. The second distinctive feature is the special nature of the striking platform. It appears to resemble a faceted striking platform, but in actual fact it is the dull working edge of a bifacial tool. It is believed that most of these flakes were produced while resharpening bifacially flaked tools (Frison, 1967; Bordes, 1961).

Blades (Fig. 17) are the last class of flakes to be discussed. A blade is defined here as a flake which is at least twice as long as it is wide and struck from a special core manufactured for the production of blades. The lack of any blade cores reported from the site and the low frequency of blades in the assemblage make one suspect that these blades may have been produced accidentally. However, the presence of Middle Woodland ceramics on the site suggest that these blades may be associated with this component.

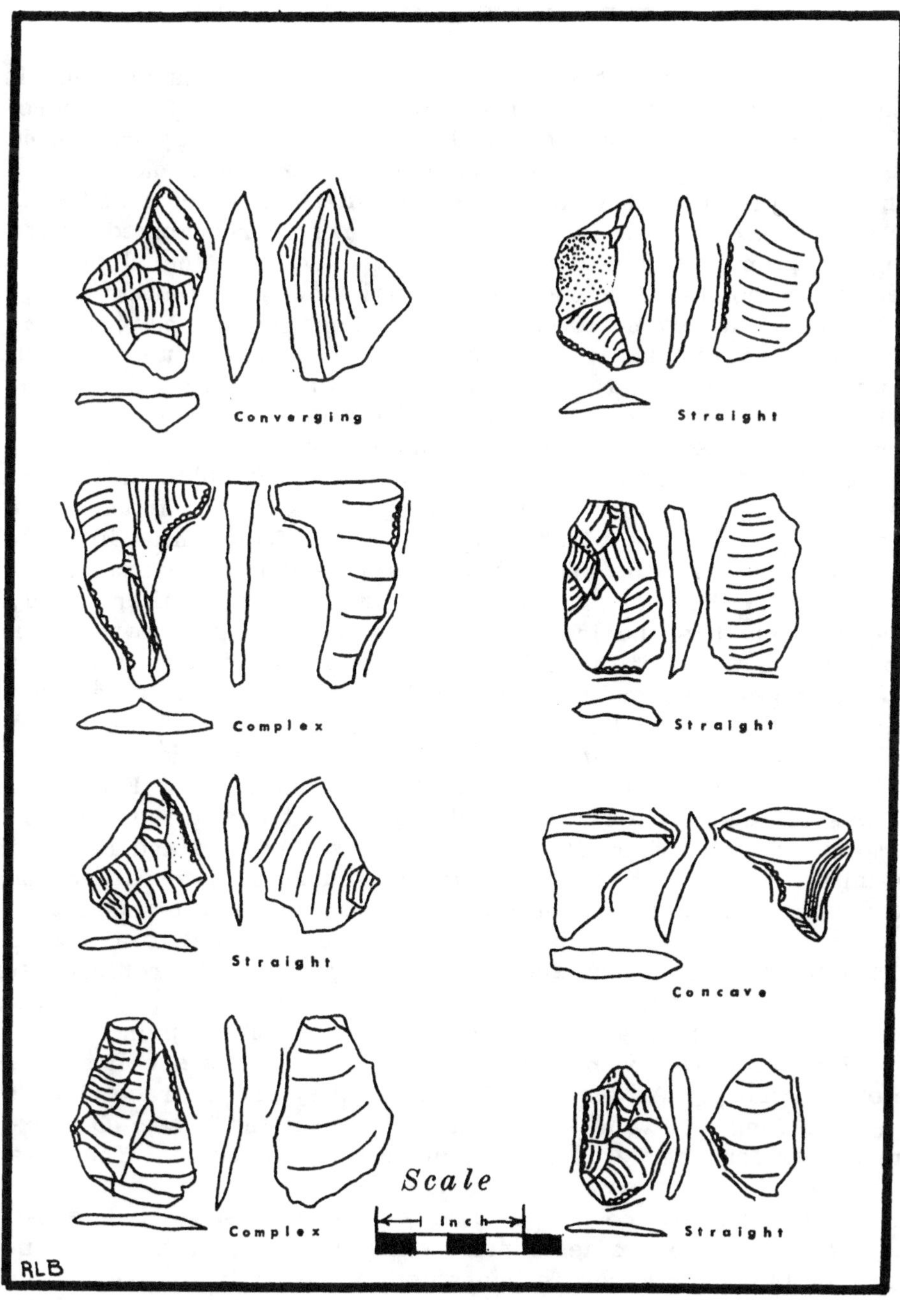

FIG. 15. Moccasin Bluff Utilized Flakes.

PROJECTILE POINTS AND BIFACIAL TOOLS

Small triangular points (Pl. 39) constitute the largest single class of artifacts in the entire collection, representing 44 percent of all tools. In shape and detail of manufacture they represent a highly variable group. They range from very well made examples which are finely flaked and have very distinctive form and shape to examples which at first glance may not be recognized as triangular points. These latter examples have only the slightest suggestion of points; they show a minimal amount of flaking and are only approximately triangular in shape. Functionally, however, they are probably just as effective as the well made points. Two of the examples are unifacial, i.e., made on a flake, while all the rest are bifacially flaked. On several of the points, pieces of the weathered cortex remain on the finished point.

Small stemmed points (Pl. 40). Three examples of such points were classified in this sample. They are all made from a similar smooth opaque stone which ranges in color from white 10YR 8/2 to pale olive 5Y 6/3. The stone has a speckled appearance resulting from the inclusion of small particles of a whiter material. One example has the inclusion of a coarse orange-brown material. The bases of two of the points have been ground to dull the sharp cutting edge, presumably to aid in hafting. There is a tendency for the stem to be slightly wider at the base than at its center.

Large stemmed points (Pl. 40). These points do not form as tight a grouping as the three small stemmed points. Each of the shapes is slightly distinctive and the chert types are different. The largest example, E on Plate 40, is coarsely flaked and rather indefinitely shaped. It may have been used as a knife rather than as a point. Example A on Plate 40 definitely had a secondary use because the tip has been modified from a point to a scraper-like working edge. The tip has the steep, step-like retouch seen on the small, thick, steep-edge pieces as well as a slight polish or sheen. Basal grinding is present on two of the points.

Expanding stemmed points (Pl. 40). Only two specimens fall into this group. As the name implies, they are characterized by a rather long and wide stem which flares at the base. One example has four serrations on each side of the blade. The base of this example has also been ground.

Small side and corner notched points. These 18 points have been grouped into six descriptive categories. A statistical summary of the six classes is presented in Appendix 9. The descriptive categories are based primarily on size and shape differences. These differences are adequately illustrated in Appendix 9 and on

Plate 41. A feature of the points in class F is particularly worthy of note. These two points differ from the others illustrated in their relatively greater thickness and by an extreme amount of wear on the tip and blade. One example of this type of wear, P on Plate 41, shows an almost rounded edge which would be completely unserviceable for penetrating the flesh of beast or bird. The nature of the wear indicates that the point may very well have been the tip of a drill used to penetrate a material such as wood or bone.

Dustin-like points are represented by two examples. The larger has the distinct medial ridge so characteristic of the Dustin points; in the smaller example this ridge is not as noticeable.

Large bifaces or knives (Pl. 42) are represented by five pieces of chipped flint. These are probably finished artifacts even though in the literature they are often referred to as blanks. They lack the step-like retouch which characterizes the small, thick, steep-edge pieces. Their relative thinness in proportion to their size suggests that they were used as tools, either as knives, or perhaps as points for spears or lances which may have been used to hunt some of the larger animals. Some slight suggestion of grinding on the basal edges of the triangular shaped blades indicates that they may have been hafted. The largest piece, example G on Plate 42, apparently broke in the process of retouch. It displays a type of fracture which a colleague, Edwin N. Wilmsen, pointed out as distinctive of accidental breakage during retouch. It is a good example of the type of tool from which the flakes of bifacial retouch were derived. On examination, only a few of the flakes that had been driven off in retouching were represented in the analysis; these were the larger flakes. Most of the flakes that had been removed were very small and were not recovered in the course of excavation.

Ovate biface pieces (Pl. 42, C, D, E) represent a distinct class of artifacts that stands out from the general collection because of the overall similarity of type of stone and shape. The stone seems to be generally of a finer grade and a lighter color than most of the stone from the site, although it differs slightly among the pieces. This, along with their ovate shape, makes them easily identifiable.

SCRAPERS (Pl. 43)

Thumb nail. These represent a class of artifacts which have been traditionally reported in the literature. They are generally triangular in shape, with the working or scraping edge along the

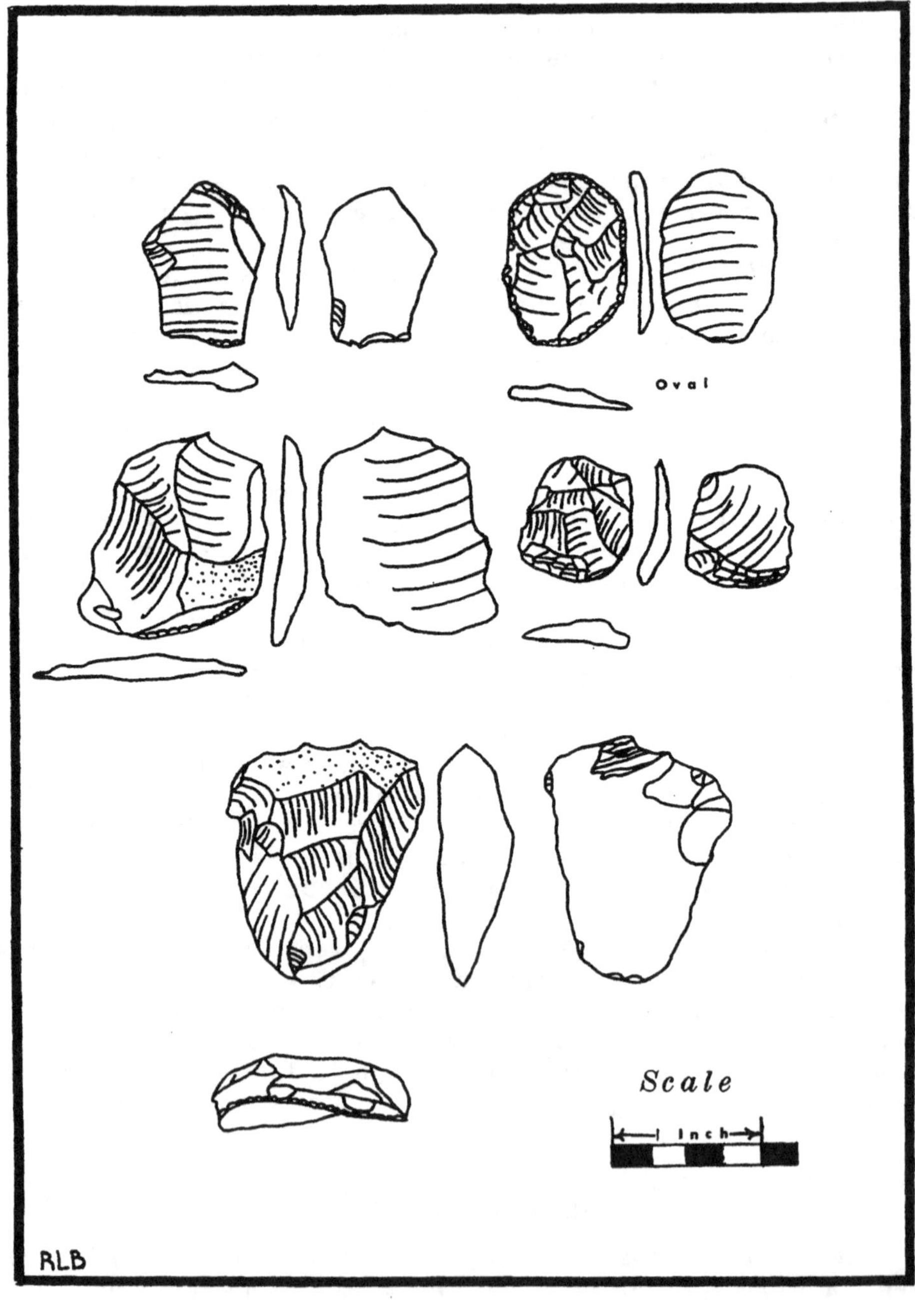

FIG. 16. Moccasin Bluff Scrapers.

widest dimension of the tool. The bottom surface is generally flat while the upper surface has a humped appearance. One example is unifacially flaked while all the rest are bifacially flaked. Seven of the eight pieces classified have the step retouch on the dorsal surface described by Crabtree and Davis (1968) which results from the resharpening of wood-working tools.

Oval scrapers. Two tools were classified as oval scrapers (see Fig. 16). They might equally well have been included with the retouched flakes since they both were manufactured on flakes, but the angle of the working edge is blunt and steeper than on the retouched flakes, which suggests that these tools were used as scraping tools rather than cutting tools. The tools are retouched around the entire circumference of the piece and any of the edges may have been used as a working edge. They also have the step retouch described by Crabtree and Davis (1968).

Hafted scrapers (Pl. 43, K, L, M, N) The hafted scrapers differ from all other scrapers in two primary ways. The first and obvious one is that they show evidence of having been hafted by the presence of a stem or notching to facilitate hafting. Their second distinctive feature is that in contrast to the other scrapers their working edge appears similar to the working edge on most of the bifacial tools, i.e., both sides of the working edge are symmetrical. On all other tools classified as scrapers the working edge is asymmetrical; the bottom edge is a plane while the top edge is convex. Plate 43 illustrates the different shapes of the hafted scrapers.

Other scrapers (Fig. 16). This class represents a series of tools of miscellaneous shape on which one or more of the surfaces have the asymmetrically shaped, steep working edge which is felt to be characteristic of scrapers. These pieces also have the step retouch.

Drills (Pl. 44) fall into three classes, a large T-shaped class, a smaller T-shaped class, and a small ovate class. The larger drills are represented by only two specimens, both of which are broken. The largest piece (example H, Pl. 44) represents the greater part of a blade of a standard type of prehistoric drill from the area. The smaller of the two (example G, Pl. 44) is slightly asymmetrical and more crudely flaked. It resembles the larger drill in its diamond-shaped cross section and in the method of retouch—flakes are removed along the edge of both surfaces in parallel fashion resulting in the formation of a ridge along the top and bottom sides of the piece. This example raises the question of how one can drill with an asymmetrical drill. The answer, of course, is that one probably cannot and that the tool in question

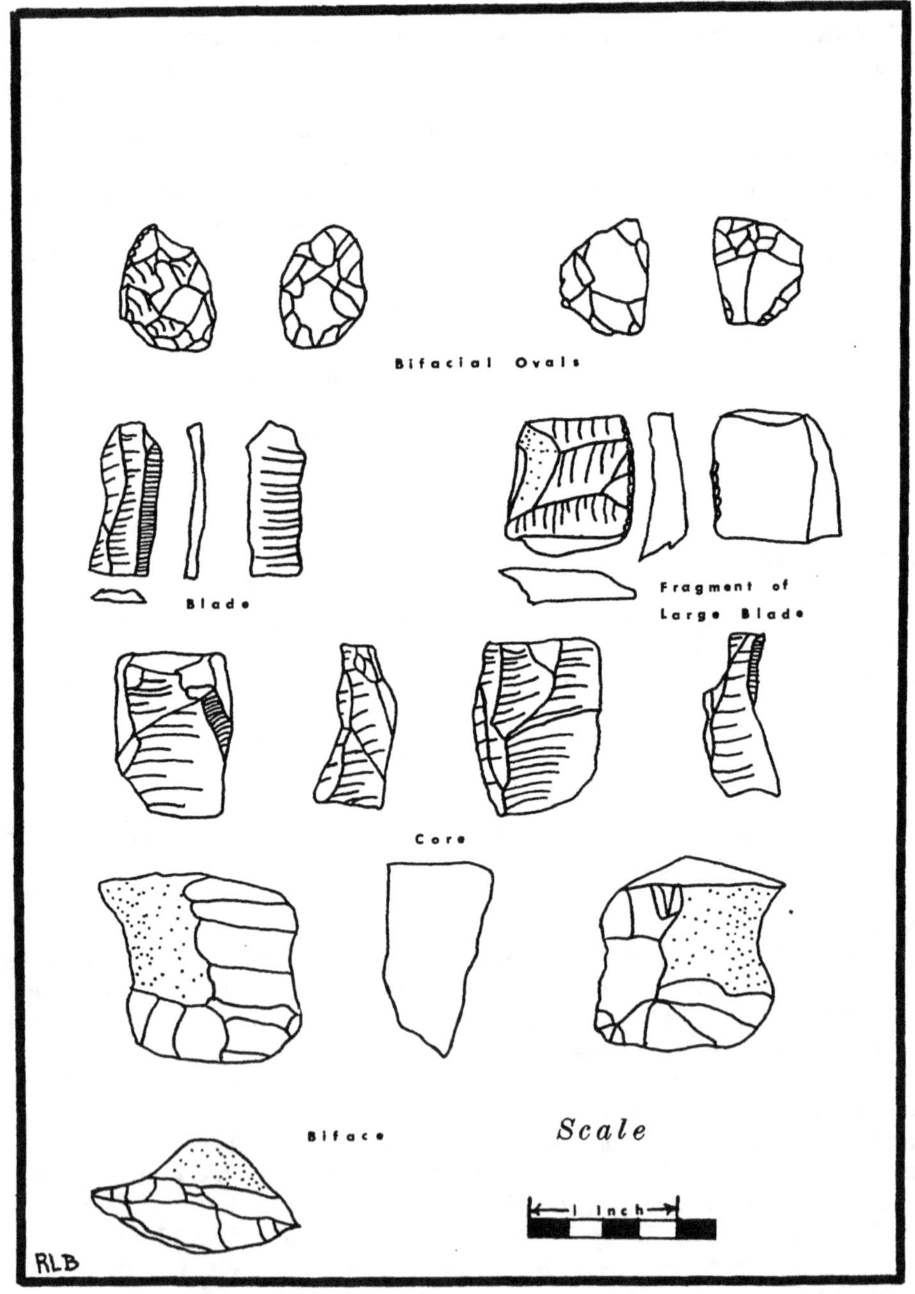

FIG. 17. Miscellaneous Lithic Tools from Moccasin Bluff.

was probably not used as a drill, but must have had some other function.

Gravers (Pl. 44, I, J, K). This somewhat bizarre-looking group of tools has as its common characteristic the small sharp projection near the top of the tool. All examples are irregularly shaped and all appear to have been broken or reworked from broken tools.

Small, thick, steep-edge pieces (Pl. 45). At first glance these tools appear to be unfinished bifacial tools, perhaps points that the Indian had difficulty thinning. However, upon closer examination, it becomes obvious that they form a separate class. A sample of 28 were examined for evidence of use and retouch. Ten of the pieces have the step retouch described by Crabtree and Davis (1968). Almost every piece had a serrated or sinuous, saw-like, denticulate edge which was experimentally determined to be effective for sawing through or incising small pieces of wood. Four of the pieces had dulled edges which, according to Wilmsen, appeared to be the result of heavy wear that often results from working bone or wood. All pieces except two are bifacially flaked; these two are unifacial. In summary, these tools may have been used in a variety of tasks which required a thick, heavy tool.

FRAGMENTS OF BIFACIAL TOOLS

A final class of chipped stone pieces consists of fragmentary pieces which are summarized in Table 8.

DISTRIBUTION OF CHIPPED STONE

The distribution of chipped stone material (Tables 9-11) tends to confirm the conclusion drawn from the distribution of the pits that the greatest concentration of material, and presumably the heaviest occupation, occurred in the area of trench C. The remaining trenches appear to have sampled the periphery of the site.

Although the significance of the distribution of material on sites is not established, what little evidence does exist (see Binford, et al., 1966) indicates that the distribution of flint on a site can be highly variable. The factors that determine the spatial distribution of chippage on a site have not been conclusively ascertained, but among those often mentioned are specialized activity areas or different occupations over time which utilize the spatial area of the site in different ways. Because the implications of

TABLE 8

TOTALS OF CHIPPED STONE

			N	%
Primary flakes			122	8.0
Block flakes			235	15.5
Simple flakes			724	47.6
Utilized and/or retouched flakes			54	3.5
concave		11		
convex		12		
complex		6		
straight		25		
Flakes of bifacial retouch			34	2.2
Blades			6	0.4
Scrapers			23	1.5
thumb nail		12		
oval		2		
hafted		3		
other		6		
Points			133	8.8
small triangular		104		
small stemmed		3		
large stemmed		4		
expanding stemmed		2		
small side and corner notched		18		
A	4			
B	2			
C	6			
D	2			
E	2			
F	2			
Dustin-like		2		
Large blade or knife			7	0.5
Ovates			3	0.2
Drills			6	0.4
Gravers			6	0.4
Small, thick, steep-edge pieces			53	3.5
Miscellaneous			5	0.3
Fragments of bifacial tools			104	6.8
tips		36		
small triangles	20			
others	16			
bases		48		
small triangles	35			
others	13			
miscellaneous		20		
Cores			4	0.3
		Totals	1519	99.9

the spatial distributions at Moccasin Bluff are unclear, only those factors which may be significant will be mentioned.

One might expect that material will be concentrated in the trenches with the highest density of pits e.g., trenches A and C. The further away from these trenches that one samples, the less material one will find. This expectation seems to be borne out by the distribution of the material at Moccasin Bluff. Examining the adjusted frequencies in Table 10, one first notices the relatively low number of primary flakes in trenches C and F. The site as a whole has a rather low ratio of flakes to finished artifacts and our understanding of the factors governing this ratio is far from adequate. Trench E has a much higher number of simple flakes than might be expected. Trench C has a larger number of flakes of bifacial retouch; trench F has a high frequency of blades. Trench C is again outstanding in having a large number of thumb nail scrapers. The number of small triangular points appears to be high in trench C, but when an adjustment is made for the 16 points from pit 92 this trench no longer appears exceptional. Trench E is noteworthy in being associated with a rather high frequency of small triangular points; trench F has fewer than expected. The number of small stemmed points and type C side notched points also have higher frequencies in C than in the other trenches. The number of small, thick, steep-edge pieces in trench C as compared to the other trenches is truly impressive. Even after making adjustments for the 11 pieces from pit 92 their frequency is still three times greater than that in any other trench. Trench C is also exceptional because it contains no tips of small triangular points while at the same time it has the highest frequency of bases of small triangular points.

The only overall hypothesis that can be ventured is that trench C—with its high frequencies of flakes of bifacial retouch, thumb nail scrapers, and small, thick, steep-edge pieces—may represent a specialized activity area, the exact nature of which is unclear.

TABLE 9

DISTRIBUTION OF CHIPPED STONE BY TRENCH

Trench	A	B	C	D	E	F	G	H	K	L	M	N	O	Total*
Primary flakes	79	5	9	4	8	2		2		1	3	1	8	122
Block flakes	110	3	28	6	32	14	1	3	2	1	18	4	12	234
Simple flakes	284	23	85	15	104	73	4	17		3	47	20	38	713
Utilized flakes	25	4	8	1	2	3	1				7		1	52
Flakes of bifacial retouch	14	1	8	1	1	2	1	1			4			33
Blades	2					3		1						6
Scrapers														
thumb-nail	6		4		1							1		12
oval	1					1								2
hafted	1				1	1								3
other	6													6
Points														
small triangular	52	7	28[a]	2	10	2	1				2			104
small stemmed	2				1									3
large stemmed	1		2			1								4
expanding base						2								2
small side and corner notched														
A	2				1							1		4
B	1					1								2
C			4			2								6
D	1					1								2
E	1				1									2
F	1		1											2
Dustin-like	1		1											2
Large blades	3		3	1										7
Ovates	2		1											3
Drills	4				1								1	6

TABLE 9 (Continued)

Trench	A	B	C	D	E	F	G	H	K	L	M	N	O	Total*
Gravers			3											3
Small, thick, steep-edge pieces	14	4	20[b]		8	1		2	1	1	1		1	53
Miscellaneous	1		1	1	1	1								5
Fragments														
tips														
small triangular	15	1			1	1	1			1				20
other	4		3		4	2		1			2			16
bases														
small triangular	19		9		3	2					1		1	35
other	7		2		2	2								13
miscellaneous	10		6		1	2							1	20
Cores	1				1						1		1	4
Total	670	48	226	31	184	119	9	27	3	7	86	27	64	1501

* Totals do not agree with totals in Table 8 because some test pits are not included in this table.
[a]16 from pit 92.
[b]11 from pit 92.

TABLE 10

DISTRIBUTION OF CHIPPED STONE BY TRENCH
(Trenches Adjusted to Uniform Size)

Trench	A	B	C	D	E	F	G	H	K	L	M	N	O
Primary flakes	42	8	17	26	22	3		5		16	6	4	40
Block flakes	58	5	53	39	89	22	13	7	16	16	36	15	60
Simple flakes	149	37	162	97	288	112	53	41		48	94	77	190
Utilized flakes	14	8	15	6	6	6	13				14		5
Flakes of bifacial retouch	7	2	15	6	3	3					8		
Blades	1					5		2					
Scrapers													
thumb-nail	3		8		3							4	
oval	1					2							
hafted	1				3	2							
other	3												
Points													
small triangular	27	11	53[a]	13	28	3	13				4		
small stemmed	1					3							
large stemmed	1		4			2							
expanding base						3							
small side and corner notched													
A	1											4	
B	1					2							
C			8			3							
D	1					2							
E	1				3								
F			2										
Dustin-like	1	2	2										
Large blades	2		6										
Ovates	1		2			2							
Drills	2				3								5

TABLE 10 (Continued)

Trench	A	B	C	D	E	F	G	H	K	L	M	N	O
Gravers			6										
Small, thick, steep-edge pieces	7	7	38[b]		22	2		5	8	16	2		5
Miscellaneous	1		2	6	3	2							
Fragments													
tips													
small triangular	8	2			3	2	13			16			
other	2		6		11	3		2			4		
bases													
small triangular	10		17		8	3					2		5
other	4		4		6	3							
miscellaneous	5		11		3	3							5
Cores	1				3						2		5

[a]30 from pit 92.
[b]21 from pit 92.

TABLE 11

DISTRIBUTION OF CHIPPED STONE WITHIN AND OUTSIDE OF PITS

	In pit	%	Out of pit	%	Total
Primary flakes	38	31	84	69	122
Block flakes	54[a]	24	178	76	232
Simple flakes	181[b]	25	543	75	724
Utilized flakes	15	28	39	72	54
Flakes of bifacial retouch	9	26	25	74	34
Blades	2	33	4	67	6
Scrapers	4	17	19	83	23
thumb-nail	3	25	9	75	12
oval			2	100	2
hafted			3	100	3
other	1	17	5	83	6
Points	60		73		133
small triangular	51[c]	49	53	51	104
small stemmed	1	33	2	67	3
large stemmed	2	50	2	50	4
expanding base	1	50	1	50	2
small side and corner notched	5	28	13	72	18
A	1	25	3	75	4
B	1	50	1	50	2
C	2	33	4	67	6
D	1	50	1	50	2
E			2	100	2
F			2	100	2
Dustin-like			2	100	2
Large blades	2	28	5	72	7
Ovates	3	100			3
Drills	2	33	4	67	6
Gravers	3	50	3	50	6
Small, thick, steep-edge pieces	19[d]	36	34	64	53
Fragments					
tips					
small triangular	4	20	16	80	20
other	3	19	13	81	16
base					
small triangular	14	40	21	60	35
other	2	15	11	85	13

[a]10 from pit 92.
[b]37 from pit 78 and 11 from pit 92.
[c]16 from pit 92.
[d]11 from pit 92.

V

CERAMICS

THE ceramic material from the Moccasin Bluff site falls into two major categories that reflect two distinct technological traditions recognized by archaeologists working in the Upper Mississippi Valley. The earliest used crushed rock as the tempering material in the manufacture of ceramics. This tradition makes its appearance with the first ceramics from the area during the Early Woodland period around 500 B.C. and continues in the northern areas until the abandonment of pottery-making in the Historic Period in the Upper Mississippi Valley and Upper Great Lakes. The second tradition is based upon the use of the ground shell of fresh water mollusks as the tempering material and is usually associated with the prehistoric cultures of the Mississippian Period. This tradition seems to make its first appearance in southwestern Michigan around A.D. 1000 and persists until the Historic Period. The grit-tempered material shows a strong developmental tradition in the area beginning with the introduction of the earliest pottery and continuing until the replacement of aboriginal pottery by items of European and American manufacture. The archaeological problem is to distinguish stylistic change through time so that a usable chronology can be constructed to adequately date the various occupations and to help interpret the developmental sequence. The methodology employed in classifying the pottery was simply to sort the pottery into groups which reflected greater or lesser amounts of similarities and differences. These groups were then examined and sorted into individual vessels. The vessels as reflected in the collected rim sherds are the units of analysis.

A total of 534 usable rim sherds were recovered in the University of Michigan excavations. A usable rim sherd for this study is one which is about the size of a dime or larger. These 534 rim sherds were sorted into 424 vessels. These 424 vessels were then grouped into the following categories.

MOCCASIN BLUFF WARE

This ware includes most of the grit-tempered vessels at the site and constitutes about 87 percent of the total sample. It includes both cordmarked and plain varieties. The ware shows certain changes in tempering material and paste through time along with certain changes in vessel form and techniques of decoration. It is probable that at certain periods several of the traits are present with greater frequency than at other periods. The ceramic tradition represented in this ware appears to cover a rather long period of time and shares the general developmental trends which are recognized for the post Middle Woodland groups in the Upper Mississippian area. The lack of stratigraphic control in this sample prevents us from testing these ideas rigorously.

Moccasin Bluff Cordmarked

Variety 1a (Pl. 12)

This group of 16 vessels is represented by 16 sherds. The surface texture has the feel of a sandy paste, that is, when the thumb is run back and forth across the surface of the sherd, it often has a more sandy, or coarse, feeling than most other sherds in the collection. The texture is uniform in composition and well consolidated. Color, using the Munsell guide, varies from reddish brown 5YR 5/4, reddish yellow 5YR 6/6, strong brown 7.5YR 5/6, light brown 7.5YR 6/4, gray brown 10YR 5/2, brown 10YR 5/3, yellow brown 10YR 5/6, pale brown 10YR 6/3, to very pale brown 10YR 7/3. The color tends to be uniform throughout the thickness of the sherd with only a slight modification of chroma between the exterior and the inner and interior surfaces of the sherd.

Tempering material is a black crushed rock composed of hornblende with some magnetite, probably deriving from a diorite source. The particle sizes vary from quite small to a fair number of large pieces which achieve a size of up to .8 cm. The amount of temper seems to be somewhat denser than the average for sherds in the collection—a fair number of the particles are visible on both the interior and the exterior surface of the sherds. The rim form is generally straight although five of the vessels have a slightly excurved or constricted neck. There is a tendency for the rim diameter at the lip to be a little thinner than at a point between one to three cm below the lip. The average diameter at the lip is .562 cm, range .5-.9 cm, while at the lower point it measures .675 cm, range .3-.8 cm. This tendency is even more pronounced for the five vessels with the excurved rim. For these the average diameter at the lip is .42 cm, while at a point one to three cm below the lip, it is .7 cm.

All sherds have a cordmarked exterior surface and a smoothed interior surface. The top of the lip is flattened or rounded; five sherds of the sample are smoothed, while the rest are cordmarked. On the exterior surface the cordmarking runs perpendicular to the lip in all cases except for one of the excurved vessels which has oblique cordmarking slanting from top left to bottom right. Two of the excurved vessels also show a slight collar of between .3-.5 cm in height. None of the sherds show any sign of cooking residue. The sherds are also of a smaller size than the sample in general—10 of the sherds are about the size of a nickel or smaller.

Variety 1b

This grouping is distinguishable from variety 1a both by paste and temper. The vessels within the group vary among themselves with regard to the shape of the rim and the lip.

Group 1: square, flattened, and cordmarked lip (Pl. 13-17). A straight rim with flattened or slightly rounded lip and cordmarking on the top of the lip characterizes this class of vessels. One example has some channeling on the interior of the rim just below the lip while all the rest of the sherds in this group have plain, smoothed interior surfaces. The group consists of 18 sherds grouped into 15 vessels. The paste is well consolidated and of uniform texture. Exterior color ranges from strong brown 7.5YR 5/6, to dark gray 10YR 3/1, gray brown 10YR 5/2, pale brown 10YR 6/3, light yellow brown 10YR 6/4, to very pale brown 10YR 7/3. The gray browns to grays are the most common. The interior surface color tends to be slightly lighter in color, the core of the sherds is quite a bit darker, with black being common.

Tempering is medium to light in density, with quartz grains, some mica scales, and a few pieces of feldspar along with other unidentified material. Temper size is generally .05 cm in size or smaller while in some cases it gets as large as .2 to .3 cm. The source of the temper seems to have been a granitic type rock. It would be interesting to compare the products obtained by crushing various types of granitic rock with a more rigorous study of the temper of the sherds to see if there is a high correlation between what is produced by crushing granitic rock and what is included as tempering material in the clay. It may be that the aborigines were more selective in the material they preferred for tempering than we now suspect.

There is little difference between the thickness of the sherd at the lip as compared with one to three cm below the lip. The mean thickness of the lip is .743 cm, range .4-.9 cm, while below it is .740 cm, range .6-.9 cm. Cordmarking is mixed and variable. In some cases it is narrow with the impressions placed perpendicular to the lip of the vessel and arranged in parallel fashion on the sides of the vessels. In other cases the cordmarking is slightly smoothed over; in still other examples, it is coarse and applied in a variable fashion.

Group 2: protruding exterior rim (Pl. 13). These three sherds represent three additional vessels that resemble the above group in most of the technical attributes but differ in the shape of the rim. They have a profile which resembles a bulging collar, i.e., the exterior surface of the rim just below the lip is slightly convex in profile, giving the sherd a somewhat distinctive appearance. Cordmarking is irregular—the top of the lip is cordmarked, but in one case the cordmarking is partially smoothed over. Average thickness of the vessel at the lip is .733 cm, range .5-.9 cm, while below the lip it is 1.0 cm, range .8-1.3 cm.

Group 3: beveled lip (Pl. 13). A third subgrouping within the variety 1b sherds is a class of 11 sherds which belong to eight different vessels. The outstanding characteristic of this group is the beveled lip. The paste and temper characteristics are similar to those described above. The average thickness of the rim is .775 cm, range .5-.9 cm; at the lip, the average thickness is the same, or .775 cm, range .7-1.0 cm. All the sherds have cordmarking on the top of the lip; the cordmarking on the exterior of the vessel is variable. Three of the vessels are unusual for their slight—.4 to .7 cm high—collar which results from the folding over onto the exterior edge of the rim of a small amount of clay from the top of the lip. Perhaps this is a by-product of beveling the lip. This group also has a greater frequency of sherds indicating a slightly constricted neck. Two of the sherds with this constricted neck are less than three cm in length as measured from the lip to the bottom of the sherd. Two of the others are over five cm in length. If all sherds were longer than five cm, the frequency of vessels having constricted necks might be greater because the two vessels represented by the longer sherds would most likely have been classified as straight had the sherds been shorter.

Group 4: lip squared and plain (Pl. 14). This is a somewhat variable class of vessels represented by 35 sherds from 28 vessels. Paste and temper are generally similar to those described above for group 1. Color of the exterior surface is dark reddish brown 5YR 3/3, reddish yellow 7.5YR 6/6, dark gray 10YR 4/1, grayish brown 10YR 5/2, pale brown 10YR 6/3, to light yellowish brown 10YR 6/4, and one black, the majority of the vessels are grayish brown to pale brown. The interior surface color is black in almost all cases; the core of the sherds is similar to the color of the exterior surface or slightly darker. Temper particles range up to .4 cm in diameter, but the vast majority are .1 cm or smaller. The rim shape is straight or constricted with the top of the lip being flattened or the edges slightly rounded. The average thickness of the sherd at the lip is .7 cm, range .6-1.0 cm, while at mid-rim it is .78 cm, range .5-1.0 cm. Exterior cordmarking is variable, the top of the lip is smoothed. Three of the sherds in this group have evidence of cooking residue on the exterior or the rim; two show this evidence on the interior of the rim.

Group 5: small collar (Pl. 15). This group of vessels is distinguished by a small collar surrounding the vessel at the exterior edge of the lip. There are 20 sherds from 15 vessels. Paste and temper are similar to the groups described above. Color of the exterior surface of the vessel is reddish yellow 5YR 6/6, dark reddish brown 5YR 3/3, dark gray 10YR 4/1, gray brown 10YR 5/2, and light yellowish brown 10YR 6/4; the majority of the vessels are dark gray to gray brown. Rim form is straight or slightly constricted, with the top of the lip flattened in most cases. Thickness of the rim at the lip is .73 cm, range .5-1.0 cm, while at mid-rim it is .72 cm, range .5-.9 cm. The vessels have a slight collar which varies in height from .4 to .9 cm. The cordmarking may be variable, but most of the sherds have parallel cordmarking placed perpendicular to the lip. Cooking residue is present on the interior surface of two of the vessels. One of the vessels has a drilled hole about two cm below the lip.

Group 6: smoothed exterior surface, plain lip (Pl. 16). The final sub-group in this class is characterized by a partially smoothed-over exterior surface finish and plain surface top of lips. Twelve sherds representing 12 vessels are included in this group. Paste and temper characteristics are similar to those recorded for the other vessels described above. Color is predominantly gray brown; one sherd is a yellowish red 5YR 5/8 in color. Eight of the vessels show an excurving rim profile even though most of them are shorter than three cm in length. The top of the rims are smoothed and flattened; six of the sherds have a slight thickening of the lip resulting from the process of flattening the top of the lip. This thickening causes the average thickness at the lip to be greater than the thickness half way down the sherd: the average thickness of the sherd at the lip is .811 cm, range .6-1.1 cm; half way down the sherd, it is .733 cm, range .6-1.0 cm. The exterior surface has been cordmarked and then partially smoothed over, giving the sherd a somewhat distinctive appearance. Five sherds have evidence of cooking residue on either the interior, exterior, or the top of the sherd.

Moccasin Bluff Collared (Pl. 18)

This is a grouping of 15 sherds from 14 vessels which are distinguished by a good collar on the neck of the vessel and, in some cases, castellation. The group may be subdivided into two separate classes, A and B, which differ in paste and temper. Group A, six vessels, has the reddish and pale brown colors noted in variety 1a and is tempered by the same black temper described for that group. Group B, six vessels, tends to cluster in the gray-brown range with temper similar to variety 1b. Group A sherds are thinner than those in group B: the mean thickness at the lip for group A is .52 cm as contrasted to .662 cm for group B. The average thickness of the rim below the collar is .675 cm for group A and .760 cm for group B. The height of the collar varies between one and two cm for group A and 1.5 to 2 cm for group B. Castellations are present on two sherds from each group. One castellated sherd from group B has elongated impressions approximately one cm in length and .5 cm wide, placed about 1.5 cm apart on the interior edge of the rim. The impressions begin at the lip and extend downward. Cooking residue is not present on any of the sherds in either group; cordmarking is mixed and not distinctive.

Moccasin Bluff Modified Lip

Group 1: Cord-wrapped-stick impressions (Pl. 19) This group of vessels is distinguished by the presence of cord-wrapped-stick impressions on the top of the lip. Twenty-two sherds from 19 vessels are included in this class. Paste and temper are generally similar to that described for variety 1a vessels, although five of the vessels have characteristics associated with variety 1b vessels. Color includes yellowish red 5YR 5/6, light brown 7.5YR 6/4, dark gray 10YR 4/1, dark gray brown 10YR 4/2, gray brown 10YR 5/2, brown 10YR 5/3, light brownish gray 10YR 6/2, pale brown 10YR 5/3, with pale brown and brown being the most prevalent. Rim form is fairly straight; most sherds being below three cm in length. The sherds tend to be slightly thicker at the lip than further down the body: dimensions for the thickness at the lip average .757 cm, range .6-1.2 cm; further down the rim they average .688 cm, range .4-.9 cm.

Cordmarking tends to be fine, with about seven rows of parallel cord marks per centimeter. One sherd has a heavier, irregular cordmarking, and also has a small collar .5 cm high. The unique decorative feature of these sherds is the modification of the top of the lip either with a cord wrapped stick or, in one case, with punctates. The impressions are variably placed and vary from .3 cm to .5 cm in width (one is 1.0 cm). They are placed directly across the lip, obliquely across the lip, obliquely across the exterior edge of the lip, or lengthwise along the top of the lip. In most cases they lie parallel to one another; however, in one example, they are arranged in opposing fashion obliquely across the top of the lip in a V pattern. The impressions are generally placed between .5 and .6 cm apart although in one example they are spaced more than 1.5 cm apart and in another, they are 2.0 apart. Three sherds differ from the general pattern and from one another. On one, the only decorations are .35 cm wide punctates on the top of the lip placed 1.5 cm apart and between .5 and .5 cm deep; on another, the stick impressions are placed on a 1.0 cm high bead-like collar; on the third, there are opposing diagonal slashing incisions on a .8 cm high collar. No cooking residue is visible on any of the sherds.

Group 2: Paddle-edge impressed (Pl. 20) This group of five sherds from five vessels has paste and temper characteristics similar to variety 1b. Color of the sherds includes strong brown 7.5YR 5/6, very dark gray 10YR 3/1, dark gray 10YR 4/1, dark grayish brown 10YR 4/2, and yellowish brown 10YR 5/4. The core of the sherds is generally black, at times very dark gray; the interior surface is similar in color to the exterior surface or slightly lighter. Temper particles are small, generally under .1 cm, and tempering density is light to medium. Rim profiles are generally straight. Most of the sherds are less than 2 cm in length. Average thickness of the rim at the lip is .65 cm, range .5-.9 cm; below the lip, thickness averages .65 cm, range .5-.8 cm. Cordmarking is light and it is difficult to distinguish individual impressions. On the two sherds where impressions are visible the pattern is mixed and irregular. The characteristic decorative feature consists of small paddle-edge impressions placed on the exterior edge of the lip. The impressions are placed approximately 1 cm apart, have an average length of .5 cm, and are approximately .4 cm wide and .2 cm deep. Some of the impressions assume an elongated shape, while others are more rounded in form. One example has cooking residue on the interior and the exterior of the rim.

Group 3: Finger-nail impressed (Pl. 20) This small group is represented by 11 sherds from six vessels. Paste and temper characteristics show nothing unusual and approach the description provided for variety 1b sherds. Color of the exterior surface is gray brown 10YR 5/2, very dark gray 10YR 3/1, and very pale brown 10YR 7/3. The interior surface is either dark gray 2.5Y N4/ or very dark gray 10YR 5/1, while the core is dark gray to black. Temper size may approach .4 cm in size, but generally is much smaller, approximately .05 cm in diameter. The rim profile is generally straight, with the top of the lip being square in shape. One example has a thinner profile with the lip rounded. The top of the lip is generally plain although one example has cordmarking. Average lip thickness is .80 cm, range .6-.9 cm; the average thickness of the rim below the lip is .70 cm, range .6-.9 cm. Cordmarking runs vertically down the vessel sides and tends to be quite heavy and large (three impressions per centimeter); one vessel has small, faint impressions. Some of the impressions are partially smoothed over. One vessel is plain. Decoration consists of finger nail impressions of the exterior edge of the lip. These impressions vary from .8 to 1.4 cm apart and from .7 to 1.3 cm in length. Cooking residue is present on the interior surface of two vessels and on the exterior of a third.

Group 4: Lunate impressions (Pl. 20) This is a fairly homogeneous group of 10 sherds from nine vessels. There is some tendency for the paste of these vessels to have a somewhat laminar texture and, in some cases, for breaks to have a smoother, chalk-like appearance. Tempering material is variable, including black particles as well as white quartz fragments. Particle size may approach .5 cm; in a few sherds, a fair percentage of the particles are of a larger size. In other examples, the density of the tempering particle is rather light and only a few particles are actually visible. Exterior surface coloring is rather uniform, ranging from dark grayish brown 10YR 4/2, to very pale brown 10YR 7/3, and including light brownish gray 10YR 6/2, pale brown 10YR 6/3, light yellowish brown 10YR 6/4 and light gray 10YR 7/2. The interior surface is either a dark gray or a darker shade of color than the exterior surface; the core is either dark gray or black. One pale brown sherd is uniform in color throughout.

The rim profiles are generally straight; three examples are slightly excurved. Most of the sherds are less than three cm in length. The top of the lips tend to have been smoothed and the lip rounded. A small collar has been folded over on the exterior of the vessel and worked into the surface of the vessel so that in some cases it is barely visible. The thickness of the vessel at the lip averages .70 cm, range .6-.9 cm; below the rim it is .60 cm, range .5-.7 cm. The vessel exterior, at least directly below the rim, has been cordmarked and then either partially or completely smoothed over. The cordmarking seems to have been heavy (approximately three impressions per centimeter) and to have run vertically down from the lip. Decoration consists of a series of lunate impressions placed along the exterior edge of the lip. These impressions are either smoothed or contain a series of small straight parallel lines in the lunate-shaped depression. The impressions are placed between .8 and 1.9 cm apart and often extend all the way to the interior of the lip edge. No cooking residue was observed on any of the sherds.

Group 5: Lip-thickened and notched (Pl. 21) This is a somewhat mixed group of 13 sherds from 12 vessels. Their common characteristics are that the sherds are thickened at the lip and that the exterior edge of the lip is notched. Paste is variable: in some sherds it is well compacted and of good texture; in others, it may be laminar or, in several cases, even quite friable. Temper varies from crushed rock to two examples of mixed shell temper and rock, to one example of all shell temper. Some are heavily tempered with very small temper particles, while others are lightly tempered with somewhat larger sized particles. Color includes pale brown 10YR 6/3, light yellowish brown 10YR 6/4, very dark gray brown 10YR 3/2, dark gray 10YR 4/1, very dark gray 10YR 3/1, and black, with the grays being the most common. The shell tempering is restricted to the pale browns and the yellowish browns. Interior surface resembles the exterior surface in color, although it is a bit darker in a few cases. The core of the sherds is usually gray to dark gray to black.

Rim shape is mostly straight—a few sherds are excurved—and all sherds have a length of less than three cm. Top of the lip is usually flat and squarish, and may or may not be cordmarked. In some cases the lip of the vessel has been thickened; in others some of the clay has been folded outward to form a slight collar or beaded-like rim. In one case it is clear that a separate strip of clay has simply been added around the exterior edge of the lip and across the top to achieve the same effect. The sherd dimensions for average thickness at the lip are 1.04 cm, range .7-1.4 cm; further down the rim, the average thickness is only .717 cm, range .4-.8 cm. Cordmarking is mixed and irregular with smoothing over occurring in a number of examples. The notching on the exterior of the lip varies from small grooves only .25 cm apart to large lunate-shaped impressions 1.5 cm apart. Some of the notches are narrow, only .5, .2, .3 cm wide; the large lunate depression may be as large as one cm. Three of the sherds have cooking residue on the interior surface of the rim.

Group 6: Punctates on the exterior edge of the lip (Pl. 21) The common feature of these six sherds representing six vessels is the presence of impressions or punctates just below the exterior edge of the lip. The group can be broken down into two distinct sub-groups, A and B. Group A consists of three sherds from three vessels. The sherds, and probably the vessels, are larger in size than those in the second group. The paste is well consolidated with irregular breaks along the edges. Temper varies from all black in one sherd to mixed colors in the others. Tempering density is medium; temper particles are visible on the exterior and the interior surfaces of the sherds. Particle size may reach .3 cm, but most of the pieces are much smaller. Rim profiles are slightly sinuous, with the top of the lip smoothed and squared. Cordmarking is irregular and heavy (about three impressions per centimeter). Thickness of the sherds at the lip averages .933 cm, range .8-1.1 cm, while below the lip it is .766 cm, range .7-.8 cm. Impressions or punctates are shallow and are placed just below the exterior edge of the lip, between 1 and 1.5 cm apart, and have an average diameter of .6 cm. No cooking residue was visible on any of the sherds.

Group B also consists of three sherds representing three vessels. Paste is also well composed, but temper is mostly white quartzite particles from crushed granitic rocks. Particle size may approach .3 cm, but most particles are much smaller. Tempering density is about medium and particles are not visible on the surface. Color is dark gray, 10YR 3/2, pale brown 10YR 6/3 and very dark gray 10YR 5/2. The interior surface tends to be the same color as the exterior surface. In the one case in which it differs, the interior surface is gray. The core is very dark gray to black. Rim profiles tend to be slightly excurved, with an average thickness at the lip of .766 cm, range .7-.9 cm; further down the rim the average thickness is .666 cm, range .6-.7 cm.

The exterior edge of the rim is slightly rounded, while the interior edge is more rectangular. The top of the lip is smoothed. The cordmarking on the exterior surface is medium to fine and in two of the sherds is smoothed over. The punctates just below the exterior edge of the lip are small and shallow. They vary in diameter from between .2 to .3 cm, may be elongated to .7 cm, and are spaced between .8 to 1.0 cm apart. One sherd has cooking residue on the exterior edge of the rim.

Moccasin Bluff Impressed Exterior Lip

Group 1: Impressed exterior lip (Pl. 22, 23, 24, 25) This group represents a heterogeneous collection of 90 sherds from 52 vessels. The paste resembles that described for variety 1b vessels and is typical of most Woodland pottery from this area. Color includes dark reddish 5YR 4/2, reddish brown 5YR 5/4, yellowish red 5YR 5/6, brown 7.5YR 5/4 and 10YR 5/3, very dark gray 10YR 3/1, dark gray 10YR 4/1, dark grayish brown 10YR 4/2, gray brown 10YR 5/2, yellow brown 10YR 5/6, pale brown 10YR 6/3, light yellowish brown 10YR 6/4, very pale brown 10YR 7/2, with the grays and the gray browns being the most common colors. Temper is crushed granitic rock with some sand. Most of the particles are less than .05 cm in diameter, but some approach .4 cm. Generally, the largest particles are about .2 cm in size. Temper density varies from medium to light in most cases with a few sherds having a heavy density.

Rim profiles vary from straight to excurved; most of the straight sherds are less than .3 cm in length, while most of the sherds showing some constriction around the neck are longer than .4 cm. The top of the rim may be either flattened and squared, cordmarked or plain, rounded on the exterior edge, or rounded on both the exterior and the interior edges. The top of the rim may be thinned or, in one case, quite thickened. The average thickness at the lip is .745 cm, range .4-1.1 cm; further down it is .759 cm, range .5-1.0 cm. Cordmarking might best be called mixed and variable. It very seldom shows any such definite pattern as vertical parallel lines running from the lip; instead it has a mixed appearance, like the bark of an elm tree. In most cases it is light, in a few cases it is smoothed over. In two cases parts of the exterior surface are completely smoothed over, leaving a plain band on the sherds. The primary form of decoration on the sherds is a series of impressions placed around the exterior lip of the sherd. These impressions may be quite variable. In some cases they are long (up to 1.0 cm), narrow (up to

.3 cm), and spaced about .45 cm apart. In other cases they are more circular (diameter about .5 cm) and spaced up to 1.5 cm apart or as close as .5 cm. In still other cases the impressions appear to have been made with the side of a finger. The impressions may be very shallow and faint, only slightly modifying the exterior edge of the lip, or they may extend all the way across the top of the lip to the interior rim of the sherd. In most cases they are placed directly on the lip edge; in several examples, however, they are applied in parallel fashion, diagonally to the edge.

Four of the vessels have a hole drilled from 1.5 to 2.5 cm below the top of the rim. One vessel from this class has finger or antler trailed impressions placed over the cordmarked surface on the shoulder of the vessel. The impression runs from the neck of the vessel at a point about three cm below the lip vertically down from the lip in parallel fashion completely around the vessel. The impressions are spaced about two cm apart. This same vessel also has four groups composed of three lug handles at each quarter section of the vessel. Eight vessels have evidence of cooking residue distributed in the following manner: 1 interior and exterior, 2 exterior and interior, 1 exterior and top of lip, 1 top of lip and interior, 3 interior.

Group 2: Smooth paste (Pl. 24) This small group is represented by five sherds from four vessels. It is distinguishable by its paste and temper. The sherds have a smooth soap or wax-like surface texture which sets them apart from the other sherds in the above group. The surface color is very dark gray 10YR 3/1, as is the interior surface; the core of the sherds is generally black. Temper is composed of some crushed rock, sand, and some shell. All the shell seems to have been leached out of the sherds, leaving only the long thin narrow impressions in the sherd that indicate its former presence. The sherds are generally thinner than those of the preceding group: the thickness of the lip is .60 cm; further down the rim the thickness is .55 cm. All rim sherds are shorter than 3.0 cm and show some constriction around the neck. One sherd has a markedly outflaring profile. The lip is smoothed and may be flattened and squarish, but most often the exterior edge of the lip is rounded. The surface of the sherds has been cordmarked and then either partially or entirely smoothed over. Decoration consists of impressions on the exterior of the lip similar to those described for the preceding group. Cooking residue is present on the interior and the exterior surface of one sherd and on the interior surface of another.

Moccasin Bluff Plain (Pl. 26)

This group of 37 plain surface, undecorated vessels composed of 48 sherds. Paste is well consolidated and is similar to the paste on most other Woodland vessels. Color includes yellowish red 5YR 5/6, strong brown 7.5YR 5/6, reddish yellow 7.5 7/8, very dark brown 10YR 2/2, very dark gray 10YR 3/1, dark gray 10YR 4/1, dark grayish brown 10YR 4/2, grayish brown 10YR 5/2, brown 10YR 5/3, pale brown 10YR 6/3, light yellowish brown 10 YR 6/4, brownish yellow 10YR 6/6, and very pale brown 10YR 7/3, with pale brown, reddish yellow, and brownish yellow being the most common colors. Tempering is generally light; some of the sherds tend toward the medium class. Temper is mostly crushed granitic rock; one sherd has black temper particles. Particles are well smoothed over and are not visible on either the interior or the exterior surface of the sherds. Rim profiles are generally straight; most of the sherds are under 3.0 cm in length. The several sherds which exceed 3.0 cm in length all have excurving rim profiles. As one might expect in this class, all sherds have a smoothed, plain surface finish on the top of the lip. The shape of the profile of the top of the lip varies from squared in 12 cases, to rounded and thinned in six cases, to just rounded in 13 cases. Three examples have a thickened lip; three others have a small bead-like band running around the exterior edge of the lip. The average thickness of the sherds at the lip is .72 cm, range .3-1.1 cm, while below the lip it averages .73 cm, range .4-1.1 cm. Cooking residue is present on the exterior of two sherds and on the interior of one other.

Moccasin Bluff Plain Modified Lip

Group 1: Finger impressed (Pl. 27, 28) This is a group of 19 sherds from 15 vessels. Paste and temper characteristics are similar to those of most of the other Woodland groupings. Color includes reddish brown 5YR 4/3, very dark gray 10YR 3/1, dark gray 10YR 4/1, dark grayish brown 10YR 4/2, grayish brown 10 YR 5/2, brown 10YR 5/3, with grayish brown and brown being the most common colors. The color of the interior surface is usually a shade darker than the exterior surface; the core of the sherd is generally dark gray, very dark gray, or black. Temper size is generally small, below .05 cm and the density is light to medium. Rim form is generally straight; most sherds are less than 3.0 cm in length. A few forms display a rather acute angle at the exterior junction of the neck and shoulder. The top of the lip is plain and may be squarish and flat or beveled. Average thickness at the lip is .813 cm, range .4-1.2 cm; below the lip it is .747 cm, range .5-1.1 cm. Decoration consists of a series of broad impressions placed on top of, and on the exterior edge of, the lip. The impressions are generally around 1.0 cm in diameter, but achieve a diameter of up to 1.5 cm. Spacing of the impressions varies from 2.5 cm apart for the largest impressions to 1.5 cm apart for the most common ones. The impressions appear to have been made with the tip or side of the finger or perhaps with a tool of finger-like dimensions. They may extend across the top of the lip from the interior edge or may simply be placed on the exterior edge of the lip. No cooking residue was recognized on any of the vessels.

Group 2: Narrow notched (Pl. 28) Group 2, composed of 14 sherds from 14 vessels, is generally similar to group 1 in paste and temper characteristics. However, four sherds in the group show much less temper than most of the sherds from either group. Rim form is straight or excurved with most sherds less than 2.5 cm in length. Color includes reddish brown 5YR 5/4, dark brown 7.5YR 4/2, brown 7.5YR 5/2, strong brown 7.5YR 5/6, reddish yellow 7.5YR 6/6, very dark gray 10YR 3/1, light brownish gray 10YR 6/2, pale brown 10YR 6/3, light yellowish brown 10YR 6/4, very pale brown 10YR 7/3. Interior surfaces are the same color as, or darker than, exterior surfaces; cores are either the same color as the exteriors or very dark gray or black. The top of the lip may be flat and squarish, or rounded on the exterior lip, or completely rounded. The thickness of the lip is .743 cm, range .5-1.1 cm; further down the rim, it averages .675 cm, range .4-1.0 cm.

The surface of the sherds is plain. Decoration consists of narrow notching on the exterior edge of the lip. The largest notches are .5 cm, but generally they range around .3 cm. Spacing varies from .5 to 1.0 cm. Notches are generally placed perpendicular to the lip; a few examples are placed diagonally. Impressions are applied with a narrow tool; in some cases, the tool appears to have been pressed into the clay and then twisted with the wrist, leaving a V-shaped impression with a slight groove in it. Impressions always appear on the exterior edge of the lip; in no cases do they extend back to the interior edge of the lip. No cooking residue was found on any of the sherds.

Group 3: Rounded lip and small notches (Pl. 28) This is a group of seven small sherds from seven vessels. Paste is similar to those above but temper is very light. Color of the exterior surface is gray brown 10YR 5/2, reddish yellow 7.5YR 6/6, and black. Interior surface is generally the same color as the exterior surface; the core of the sherd is a shade darker. The rim profile is excurving; most of the sherds are shorter than 2.5 cm in length. Top of the lip is rounded in all cases and decoration consists of little notches placed on the top of the lip. The notches are shallow—approximately .2 cm deep and .2 cm wide, and .5 cm or less apart. Two of the sherds have cooking residue on the exterior edge of the lip. Thickness at the lip averages .58 cm, range .5-.8 cm; below the lip the average is .59 cm, range .4-.8 cm.

Moccasin Bluff Notched Applique Strip (Pl. 29, 30)

This distinctive and stylistically homogeneous group of 34 sherds from 20 vessels represents a widespread style that characterizes the very late Pre-historic and early Historic periods. Paste and temper are typical of most Late Woodland ceramics. The paste is well made, well compacted, and has a durable texture. The tempering is crushed granitic rock of up to .4 cm in diameter—but most often less than .05 cm in diameter—with density varying between light to medium. Colors include dark reddish gray 5YR 4/2, strong brown 7.5YR 5/6, black 10YR 2/1, very dark gray 10YR 3/1, dark brown 10YR 3/3, dark gray 10YR 4/1, gray brown 10YR 5/2, brown 10YR 5/3, pale brown 10YR 6/3, and light yellow brown 10YR 6/4, with the grays, browns, and the pale browns the predominant colors. The interior surface often matches the exterior in color; sometimes it is a bit darker; the core of the sherds is almost always black. The rim profile is outsloping or excurvate with a flattened, squarish lip. The top of the lip is usually plain, but may be cordmarked in a few examples. The thickness of the lip averages .805 cm, range .3-1.0 cm; the thickness of the rim averages .797 cm, range .5-1.0 cm.

Decoration consists of a series of diagonal impressions encircling the vessels about 1.5 to 2.0 cm below the lip. The impressions may be placed on the exterior vessel wall or an applique strip may be added to the exterior of the vessel upon which the impressions are then placed. The height of the strip and impressions never exceeds 1.0 cm. The impressions are rarely more than .2 cm wide and are placed diagonally about .7 cm apart. The rim and neck of the vessel are usually plain or smoothed over with mixed cordmarking beginning at the shoulder and continuing down the vessel. One vessel has a hole drilled from the exterior below the notched strip. Three vessels have visible cooking residue: one on the interior rim and exterior shoulder, another on the exterior rim, and the last on the interior shoulder. One vessel has an extra set of impressions just below the lip of the vessel above the usual series of impressions.

Moccasin Bluff Scalloped (Pl. 31)

This group is a somewhat ill-defined class consisting of 20 sherds from 10 vessels. Paste and temper are characteristic of most other Late Woodland ceramics. Colors include very dark gray 10YR 3/1, very dark grayish brown 10YR 3/2, dark grayish brown 10YR 4/2, grayish brown 10YR 5/2. The interior surface color is a shade or two lighter than the exterior surface in a fair number of cases; in others, it is either the same color or a lighter tone. The core of the sherd is most often black or dark gray. The rim profile is slightly excurving; at least six of the vessels are represented by sherds 4.0 cm or greater in length. The top of the lip may be either rounded or flattened; most of the examples have a plain, smoothed lip. One example has cordmarking on the top of the lip which is smoothed in the depressions of the scallops. The exterior surface may be smoothed, partially smoothed, or cordmarked. Decoration consists of small scalloped impressions, between 1.0 and 2.0 cm in length, most likely formed by impressing the thumb or finger on the top of the lip. The impressions are placed one next to the other so that a continuous pie crust effect is produced. Two of the vessels have a 1.0 cm high collar while three others have a small lipping around the vessel on the exterior edge of the lip. Three of the vessels have cooking residue present: one on the exterior of the rim, another on the interior, exterior, and on the top of the lip. Thickness at the lip averages .74 cm, range .6-1.0 cm; below the lip the average is .7 cm, range .5-.8 cm.

BERRIEN WARE

Berrien ware is a descriptive designation referring to the series of shell-tempered pottery found at the site. It will be divided into five categories for descriptive purposes. A well made compacted paste tempered with crushed shell is characteristic of all groups.

Group 1: Well developed shoulder and high neck (Pl. 32) This group of 15 sherds from 11 vessels includes the following colors: dark gray 10YR 3/1, very dark grayish brown 10YR 3/2, dark gray 10YR 4/1, dark grayish brown 10YR 4/2, grayish brown 10 YR 5/2, brown 10YR 5/3, yellowish brown 10YR 5/4, pale brown 10YR 6/3, with the grays and the gray browns being the most common. The interior surface is usually the same color as the exterior surface; the core of the sherd is almost always black. The rim profile is characterized by a neck which ranges from 3.5 cm to 4.0 cm high and forms a right or an acute angle at the junction of the neck and the shoulder. Top of the lip is smoothed and flattened; four examples have broad, shallow, finger-like impressions on the top of the lip that are very faint and barely noticeable. Exterior surface finish is always plain with no signs of cordmarking. The thickness of the rim at the lip averages .777 cm, range .5-1.0 cm; just above the junction at the shoulder, the thickness averages .794 cm, range .7-1.1 cm. In five cases there is a slight lipping on the exterior edge of the lip. Six of the vessels have evidence of cooking residue: two on the interior surface, one on the interior and the exterior surface, one on the exterior surface, one on the exterior surfaces and the top of the lip, and one on the shoulder.

Group 2: Developed shoulder and short neck (Pl. 32, 33) This group of nine sherds from seven vessels includes the following colors: very dark gray 10YR 3/1, dark gray 10YR 4/1, light yellowish brown 10YR 6/4, grayish brown 10YR 5/2. Interior surface color is similar to the exterior and the core of the sherds is mostly black. Rim profile again forms a right or an acute angle at the junction of the neck and the shoulder; but the rim or neck height is only between 2.0 and 2.5 cm. The rim shows some tendency to be thinned at the lip: the average thickness at the lip is .642 cm, range .5-.7 cm, while just above the junction of the neck with the shoulder, the average thickness is .757 cm, range .6-1.0 cm. All surfaces are smoothed and the top of the lip, as a result of the thinning perhaps, has a rounded contour. Six of the vessels have small notches or impressions on the top of the lip. These may be between .4 and 1.0 cm wide and spaced between 1.5 cm for the wider notches to .7 cm apart for the smaller ones. The larger impressions may have been made with a finger; the smaller ones were probably produced with a tool. Two vessels show cooking residue, one on the exterior and on the interior surfaces, and one on only the interior surface. One of the sherds has a large (1.1 cm) squarish hole made while the clay was still soft, and may represent part of a colander.

Group 3: Sloping shoulder and plain lip (Pl. 33) This is a group of 16 sherds from 11 vessels. Colors include reddish brown 2.5YR 5/4, reddish yellow 5YR 6/6, very dark gray 10YR 3/1, dark brown 10YR 3/3, gray brown 10YR 5/2, and pale brown 10YR 6/3, with dark gray and pale brown predominating. Rim profile is excurving or mildly outsloping without the marked angle at the junction of the neck and the shoulder seen in the two previous groups. Top of the rim tends to be rounded. The sherds as a whole are thinner than those of most of the other groups: the average thickness of the rim at the lip is .583 cm, range .4-.7 cm; further down the rim it is .633 cm, range .4-.9 cm. All sherds have plain surfaces with no decoration, except for one sherd, which has broad 1.0 cm, shallow, opposing, or inverted impressions on the shoulder. The impressions were probably made with the finger. One sherd has a loop handle; another has a small (.35 cm) hole drilled from both sides. Another vessel has the remains of what may have been a notched applique strip encircling the vessel. One of the vessels has cooking residue on the interior surface; another has residue on the interior surface and on the shoulder of the vessel.

Group 4: Sloping shoulder and modified lip (Pl. 34) This group of 10 sherds from five vessels is characterized by only two colors: gray brown and very dark gray. The rim profiles are outsloping or excurvate, but not as sharp as the first two classes described. The top of the rims is generally rounded. Four of the vessels have a series of notches on the exterior of the edge on the rim and one has small (.2 cm) impressions on the top of the lip .4 cm apart. The notches only range up to .5 cm in width and are only .8 cm apart, measured from the center of one notch to the center of the one next to it. Surfaces are mostly smoothed or plain; one sherd has mixed cordmarking. Three of the sherds have decoration on the shoulder of the vessel consisting of finger-impressed, or tool-incised, trailed lines with small punctates or finger impressions. Thickness of the rim at the lip is .66 cm, range .4-.9 cm; further down on the rim, the average thickness is .76 cm, range .6-1.0 cm. All of the sherds in this group have evidence of cooking residue: three on the interior and the exterior surfaces of the rim, one on only the exterior; and the last on only the interior surface.

Group 5: Miscellaneous (Pl. 35) This is a heterogeneous group of 22 sherds from 17 vessels. These are all shell tempered sherds which do not clearly fall into any of the other groupings. Colors of the exterior surface include reddish brown 5YR 5/3, reddish yellow 7.5YR 6/6, very dark gray 10YR 3/1, dark brown 10YR 3/3, dark gray 10YR 4/1, gray brown 10YR 5/2, pale brown 10YR 6/3, light yellowish brown 10YR 6/4, with the dark grays and the very dark grays being the most common colors. Thickness at the lip for the group averages .81 cm, range .6-1.0 cm; below the lip the average is .74 cm, range .5-1.0 cm.

The vessels can be grouped into five categories based on the treatment of the top of the lip: (a) This consists of a group of four vessels represented by 19 sherds which have small (.2 to .5 cm) tool impressions on the top of the lip. The impressions are spaced .5 to .8 cm apart. One vessel in this group has cord impressions at the junction of the neck and shoulder. (b) This is a group of three vessels represented by three sherds which have broader impressions (.6 to .8 cm wide) made perhaps with the side of a finger. The impressions are spaced one directly next to the other. Two vessels of the group are cordmarked while the rest are plain. (c) This consists of six sherds from six vessels with impressions on the exterior of the lip similar to those on the Moccasin Bluff Impressed Exterior Lip vessels. Three of these vessels are cordmarked while the rest are plain. One of the plain vessels has a small lug handle. (d) This is a group of four sherds representing three vessels which have a scalloped or pie crust decoration on the top of the lip. These vessels have plain surfaces, but one has a strap handle and another a lug handle. (e) This consists of one sherd representing one vessel. It is simply a shell temper vessel with a cordmarked surface and cordmarking on the top of the lip.

MIDDLE WOODLAND POTTERY (PL. 36)

This series of 20 sherds from 20 vessels is very characteristic of previously described Middle Woodland pottery types. The surface texture is often sandy and coarse; the temper is crushed rock and is medium to heavy in density. Color includes light reddish brown 5YR 6/3, very dark gray 10YR 3/1, grayish brown 10YR 5/2, yellowish brown 10YR 5/4, pale brown 10YR 6/3, and light yellowish brown 10YR 6/4. Rim profiles are generally straight, the top of the lip is smoothed and flattened; the exterior edge of the rim sometimes has a slight lipping. Surface finish on all sherds is plain, with two examples of a possible smoothed-over cordmarking. Decoration includes cordmarked-stick impressions on the external edge of the lip, internal punctates, internal punctates forming nodes on the exterior of the sherd, crescent-shaped, finger nail-like impressions arranged in parallel rows around the vessel, notching on the internal edge of the lip, parallel rows of dentate stamping running down from the lip of the vessel, annular punctates, crescent-shaped dentate stamping, rocker dentate running horizontally parallel to the lip, cross-hatched incising, brushed sherds, and Havana plain sherds. Each sherd, in fact, is unique except for the three brushed sherds. No cooking residue is present on any of the sherds.

MISCELLANEOUS SHERDS

Miniature Pots or Children's Vessels

These include five sherds from five vessels. Paste is well compacted and smooth. Temper is variable: three of the vessels are temperless, one is shell-tempered, and one is grit-tempered. Two of the vessels have an excurvated lip and decoration while the other three have a barrel-shaped rim profile. Decoration on one vessel consists of three parallel, vertically incised lines (Pl. 37, M), while on the other vessel (Pl. 37, N), there are two rows of lightly incised inverted V's.

The remainder of the miscellaneous sherds are illustrated in Plate 37.

DISTRIBUTION OF VESSELS ON SITE

An examination of the distribution of the ceramic material on the site is in part hindered by the sampling method used in the excavations. One can gain some indication of the possible implication of the surface distributions by looking at the distribution of vessels by trench (Table 13). Because of the low frequencies in most of the classes, statistical tests, useful for evaluating the distributions, were not possible. The results also tend to be distorted because of the small size of some of the excavation units: the recovery of one sherd from a small unit produces a large frequency when the units are adjusted for size. It is therefore necessary to examine the adjusted frequencies with an eye to the raw data and to eliminate those cases which cause the distortions. With these considerations in mind, the most meaningful comparisons are between trench A and trench C, and occasionally with trench F.

In examining the adjusted frequencies in Table 14, certain items appear significant. Trench C contains a higher density of material than do any of the other trenches. Items notably concentrated in trench C are Moccasin Bluff Cordmarked Variety 1a, Variety 1b, group 4 (lip squared and plain), Moccasin Bluff Modified Lip group 1 (cord-wrapped stick), group 3 (finger nail) and

TABLE 12

SUMMARY OF CERAMIC TYPES

	No. of Sherds	% of Sherds	No. of Vessels	% of Vessels
Moccasin Bluff Ware				
Moccasin Bluff Cordmarked				
Variety 1a	16	3.0	16	3.8
Variety 1b				
Group 1: square and flattened lip/corded	18	3.4	15	3.5
Group 2: protruding exterior rim	3	0.6	3	0.7
Group 3: beveled lip	11	2.0	8	1.9
Group 4: square and flattened lip/plain	35	6.6	28	6.6
Group 5: small collar	20	3.7	15	3.5
Group 6: exterior smoothed/ lip plain	12	2.2	12	2.8
Moccasin Bluff Collared	15	2.8	14	3.3
Moccasin Bluff Modified Lip				
Group 1: cord-wrapped stick	22	4.1	19	4.5
Group 2: paddle-edge impressed	5	0.9	5	1.2
Group 3: finger-nail impressed	11	2.0	6	1.4
Group 4: lunate impression	10	1.9	9	2.1
Group 5: lip thickened and notched	13	2.4	12	2.8
Group 6: punctates	6	1.1	6	1.4
Moccasin Bluff Impressed Exterior Lip				
Group 1: impressed exterior lip	70	13.1	52	12.3
Group 2: smooth paste	5	0.9	4	0.9
Moccasin Bluff Plain	48	8.9	37	8.7
Moccasin Bluff Plain-Modified Lip				
Group 1: finger impressed	19	3.6	15	3.5
Group 2: narrow notched	14	2.6	14	3.3
Group 3: rounded lip and small notches	7	1.3	7	1.6
Moccasin Bluff Notched Applique Strip	34	6.4	20	4.7
Moccasin Bluff Scalloped Lip	20	3.7	10	2.4
Berrien Ware				
Group 1: well developed shoulder-high neck	15	2.8	11	2.6
Group 2: well developed shoulder-short neck	9	1.7	7	1.6
Group 3: sloping shoulder-plain lip	16	3.0	11	2.6
Group 4: sloping shoulder-modified lip	10	1.9	5	1.2
Group 5: other	22	4.1	17	4.0
Middle Woodland Pottery	20	3.7	20	4.7
Miniature Vessels	5	0.9	5	1.2
Miscellaneous	23	4.3	21	5.0
Totals	534	99.6	424	99.8

TABLE 13

DISTRIBUTION OF VESSELS BY TRENCH

Trench	A	B	C	D	E	F	G	H	K	M	N	O	Other	Total
M. B. Cordmarked														
Variety 1a	3	1	5	1	2	1		1				1	1	16
Variety 1b														
Group 1	5		2		1	2		1					4	15
Group 2	2				1									3
Group 3	6		1										1	8
Group 4	8		5		4	3		5				1	2	28
Group 5	9		2		2	1		1						15
Group 6	5		4		1			1	1					12
Collared	4		2	1	3		1			1		1	1	14
Modified Lip														
Group 1	4		5	1	1	1		1	1		2	2	1	19
Group 2	1	2			1			1						5
Group 3	1		3			1				1				6
Group 4	6	1			1								1	9
Group 5	10		1										1	12
Group 6	2		1		1			1					1	6
Impressed Exterior														
Group 1	25	4	3		5	9		1				2	3	52
Group 2	3		1											4
M. B. Plain	15	2	3		10	3		1		1			2	37
M. B. Plain Modified Lip														
Group 1	11		1		1	1			1					15
Group 2	7	1	3					2			1			14
Group 3	4	1	1			1								7
M. B. Notched Applique Strip	7	2	4		2	2							3	20
M. B. Scalloped Lip	6		1		1			1					1	10
Berrien Ware														
Group 1	4		4		1	1			1					11
Group 2	3	2	1			1								7
Group 3	6	1	4											11
Group 4	2		3											5
Group 5	10		5		1	1								17
Middle Woodland Vessels	7		3		3	1		1	1	2			2	20
Miniature Vessels	2		2										1	5
Miscellaneous Vessels	5	2	6		5					1			2	21
Total	183	19	76	3	47	29	1	18	5	6	3	7	27	424

TABLE 14

DISTRIBUTION OF VESSELS BY TRENCH
(Trenches Adjusted to Uniform Size*)

Trench	A	B	C	D	E	F	G	H	K	M	N	O	Other
M. B. Cordmarked													
Variety 1a	2	2	10	6		2		2				5	
Variety 1b													
Group 1	3		4			3		2					
Group 2	1												
Group 3	3		2										
Group 4	5		10			5		12				5	
Group 5	5		4			2		2					
Group 6	3		8					2	8				
Collared	2		4	6			13			2		5	
Modified Lip													
Group 1	2		10	6		2		2	8		8	10	
Group 2	1	3						2					
Group 3	1		6			2				2			
Group 4	3	2											
Group 5	5		2										
Group 6	1		2					2					
Impressed Exterior Lip													
Group 1	13	6	6			14		2				10	
Group 2	2		2										
M. B. Plain	8	3	6			5		2		2			
M. B. Plain Modified Lip													
Group 1	6		2			2		5	8				
Group 2	4	2	6								4		
Group 3	2	2	2			2							
M. B. Notched Applique Strip	4	3	8			3							
M. B. Scalloped Lip	3		2					2					
Berrien Ware													
Group 1	2		8			2			8				
Group 2	2	3	2			2							
Group 3	3	2	8										
Group 4	1		6										
Group 5	5		10			2							
Middle Woodland Vessels	4		6			2		2	8	4			
Miniature Vessels	1		4										
Miscellaneous Vessels	3	3	11							2			

*Figures rounded off to the nearest whole number.

the Berrien ware group. Concentrated in trench C are the Moccasin Bluff Modified Lip group 5 (thickened and notched) and Moccasin Bluff Impressed Exterior Lip group 1 (impressed exterior lip). This latter group also appears with great frequency in F. Finally in trench C we have the Moccasin Bluff Modified Lip group 1 (finger impressed). Moccasin Bluff Impressed Exterior Lip tends to be concentrated in trenches A and F. This distribution is particularly interesting since the general tendency is for material to occur in greater density in trench C. In addition, Berrien ware tends to be concentrated in trench C. These two patterns are worthy of further investigation.

Investigating the distribution of material within and outside of the pits (Table 15), the general tendency is for material to be located outside of the pits more often than within them. Notable exceptions are Moccasin Bluff Cordmarked, variety 1b, group 6 (smoothed exterior surface, plain lip) and Berrien ware. The Moccasin Bluff Cordmarked Modified Lip group and the Middle Woodland vessels are more generally found outside of the pits. Some of the possible implications of these distributions will be explored in a later chapter (see pp.

Finally in attempting to examine the distribution of the vessels by level (Appendix 12), the lack of comparability of material from trench to trench makes interpretation of the data somewhat questionable. Level two in trench F is not comparable to level two in trench C. A trench-by-trench comparison yields frequencies too low to be meaningful. There is a tendency for the Moccasin Bluff Cordmarked Collared vessels to be concentrated in level 1 as are the Moccasin Bluff Cordmarked Impressed Exterior Lip group 1 (impressed exterior lip). The Moccasin Bluff Plain vessels have a tendency to be concentrated in level 2.*

BODY SHERDS (FIGS. 18-21)

Body sherds from the site were analyzed along two dimensions, surface treatment and temper. Surface treatment was divided into six categories: cordmarked, plain, fabric, brushed, decorated, and indistinct. Temper was grouped into seven classes: coarse and sandy, black, typical, temperless, mica, mixed, and shell. The categories of surface treatment are largely self-explanatory. The classes of temper call for some elaboration. The coarse and sandy group includes rather large pieces of crushed rock in fair density with particles of tempering often visible on both the exterior and the interior surfaces of the sherd. This type of temper is often

*See Appendix 12 of the author's dissertation (of the same title, completed at the University of Michigan, 1971) for complete distribution list of vessels by level.

TABLE 15

DISTRIBUTION OF VESSELS IN AND OUT OF PITS

	No. of vessels in pits	No. of vessels out of pits	?	Vessels on surface
Moccasin Bluff Ware				
M. B. Cordmarked				
Variety 1a	8	7		1
Variety 1b				
Group 1	2	9	2	2
Group 2	1	2		
Group 3	4	3		1
Group 4	9	17		2
Group 5	4	11		
Group 6	8	4		
Collared	4	10		
Modified Lip				
Group 1: cord-wrapped stick	2	16		1
Group 2: paddle edge	0	5		
Group 3: finger nail	2	4		
Group 4: lunate impression	0	8	1	
Group 5: thickened and notched	2	9		1
Group 6: punctates	2	4		
Impressed Exterior lip				
Group 1	19	30		3
Group 2	3	1		
M. B. Plain	11	24		2
M. B. Plain-modified lip				
Group 1	5	10		
Group 2	3	11		
Group 3	3	4		
M. B. Notched Applique Strip	9*	11		
M. B. Scalloped	4	5	1	
Berrien Ware				
Group 1	6	5		
Group 2	2	5		
Group 3	6	5		
Group 4	4	1		
Group 5	8	9		
Middle Woodland Pottery	3	15		2
Miniature Vessels	3	2		
Miscellaneous	7	12		2
Total	144	259	4	17

*Two of these nine vessels were found in a pit excavated by local archaeologists.

FIG. 18. Miscellaneous Grit-Tempered Body Sherds.

A. Cord-wrapped stick impressions on plain 37748 Trench A.

B. Cord-wrapped stick impressions on plain 37748 Trench A.

C. Incisions on plain 29457 Trench A.

D. Incisions on plain 29688 Trench A.

E. Punctate with corded surface below. 29699 Trench.

F. Punctate on plain 37759 Trench C.

G. Incisions over cord 37421 Trench C Pit 26B.

H. Cord impressions over cordmarked surface 37560 Trench C Pit 88.

I. Cord-wrapped stick impressions over corded surface 37413 Trench K.

J. Punctates and incisions on plain 29654 Trench A Pit 9.

K. Irregular punctates with corded surface below 37855 Trench C.

L. Incisions and punctate on plain 29906 Trench F.

A
B
C
D
E
F
G
H
I
J
K
L
1 inch
Scale
RLB

FIG. 19. Miscellaneous Shell-Tempered Body Sherds.

A. Incisions and punctates on plain surface 37447 Trench C Pit 51.

B. Incisions and punctates on plain surface 37766 Trench C.

C. Incisions and impressions on plain surface 29391 Trench A.

D. Incisions over cordmarked surface 37438 Trench C Pit 63.

E. Incisions over cordmarked surface 37497 Trench C Pit 86.

F. Incisions and punctates on plain surface 37440 Trench C Pit 86.

G. Incisions and punctates on plain surface 37420 Trench C.

A
B
C
D
E
F
G
1 inch
SCALE
RLB

FIG. 20. Decorated Middle Woodland Body Sherds.

A. Circular impressions on plain surface 37636 Trench F.

B. Circular punctates on plain surface 29877 Trench E.

C. Incised lines on plain surface 37856 Trench C.

D. Annular punctate over cordmarked surface 29978 Trench F.

E. Tear drop shaped punctate on plain surface 37543 Trench O Pit 49.

F. Circular impressions with cordmarking below 29891 Trench F.

G. Crescent punctates on plain surface 37896 Trench A Pit 17.

H. Incising and punctates on plain surface 29999 Trench F Pit 79.

I. Incising and punctates on plain surface 29538 Trench B.

J. Incising or impressions on plain surface 29976 Trench F Pit 73.

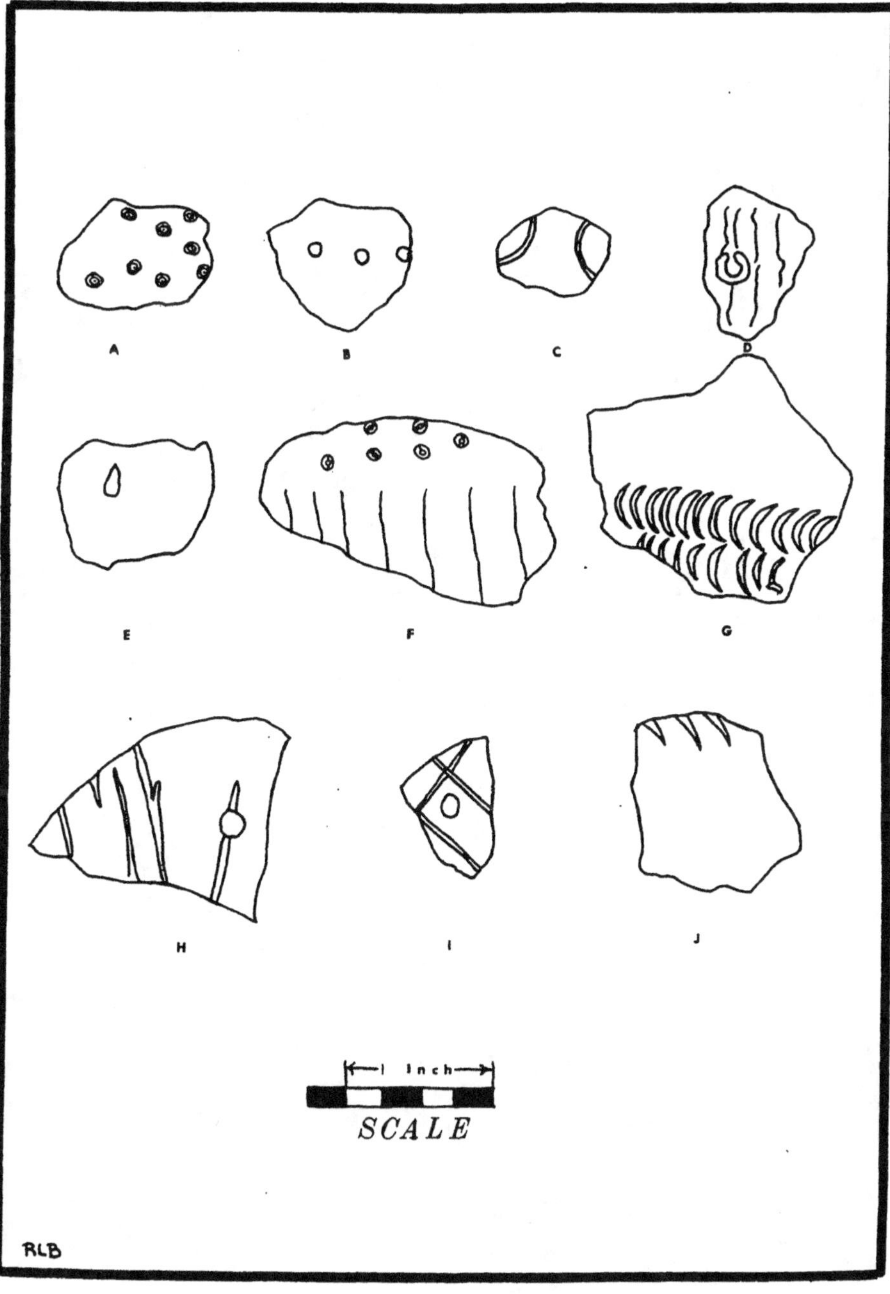
A
B
C
D
E
F
G
H
I
J
1 Inch
SCALE
RLB

FIG. 21. Dentate Stamped Sherds.

A. 37413 Trench K.

B. 37459 Trench C Pit 54.

C. 29914 Trench F.

D. 37408 Trench K.

E. 29909 Trench F.

F. 29891 Trench F.

G. 29877 Trench F.

H. 29895 Trench F.

I. 29952 Trench E.

J. 29920 Trench F.

K. 29461 Trench A.

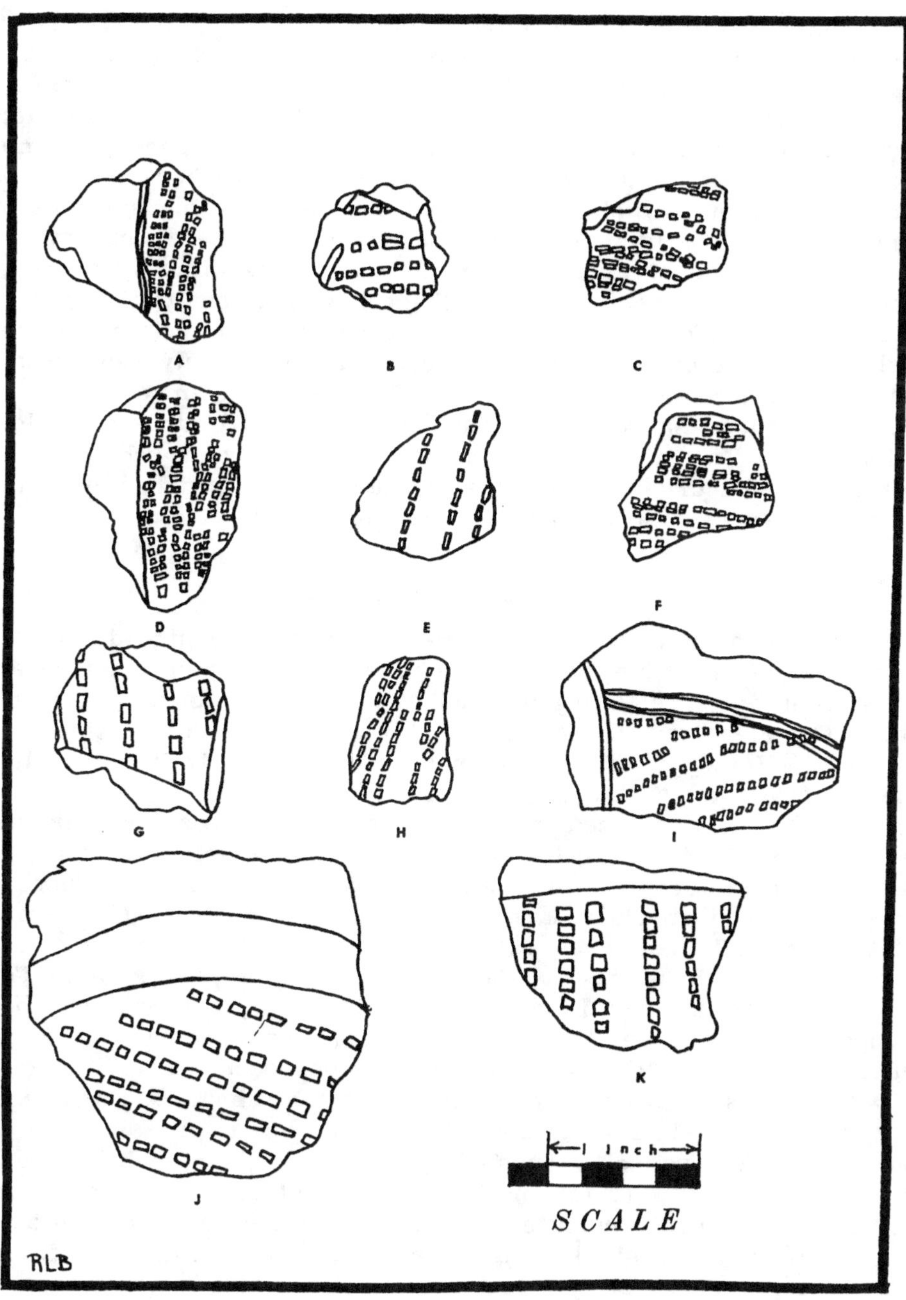
A
B
C
D
E
F
G
H
I
J
K
1 inch
SCALE
RLB

associated with ceramics of the Middle Woodland period. Black temper refers to sherds which have a high percentage of black temper particles included within them. Temper is often visible on the surfaces of these sherds, but the particle size is smaller than in the coarse and sandy variety. Typical temper is the most common variety of tempering. It consists of crushed rock in moderate amounts and is generally not visible on the surfaces of the sherds. The temperless group refers to those sherds which have an absence of visible temper. Mica refers to a class of sherds which seems to have an abundance of mica particles included within the paste. Whether greater amounts of mica were deliberately selected or whether these sherds merely represent random fluctuation could not be established. The mixed class refers to those sherds which have a mixture of grit temper along with shell. The final class consists of those sherds which are tempered with crushed fresh water shell. The frequencies of the various classes of body sherds is given in Table 16.

Decorated Body Sherds

The decorated body sherds were grouped into nine design categories (see Table 17). These nine categories may not be exclusive units representing distinct and separate motifs. Some of the categories may be fragments or parts of designs in other classes. However, there is no internal evidence from the collection to suggest that this is the case.

Motif 1 is composed of a series of parallel, obliquely incised, narrow (.3 cm) lines on the shoulder of the vessel. The incising if found on either grit- or shell-tempered sherds and is placed on cordmarked or plain surfaces. Several of the sherds indicate that at least five of these parallel incisions may be present on one design unit. A look at the adjusted frequencies in Table 17a indicates that this motif most often occurs on plain surface, shell-tempered vessels that tend to be concentrated in trench A. It is interesting to note that when the motif does occur on grit tempered vessels, it is most often found on a cordmarked surface.

Motif 2 consists of broad (.8 cm), shallow impressions on the shoulder of the vessel. These impressions appear to have been made either with a finger or finger-like tool such as an antler. Some of the sherds indicate that several of the vessels have at least four of these shallow impressions in their design motif. The impressions are placed on grit- or shell-tempered vessels and on cordmarked or plain surface vessels. The distribution of this motif is somewhat interesting: the adjusted frequencies (Table 17a)

TABLE 16

BODY SHERDS

Temper	Coarse and Sandy	Black	Typical	Temperless	Mica	Mixed	Shell	Total
Surface Treatment								
Cordmarked	181[a]	418	3450	2	64[c]	4	358[d]	4477
Plain	192[b]	92	1037		31	4	775[e]	2131
Fabric			3			1		4
Brushed	4		1					5
Decorated	39	4	125	1	2	1	178[f]	350
Indistinct	21	26	1319	—	8	—	108	1482
Total	437	540	5935	3	105	10	1419	8449

[a]24 sherds with carbon deposits and 4 with drilled holes.
[b]3 sherds with carbon deposits and 6 with drilled holes.
[c]1 sherd with carbon deposit.
[d]6 sherds with carbon deposits and 3 with drilled holes.
[e]15 sherds with carbon deposits and 11 with drilled holes.
[f]5 sherds with carbon deposits.

TABLE 17

DISTRIBUTION OF DECORATED SHERDS BY EXCAVATION UNIT

	1				2				3				4		5	
	Temper				Temper				Temper				Temper			
	Grit		Shell		Grit		Shell		Grit		Shell		Grit	Shell	Shell Temper	
	Surface				Surface				Surface				Surface		Surface	
Tr.	C*	P*	C	P	C	P	C	P	C	P	C	P	Plain	Plain	Corded	Plain
A	14	2	24	41	24	1	18	8	4	2	2		2	1		11
B	1		2		1		1			1	1					1
C	3	2	6	8	2	1	7	15	1		1				2	2
D				0			1									1
E		1	1	4		1	1		2							
F	2	3		1	6	1			1	1			1			3
H			1	1												
K									1							
O					1		3									2
Total	20	8	34	55	34	4	31	23	9	4	4		3	1	2	20

*C= Corded
P= Plain

TABLE 17a

DISTRIBUTION OF DECORATED SHERDS BY EXCAVATION UNIT
(Trenches Adjusted to Uniform Size)

Tr.																
A	7	1	13	22	13	1	9	4	2	1	1		1	1		6
B	2		3		2		2			2	2					2
C	6	4	11	15	4	2	13	28	2		2				4	4
D							6									6
E		3	3	11		3	3		6							
F	3	5		2	9	2			2	2			2			5
H			2	2												
K									8							
O					5		15									10

TABLE 17 (Continued)

DISTRIBUTION OF DECORATED SHERDS BY EXCAVATION UNIT

Trench	6 Shell Temper Surface Corded	7 Shell Temper Surface Plain	8 Shell Temper Surface Corded	9 Shell Temper Surface Plain	Total
A	1	1	1		157
B				1	9
C					50
D					2
E					10
F					19
H					2
K					1
O					6

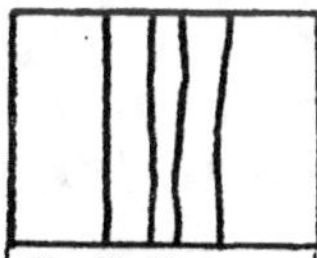

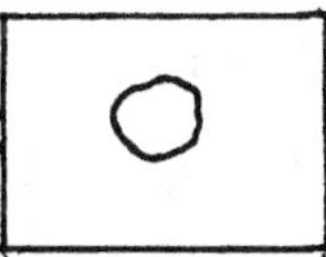

show a marked concentration in trench C. This contrasts with the distribution of motif 1, which has a higher frequency in trench A. Both motifs appear on shell-tempered ware.

An interesting nuance of this distribution is the frequency of grit-tempered, cordmarked surface sherds with motif 2 concentrated in trench A. It suggests that the distributions for this motif may depend upon the ware with which it is associated. Looking at the shell-tempered ware with motif 2 in trench A, another interesting aspect presents itself. Here, contrary to the general trend—most grit-tempered, decorated sherds tend to be cordmarked and most shell-tempered ware tends to be plain—motif 2 occurs more often on shell-tempered ware with a cordmarked surface. The significance of these differences is not clear at present and may simply be due to sampling error.

Motif 3 consists of small (.3 cm) punctates or impressions placed on the shoulder of the vessel. The impressions are not as deep as normally seen in Woodland pottery; the term impression will be used, therefore, to indicate an indentation of the surface of the vessel which does not have the clean sharp features of a normal punctate. Frequencies of this motif are low but the lack of shell-tempered, plain surface sherds associated with this motif may be noteworthy.

Motif 4 is represented by a few sherds which consist of a narrow, shallow incised line associated with several punctates or, rather, small shallow impressions and at least one large shallow impression. The large impressions looks as if it could have been made with a thumb. Frequencies are too low to arrive at any clear statement of the distribution.

Motif 5 consists of a combination of motifs 1 and 3. A series of narrow, incised parallel lines are combined with a series of the small, shallow, circular impressions. This motif is found mainly on shell-tempered, plain-surfaced vessels and seems to be distributed widely over the site.

The remaining motifs are illustrated in Table 17 and require little comment here. Motif 6 consists of two shallow parallel, incised lines; motif 7 combines incised lines and a large, shallow thumb print impression; motif 8 is simply a large shallow thumb impression; and motif 9 is two diagonal, parallel lines and a large shallow thumb impression.

The distribution of the Middle Woodland sherds on the site is also worthy of notice (see Table 18): decorated Middle Woodland body sherds are concentrated in trench F. These are the only data which tend to confirm the excavators' impressions of a concentration of Middle Woodland material in the southern area of the site. The somewhat less strong tendency from trench K might also tend to confirm this conclusion but the frequencies involved are low. Table 19 shows the distribution of the decorated body sherds by pit.

Discussion

The distribution of body sherds by trench with trenches adjusted to uniform size (Table 21) tends to corroborate the data

TABLE 18

DISTRIBUTION OF DECORATED MIDDLE WOODLAND SHERDS

Trench	A	B	C	D	E	F	H	K	O	M	Total
Number of Sherds	4	1	4		2	13		2	1	1	28
Adjusted Frequencies	2	2	8		6	20		16	5	2	

TABLE 19

DISTRIBUTION OF DECORATED SHERDS BY PIT

	1				2				3				4		5	
	Temper				Temper				Temper				Temper		Temper	
	Grit		Shell		Grit		Shell		Grit		Shell		Grit	Shell	Grit	Shell
	Surface				Surface				Surface				Surface		Surface	
Pit	C	P	C	P	C	P	C	P	C	P	C	P	Plain	Plain	Corded	Plain
9	1		1					1								
10			2	3			1									
15	1	1	2	2	1		2	1						1		1
17	1				1			1					1			2
22			2								1					
22A				2				1								
29A			1	1												
34				2			2		1							
34B	1		1						1							
44					1	1										
49							1									1
50								3								
51							2	2	1							
71		1			2											
73				1												1
85				1	1											
86			1								1				1	
88	1		1				1									
90							2									
Pits Having Only One Decorated Sherd																
		14	8	14	20	12	96	4	80							11
				30				33								68
			40					91								
			32													
			63													
			84													

TABLE 20

DISTRIBUTION OF BODY SHERDS BY TRENCH

Trench	A	B	C	D	E	F	G	H	K	L	M	N
Grit-tempered												
Cordmarked	951	50	247	1	331	66	4	118	30	18	25	6
Plain	288	27	17	1	312	83	4	49	8	10	16	3
Indistinct	341	23	37		256	135		15	5			
Other	11											
Shell-tempered												
Cordmarked	175	4	81		5			4	4		3	
Plain	180	18	107		22	13	1	10	1			
Indistinct	42	3	7		5	4			4			
Other												
Black												
Cordmarked	48		20	1	31	7		20	20	6	5	
Plain	7	2	2	1	23	3		16	3		2	
Indistinct	6		1		4	4		1				
Other											1	
Coarse and Sandy												
Cordmarked	50		8	2	8	20		62	9	24	5	6
Plain	37	2	2	8	24	20	5	18	10			10
Indistinct	5		2		2	1					1	
Other	4										1	

on the distribution of rim sherds and decorated body sherds. Trenches A and C appear to have the heaviest density of material; trench A has a high density of grit-tempered sherds and trench C has a higher density of shell-tempered material. Trenches F, H, and K have high adjusted frequencies (and in some cases higher absolute frequencies) of coarse and sandy tempered material which represents the Middle Woodland from the site, again indicating a Middle Woodland occupation in this area, something suspected by the excavators. Trenches H, K, and L also have higher frequencies of black-tempered pottery. This type of pottery is felt to represent late Middle Woodland and early Late Woodland ceramics in this area, although it is not confined exclusively to ceramics from this period.

TABLE 21

DISTRIBUTION OF BODY SHERDS BY TRENCH
(Trenches Adjusted to Uniform Size)

Trench	A	B	C	D	E	F	G	H	K	L	M	N
Grit-tempered												
Cordmarked	500	80	469	6	917	102	53	286	240	288	50	23
Plain	152	43	32	6	864	128	53	118	64	160	32	12
Indistinct	179	36	70		709	208		36	40			
Other	6											
Shell-tempered												
Cordmarked	92	6	154		14			10	32		6	
Plain	95	29	203		61	20	13	24	8			
Indistinct	22	5	13		14	6			32			
Other												
Black												
Cordmarked	25		38	6	86	11		48	160	96	10	
Plain	4	3	4	6	64	5		39	24		4	
Indistinct	3		2		11	6		2				
Other											2	
Coarse and Sandy												
Cordmarked	26		15	13	22	31		150	72		10	23
Plain	19	3	4	52	66	31	67	44	80			38
Indistinct	3		4		6	2			384		2	
Other	2										2	

The distribution of body sherds according to features combined with information about rim sherds and radiocarbon dates (Table 22) suggest a chronological ordering for this material. The earliest group of features seems to indicate an occupation from around A.D. 1050. The group is characterized by grit-tempered and cordmarked surface pottery (45-75 percent) with fair amounts of grit-tempered and plain surface pottery and some shell-tempered and cordmarked surface pottery. The next grouping of features was apparently created by an occupation around A.D. 1200 and is mostly grit-tempered, cordmarked pottery. The last group appears to have been made by groups occupying the site at A.D. 1600. These features are 25-45 percent grit-tempered pottery

TABLE 22

POSSIBLE CHRONOLOGICAL ORDERING OF FEATURES[3]
(Suggested by % of different types of body sherds present, supporting evidence of rim sherds, and radiocarbon dates)

Earliest
45-75% grit-tempered cordmarked, some grit-tempered plain, and some shell-tempered corded

Number	Type	Trench
9	Pit and hearth	A
10	Pit	A
11	Pit	A
14	Pit	A
15	Pit, A.D. 1060	A
20	Pit	B
22	Pit	B
23	Pit	B
30A	Pit	A
33	Pit	A
34	Pit	A
46	Pit	A
54[1]	Hearth	C
64	Pit	D
76	Hearth	C
85	Pit	C
86	Fire Pit A.D. 1090	C
87	Pit	C

Latest
25-45% grit-tempered cordmarked, 25% or more shell-tempered plain

Number	Type	Trench
4	Pit	A
17	Pit	A
21	Fire Pit A.D. 1640	B
26A	Pit	C
29	Pit	A
34A[2]	Pit	A
37C	Pit	A
51[2]	Fire Pit	C
68	Burial 3	C
84	Pit	C
91[2]	Fire Pit A.D. 1590	C
95	Pit	C
96	Pit	C

Intermediate
75% or more grit-tempered cordmarked

Number	Type	Trench
1	Pit	A
3	Hearth	A
12	Pit	A
26B	Pit	C
30B	Pit	A
30C	Pit	A
32	Fire Pit	A
36	Pit and hearth	A
37A	Pit	A
37B	Pit	A
39C	Pit	A
47	Hearth	D
48	Hearth	D
49	Pit, A.D. 1210	O
62	Fire Pit A.D. 1150	C
66	Fire Pit	N
75	Hearth	F
76	Hearth	F
78	Pit and hearth	F
80	Hearth	E
82	Hearth	F
83	Pit	H
88	Pit	C
90[2]	Pit	C
92[2]	Pit	C

Other
50% shell-tempered plain, probably latest

Number	Type	Trench
50	Fire Pit	C
73	Pit	E

High % shell-tempered, cordmarked surface, probably earliest

Number	Type	Trench
39A	Pit	A
40	Pit	A
50A	Fire Pit	C
63	Pit	C

[1]Placement by radiocarbon date.
[2]Placement by associated rim sherds.
[3]Features omitted from this table have little or no pottery.

with cordmarked surface and 25 percent or more shell tempered pottery with plain surface representing Huber ceramic types. Two minor groupings represent the extremes of the tendencies characterizing the earliest and the latest groups. One of these groups includes features with 50 percent or more of the shell-tempered, plain-surface pottery; the second group contains high percentages of shell-tempered, cordmarked surface pottery. These groups are separated simply to call attention to their presence in the sample. Chronologically, they are to be placed with the other features.

The fact that this sequence parallels in part the sequence reported from the Fisher site (J. W. Griffin, 1946) should give those concerned with this problem some food for thought.

Finally, a note of caution: in many of the pits the frequency of ceramic material is low and only suggestive, at best. In addition, data on the pits themselves and associated material are rudimentary and not to be heavily relied upon. This chronological ordering of features is therefore referred to as a "possible chronological ordering."

VI

STONE AND BONE OBJECTS

STONE OBJECTS

Hammer and Anvil Stones

Eleven hammer and/or anvil stones were present in the Museum collection (see Table 23). These granitic stones of various shapes and sizes were used for hammering and/or as anvils on which to place objects that were being hammered. A number of the stones have an elliptical cross-section and a circular circumference; others assume a variety of shapes. The ends and sides often show battering and abrasion resulting from hammering; in some cases they also have pitting on one or both of the larger, flatter surfaces. This pitting results either from the fact that objects were hammered with this part of the stone or from the fact that objects to be hammered were placed on the stone at this point and then struck with another stone. The flat sides of some of the stones seem almost polished or smoothed, except for the pitting in the central part of the surface.

Celts (Pl. 47)

Two badly battered and fragmentary celts are present in the Museum collection. Both are made from a granitic stone and were apparently discarded after breakage. The working edge of the celt was formed by beveling each side through grinding to achieve the desired cutting edge.

Abrading Stone

One small abrading stone, sometimes known as an arrow shaft straightener, was recovered from pit 15, trench A. It is made from granular sandstone typical of these objects in the Upper Great Lakes. One side has a 1.32 cm wide groove apparently formed by abrading the shafts of arrows and other elongated objects to smooth them.

TABLE 23

HAMMERSTONES

Cat. No.	Location	Width (cm)	Diameter (cm)	Thickness (cm)	Weight (gms)	Comments
29984	Tr. H	7.62	7.22	2.78	253.3	Depression in center; abrasion around edge
37903	Tr. A Pit 40	8.10	9.45	4.75	767	Pitted edges; depression in center; and smooth sides
37684	Surface	11.67	10.34	5.95	1095	Edge pitting; depression in center
37443	Tr. C Pit 51	7.72	10.76	4.77	697	Pitted edges; pitted depression on side and center
29728	Tr. C	5.12	4.78	Irreg.	302.8	Pitting on points of irregularly shaped stone
37448	Tr. C Pit 87	7.2	6.53	5.1	367.4	Edge pitting; smooth sides
37755	Tr. A	4.29	4.14	5.25	168.8	Irregular shape; pitting on various surfaces
29565	Tr. A Pit 15	5.57	5.75	Irreg.	272.84	" "
29577	Tr. A Pit 15	5.93	6.9	2.79	161.85	Slight pitting in various places
29577	Tr. A Pit 15	8.07	6.14	4.44	415.5	Slight pitting on various surfaces
37508	Tr. C Pit 92	3.36	3.02	Irreg.	60.5	Pitting on two ends

TABLE 24

CELTS

Cat. No.	Location	Length (cm)	Width Midpoint (cm)	Thickness (cm)	Weight (gms)
29651	Tr. B Pit 26	16.9	5.58	2.63	43.15
29348	Tr. A	—	—	1.53	63.95

Cat. No.	Location	Length (cm)	Width (cm)	Thickness (cm)	Weight (gms)
29571	Tr. A Pit 15	3.59	2.76	1.26	12.75

Stone Pendants (Pl. 48)

Two objects of stone were recovered and classified as pendants (see Table 25). One of the stones (Pl. 48, G) was complete; the other (Pl. 48, I) was fragmentary. The two objects were classified as pendants because of the presence in each of a hole, probably used for suspension. Both objects seem to have been made from the same material, a soft, fine sandstone. The complete pendant appears to have had the front edges ground to give a rounded contour, while the edges on the back side are rectangular. The other object appears to be unmodified except for the hole piercing it. Both objects were found in the same pit.

TABLE 25

STONE PENDANTS

Cat. No.	Location	Width (cm)	Thickness (cm)	Length (cm)
29678	Tr. B Pit 23	3.1	0.79	4.8
29684	Tr. B Pit 23	fragmentary		

Green Argillite (Pl. 48)

One fragment of green argillite was also recovered. This piece was obviously a fragment of a larger piece that was not recovered. It is relatively uninteresting except for the fact that the edge has several notches, apparently resulting from the use of the stone. The top surface of the stone is covered with striations which may have resulted from the cutting of material on the stone.

Cat. No.	Location	
29435	Tr. A	fragmentary

Burned Limestone

Two pieces of reddish colored limestone were also included among the cultural materials. These two stones initially appeared to represent pestles used to crush red ocher for pigment. However it has been suggested by Dr. Henry Wright that they may represent burned limestone which achieved its reddish color as a result of having been fired. The red outer coating of the stone could then have been rubbed off and used as a pigment. A thorough examination of the stones indicated that this second idea was most likely.

Cat. No.	Location
29990	Tr. H
29765	Tr. A Pit 11

Pipes (Pl. 48)

Six items from the collection were classified as pipes or stone being worked into pipes (see Table 26). None of the specimens was complete. The most convincing piece (Pl. 48, A) is a top to bottom half section of the bowl of a pipe made from a soft, very fine sandstone-like rock. The stone has a texture more silty than many sandstones. It has been shaped into a barrel-like form and two holes have been drilled into it, one from the top and the other from the side at right angles to the first.

The second piece (Pl. 48, B) appears to be another pipe bowl fragment. This piece is made from fired clay and is shell-tempered. This piece may be a clay tube rather than a pipe, perhaps a shaman's sucking tube. The fragmentary nature of the item leaves the question unresolved. Only the central cavity of the item is visible. A connecting channel at right angles to the central one is not present. The object appears to be tapered from top to bottom to form a conical shape.

Two additional pieces (Pl. 48, E, F) are sedimentary limestone rocks which have been shaped by grinding probably to form the bowl of pipes. One piece (Pl. 48, F) has a triangular cross-section; the other piece (Pl. 48, E) has a more or less trapezoidal cross-section. Both pieces have the beginnings of a hole being drilled into the top, suggesting their future use as pipes. It is not clear why the items were never finished. Neither of them has any obvious defects or imperfections.

Finally two fragments of what appear to be parts of the bowls of clay pipes were recovered. One fragment is plain (Pl. 48, D) while the other (Pl. 48, C) has at least three incised lines running parallel to the rim encircling the bowl.

TABLE 26

PIPES

Cat. No.	Location	Comments
29846	Tr. A Pit 36	Fragment of pipe bowl
37549	Tr. D Pit 64	Fragment of pipe bowl or tube
29588	Tr. A Pit 15	Unfinished pipe bowl
37498	Tr. C Pit 92	Unfinished pipe bowl
29649	Tr. B Pit 20	Fragment of clay pipe
No Number	Unknown	Fragment of clay pipe

BONE TOOLS

Bone Cylinders (Pl. 49)

Six items have been identified as bone cylinders (see Table 27). These are small, long, thin, solid pieces of bone shaped into a cylindrical form, and at times have been referred to as flaking tools. The ends are sometimes polished. The occurrence of two of these objects in Pit 92 along with a large number of points and small, thick, steep-edge pieces would tend to support the theory that they represent bone flaking tools.

TABLE 27

BONE CYLINDERS

Cat. No.	Location	Length (cm)	Diameter (cm)
29580	Tr. A Pit 15	4.40	1.05
29580	Tr. A Pit 15	4.67	1.10
37510	Tr. C Pit 92	4.04	.92
37510	Tr. C Pit 92	6.36	1.24
29760	Tr. A Pit 29	4.69	1.15
No Number	Tr. A Pit 39B	3.38	1.03

Beaming Tools (Pl. 49)

Five fragments of bone beaming tools were recorded in the collection (see Table 28). They represent either the distal or the proximal ends of deer metatarsal. All of the pieces seem to have been discarded after having broken in half during use. No complete piece was found. All show the characteristic wear pattern found on these types of tools, the arched wearing away of the central portion of the bone, probably from scraping hides laid over a log.

TABLE 28

BEAMING TOOLS

Cat. No.	Location	Comment
29590	Tr. A Pit 15	Distal end
29777	Tr. A Pit 32	Distal end
29653	Tr. B Pit 20	Proximal end
29941	Tr. C Pit 67	Proximal end
29937	Tr. C Pit 50	Proximal end

Antler

A number of different types of antler objects were recovered from the site. Most of the items were tines, perhaps used as flaking tools. Other items included are celt-like pieces of elk antler, one antler point, a nearly complete piece of deer antler, and a large piece of elk antler.

Ten antler tines (Pl. 50) were identified. The only noticeable feature of these objects was that the tips were usually worn down to a blunt point from their naturally more pointed shape.

Several spatulate or celt-like objects were also recovered (Pl. 51). These objects can be divided into two classes. The first class consists of broad flat objects with one blunt end and one end, probably the middle of the original object, with the remains of a drilled hole in the center of the broad surface. Three of these items were recovered and all seem to have been broken at the center where the hole was drilled. All were made from pieces of elk antler. The second class consists of two pieces, probably also elk antler, similar in general shape to the first class but lacking the drilled hole on one end. The other end, instead of being blunt, is shaped into an adz or celt-like shape. Both ends seem somewhat polished from use.

TABLE 29

ANTLER TINES

Cat. No.	Location
29772	Tr. A Pit 34B
29522	Tr. A Pit 10
29658	Tr. A Pit 11
29599	Tr. A Pit 15
29447	Tr. A Pit 12
29477	Tr. A Pit 12
37836	Tr. C
29938	Tr. C Pit 50
29579	Tr. A Pit 15
No Number	Tr. C Pit 91

TABLE 30

SPATULATE PIECES

Cat. No.	Location	Length (cm)	Width (diam.) (in cm)	Thickness (cm)	Comments
37495	Tr. C Pit 95	11.33	3.5	1.1	Celt-like
No Number	Tr. C Pit 90	6.41	3.81	1.04	Celt-like
No Number	Unknown	5.89	3.07	1.00	Blunt end drilled hole
No Number	Unknown	8.80	3.36	1.05	Blunt end drilled hole
No Number	Unknown	9.05	5.20	0.92	Blunt end drilled hole

One antler point (Pl. 50, C) was noted as coming from the site. This small cylindrical object was modified to form a point at one end and a small socket was drilled into the other end of the bone.

Cat. No.	Location	Length	Width
37445	Tr. C Pit 51	4.08	1.49

Finally, two large pieces of antler were found. In pit 34A was a nearly complete right deer antler and in pit 15 was a large fragment (14 in) of elk antler, with the stub of one tine having a polished appearance. These pieces are sometimes called picks, and may be a form of digging implement.

A piece of long bone, described below in chart form, had been modified to form a long narrow object (Pl. 51, H). This piece of bone was then incised on the outer side with a long, narrow groove. This groove is somewhat triangular in cross-section and smoothed along its entire length.

Cat. No.	Location	Length (cm)	Width (diam. in cm)	Thickness (cm)
37688	Tr. A Pit 33	20.3	2.86	1.30

Bone Awls (Pl. 50)

Three bone awls were recorded from the site (see Table 31). One was made from a deer ulna, another from a long bone fragment, and the final one from a mammalian mandible fragment.

TABLE 31

BONE AWLS

Cat. No.	Location	Comments
No Number	Tr. H	Deer ulna
29780	Tr. A Pit 32	Long bone fragment
No Number	Tr. B Pit 22	Mammalian mandible fragment

Miscellaneous

Two remaining pieces of bone are unique. One is a short tube or large bead (Pl. 51, B). The object was cut from a large bird bone and both ends were polished. The other piece is a fragmentary piece of deer bone pierced with a circular hole (Pl. 51, A).

Cat. No.	Location	Length (cm)	Width (cm)
Bird Bone			
29573	Tr. A Pit 15	3.25	1.50
Perforated Deer Bone			
37755	Tr. A		

Elk Scapulae (Pl. 52, 53)

Three worked elk scapulae were recovered from the site (see Table 32). These bones have a distinctive type of wear pattern which has led many people to refer to them as hoes. The inferior border of the bones has a smoothed and polished appearance. The smoothed and polished pattern continues into the central part of the blade surface where the border becomes U-shaped. At about mid-point in the blade, a hole is punched through the thin bone. Apparently as the item was used, the central part of the inferior surface, being thinner, wore more rapidly and became more U-shaped until it joined with the hole. At this point the tool was discarded. All specimens have the acromion process removed and two lack the coracoid process. Little wear was noted around the neck, but the borders of the hole in the blade do show some smoothing. This tool was probably used as a hoe. A similar type of specimen is on exhibit in the American Museum of Natural History in New York City, however, and this specimen is said to have been used by the Fox Indians for shredding bark. Strips of bark were drawn back and forth through the hole in the bone. The specimen in the Museum was unavailable for detailed examination to determine whether it shows evidence of the characteristic wear pattern along the inferior border of the bone.

Two final items of bone recovered from the site are carapaces from turtles identified as *Terrapene carolina.* Both shells were found intact and most likely served as containers. The shells did not appear to have been modified in any way.

TABLE 32

ELK SCAPULAE

Cat. No.	Location	Comments
No Number	Tr. C Pit 68	Left scapula
No Number	Tr. C Pit 92	Right scapula
No Number	Tr. A Pit 15	Right scapula

TABLE 33

TURTLE CARAPACES

Cat. No.	Location	Comments
29655	Tr. A Pit 9	Terrapene carolina
29755	Tr. B Pit 22	Terrapene carolina

RED OCHRE

Seven pieces of red ochre were present in the Museum collection. They were distributed in the following fashion:

Piece 1	Tr. A Pit 15	2.03 gms
Piece 2	Tr. C Pit 70	101.05 gms
Piece 3	Tr. A	33.35 gms
Piece 4	Tr. A Pit 17	71.52 gms
Piece 5	Tr. C Pit 51	58.40 gms
Piece 6	Tr. A	15.32 gms
Piece 7	Tr. A	10.00 gms

VII

CULTURAL AND CHRONOLOGICAL RELATIONSHIPS

INTERNAL evidence at the Moccasin Bluff site for cultural and chronological differentiation is not very significant. A survey of the variety of material described from the site indicates a long history of occupation covering a number of known cultural groupings. In order to unravel the complex history presented here, the material from Moccasin Bluff will be compared with better dated material from the surrounding area and this information supplemented with what supporting evidence exists from the site itself.

ARCHAIC OCCUPATION

The earliest traces of occupation at the Moccasin Bluff site date to the Middle and Late Archaic period. This period is represented at the site by the presence of various types of projectile points known to be representative of this horizon from other sites in the midwestern United States. None of the points found in the course of the Museum's excavation can be placed in this period with any degree of certainty. However, the Birdsell collection from the site contains a number of points which seem representative of this period. Birdsell collected widely over the semi-circular area enclosed by the hills to the west of the site, and it is likely that these points came from areas which were not sampled by the Museum's excavations. Plate 59 illustrates two points which probably fall into this period: they are two side-notched points (O, R) which are related to the Raddatz Side-notched points of Wisconsin and Illinois. Raddatz points have been found in Middle and Late Archaic context at the Raddatz Rockshelter (Wittry, 1959) and at the Durst Rockshelter (Wittry, 1959), both in Wisconsin, and similar type points have been found at the Modoc Rockshelter in Illinois in Middle to Late Archaic horizons (Fowler, 1959). The Faulker Side-notched point of the Wabash River Valley in Illinois and Indiana is also related to the Raddatz Side-notched and the side-notched points from Moccasin Bluff

(Winters, 1967). Similar points from Michigan have been described by Binford and Papworth (White, et al., 1963), who called them Hodges and Davis points and assigned them to Late Archaic horizons.

A second type of point can also be placed in this time period. These are the bifurcate-base points illustrated on Plate 58, R-W. These points seem to be related to the smaller, triangular-bladed, bifurcate-base points discussed by Fitting (1964a). Points of this type have been reported from a wide area in the Eastern United States ranging from Texas to West Virginia. Winters (1967) records them in the Wabash River Valley in Illinois, while Munson and Downs (1966) describe them from central Illinois, and Dragoo (1959) notes their presence in the Upper Ohio Valley. Fitting (1964a) suggests that these points fall into the Late Archaic period. This dating is supported by the radiocarbon date (Y-486) from the Rohr shelter, which contained similar points in the earliest level, dated at 3352 B.C. ± 90 (Dragoo, 1959; Deevey, et al. 1959:161). However, the Le Croy points, a type very similar to the bifurcated-base point from Moccasin Bluff, have recently been radiocarbon dated at the St. Alban site in West Virginia at 6300 B.C.± 100 (Y-1539) (Broyles, 1966:40-41). This date seems to reflect more accurately the true temporal position of these points.

LATE ARCHAIC-EARLY WOODLAND OCCUPATIONS

The next period represented at the site is the Late Archaic-Early Woodland period. Clearly diagnostic artifacts from the Late Archaic period are not present in the collections at the Museum. Most of these objects (turkey tail points, rolled copper beads) are usually associated with burials, and no burials from this period are known at the Moccasin Bluff site. Settlement sites from the Late Archaic are very poorly known, but there is some suggestion that an Early Woodland settlement may have existed at Moccasin Bluff. A number of stemmed points are represented in both the Museum and the Birdsell collections (Pl. 40, A, B, C, G, H, I; Pl. 54, G, O, P; Pl. 60, R, U, V). Similar types of points have been reported from the Schultz site in the Saginaw Valley, Michigan. These points were found to occur stratigraphically below a Middle Woodland occupation and were radiocarbon dated to 530 B.C. (M-1525, 2490 ± 130) (Crane and Griffin, 1966). These small stemmed points seem closely related to the Durst stemmed type from Wisconsin (Wittry, 1959) and to the Saratoga type cluster and Kramer points from Illinois (Winters, 1967; Munson, 1966). At the Schultz site the points were associated with plano-convex ovate bifaces; several such bifaces from Moccasin Bluff can be seen in the Birdsell collection (Pl. 56, E; Pl. 60, E, F, G). The points at the Schultz site were also associated with a variety of Marion Thick pottery known as Schultz Thick. Munson (1966) has postulated an association of Marion Thick pottery and Kramer points; the Morrow site in Indiana (Faulker, 1964a) has produced an association of Marion Thick pottery, stemmed points, and ovate blades.

No sherds which could be referred to as Marion Thick were found in the material excavated by the Museum at Moccasin Bluff. The Birdsell collection, however, did contain a number of sherds which could be placed in this category. Twenty-three body sherds, having exterior and interior cord markings, were selected from the collection. In paste and in temper these sherds were identical to Havana Cordmarked sherds and differed from them only because of the presence of interior cordmarking. Measured for thickness, these sherds ranged between 0.7 cm and 1.67 cm, with an average thickness of 1.0 cm. Griffin's original description of Marion Thick noted that the range of thickness was between 1.0 and 1.5 cm (J. B. Griffin, 1952). The range of this group of sherds is much wider, but the mean falls just within the range noted by Griffin. The similarity between Marion Thick sherds and Havana Cordmarked sherds is so great at Moccasin Bluff that a number of Havana Cordmarked sherds are much thicker than most of the Marion Thick sherds. This suggests that an occupation at Moccasin Bluff might have been transitional between Early Woodland and Middle Woodland. However, the absence of any clearly recognizable Early Middle Woodland types does not support this conclusion. Marion Thick pottery was also found at the Bowmanville Site along the north branch of the Chicago River within the present limits of the city of Chicago and at the Plum Island Site near Starved Rock, Illinois (Fenner, 1961, 1963). At both of these sites, such Early Middle Woodland types as Morton Incised and Sister Creeks Punctated indicate continuity with the following Middle Woodland occupations. In northwest Indiana, sites such as Mathis have been reported as having an association of Marion Thick pottery, a grooved axe, slate plummet, a slate gorget, and stemmed and notched points (Faulkner, N.D.).

MIDDLE WOODLAND OCCUPATION

The Middle Woodland period is strongly represented at the Moccasin Bluff site. The Early Middle Woodland period is only suggested by material from the site. One possible Sister Creeks

Punctated sherd was identified in the Birdsell collection. Brown claims to have identified sherds of Fettiė Incised and Neteler Stamped, from Moccasin Bluff probably from the Young collection in the Illinois State Museum (Brown, 1964). Early Middle Woodland types have been identified by Charles Faulkner (N.D.) for a number of sites in the Kankakee Valley in northwestern Illinois. These sherds are not very abundant but are found in small numbers in collections from several sites: Watson, Schoon, and Wunderink (Faulkner, N.D.). That continuity exists between the Early and Middle Woodland period in this area is suggested by material from the Schoon site. This site produced one of the larger groups of earlier Middle Woodland ceramics. It was especially rich in Sister Creeks Punctated sherds and produced a Marion Thick-like sherd with interior and exterior cordmarking but decorated on the outer rim with fingernail punctating similar to Sister Creeks.

At Moccasin Bluff there is a sample of Havana Ware characterized by Naples Stamped, Havana Zoned Dentate, and other Havana types in minor numbers. One Hopewell Plain bowl as well as a sherd of Hopewell Rocker Dentate were found in the Birdsell collection (Pl. 79). There is a suggestion in the Birdsell notes that the Hopewell Plain vessel came from a burial group in the southern area of the site. In addition to the burial group there is also some indication of the former existence of a small mound in this southern area of the site. Two corner notched projectile points are listed as coming from this mound (Pl. 59, P, Q). These are elongated, corner notched points made from a blue-gray flint. The elongated blades of these points are rather distinctive and unusual for Hopewellian sites. However, the Summerville Mounds in the valley of the St. Joseph River have yielded points that are almost identical to the two illustrated here (Quimby, 1941); one point from the Goodall Mounds in Indiana (Quimby, 1941, Pl. 14, No. 14) is similar in form.

Other material in the Birdsell collection probably relating to this same occupation are the two slate gorget fragments, drilled from both sides (Pl. 61, B, C). These are similar to slate gorgets found at the Summerville site and the Marinetta Mounds, both in the valley of the St. Joseph River. A third gorget found in the same southern area of the site, may also be related; however, the form differs significantly from the other two (Pl. 61, E). It is a type known from late Adena sites in Ohio and West Virginia, where it is called a semi-keeled gorget. The gorget is plano-convex in cross-section and the holes are drilled only from the plano side. It is made from a reddish, lighter-weight material than the slate fragments. The small round stone illustrated at the top of Plate 61 also most likely belongs to the Middle Woodland component. Ten such stones were originally found, but only five remain in the Museum collections. They are similar to those from the Goodall site illustrated by Quimby (Quimby, 1941, Pl. 12). Stone celts (Pl. 47, Pl. 62 F, G) are also commonly associated with Middle Woodland sites and should be placed here. An elongated stone object shown in Plate 62, C is similar in shape to a stone celt illustrated from the Goodall site (Quimby, 1941, Pl. 11). The stone from Moccasin Bluff, however, has a rounded, blunt end in contrast to the pointed bit of the celt from the Goodall site. The mica fragment listed in Appendix 17 is commonly found associated with many Hopewellian sites in the Upper Great Lakes. It has been found at the Goodall site, the Summerville Mounds, and the Marinetta Mounds as well as the Adler Mounds in northern Illinois (Winters, 1961) and the Wilson site in the Wabash Valley (Neumann and Fowler, 1952).

A copper celt (Pl. 64C) collected by Birdsell is also part of the Middle Woodland occupation at Moccasin Bluff. These celts are common on Hopewellian sites and have been reported from Summerville, Norton and the Goodall sites by Quimby (1941).

The notched points illustrated in Plate 41 also seem to be related to this Middle Woodland occupation. Although they are listed in five separate classes, they could reliably be grouped into one class in the light of the data from the Schultz site. At the Schultz site, similar points are called small expanding stemmed points and large expanding stemmed points. Groups A-E of the notched points from Moccasin Bluff would easily be accommodated into the Schultz groupings. At the Schultz site, these points were found stratigraphically associated with the Middle Woodland levels. A Norton Corner Notched point is illustrated on Plate 59 L. This type of point is well known from Hopewellian sites. It is represented in collections from the Norton site to the north of Moccasin Bluff and at the Goodall site to the south of Moccasin Bluff. Apparently also associated with Hopewellian sites is a form of the corner notched point reworked into a hafted scraper which is also sometimes called a blunt. Plate 63 E, F, G illustrate three of these tools from the Birdsell collection. Brown (1964) mentions these types of tools in the Young collection from the Goodall site and Winters (1961) mentions them as associated with material from Adler. At the Schultz site two similar hafted scrapers of this type were associated with the Middle Woodland levels.

LATE WOODLAND OCCUPATION

During the later part of the Middle Woodland period and continuing into the early part of the Late Woodland there is a trend from ceramics decorated with dentate, stamped, or incised decoration to a large amount of cord-impressed and cord-wrapped stick decoration. This trend has been noted by J. B. Griffin (1952) and Wray and MacNeish (1961). The period of transition from Hopewellian assemblages to complexes clearly recognized as Late Woodland is well represented at Moccasin Bluff. A number of ceramic groupings from the site seem to represent occupations from this period. The Moccasin Bluff Cordmarked variety 1a sherds are probably most closely related to the earlier Middle Woodland material. Their paste, temper, and method of manufacture would seem to imply a close association with earlier material. The Moccasin Bluff Cordmarked variety 1b, with its various subgroups, also should be related to this period. The variety 1a sherds probably appear at the tag end of the Middle Woodland and develop into the variety 1b sherds in Late Woodland times. The group 1b sherds have paste and temper characteristics which are more similar to the general type of Late Woodland wares found in the area. The Moccasin Bluff Modified Lip sherds also seem to reflect the movement away from the more "classic" Hopewellian types to the early Late Woodland wares. The Moccasin Bluff Collared sherds probably begin appearing late in this period, perhaps as early as the closing centuries of the first millenium. They can be separated into two groups. Group A has paste and temper characteristics which relate it to the Moccasin Bluff Cordmarked variety 1a sherds, while group B is more similar to the recognized Late Woodland wares in paste and temper. Many of the Moccasin Bluff Plain sherds and Plain Modified Lip sherds may also belong to this period.

At Spoonville, a Hopewellian site in the Grand River Valley to the north of Moccasin Bluff, there are sherds which are very similar in paste and tempering to the Moccasin Bluff Cordmarked variety 1a group. The Crockery ware from Spoonville commonly has cord impressions up to the lip and a rim profile that resembles the Moccasin Bluff material (Flanders, 1965).

In northern Indiana, Faulkner (N.D.) reports pottery similar to Moccasin Bluff Cordmarked in the Weise and the Wunderink mounds. He feels that the Wunderink mound was built in the early Late Woodland period. The situation at the Weise mound is more complex, but on the basis of the artifacts present, it should date from the terminal phases of the Middle Woodland period (McAllister, 1932).

The Moccasin Bluff Modified Lip sherds also seem to be part of this complex. The paste and temper characteristics of some of the sherds (Pl. 19, D) show similarities to Moccasin Bluff Cordmarked variety 1a and to material from the Spoonville site. At Spoonville Flanders' Crockery Flared type has cord-wrapped stick impressions across the top of the lip as well as transverse notching with a sharp tool on the lip. This lip treatment parallels the Moccasin Bluff Modified Lip group 1 sherds. The relative absence of the Crockery Cambered types at Moccasin Bluff might suggest that the bulk of the occupation at Spoonville is slightly earlier in time than most of Moccasin Bluff. The Crockery ware is probably more representative of a chronological placement closer to the period when Baehr material was being produced in Illinois. Further to the north, Hinsdale unearthed a vessel similar to Moccasin Bluff Modified Lip from the West Twin Lake site Mound 8. This pot was found with flexed burial in the mound associated with 15 side-notched points, an antler point, two two-holed slate gorgets, an elbow-shaped clay pipe, four bone harpoons, and two antler tines with beaver incisors inserted in them (Hinsdale, 1929). A radiocarbon date was run on material from this mound which gave a date of A.D. 950 (M-1084 1000±100) (Crane and Griffin, 1968). Whether this date actually dates the pot is unclear because the date was run on skeletal material from the mound. Two intrusive bundle burials were found in the same mound. It is likely that the bone used for the radiocarbon date may have come from these bundle burials. The bones used for the date were femurs and the original report indicates that the right femur of the burial associated with the pot was very pathological. There is no mention of pathology on the femurs submitted for the radiocarbon date which may indicate that femurs from another burial may have been dated. A similar pot is reported by Hinsdale from Mound 1 of the Brooks group. Quimby's type III sherds in his report on the Goodall Focus are also related to this material (Quimby, 1941). Quimby mentions the vessel reported by Hinsdale from the Brooks site, as well as a pot and some sherds from the Summerville site and the Goodall site which are also related to the Moccasin Bluff Cordmarked Modified Lip sherds.

From the Lower Muskegon Valley Prahl reports a number of sites which are related to this horizon (Prahl, 1970). At the Parsons Mound 1 he describes a vessel whose lip has been given a scalloped effect due to a cord-wrapped stick or paddle impressed on the surface. The Mallon Mound group seems to be a series of mounds which falls into this period. Almost all the vessels from these mounds have modification of the top of the lip in some fashion or other. The Jancarich Earth enclosure also produced pottery which is similar to these wares. Some of this Lower Michigan material is beginning to approach the simpler forms of the Mackinac wares described by McPherron (1967). The Mackinac phase A at the Juntunen site has been dated by radiocarbon to A.D. 835±75 (M-1142) (Crane and Griffin, 1961).

To the south of Moccasin Bluff in Starke County, Indiana, is the Brems site. Analyses of the Birdsell collection from this site in the Museum of Anthropology, The University of Michigan is presented in Appendices 13 and 14. This site has a strong component of Moccasin Bluff Cordmarked variety 1a and Moccasin Bluff Modified Lip sherds. Two radiocarbon dates from two different pits at the site have been run: the earliest is A.D. 555±300 (M-48A, 1400±300) and probably dates this occupation; the later is A.D. 1455±250 (M-48B, 500±250) and may date a later Huber occupation of the site (Crane and Griffin, 1958).

Further to the west, similarities are noted to material from the Bowmanville site where impressions on the top of the lip are known from some sherds (Fenner, 1961). Cord-wrapped stick impressions are present on some of the Havana Cordmarked vessels (Pl. 78) and it is not unusual to find this decoration on Naples-type vessels. This type of decoration carries over into the following period on some of the Moccasin Bluff Modified Lip vessels (Pl. 75). Sherds similar to those from Moccasin Bluff Modified Lip group 6 are attributed by Quimby to the Goodall site (Quimby, 1941, Pl. 13, No. 34, 35). Sherds of this group 3 type, especially those in Plate 20, I, J, and K, seem related to material in the Wabash Valley known as Stoner Cordmarked (Winters, 1967). Winters feels that the Allison complex, of which the Stoner Cordmarked sherds are a part of the assemblage, is associated with the later part of the Middle Woodland period.

The Swanson complex pottery mentioned by Brown (1961) seems to be related to the early Late Woodland period. This pottery, because of its cordmarking to the lip, its modification of the top of the lip, its general vessel shape, seems to be more closely related to this period than to the terminal Woodland or early Historic period, where Brown places it on the basis of its association at Starved Rock and the Hotel Plaza sites.

To the east, relationships can be seen to the Wayne ware of the southeastern Michigan (Fitting, 1965). Fitting sees the Wayne ware as developing out of the late Middle Woodland base in the area and into the Late Woodland Younge tradition. This situation parallels that found in western Michigan.

Across the lake on the Door Peninsula of Wisconsin, Mason has identified and dated a complex related to this period. This complex, called Heins Creek ware, is related to the Moccasin Bluff material through similarities in tempering and vessel manufacture as well as decoration (R. J. Mason, 1966:202-204). The closest related type is Heins Creek Cordmarked which has the fully cordmarked exterior and is decorated on the top of the lip by scalloping or shallow notching with a plain or cordwrapped paddle edge. The other types from Heins Creek, although closely related to the above, are more elaborate, decorated by various types of stamping and cordmarking. The heavy incrustations of burned food adhering to the interior surfaces of these sherds have been radiocarbon dated to A.D. 720 (I-678, 1230±150) (R. J. Mason, 1966:27-28). The projectile points at Heins Creek reported by Mason were all triangular.

In the last centuries of the first millenium after the birth of Christ, the trend toward cordmarking up to the lip of the vessel continues, as does the tendency to constrict the neck of the vessels. At Moccasin Bluff, the top of the lip receives less attention while the exterior edge of the lip begins to assume greater importance as a focus for decoration. Sites characterizing this period are not well known in the Moccasin Bluff area, but one marker along the path may be the Spring Creek site in Muskegon County, Michigan. This site with its simple cordmarked vessels, its collared vessels, and its decoration by punctations, cordwrapped stick impressions, and occasional incised lines, has been radiocarbon dated to A.D. 960±75 (M-512, 990±75) (Crane and Griffin, 1958). At Moccasin Bluff many, if not most, of the Moccasin Bluff Cordmarked variety 1b sherds are representative of a similar horizon. These sherds show a continuum with the earlier material. The temper and the paste are more typical of Late Woodland material generally: temper consists of mixed granitic rock, black temper being less common; the paste is brown, gray-brown, to gray and black in color. Vessel form varies from examples with relatively straight profiles to others which show a fair degree of constriction in the neck. All traces of plain pottery seem to have disappeared by this time; it is almost unknown at the Heins Creek site in Wisconsin and at the Spring Creek site. Some smoothing is associated with the Wayne ware material but it seems to increase in frequency in the later horizons (Fitting, 1965:135, Fig. 19).

Collared ware also begins to appear during this period. There may be a development from examples with weakly developed, small collars and thinner vessel walls to thicker and more massive collars. The earlier types may be represented by the group A collared vessels at Moccasin Bluff, some of the collared sherds at the Spring Creek site, and some of the collared sherds at the Brems site (see Appendix 18). The later group B collared vessels are more similar to Aztalan Collared from Wisconsin (Baerreis and Freeman, 1958) and to Starved Rock Collared in northern Illinois (Hall, 1962b). One sherd of Starved Rock Collared is represented in the Moccasin Bluff collection (Pl. 18, M). These later collared forms may date around A.D. 1200 (Baerreis and Bryson, 1965:209).

By A.D. 1100 Moccasin Bluff Impressed Lip vessels appear as the major indication of occupation at the site. This occupation is probably the largest of the site, judging by the amount of pottery present. Most of the material from the site, as well as most of the features on the sherds, are associated with this or with later occupations, dating from A.D. 1060 to A.D. 1210 (M-1941, 890±110; M-1936, 890±110; M-1938, 860±110; M-1940, 800±110; M-1939, 740±100) (Crane and Griffin, 1970).

The pottery, Moccasin Bluff Impressed Lip which seems to be a local development from earlier Late Woodland material, is closely associated with material from northern Illinois and northwestern Indiana, usually referred to as Upper Mississippian. Upper Mississippian Fisher and Langford material and Oneota-related Huber material are all intimately connected in this area. Their exact relationship and chronological ordering is not clear at the present time. What is clear is that the occupants at Moccasin Bluff, while maintaining their own identity, were heavily influenced by all three of these related ceramic groups and presumably by their maker or makers.

The relationship of the Moccasin Bluff Impressed Exterior Lip sherds to the Fisher and the Langford material can be clearly seen in Plate 25. This vessel has the modification on the exterior edge of the lip after which this type is named. The same form of decoration is found on Fisher and such related ceramics as the Fifield series from northwestern Indiana (Faulkner, 1970). The presence of small nipple-like lugs grouped at 90 degree intervals around the exterior edge of the lip of the vessel is similar to the lugs associated with Fisher and the Fisher-like Fifield pottery. Perhaps the most characteristic feature is the decoration, which consists of a series of broad (9 mm wide) impressions running from the neck to the shoulder. This type of decoration is related to Fifield Bold (Faulkner, 1970), Langford Bold (Brown, et al., 1967) and to Koshkonong Bold from Oneota sites in Wisconsin (Hall, 1962a:72-75). Both Fifield and Koshkonong are shell-tempered types; Langford Bold is grit-tempered. Since the related type at Moccasin Bluff is grit-tempered, there has been some tendency to refer it more closely to the Langford material. However, it is the author's opinion that the decoration on Moccasin Bluff Impressed Exterior Lip is probably more closely related to the shell-tempered Fifield material, to the south of Moccasin Bluff than to the Langford material to the west. The decoration on the exterior of the lip and the lugs are more common in the Fisher and related material than in the Langford material. The people of Moccasin Bluff appear to have adopted this form of decoration through their contact with the populations in northwestern Indiana.

Further evidence for contact between Moccasin Bluff and the shell-tempered material to the south is supported by the occurrence of sherds similar to Fisher Cordmarked. These sherds, grouped into the Berrien ware group 5 class, represent shell-tempered, cordmarked sherds with decorated lips. Decorated body sherds associated with these rim sherds are listed in Table 17. Motifs 1, 3, 4, 5, 7, 8, and 9 are closely related to Fifield Trailed sherds; 2 and 6 are examples of Fifield Bold (see Faulkner, 1970). Several of the sherds in the Berrien ware group 4 are also related to the Fifield Trailed type. A number of shell-tempered, cordmarked sherds from the Birdsell collection also have lug handles, which indicate a similarity to the Fifield material.

The Berrien ware groups 1, 2, 3 are good examples of Huber ware (Faulkner, 1970). This pottery is best known from the Anker site (Bluhm and Liss, 1961), the Oak Forest site (Fenner, 1961) and the Huber site (J. B. Griffin, 1943). It is a shell-tempered, often plain surface pottery with incised trailed lines or "finger grooves" on the shoulder of the vessel. Rims are either short or medium high and range from gently outsloping to rather acute outsloping examples. Top of the lip is plain and flattened or has broad, shallow impressions or narrow notches. Surface finish is plain at Moccasin Bluff, but cordmarked examples do occur at other sites. Decoration somewhat resembles Fifield Trailed: motifs 1 (trailed line) and 2 ("finger grooves," and fine trailed lines and punctates) from Table 17 are common to both groups. The trailed lines on the Huber material are generally much thinner than on the Fifield. The Huber examples are generally from 1 to 1.5 mm wide while the Fifield examples are generally around 4 mm wide. Motif 2, "finger grooving," occurs on plain sherds in the Huber material, whereas it is most often found on cordmarked sherds in the Fifield examples. The design is also applied differently: in the Fifield examples, the design is placed on the shoulder as if radiating out from a point at the center of the vessel; in the Huber examples, the impressions are opposed diagonals with punctates filling the triangular spaces between the impressions. Roundish strap handles are also associated with the Huber complex.

The Huber material is most certainly later than Fisher-Fifield material. In the Chicago area, it is associated with Historic material at Oak Forest (Bluhm and Fenner, 1961:145) and the Palos site (Munson and Munson, 1969:185). Some evidence of a chronological difference at Moccasin Bluff is suggested by data presented in Table 17. In design motif 2, which is common to both the Fifield and Huber material, there is a difference in the distribution of the material. Shell-tempered, cordmarked ware most often associated with the Fifield ware is found to be concentrated in trench A; shell-tempered, plain sherds with the same motif, more common in Huber material, is concentrated in trench C. The difference in distribution in this case most likely reflects different utilization of these two types of pottery at different occupations of the site. A later placement of the Huber-Berrien material is also suggested by two radiocarbon dates—A.D. 1590 and A.D. 1640 (M-1936, 360$\pm$100; M-1935, 310$\pm$100) (Crane and Griffin, 1930)—from Moccasin Bluff. The association of this Huber-Berrien material with a relatively higher percentage of Huber-like plain surface, shell-tempered body sherds in pits 91 and 21 (see Table 20) suggests that these dates may relate to the Huber-Berrien occupation.

To summarize the relationship of the Moccasin Bluff Modified Lip sherds to the material to the south and west of Moccasin Bluff, the situation appears to be as follows. Very little, if any, pottery directly assignable to Moccasin Bluff Modified Lip can be detected in this area. The Kankakee Valley of northeast Illinois seems to be the repository of Fisher-related materials, as reported from the Griesmer and Fifield sites (Faulkner, 1970). Survey in this area by Faulkner has failed to reveal any significant amount of Moccasin Bluff Modified Lip sherds or Langford material. The influence of this material can be seen at Moccasin Bluff by the presence of similar shell-tempered, cordmarked pottery of the Fifield Trailed and Fifield Bold types. These types are classified at Moccasin Bluff under the category of Berrien ware groups 4 and 5. Some of the Moccasin Bluff Modified Lip vessels apparently also used trailed designs and "finger grooving" as decoration (see vessel in Pl. 25). Analysis of the decorated body sherds also indicates that the grit-tempered, cordmarked sherds, related in part to the Moccasin Bluff Modified Lip vessels, are probably associated with this assemblage. Fisher material has been radiocarbon dated at the Lawrence site in Whiteside County, Illinois: these dates run from A.D. 1160±110 to A.D. 1270±110 (M-1593, 790±110; M-1592, 780±110; M-1594, 690±110; M-1594, 680±110) (Crane and Griffin, 1966:267). These dates are in very close agreement with the dates associated with similar material obtained from Moccasin Bluff.

The Upper Illinois River Valley is largely characterized by the presence of Langford material at such sites as Gentleman Farm (Brown, et al., 1967), Plum Island (Fenner, 1963), the Zimmerman site (Brown, 1961), and the upper levels of the Fisher site (Langford, 1927, and J. W. Griffin, 1946). Other sites, such as the Oakwood Mound (Skinner, 1953) and Robinson Reserve (Fowler, 1952) are along the Des Plaines River south and west of Chicago. The Mississippian pottery from these sites is overwhelmingly Langford ware. Small amounts of Fisher ware occur on most of them. The Fisher site, which has a large amount of shell-tempered ware, is perhaps the only exception, but until the material is studied in its entirety, its position will remain unclear. The Langford pottery has been dated by radiocarbon to between A.D. 1200 and 1500 (Brown, et al., 1967:43).

The Huber pottery is centered in the Chicago area and is known from the Huber site (J. B. Griffin, 1943:284-286), the Oak Forest site (Bluhm and Fenner, 1961) and the Anker site (Bluhm and Liss, 1961). The beginnings of the Huber tradition is not well-defined at the present time, but it certainly continues into the early Historic period at the Oak Forest site and at the Palos site (Munson and Munson, 1969). Moccasin Bluff has a clear occupation associated with Huber-Berrien pottery and the late radiocarbon dates from Moccasin Bluff support the late Prehistoric position of this ware. Little, if any, influence from Moccasin Bluff is evident in any of the collections from the above-mentioned sites.

To the north of Moccasin Bluff, the evidence is very slim. In Kent County at the mouth of the Thornapple River, where it flows into the Grand River, material related to Moccasin Bluff Modified Lip pottery has been reported from a number of local collections (Pl. 81). This site, known locally as the Ada site, is reported as having both grit-and shell-tempered pottery. Pots are globular in shape, with the rim slightly outflaring, and impressions on the exterior edge of the lip. Wide handles are known to be present. Decoration is similar to motif 5 illustrated in Table 17 (Quimby, 1937).

At the Dumaw Creek site in Oceana County, Michigan, pottery resembling Moccasin Bluff Modified Lip has also been found

(Quimby, 1966; and private collections). This pottery has a coarser, more sandy texture and is usually more heavily tempered than is the material from Moccasin Bluff. Quimby has dated this site as late Prehistoric, perhaps A.D. 1605 to 1620. While these dates are probably valid for the burials that Quimby dated, some of the pottery from the site may be stylistically related to material from the early Late Woodland period.

On the basis of the above material and of collections in the Kent County Museum, the Muskegon County Museum, and the Traverse City Museum, it seems that material similar, if not identical, to Moccasin Bluff Modified Exterior Lip is common along the western edge of the state. Moccasin Bluff appears to be located near the southern limit of this distribution. The further north of the Grand River, the more the material begins to approach the material from the Juntunen site. Few specific resemblances can be noted to material in southeastern Michigan.

Two additional ceramic groupings which most certainly belong in the very late Prehistoric, if not proto-Historic, are the Moccasin Bluff Scalloped sherds and the Moccasin Bluff Notched Applique Strip sherds. The Moccasin Bluff Scalloped sherds are similar to the vessel Quimby reported as coming from burial 1 at Dumaw Creek (Quimby, 1966a:65). He felt that these burials dated between A.D. 1605 and 1620. Huber pottery is not uncommonly found with slight modification of the top of the lip, resulting in a faint scalloped effect. The association of Huber material with Historic material would again not be out of line with the late date for Moccasin Bluff Scalloped, assuming there is some connection between the two groups. This assumption is strengthened by the association of both types at Moccasin Bluff. Scalloped rim sherds are not uncommon to collections from western Michigan and are found as far north as the Straits of Mackinac (McPherron, 1967; Pl. X, XXIII). Scalloping is also not unusual on Oneota ceramics, which generally have a late Prehistoric date.

Moccasin Bluff Notched Applique Strip is another type which is certainly late in its associations. One complete vessel of this type was found at the Ada site, in Kent County, Michigan (Herrick, 1958). This pot was found in a field along with a fair amount of Historic material dating from the period of French dominance, i.e., pre-A.D. 1760. Association between the pot and the trade goods is not secure, but it is nevertheless suggestive of a late date, perhaps around A.D. 1600. A similar type of pottery was reported from the Bell site in Winnebago County, Wisconsin (Wittry, 1963:27). The Bell site pottery is shell-tempered and similar to pottery in the Starved Rock area in Illinois called

LaSalle Filleted. The Bell site is reported as a Fox Indian village dating from the period between A.D. 1680 and 1730. Similar material is known from the Whittlesey sites in northern Ohio. In Ohio this material occurs in both shell and grit temper, with grit being the most common (Greenman, 1937:355). James E. Fitting, in a reanalysis of this material, named this pottery Tuttle Hill Notched (Fitting, 1964b). He concluded that this type of pottery was late in the sequence he examined. One radiocarbon date from Moccasin Bluff, M-1935, may date this pottery. It was run on charcoal association with sherds of this type from pit 21. A date of A.D. 1640±100 was reported from this sample (Crane and Griffin, 1970).

More broadly, similar sherds are known from Fort Ancient sites, such as Fox Farm (J. B. Griffin, 1943:Pl. CIII). At these sites the ware is usually shell tempered.

Finally, a few miscellaneous sherds deserve special mention. The miniature vessels illustrated in Plate 37, M, N, are all suggestive of similar material associated with Huber and Oneota sites (Faulkner, 1970:113). Miniature vessels are often found on these sites and the incised designs are suggestive of those found on Huber Trailed vessels.

One sherd illustrated in Plate 37 K is representative of Parker Festooned (Lee, 1958). This type is well-known in southeastern Michigan, southwestern Ontario, and northern Ohio where it is a marker for the late Prehistoric period, after A.D. 1400 (Fitting, 1965:142-150). The author has also identified a sherd of Parker Festooned in the Younge collection from Moccasin Bluff in the Illinois State Museum.

From the Birdsell collection there is one example of the base of a water bottle (Pl. 80). This vessel has a maximum exterior diameter of 13 cm and an approximate height of 8.9 cm from the base to the junction of the neck and shoulder and is a good example of Saint Clair Plain (J. B. Griffin, 1949:34). It is probably most closely related to Middle Mississippian material in the Central Illinois River Valley known as the Spoon River Focus (Wray, 1952; Cole and Deuel, 1937). A similar water bottle is reported from the Huber-related Anker site. The Anker material is slipped and painted, which is not characteristic of material from this area.

NONCERAMIC ARTIFACTS

A survey of the nonceramic artifacts reveals some interesting and informative data. Although the occupational periods reflected in the ceramic material reveal a fairly broad expanse of time, it is not possible at present to divide the nonceramic material into a similar number of identifiable units. The nonceramic material will therefore be treated as a unit, even though it may be possible to identify separate components at some future time.

The most prevalent artifact other than pottery is the small triangular point (Pl. 39). Such points are widely known throughout the midwest as markers for the Late Woodland and Mississippian periods. Faulkner, in his study of the Kankakee Valley, argues for the possible presence of at least two groups of these points: the first (type I) is a long and narrow point with a length-width ratio of .49 associated with Huber material; the second (type II) is a shorter form with a length-width ratio of .73 associated with Fisher material. These two distinct groups are not in evidence at Moccasin Bluff. Almost all of the points at Moccasin Bluff would fall into Faulkner's shorter type II group. A few individual points would qualify for inclusion in his type I class, but their number is small. When the length-width ratios for the points from Moccasin Bluff are plotted on a graph, a unimodal distribution results.

Another article of interest for comparative purposes is the ovate or double pointed blades or knives (Pl. 42, C, D, E). These tools were listed as diagnostic of the Upper Mississippian phase by McKern (1945:134) and similar forms occur at the Griesmer site (Faulkner, 1970) and Anker (Bluhm and Liss, 1961:Fig. 59), both of which are Oneota-related Huber sites. They also are reported from Plum Island (Fenner, 1963:Fig. 36J), a Langford tradition site, and seem common on such sites in northern Ohio as Fairport Harbor (Morgan and Ellis, 1943:10), Tuttle Hill and South Park (Greenman, 1937:Figs. 13, 14), and Reeve (Greenman, 1937: Fig. 8). Such blades are not listed by Griffin in his analysis of the Fort Ancient material (J. B. Griffin, 1943:Table XIV) and a search of the literature fails to reveal any examples on Fort Ancient sites.

The scrapers also have a distribution similar to the ovate blades. End scrapers are commonly found on Oneota sites, but they are generally unifical (McKern, 1945:133). At Moccasin Bluff, only one end scraper was unifically flaked, while all the rest were bifacially flaked. At the Fifield site in northern Indiana most of the end scrapers were bifacially flaked and similar to those from Moccasin Bluff (Faulkner, 1970:198). Similar end scrapers also are reported from the Whittlesey sites in northern Ohio (Morgan and Ellis, 1943:11; Greenman, 1937:Figs. 13, 15). J. B. Griffin noted the general absence of end scrapers in the Fort Ancient sites (1943:301). Two oval scrapers were reported from Moccasin Bluff. These scrapers are similar to types reported from the Fairport Harbor site by Morgan and Ellis (1943:11).

Drills from the late Prehistoric period seem to be of three general types: the double pointed, the expanding base, and the distinct T-shaped drills. All are found at Moccasin Bluff. The double pointed drills appear to be widespread, occurring in all groups discussed here. The expanded base drill is commonly found at most of the sites discussed here. While no examples of the expanded base drill were found in The University of Michigan excavations, several examples are present in the Birdsell collection (Pl. 57). The T-shaped drill is rarely found on Oneota sites or in Langford tradition sites in northern Illinois or in sites from the late Prehistoric period in northwestern Indiana. It is more commonly found in Fort Ancient sites.

A final class of interesting chipped stone tools is the small, thick, steep-edge pieces. This seems to be a fairly widespread type but its presence is sometimes difficult to ascertain because it is not uniformly reported in the literature. Faulkner (1970:133) reports thick, triangular blades from the Griesmer site which may be similar to the small, thick, steep-edge pieces from Moccasin Bluff. Similar tools are reported from the Gentleman Farm (Brown, et al., 1967:30), Zimmerman (Brown, 1961:54), Plum Island (Fenner, 1963:Fig. 36*b*) and the Fisher site where they appear to be similar to Griffin's type 1 scraper (J. W. Griffin, 1946:42). Similar tools are also present at the Chicago-area Huber sites (Bluhm and Liss, 1961:Fig. 59; and Bluhm and Fenner, 1961:Fig. 77*c*), but as far as is known, none have been reported from Oneota sites in the Wisconsin area. Small, thick steep-edge pieces are not reported from Whittlesey sites and are not usually mentioned in connection with Fort Ancient sites, although they seem to be presented at the Graham Village site (McKenzie, 1967:73).

If we look at the ratio of debitage to finished tools, we find that at Moccasin Bluff there are about 4.7 flakes for every tool; a rather low ratio, which might imply that a fair part of the flint knapping was done elsewhere. Fitting noted a similar situation at the Spring Creek and the Riviere au Vase sites (Fitting, 1968:70; 1965:47). At the Griesmer site in northwestern Indiana a similar comparison results in a ratio of eight flakes for every finished artifact (data calculated by the author from Faulkner, 1970). It should be noted that the Griesmer site had 59 cores, compared with the four from Moccasin Bluff. These comparisons, while not entirely conclusive, certainly suggest differences in cultural behavior between different populations. Wider use of these comparisons is hampered by the lack of standardized procedures for analysis and reporting of the data as well as by the lack of analysis of the manufacturing techniques, since different techniques of manufacture would probably lead to different ratios of material.

Since stone tools are often the artifact class which most closely articulates an aboriginal population with certain of its economic activities, this class of artifacts is probably a most sensitive indicator of these economic activities. Much of the variation in the types of stone tools among sites can probably be better understood if the variation in the tools were integrated with the variation in the economic activities carried out at the site.

Two classes of stone tools are particularly prominent at Moccasin Bluff: the small triangular points and the thick bifaces. The points were certainly used as arrow or spear heads for the hunting of deer and elk and other game and may have been used to point the shafts used to spear sturgeon. The thick bifaces—if they were, in fact, wood-working tools, as has been postulated—may have been used for the preparation of shafts of the arrows and spears as well as for other wood-working tasks. Small triangular points constitute 44 percent of all tools from Moccasin Bluff. At the Griesmer site, they account for 26 percent, at the Anker site, they represent 32 percent, and at Oak Forest they represent 28 percent of all the tools. Perhaps the high percentage at Moccasin Bluff results from the sturgeon spearing at this site, an activity which is not represented at any of the other sites.

The remaining tools, such as the utilized flakes, the ovate blades, which seem to have served as knives, the drills, and the gravers, are all familiar tools and their presence here deserves no special comment.

If one compares the total number of ceramic vessels to the total number of stone tools at Moccasin Bluff, a ratio of two ceramic vessels to each stone tool is obtained. This compares with a ratio of four vessels for each finished stone tool at the Spring Creek site. Fitting has suggested that the greater number of vessels would indicate an emphasis on female activity at Spring Creek and the likelihood that more females were actually present at the site than males (Fitting, 1968:70). While it may be true that there were more females at the site than males, the proposed sex ratio difference requires further documentation. This sort of ratio, however, may be useful in comparisons between sites to indicate functional differences in the types of activities. It would seem that at Spring Creek, activities involving ceramic vessels had a greater importance than at the Moccasin Bluff site. Why this might be so is not clear at this time. At the Griesmer site, the ceramics were not analyzed into vessels so the comparison must be based on the total sherd counts: at Griesmer, there are five sherds per stone tool or one piece of flint for every sherd; at Moccasin Bluff, there are 38 sherds per tool or six sherds for every piece of flint; at Spring Creek, there are 75 sherds per tool or 10 sherds for every piece of flint. Allowing for the differences in sampling the sites and analyzing the material, these ratios may indicate that flint chipping was carried out at the Griesmer site while very little chipping was done at Moccasin Bluff and at Spring Creek.

In looking at the distribution of the flint in Table 10, two figures seem especially interesting: the concentration of flakes of bifacial retouch and small thick bifaces in trench C. These concentrations may indicate that this area was a specialized activity area.

Hammer stones and celts are commonly found on many late Prehistoric sites, so their presence at Moccasin Bluff is not surprising. The abrading stones at Moccasin Bluff are similar to the rectangular, single grooved type often noted as being typically Oneota (McKern, 1945:130-131). Several similar arrowshaft finishers have been reported for the Fort Ancient Madisonville site in Ohio (Hooton and Willoughby, 1920:Pl. 6).

Stone pendants and balls generally similar to those from Moccasin Bluff have been reported from the Zimmerman site (Brown, 1961:55).

Most of the bone tools—the bone cylinders, beaming tools, antler tines, antler points, bone awls, and bone beads—are apparently widely distributed in the late Prehistoric period. Several items of the bone assemblage, however, deserve special mention. The spatulate pieces of antler, sometimes called antler chisels, antler gouges, or antler scrapers, have a somewhat irregular distribution. They are not reported from most of the sites in northwestern Indiana or northern Illinois. Possible examples occur at the Plum Island site (Fenner, 1963:Fig. 31) and at the Fisher site (Langford, 1927:Pl. XIX; and J. W. Griffin, 1946:28). McKern illustrates a possible example for the Lake Winnebago site (1945:Pl. 27). Spatulate pieces of antler are apparently most common on Whittlesey sites in northern Ohio (Morgan and Ellis, 1943:21; Greenman, 1937:Fig. 28; Greenman, 1935:16). Some possible examples occur in Fort Ancient sites such as Campbell Island Village (Mills, 1926:27), but most of these are larger and are usually referred to as hoes (Hooton and Willoughby, 1920:Pl. 14).

Perforated deer bone similar to the one from Moccasin Bluff also seems to have a more eastern distribution. One example is reported from the Gentleman Farm site (Brown, et al., 1967:Fig. 12) and others are reported from the Fisher site (J. W. Griffin, 1946:29). J. B. Griffin lists the presence of similar bones at four Fort Ancient sites (1943:Table XIV).

The elk scapula tools are most commonly referred to as hoes. They occur at the Griesmer and the Fifield sites in the Kankakee Valley in association with bison scapulae (Faulkner, 1970:201-202). They are also found at the Anker and the Oak Forest Huber sites and in other Oneota-related sites (Bluhm and Liss, 1961:Fig. 67; Bluhm and Fenner, 1961:Fig. 80). These tools are not reported for the Whittlesey sites and are generally not found on Fort Ancient sites, although several examples are reported from the Campbell Island site (Mills, 1926:24). One example is reported from the Middle Woodland Norton Mounds (J. B. Griffin, et al., 1970:Pl. 177).

The musical rasp also has a spotty distribution. Skinner (1951) reports an example from the Fifield site just to the south of Moccasin Bluff and Bluhm and Liss (1961:Fig. 67) report an example from the Anker site. Other examples are known from Whittlesey sites and from Fort Ancient sites in Ohio (Greenman, 1937:Fig. 20; Morgan and Ellis, 1943:24; Hooton and Willoughby, 1920:Pl. 15).

Finally, the piece of grooved antler is similar to only one other artifact reported in the literature from the Upper Great Lakes area. This is a generally similar piece illustrated from the South Park site in northern Ohio (Greenman, 1937:Fig. 20). The item from South Park, however, has two grooves rather than one groove, as at Moccasin Bluff.

The pipe complex at Moccasin Bluff also points to some interesting relationships. The pipes are made from stone and clay as are many of the pipes in the Upper Great Lakes from the late Prehistoric period. The principal form at Moccasin Bluff is the stemless pipe. Only one pipe stem was identified and it was in the Birdsell collection (Pl. 64 E). Two types of stone pipes are found at Moccasin Bluff: one is the vase or bowl-shaped pipe while the other is the more blocky type. The blocky pipe is known only from two unfinished examples. These pipes have their closest relationships with the Whittlesey and Fort Ancient material in Ohio. Stemless pipes and one rectangular block pipe are reported from the Anker site, but most of the pipes at Anker are of the disk pipe or stemmed and effigy types (Bluhm and Liss, 1961:Fig. 64). The pottery pipes are found in most of the assemblages discussed for the late Prehistoric period. It is also noteworthy that the Dumaw Creek pipes too have their closest ties to the more eastern pipe complex, although a few more stemmed pipes are found at Dumaw Creek than at Moccasin Bluff (Quimby, 1966 :50-54). Specimens similar to the clay, shell-tempered pipe are known from Wisconsin; a modified tube-shaped pipe which may represent a complete specimen of the fragment found at Moccasin Bluff is reported from the McClaughry Mound group in Marquette County, Wisconsin (West, 1934:294, Pl. 35).

Pipes may very well be valuable indicators of ethnic relationships in this area. It is well documented that historically pipes played an important role in the ritual and ceremonial life of the Indian groups. The importance of pipes can be projected back into the Prehistoric period where they are often found as offerings associated with burials.

Barrett gives a description of pipes and pipe smoking among the Chippewa and Menominee (1911:353-357). He describes two types of pipe made from different materials and having different shapes. Ceremonial pipes are almost exclusively stemmed and made from catlinite, such as the calumet; in some instances there is a similarly shaped form made from a black stone which is referred to as a chief's pipe. The other type is a stemless pipe made from limestone or from sandstone and includes the stone pipes found at Moccasin Bluff. This stemless pipe is used for everyday smoking. If we can generalize from the Chippewa and Menominee to other Central Algonkian groups, then we might be able to trace cultural relationships by means of association with different types of pipes. It may also be of interest that Barrett illustrates a turtle carapace which is used as a tobacco tray (1911:Pl. XXIV, Fig. 6). Perhaps the turtle carapaces at Moccasin Bluff and the carapaces found in many of the Hopewellian mounds in Michigan (which often also included pipes of various types) were used in a similar fashion.

VIII

ADAPTATION AND SUBSISTENCE

IN THIS report no detailed analysis of the ecology and adaptation of the inhabitants of the Moccasin Bluff site will be attempted. Much of the information necessary for such an analysis is not presently available, either from the archaeological or from the biological fields. Here the available data from the Moccasin Bluff site will be presented and those data which appear to be of major importance to the population will be discussed in greater detail. Specifically, this discussion is restricted to those occupations after A.D. 1000 since little of the plant and animal material can be directly associated with the earlier occupations.

CHARCOAL

Table 34 lists the species of identified charcoal and its distribution at the site. Although the sample is small and not definitive, it is suggestive of the setting of the site. The types of species and their frequencies suggest a location on a bluff overlooking the river where both river bottom and upland species may have been gathered. Although the site is located in an area usually considered a beech-maple forest, reconstruction of the original forest from land survey records shows that the area had a high degree of variability and the site itself is located in an extension of the more southern oak-hickory forest (Kenoyer, 1934). Even so, the absence of beech is peculiar since an extensive beech-maple forest occurs within a short walk of the site. However, William Benninghoff, of The University of Michigan Botany Department, has pointed out that beech does not produce much dead fall and that which is produced is small and decomposes rapidly so that little would be available for firewood. Further information on the production of dead fall by various species and the rates of decomposition of that material would undoubtedly help to clarify the occurrence of the various species in the sample.

TABLE 34

CHARCOAL IDENTIFIED FROM MOCCASIN BLUFF

Pits	15	21	28	49	54	62	84	85	86	88	91	92	96	Tr. N	Tr. E	Total
Quercus bicolor (Swamp White Oak)		x		x	x	x		x	x	x	x		x			9
Quercus alba (White Oak)			x	x		x	x									4
Carya sp. (Hickory)	x					x			x						x	4
Acer sp. (Maple)						x	x		x							3
Celtis occidentalis (Hackberry)				x		x			x							3
Castanea dentata (Chestnut)						x			x							2
Platanus occidentalis (Sycamore)	x					x										2
Betula sp. (Birch)														x		1
Carya ovata (Shagbark Hickory)		x														1
Populus sp. (Aspen, Poplar, or Cottonwood)				x												1
Quercus sp. (Oak)												x				1
Quercus rubra (Red Oak)											x					1

Identification by Fel Brunett and Wilma Koschik of the Museum of Anthropology, The University of Michigan.

It is also interesting that of the 12 species present, nine are potentially useful as food plants: the oaks, hickory, maple, hackberry, and chestnut. The oaks, hickory, and the maple also provide tough, strong wood for the manufacture of implements and tools.

FOOD PLANTS

Yarnell identified the following plant remains from Moccasin Bluff: acorn, walnut, Canadian plum, and butternut (Yarnell, 1964: 21, 196). In addition, Fel Brunett identified the remains of a hickory nut fragment. The role of nuts in the diet of aboriginal peoples has been noted for quite some time and has recently been detailed by Yarnell (1964) and Ford (1969). Both writers note that productivity in the various species varies greatly: the acorn of the red oak, for example, requires two years to mature, while that of the white oak matures in one year. Good crops may occur only every four to 10 years for the white oak, while the red oak may have a good crop every two to three years. Present evidence indicates that annual productivity of nut trees is less reliable in the Upper Great Lakes area than it may have been further to the south, and therefore groups in the Upper Great Lakes area were probably less dependent on nuts as a staple food source than more southerly groups may have been (R. I. Ford, personal communication). Ethno-historical sources also indicate that nuts, although used by groups in the area, are more often regarded as an emergency food source to be utilized in the event that more usual and desirable food sources fail. Nuts, therefore, were probably gathered by groups in the area to supplement more reliable and staple food sources and to add variety to the diet; but most likely were not regarded as a major resource.

Nuts could be gathered from late summer through the fall and in many cases stored for as long as a year for use during the winter and spring. In addition to the Indian, many other species—mice, squirrels, turkeys, elk, deer and many insects—also competed for them (Shelford, 1963:27-28).

Another plant that was probably collected, but for which there is only indirect evidence, is the white water lily *Nymphaea tuberosa*. This plant has been identified from the Griesmer site and the Rader site in northern Indiana (Faulkner, 1970:161; 1964*b*). At the Griesmer site, the tubers were found in pits that were similar to the fire pits at Moccasin Bluff. Similar pits were reported from the Gentlemen Farm site, the Zimmerman site, and the Plum Island site (Brown et al., 1967; Brown, 1961; Fenner, 1963). The early explorer, La Salle, reporting from the Illinois Valley in 1680, noted the Indian use of these plants and wrote the following description of the roasting or baking of the tubers:

> The land produces many good roots to eat, like wild onions, Ouabipena, another excellent root long as a finger and as big, potatoes, garlic, the ognonnet, and macopins.[1] These last serve as provisions for most of the savages, whom it seems that the bounty of the country makes lazier than any of the others in America. They get these roots in the swamps. They are as large as an arm; others are smaller. They make a hole in the earth, where they put a bed of rock reddened in the fire, then one of leaves, one of macopin, one of reddened rock and so on up to the top, which they cover with earth and leave the roots to sweat for two or three days, after which they boil them and eat them alone or with oil. Color is red if cooked, whitish if not cooked. They are preserved a long time if dried. (Margry, 1878-1888, Vol. 2)

Richard I. Ford of the Ethnobotanical Laboratory at the Museum of Anthropology, The University of Michigan, thinks that the plant was best collected in the late fall or early spring. These are the times when the tuber is at its maximum potential, since it stores nutrients during these periods to send up its flower during July and August. The presence of sturgeon bones in many of the pits might suggest that tubers were utilized most frequently in the spring when the sturgeon were speared during their spring spawn. Evidence from the Griesmer site also indicates that spring and early summer was the likely time of occupation at that site and the time for collecting and preparing the tubers (Faulkner, 1970: 168).

A sample of maize was also recovered from Moccasin Bluff. Yarnell, working from photographs, (Pls. 83 and 84) identified the sample as Eastern corn (Yarnell, 1964:115). Ford reached similar conclusions in his study (see Appendix 15). The maize was found in two small, six-inch diameter pits. These pits were probably used to produce smoke to prepare hides as illustrated by Densmore (1929:Pl. 75). The importance of maize in the subsistence pattern of the Indians of southwestern Michigan is not yet clear. That it was grown in the late Prehistoric period along with beans and squash seems certain (Yarnell, 1964). Details

[1] This reference to macopins is probably botanically confused. A note in Brown (1961:29) says that this description probably refers to the American or yellow lotus, *Nelumbo lutea*. The identification of *Nymphaea* at the Griesmer site is even more specific. Recent work by Williams indicates that *Nymphaea tuberosa* and *Nymphaea odorata* are not two species, but one with a variable response to the environment (Williams, 1970).

concerning the location of the fields, techniques of cultivation, amounts harvested, and the integration of crop plants into the native subsistence cycle are notably absent. The role of the crop plants might become clearer if there were some indication of the size of the population at sites such as Moccasin Bluff. It might then be feasible to estimate the quantity of the various plant and animal species used for food and to piece together the relative importance of each group in the total diet of the Prehistoric population. However, such estimates of population size are not available for Moccasin Bluff.

The relatively large number of pits at Moccasin Bluff may indicate that maize was stored for future use after the harvest. Hinsdale (1927:40) mentions the common occurrence of storage pits associated with Indian settlements and fields. The unusually large numbers of the right mandible of young deer in the faunal remains studied by Cleland also suggest the preparation of maize. He indicates that these jaw bones were used as sickles or scrapers to remove the green corn from the cob (Cleland, 1966:219).

FAUNA

The fauna from the site was analzyed and reported by Cleland (1966). His study collection consisted of the bones from eight pits donated to the Museum of Anthropology, The University of Michigan, by John Birdsell. The faunal material recovered in the excavations made by the Museum party in 1948 was sent to William Adams at Indiana University. A listing of the identified bones was received from Mr. Adams. In addition the author, with the aid of Dr. Henry van der Schalie of the Museum of Zoology at The University of Michigan, identified the mussel remains. A listing of all species is presented in Table 35.

Cleland's study of the fauna indicates that three species (deer, elk, and sturgeon) contributed 82 percent of the meat utilized at the site. Table 36 is a revised version of Table 39 from Cleland's report. Cleland, following White (1953), overestimates the average live weights of most of the mammal species listed in the table. In most cases, the weights given are for adult male members of the species and not those of a normal population. The figures listed for average live weight in Table 36 are the author's estimates of the average live weight of all members of the population, excluding fawns and calves. Cleland reports that the deer remains at Moccasin Bluff conform to the age distribution of an average deer population. Therefore, it is probably more accurate to use the average live weight for a population than to calculate the

TABLE 35

FAUNAL REMAINS FROM THE MOCCASIN BLUFF SITE

	No. of Bones	%
Deer, *Odocoileus virginianus*	934	35.2
Beaver, *Cástor canadensis*	178	6.8
Dog, *Canis familiaris*	58	2.2
Elk, *Cervus canadensis*	39	1.5
Porcupine, *Erethizon dorsatum*	31	1.2
Raccoon, *Procyon lotor*	18	.7
Woodchuck, *Marmota monax*	15	.6
Bear, *Ursus americanus*	4	.2
Muskrat, *Ondatra zibethicus*	4	.2
Wolf, *Canis lupus*	3	.1
Cottontail Rabbit, *Sylvilagus floridanus*	3	.1
Otter, *Lutra canadensis*	2	.1
Red fox, *Vulpes fulva*	2	.1
Striped skunk, *Mephitis mephitis*	2	.1
Gray squirrel, *Sciurus carolinensis*	1	
Bobcat, *Lynx rufus*	1	
Mole, *Talpidae*	1	
Bison or Bos?	1	
Pig, *Sus scrofa*	1	
Cat, *Felis domestica*	1	
Turkey, *Meleagris gallopavo*	68	2.6
Canada goose, *Branta canadensis*	1	
Herring gull, *Larus argentatus*	1	
Wood duck, *Aix sponsa*	1	
Swan, *Cygnus*	1	
Duck, *Anas*	1	
Snapping turtle, *Chelydra serpentina*	14	.5
Softshell turtle, *Trionyx*	13	.5
Blanding's turtle, *Emys blandingi*	7	.3
Map turtle, *Graptemys*	3	.1
Painted turtle, *Chrysemys*	1	
Sturgeon, *Acipenser fulvescens*	1,239	46.7
Channel catfish, *Ictalurus punctatus*	2	.1
Walleye, *Stizostedion vitreum*	2	.1
In addition to the above species identified by Cleland (1966, Table 38), two other species were identified by William R. Adams of Indiana University:		
Mountain lion, *Felis concolor*	1	
Coyote, *Canis Latrans*	4	
Mollusca		
Elliptio dilatatus Raf. form *sterkii*	11	
Amblema costata form *plicata*	6	
Lampsilis ventricosa Barnes	5	
Pleurobema cordatum form *pauperculum* Simpson	5	
Actinonaias carinata	4	
Ligumia recta Raf. form *latissima*	4	
Actinonaias ellipsiformis	3	
Lasmigona costata Raf.	1	
Unidentifiable fragments	27	

TABLE 36

AMOUNT OF MEAT PROVIDED BY MAJOR ANIMAL SPECIES

Species	Number of Individuals	Average Live Weight (lbs.)	Live Weight, Usable Meat (%)	Usable Meat/ Individual (lbs.)	Usable Meat of Species (lbs.)	Total Usable Meat (%)
Deer	53	100	50	50	2,653	39.2
Elk	9	493	50	246	2,214	33.4
Sturgeon	30	45	80	36	1,080	9.3
Beaver	20	55	70	38.5	770	6.6
Bear	3	300	70	210	630	5.4
Dog	12	40	50	20	240	2.1
Porcupine	16	15	70	10	160	1.4
Raccoon	9	25	70	17.5	158	1.4
Turkey	15	12	70	8.5	128	1.1

percentages on the basis of only adult males. The calculations based on the newly determined average live weights, while they do not change the order of importance, certainly markedly change the relative importance of the major species. In the revised table, elk contribute almost as much to the total diet as deer. Elk bones may be underrepresented in the remains at Moccasin Bluff since a large animal was probably butchered at the kill site in such a way as to separate as much of the meat from the bones as possible so that only the usable meat would have to be brought back to the camp. The deer being lighter may have been returned to the camp with more of their remains intact and therefore perhaps appear more prominent in the totals. A restudy of the animal bone with some of these impressions in mind may help to clarify some of the questions and perhaps even throw new light on some of the practices of the inhabitants at this site. The three most important species will be examined in greater detail in an attempt to understand their relationship to the aboriginal peoples.

The deer represent the most important meat source, as estimated in Table 36. A brief review of the ecology of the white-tailed deer indicates why this species was so important to the Indian populations. The first factor to be considered is the productivity of the herds. It seems clear that the whitetail is a highly productive species. The potential rate of increase has been reported to be as high as an annual rate of 104 percent with rates of 60, 40, and 30 percent not unusual. The actual rate of increase is dependent upon the density of the population in relation to the available food supply, specifically to the available winter food supply. Deer herds can easily be subject to an annual harvest of 33 percent with little to no damage to the herd.

Other predators, such as wolves, mountain lions, and domesticated dog, also took their toll of the deer herds. Four wolves have been known to kill approximately 100 in one three-square-mile area in the Upper Peninsula of Michigan and one mountain lion is said to be able to kill as many as 50 deer per year.

Cleland's study indicated that the people of Moccasin Bluff hunted deer throughout the year. While this is probably true, many historical accounts refer to a fall hunt in which deer were driven and many were taken at one time. The normal age distribution of the deer bone at Moccasin Bluff indicates that drives may have been employed by the people there. During the fall, the deer are at their maximum weight and the deer have obtained their heavier winter coats. October seems to be the ideal time for the hunt since the bucks have not yet hardened their muscles in training for the rut and are more tender and fatter than they would be in November. It is also a time when hunting can result in unplanned reduction of the herds in preparation for the scarcity of browse during the winter months and so may indirectly aid the herd's development. The Indians may also have aided the deer populations by clearing fields for the planting of maize, creating more forest edge upon which the deer could then feed.

Even in winter when few other resources were available, deer provided a valuable food source. Winter hunting was assisted by the snow which made the animals easier to track. Snow also made escape more difficult because deep snow forced the deer to leap from spot to spot rather than allowing them to run over open ground making them tire more easily, while allowing the hunters to move more rapidly over the snow on snowshoes.

In summary, the deer provided an ideal resource for the aboriginal peoples. They converted unpalatable plant resources into a desirable food source, they were easily harvestable, readily renewable, available in large packages, highly productive, and utilizable for clothing and as a source of raw material for tools as well as food. No other species could match the deer in all these qualities (Taylor, 1956).

The elk appear to be second in importance as a source of meat at Moccasin Bluff. A survey of elk behavior and ecology indicates that there are a number of important differences between deer and elk. On the whole, elk are almost five times larger than deer (see Table 36). The rate of increase for elk appears to be only about 27 percent per year as contrasted to deer which appear to increase at the average rate of 40 percent per year and seem to have the potential to increase at a rate of 100 percent per annum under favorable conditions. Under favorable conditions, deer usually give birth to twins, while elk rarely twin. The rate of growth is lower in elk, averaging about two and one half years for the cows to reach sexual maturity; in deer cows often achieve sexual maturity in one year. The elk also is tolerant of a greater variety of habitats than the deer. It is often found on the prairies as well as the woodland, while the deer is mostly confined to the woodland. Elk also have a tendency to herd which is not as marked in the deer. This herding tendency may be restricted to the western elks, since the habits of the eastern elks were not studied directly because of their early elimination from the eastern part of North America.

In the spring of the year, the elk are usually scattered over the landscape, but during the summer, cows, calves, and younger bulls begin to herd. The older bulls remain isolated. During the rut between September and October, the bulls form herds with the cows, usually each breeding bull controlling a group of cows. This condition persists until the rut is over. The carrying capacity of the elk on the eastern range is not known, but conditions in the west indicate that a capacity of 12 acres per head may be reasonable. The figure may be a little high when one considers that the western herds have access to more grassland than the eastern herds. However, the prairie peninsula in the midwest may represent a situation comparable to the western one. A number of the elk would be taken by such predators as the mountain lion, the principal killer, the bobcat, wolf, coyote, and dog. All of these predators were found among the faunal remains at Moccasin Bluff. In addition, the elk and the deer would share the same range and compete for many of the same resources, i.e., browse and mast. What the ratio of deer to elk would have been in this part of the country is not clear and, in part, may have depended upon the human predation (Murie, 1951; McCullough, 1969).

The sturgeon is the final animal to be considered here. This fish, the largest in the lakes, was probably taken by the Indians during its spring spawn. The sturgeon migrate up the rivers in the spring, probably during the middle of May in the St. Joseph River, when the water temperature in the river is between 57 and 60 degrees Fahrenheit. The spawn lasts only a week or two at most. The sturgeon travel up the river to the highest rapids they can reach, and, when conditions are favorable, deposit their eggs. The St. Joseph River opposite Moccasin Bluff is broad and shallow. It is traditionally said to be a good place to ford the river and seems to be an ideal place for sturgeon to spawn. Other species of fish, such as walleye, sucker, and pike, are also known to spawn in the river. Walleye pike are the first to spawn, choosing the first rapids of the stream when the water reaches a temperature of 38 to 40 degrees Fahrenheit, soon after the ice has left the river. A small number of walleye bones were recovered from the site. The common white sucker spawns after the walleye and before the sturgeon. The sucker spawns among the rocks in any rapids, but it cannot maintain its position in water as rapid as the sturgeon. The pike chooses the quiet backwaters of the river as its spawning place. A knowledge of the characteristics of the river bed should enable one to locate other areas favorable for settlement and to see if other species such as walleye may have been taken at other spots along the river or if they seem to have been ignored entirely by the aboriginal people because of conflict with another species in the scheduling of their subsistence activities.

Detailed information on size of sturgeon is scarce in the literature. Cleland (1966:Fig. 39) uses an average live weight of 45 pounds for the sturgeon, but Hinsdale (1932:16) gives an average figure of 60 pounds. The record sturgeon caught from Lake Michigan was 310 pounds, and sturgeon over 100 pounds were not uncommon. The growth of the sturgeon is slow: the male reaches sexual maturity some time between the age of 12 and 22 years, depending upon the area and local conditions, while the female reaches maturity between the ages of 14 and 33 years. When maturity is reached, the individual sturgeon spawns only once every four to seven years, depending upon conditions. Presumably, some sturgeon spawn every year, providing an annual harvest for the Indians. It is known that many immature sturgeon go up the rivers in the spring at the time mature fish are on their spawning migration. Any estimates of the numbers and types of fish annually entering the river are premature at this time, but indications are that the river was thick with sturgeon every spring.

In addition to spawning in the rivers, the sturgeon are also known to spawn in the lakes where conditions are favorable, i.e., in the presence of rocks—sturgeon eggs need to adhere to rocks—and of water movement through wave action—to disperse the eggs so that they settle individually and do not stick together in a large mass, smothering one another through lack of contact with air. In Lake Michigan, lake spawning has been reported from south Chicago, Point Sable, and especially at Saugatuck. Since the lake waters do not warm as rapidly as the rivers, the sturgeon may collect for spawning in the lake about two weeks later than in the nearby rivers, giving the Indians an opportunity to exploit both sturgeon runs if other subsistence activities did not interfere (Harkness and Dymond, 1961; Probst and Cooper, 1955).

MOLLUSCA

The naiad or mussel fauna from Moccasin Bluff, although not large, are nevertheless interesting. The most striking aspect of the collection is the presence of forms from two distinct ecological zones lake dwelling species and riverine forms. The lake dwelling forms are represented by *Elliptio dilatatis* Raf. form *sterkii*, *Amblema costata* form *plicata*, *Pleurobema cordatum* form *pauperculum* Simpson and *Ligumia recta* Raf., while the river species are represented by *Actinonaias carinata* and *Actinonaias ellipsiformis*, the latter usually being found in small creeks. *Lampsilis ventricosa* Barnes and *Lasmigona costata* Raf. are two widespread forms which are found in lakes as well as rivers and probably represent the river forms in this instance. The presence of these lake forms of mollusks at the site implies that the Indians went down to the lake shore, probably to the mouth of the St. Joseph River, to collect mollusks and to bring them back to their settlement. What possible attraction can the mollusks have had for the prehistoric people? Their small number seems to imply that their contribution to the diet was small or insignificant. Perhaps they were used as tools or implements.

Mollusk shells are known to have been used for at least four purposes by Indians of the Upper Great Lakes: they were ground up and used as temper in ceramic vessels; they served as spoons for the people of the Upper Illinois Valley; they were employed by these same people to cut corn kernels from the cobs; and they were reported to have been used by the Fox Indians to remove the scales from fish. No signs of any of these usages were recognized on the material examined here. The lake forms of naiade, which seem to have been preferred, are typically heavier and often smaller than the river forms of the same species. This would suggest the possible use of the shells as tools, since the heavier, thicker-shelled forms would be more serviceable. If one plots the occurrence of right and left valves by species, there seems to be a suggestion of a preference for the left valve over the right in the lake forms (or perhaps the right valve over the left valve with the right valve being utilized while the left valve is discarded).

Among the locations in which these mussels would be found along the lake are areas frequented by the lake-spawning sturgeon in their spring spawn. This correlation might suggest that the Indians were collecting shells at the same time that they were ex-

TABLE 37

DISTRIBUTION OF RIGHT AND LEFT VALVES BY SPECIES OF MOLLUSK

	Left	Right
Elliptio dilatatus Raf. form *sterkii* (lake)	8	3
Amblema costata form *plicata* (lake)	4	2
Lampsilis ventricosa Barnes (lake or river)	3	2
Pleurobema cordatum form *pauperculum* Simpson (lake)	6	
Actinonaias carinata (river)	2	2
Ligumia recta Raf. (lake)	2	2
Actinonaias ellipsiformis (small creek)	1	2
Lasmigona costata Raf. (lake or river)	1	
Unidentifiable fragments	2	3

ploiting the sturgeon at these sites, perhaps using the shells to aid them in the preparation of the sturgeon. As more information becomes available, some of these suggestions may be resolved.

In summary, the subsistence pattern that emerges, although fragmentary at this stage of our knowledge, is nevertheless an interesting one. Moccasin Bluff was apparently a mixed economy of food production along with a considerable amount of hunting and wild plant gathering. The area itself is a highly productive one: the mosaic of beech-maple, oak-hickory forests along with prairie areas, swamps, marshes, riverine environment, lake shore, and lake area itself, both inland lake and Lake Michigan, forms a variable and plentiful environment. The problem facing the prehistoric peoples was not so much one of where to locate food, but of which species to select and when to collect them. As could be expected, they seem to have selected those species which were annually reliable, highly productive, and which could be collected with the least amount of effort. Deer, elk, and sturgeon provided a stable resource base which could be annually harvested without endangering the continual supply of these species. Agricultural products also meet these requirements, but the work involved may have been greater than the collecting of wild species. The importance of agriculture and its integration into the subsistence pattern of these groups remains unclear. Perhaps Moccasin Bluff records a transitional situation. If the development of these societies had been allowed to proceed without the disruption of white contact, population may have gradually increased, putting pressure on the wild resources and requiring greater emphasis upon food production to support the greater density of people. Comparative studies of the expansion of food production economies and the evolution of subsistence systems in the temperate areas of Europe along with those in North America may produce some valuable insights about the response of human populations and eco-systems to the introduction and role of food production.

Among the plant food collected, the tubers of the white water lily may have played an important role in the diet of the inhabitants of this site. Other foods, such as nuts and fruits, while contributing to the diet, were probably of secondary importance. The role of sugar maple, an important tree in the surrounding forests and a potentially important resource, is unknown. Other species that appear to have been plentiful in the area, such as migratory water fowl and such fish species as walleye and suckers, are not represented at Moccasin Bluff either because the group occupied other sites in their seasonal cycle or because these species were largely ignored by the people as a result of the fact that the adaptive patterns they established in order to assure full utilization of technology and of populations did not require their exploitation. Much more work needs to be done in this area before more reliable answers can be found for some of these questions.

IX

ETHNIC IDENTIFICATION

THE ethnic identification of the inhabitants of the Moccasin Bluff site is a question which cannot be satisfactorily resolved at this time. It may, however, be useful to review the status of the problem and to examine the possible lines of evidence that may lead to a more certain identification at some future date.

A number of factors presently cloud the problem of ethnic identification. The primary stumbling block is the lack of detailed knowledge about the material remains of most groups who are historically known to have occupied the area; i.e., at present, little is known about Miami material culture. Only suggestions or inferences about its form are possible here. A second major factor working against the resolution of the problem of ethnic identification is the lack of accurate information concerning the location of the various historically recorded tribes before the period of contact. The Iroquois wars, the fur trade, and the introduction of disease dislocated and decimated many of the groups, creating a regrouping and realignment in the region during the Historic period that does not accurately reflect the late Prehistoric period. A third complicating factor is the lack of anthropological knowledge concerning the relationship between material remains and ethnographically recorded and recognized cultural units. Often a one-to-one correlation is assumed between material culture and ethnographically recognized units; but the sparse information presently available concerning this relationship indicates that the situation is fluid, with a variety of historical, geographic, and cultural factors all interacting to influence the eventual distribution of material (see Clark, 1968:358-398 for a discussion of this problem). The last major obstacle to the resolution of the problem of ethnic identity is the lack of precise chronological and spatial control on much of the archaeological material from the Upper Great Lakes area. Most regions have yet to be adequately surveyed, and the spatial relationship of the material still remains to be plotted. At the same time chronological control on many of the artifacts is not sufficiently rigorous to adequately isolate specific material chronologically. Like Moccasin Bluff, most sites were reoccupied over many years by groups with different material cultures. These sites have little or no stratigraphic separation of material and chronological control is often minimal. Considering all these handicaps, what can be discovered about the ethnic identity of the Moccasin Bluff populations?

The first historic reference to the inhabitants of the area is La Salle's account of 1679, which identifies a Miami encampment as occupying the portage between the St. Joseph River and the Kankakee (Anderson, 1901:77). From this period until the early 1800's, the Miami are closely associated with the region of northern Indiana and the St. Joseph River valley. An account of their history in the locality is given by Temple (1958). How great an antiquity the Miami had in this territory is unclear, but they have the strongest historic claim to the region. In 1679, in addition to their settlement on the St. Joseph River, they also seem to have had other settlements in the Chicago area and around Green Bay in Wisconsin (Thwaites, 1896, Vol. LXII:71-73).

In addition to the Miami, the Potawatomi also have strong historical ties to the region. They appear to have made their first settlement in southwestern Michigan along the St. Joseph River in 1695 and are not recorded historically as having occupied the area previous to this time. Some groups of Potawatomi have remained in the vicinity of southern Michigan until the present.

Only two historic groups from the Upper Great Lakes have been associated with archaeological material with any degree of certainty: the Winnebago have been associated with the Oneota culture of Wisconsin (J. B. Griffin, 1960; Hall, 1962*a*) and the Fox Indians have been associated with the dominant culture at the Bell site in Wisconsin (Wittry, 1963:1-57). Other archaeological assemblages, which have been attributed to various ethnic groups but whose associations are not very secure, are the Huber material, the Langford tradition with its Heally complex, and the Dumaw Creek material.

The Huber material has been attributed to a Chiwere-Siouian group by Quimby (1960:105; 1966*a*:40) and more specifically to the Siouian-speaking Winnebago by Hall (1962*a*:156). Emily Blasingham records the tradition that prior to white contact, the Miami inhabited the area of southeastern Wisconsin and northeastern Illinois (1961:163). This would presumbly make them responsible for the Huber culture. Faulkner (1970:278, 297) apparently concurs with Blasingham or possibly follows her in suggesting that the Central Algonkian Miami were the people responsible for the Huber culture.

Quimby notes the possibility that the Huber culture which he calls Blue Island may represent a group of Miami strongly influenced by the Winnebago (Quimby, 1966*a*:40). Included in the Birdsell Collection is a small group of sherds from a site known as Brandywine Creek. This site, located one mile south of Niles, Michigan, 300 yards east of the St. Joseph River and 250 yards south of the location of Fort Saint Joseph, may mark the location of a Miami village which is recorded as having occupied this location in the early Historic period, A.D. 1693 (Hinsdale, 1931; Special Bulletin, W. L. Coffinbury Chapter, Mich. Arch. Soc., 1955). An analysis of the sherds in the collection clearly shows that the vast majority of the material can be included in the category, Huber Cordmarked, as defined by Faulkner, 1970: 25 shell-tempered rim sherds from at least eight vessels of Huber Cordmarked, one rim sherd of Moccasin Bluff Collared, 137 body sherds of Huber Cordmarked vessels, and five grit-tempered, cordmarked body sherds. If, in fact, Brandywine Creek is the site of the A.D. 1693 Miami village it may indicate that the Huber assemblage is to be associated with the Miami. Admittedly, this is fairly shaky evidence, but when considered in the light of the association of Historic material with Huber artifacts in the Chicago area (see Munson and Munson, 1969; Bluhm and Fenner, 1961), one can make an arguable case for the association of the Prehistoric Huber material with the Historic Miami Indians who are reported to have occupied the region in the early Historic period.

The Fisher complex, although still not clearly defined and described, has almost consistently attributed to an Algonkian-speaking people. J. B. Griffin (1943:302) states his opinion that it is the product of an Algonkian group, while Quimby (1952:106) feels that it represents the remains of either the Potawatomi or the Miami, although in a later work (1960:102) he states only that it is the material remains of an Algonkian-speaking people.

The Langford tradition, which Brown (1961:76) traces to the Historic period at the Zimmerman site where it is recognized as the Heally complex, is attributed by him to the Kaskaskia group of the Iliniwek or possibly all of the Iliniwek, or perhaps even some of the Miami. The Danner complex from this site is associated with the Shawnee, presumably because of its close relationship to Fort Ancient material, which has been suggested as being Shawnee (J. B. Griffin, 1943:34-35). Since the Langford tradition would include the later grit-tempered material at the Fisher site, it is not clear if the earlier shell-tempered pottery would also be referred to this Iliniwek identification.

The Dumaw Creek assemblage was originally attributed by Quimby (1966*a*:88) to the Sauk or Kickapoo on the basis of the identification of the Bell site as a Fox village and the presence at this site of pottery which Wittry calls Type II (1963) and Quimby feels is similar to the Dumaw Creek pottery. Wittry speculates that the Type II pottery is possibly Sauk on the basis of the close historical and linguistic relationship between the Fox and the Sauk. Quimby follows Wittry and suggests that Dumaw Creek is Sauk. His second guess is that the site may be Kickapoo, based on the close linguistic ties between the Kickapoo and the Sauk and Fox. In a later report, Quimby's opinion has changed, and he feels that Dumaw Creek most likely represents the Potawatomi, since the site is located in what he feels was traditional Potawatomi territory (Quimby, 1966*b*:33).

Given the above discussion, it may be of interest to reexamine the ethnic identification of the Dumaw Creek site. Quimby, in his latest reference to the site, attributed the material to the Potawatomi (1966*b*:33). In this same work, he effectively argues that Summer Island was the location of the anchorage lying just at the opening into Green Bay, visited by the explorer La Salle in his "bark" in the late summer and fall of 1679. La Salle found the island inhabited by the Potawatomi. Brose has recently completed excavations on Summer Island and has identified a proto-historic component, called Summer Island III, which may represent the material remains of the Potawatomi (Brose, 1970*a*:199-214). However, Brose has emphasized that while Summer Island may not have been the island visited by La Salle, he would not expect a great difference in material culture between Summer Island III and the actual historical Potawatomi village (Brose, 1970*b*:27-28). Since Summer Island III seems to be the best candidate representing the material remains of the Potawatomi in the Upper Great Lakes at this time, it may be interesting to compare this material with that from Dumaw Creek, also a supposed Potawatomi village.

If we compare the pottery one notices that the two most common vessel types from Summer Island III, Bay de Noc Notched Lip and Garden Incised, are not well represented at Dumaw Creek as it is presently reported in the literature. A third minor group from Summer Island III, Summer Island Cordmarked, is similar to material from Dumaw Creek and corresponds to what has here been called the Moccasin Bluff Impressed Exterior Lip group. The best described ceramic type from Dumaw Creek are the scalloped vessels associated with the burials and with the radiocarbon date of A.D. 1680+ (M-7070) (Crane and Griffin, 1961:110). This scalloped ware appears to be unrepresented at Summer Island III. A look at artifact groups other than pottery indicates that similarities include triangular projectile points, bipolar core, copper beads, copper tinkling cones or points, copper snake effigy pendants, and stone celts. Conspicuously absent from Summer Island III, but present at Dumaw Creek, are ovate blades and ovate drills. In addition, the burial complex at Dumaw Creek, at present, appears to be unique in the Upper Great Lakes. The shell pendants, the shell effigy claws, the marine shell beads, and the weeping eye motif are unusual for the area. A shell pendant or mask in the collection of the Museum of Anthropology, The University of Michigan, found with a child burial near Lansing, Michigan, is the only other example of this type of artifact and burial custom presently reported from the area (see Pl. 82). The pipe complex associated with Dumaw Creek is also unrepresented at Summer Island III. These comparisons between Summer Island III and Dumaw Creek, while only suggestive, do indicate that there are sufficient differences between the two assemblages to warrant caution when equating both with the Potawatomi. The comparisons themselves are not above suspicion. No formal comparisons have been made because the sample from Summer Island III is so small. Furthermore the Dumaw Creek site is not adequately enough reported or understood at present to make formal comparisons fruitful. Looking at the pottery in the Rider collection, the site appears to have a greater time depth than is indicated by the radiocarbon dates: also the scalloped pottery associated with the burials is not particularly abundant in the surface collections from the village area. Furthermore the surface collection from the living area at Dumaw Creek is not reported in sufficient detail (frequency counts of stylistic variation are absent) to warrant formal comparisons at this time. It is preferable to keep the burial complex at Dumaw Creek separate from the village material until the refuse material is more clearly described and the relationship between the two is more firmly established. Finally, even if the assemblages from Dumaw Creek and Summer Island III do prove to be distinct as a result of a more formal comparison, this is still not an adequate basis for claiming that they represent different ethnic entities since we do not know how much formal variation is to be associated with what we may ethnographically refer to as Potawatomi culture.

Finally, the Moccasin Bluff site itself has received some comment with respect to its position in the prehistory of the Upper Great Lakes. Quimby (1952:106) mentions the site and states his opinion that it probably represents the remains of the Potawatomi or the Miami.

However, linguistically and historically the Potawatomi are more closely associated with the Ottawa and Chippewa to the north. The first French reports of the late mid-seventeenth century place the Potawatomi in the area of Green Bay, Wisconsin and the Sault (Thwaites, 1896, Vol. XVIII:231; Vol. XXIII:225). They do not historically appear to enter the St. Joseph River valley until 1695 (Temple, 1958:128).

Earlier references to the Assistaeronons or Atsistaehronons, living on the west shore of Lake Huron, by Champlain (Bigger, 1925, Vol. 3:97) are equated by some commentators with the Potawatomi (Kinietz, 1940:308) and by others with the Mascoutens (Mooney and Thomas, 1907:810-812). The word, Potawatamink, in Chippewa, a language closely related to Potawatomi, means "People of the place of fire." This is the same as the Huron word "Asistaguerouon," meaning "People of the place of fire." The Potawatomi, Ottawa, and Chippewa also had a confederation which was sometimes called "The Three Fires" (Temple, 1958: 126). The "Mascoutens," an Algonkian word meaning "People of the prairie," were sometimes also associated with the Assistaeronon or "fire people" of the Hurons. In the Chippewa dialect, "fire" is "ishkote," which is similar to "Mashkote" meaning "prairie" (Mooney and Thomas, 1907:810-811). The linguistic similarity of the Algonkian words for fire and prairie is interesting, considering the practice of buffalo-hunting by which one sets fire to the grass on all sides of the herd except for the few places at which the hunters gathered and killed the beasts as they try to escape (Kinietz, 1940:173). One can see that this situation is ripe for confusion. Was the "Fire Nation" the Potawatomi or the Mascoutens, or were the Mascoutens simply a band of the Potawatomi? Does "Mascouten" actually mean "fire" or "prairie"? To complicate matters even further, Trowbridge (1938) states that the Maskoateeau, "People of the prairie," were a band of the Kickapoo. A study of the linguistic relations of these various groups apparently indicates that the language of the Mascouten was understood by the Sauk, Fox, and Kickapoo, whereas Potawatomi is more divergent than these three and is more closely related to the Ottawa and Chippewa languages (Temple, 1958:157). Father Dablon, reporting in the Jesuit Relations of 1671, aware of the confusion which existed at the time, attempted to clarify this problem when he stated, "Fire Nation is erroneously so called; its correct name being Maskoutenech, which means 'a treeless country', like that inhabited by these people, but as, by changing a few letters, this word is made to signify 'fire', therefore the people have come to be called the 'Fire Nation'" (Thwaites, 1896, Vol. LV:199). This seems to imply that the "Fire Nation" really refers to the prairie people which really refers to the Mascouten.

Mascoutens were encountered by La Salle during his trip across southern Michigan in 1680. Near a location that seems to have been just north of present day Jackson, Michigan, La Salle mentions an encounter with Mascoutens (Margry, 1878:60). An account of this same journey, published by Clifford Prator, mentions that a party of Potawatomis were met by La Salle in the vicinity of the Kalamazoo River in northeast Kalamazoo County (Prator, 1941:114). In checking the original account used by Prator, the group encountered is actually referred to as the Ouapous (Margry, 1879:60). No evidence could be found to link the name Ouapous with the Potawatomi or with any other historically known group. Although this evidence seems to strengthen the case for a Mascouten occupation of central Michigan, the evidence is not completely clear since in the same account, La Salle, referring to southern Michigan, states that, "The Indians do not hunt there because it is situated between five or six tribes which are at war with one another, who, because they fear one another, dare not go to those parts without the greatest precaution" (Margry, 1878:60). This passage indicates that most of southern Michigan in 1680 was a no-man's land and free of permanent occupation. In short, the historic accounts referring to the aboriginal occupation of Michigan appear to be vague, confusing, conflicting, and to offer little assistance in satisfactorily locating the prehistoric occupants. No historic reference could be found to give undisputed title to the Potawatomi.

If one is persuaded by the Sauk traditions which apparently are supported by those of the Potawatomi, Ottawa, and Chippewa, which place the Sauk in the Saginaw Valley (Blair, 1911, Vol. I: 291; Vol. II:146) and by Father Francois Bressani, who in 1657 prepared a map which placed the Fox in the thumb area of Michigan (Wahla, 1966:48-51), where might the Kickapoo and the Mascoutens be located? It may be possible that they inhabited the western portions of Michigan, perhaps the valleys of the Grand and St. Joseph rivers.

The Miami, who are a very strong contender for the occupancy of the southwestern Michigan area, may have been located in the valley of the Kankakee and south, and perhaps around the southern end of Lake Michigan and the Chicago area. This suggested placement of the Kickapoo and the Mascouten in the southwestern portion of the state also accords well with the close linguistic and cultural relationship between the Kickapoo and the Shawnee, as well as the Sauk and Fox. (For recent discussions of Kickapoo history, see Silverberg, 1957 and Dillingham, 1963.)

In summary, it is conjectured that the archaeological, shell-tempered, Huber-Berrien material from Moccasin Bluff may represent the material culture of a central Algonkian group, possibly the Miami. Some of the late Prehistoric grit-tempered material, such as the Moccasin Bluff Scalloped group, may represent another Central Algonkian unit, possibly the Kickapoo, Sauk, Mascouten or Potawatomi. It may be possible that the Moccasin Bluff Notched Applique Strip ceramic group may be closely related to material from the Cleveland, Ohio area and may represent the remains of groups dispersed by the Iroquois raids prior to 1680. The author is fully aware of the current distaste among archaeologists for associating pottery groupings with particular ethnic groups, and, in fact, shares that distaste: However, in the present case the distinctiveness of these ceramic complexes and their close chronological relationship leads him to suspect that there may be some merit in this present position. Only further work will indicate if these suppositions are justified. The bulk of the ceramic material from the site remains unidentified as to specific group, but can probably be attributed to a central Algonkian people.

X

SUMMARY AND CONCLUSIONS

THIS analysis of the material from Moccasin Bluff has revealed a series of occupations covering a fairly long period of time. The first settlement is represented by the bifurcate-base points from the Birdsell Collection which, based on their similarity to the Le Croy points from West Virginia, may date as early as 6300 B.C. Other Archaic occupations may be represented by Raddatz and Lamoka-like points. These early occupations seem to have been small camps, of which few traces were uncovered in the Museum excavations. Perhaps pit 13, which is under pit 3, represents a feature from one of these earlier occupations, but the limited amount of material associated with this pit makes any identification impossible.

During the Early Woodland period, there is the first of a long series of Woodland occupations which continue until just before the Historic period. The Early Woodland occupation is represented by Marion Thick pottery from the Birdsell Collection and stemmed points from both the Museum excavations and the Birdsell Collection. The absence of Marion Thick pottery from the Museum's excavations indicates that the Early Woodland occupation area was not sampled by the field party and therefore its exact location on the terrace is not known. Indications are that it may be somewhere near the small marsh at the southern end of the terrace. No features are known from this occupation. The close relationship between the Marion Thick pottery and the Havana series ceramics from the following Middle Woodland period indicates a continuity of occupation in the region. The two forms are hardly distinguishable except for the interior cordmarking on the Marion Thick pottery. Thickness in the two groups overlaps.

Pottery distinctive of the early Middle Woodland period, although only suggested at Moccasin Bluff, is reported from a number of sites in northwestern Indiana (see discussion on p. 103 ff.). The intermediate phase of the Middle Woodland period is well represented by ceramics and related objects. In addition to the

Havana Cordmarked, Havana Zoned Dentate, Naples Stamped, and other Havana series pottery found on the site, a small number of Hopewell types were also found. There is some suggestion that a small burial mound once stood in the southern area of the site and contained a small Hopewell bowl along with some elongated, corner-notched points and possibly some slate gorgets and a copper ax. None of the features from the site can be conclusively associated with this occupation, but it is very likely that some of the hearths located in trench F are related to this settlement.

The distribution of both decorated and plain body sherds as shown in Tables 18 and 20 indicates that the Middle Woodland material tends to occur in higher densities in trenches F, K, and L. Hence, by association, the higher density of hearths in trench F may also be representative of this occupation. Table 10, which presents the distribution of the chipped stone material, indicates a concentration of blades in trench F. This information would also confirm the fact that the Middle Woodland occupations were concentrated in this area, since blades are a characteristic feature of many Hopewellian lithic assemblages.

The presence of a semi-keeled gorget, distinctive of the Late Adena and Hopewell sites from West Virginia and Ohio, may point to contact with this area. It has been suggested that the Ohio Hopewellian peoples sent out adventurer-traders to obtain obsidian from Yellowstone National Park in the western United States (J. B. Griffin, 1965:146). This position appears plausible when one considers the source and the distribution of obsidian in the eastern United States. When one contrasts the distribution of obsidian in archaeological sites throughout the eastern United States with the distribution of obsidian in archaeological sites throughout the Near East, there appears to be a difference between the two areas in the distribution of obsidian. If the Near Eastern evidence represents a pattern resulting from inter-tribal trade (Renfrew, et al., 1968), then the distribution in the eastern United States may represent a different pattern. If this comparison is indeed valid, then the presence of this gorget at Moccasin Bluff may be an indication that one of the routes used by these possible adventurer-traders to journey to the sources of native copper in the Lake Superior region may have passed by the site.

The relationships of the Havana tradition are clearly with the Illinois Valley. The strong ties with this ceramic tradition and the near certainty that the limestone-tempered Hopewell plain bowl was probably manufactured in the lower Illinois Valley indicate close connections between the Michigan and the Illinois material. J. B. Griffin has argued that a movement of population from Illinois into northwestern Indiana and southwestern Michigan is needed to account for the appearance of the Hopewellian material in the Michigan area (1967:12). While a movement of people is certainly possible, it has yet to be satisfactorily demonstrated that it actually took place.

It seems clear that the area was inhabited by groups during the Early Woodland period who were similar to the then contemporary groups in Indiana and Illinois. Burial ceremonialism is also well-demonstrated for the Michigan area for the Late Archaic period. The elaboration of burial ceremonialism and the continuation of contact and communication with the Illinois area during the Middle Woodland period should not seem unusual and need not call for the movement of population into Michigan to explain the cultural development. The similar appearance in Moccasin Bluff and other nearly Middle Woodland sites of ceramics and the elongated corner-notched points found at Moccasin Bluff Summerville, and Goodall, as well as the slate gorgets—which may carry forward a gorget tradition begun in the Late Archaic period with the appearance of shell, sandal sole, gorgets from Glacial Kame sites—all point to a basically local development of the Middle Woodland in the area that was stimulated by the same contact and communication as had existed in the region during previous periods. When more information on the subsistence-settlement system of both the Illinois Valley groups and the southwestern Michigan Middle Woodland groups becomes available, this observation can be more firmly substantiated. At the present time, Middle Woodland subsistence and settlement systems in southwestern Michigan are almost unknown. Were it not for the presence of the burial mounds, the existence of a Middle Woodland occupation in the area would hardly be known. The location and systematic excavation of one good settlement site should go a long way toward clarifying this question. Moccasin Bluff offers little aid in this problem. Middle Woodland groups certainly had camped here, as is indicated by their pottery and possibly by their hearths; they probably even buried their dead here, as indicated by the possible burial mound. The occupation, however, was light and the function of the settlement remains unclear.

The end of the Middle Woodland period shall be defined here as the time of the disappearance of the Havana and the Hopewell series pottery from the archaeological assemblages of the area. This transition seems to be well under way by at least A.D. 500, and possibly sooner. The period can be viewed as the early Late Woodland or as a transitional period between the Middle and Late Woodland, since many important traits such as burial mounds persist until much later. The distinctive ceramic marker for this period is the Moccasin Bluff Modified Lip vessel. Little other material can be associated with this period with any degree of certainty. Some of the small side- and corner-notched points may belong to this horizon, as well as the Moccasin Bluff Cordmarked variety 1a sherds. None of the features from the site can be associated with this horizon. The only distributional data which indicates any differences in association for this material appears in Table 15, which presents the distribution of rim sherds occurring within pits and outside of pits. This distribution clearly indicates the Moccasin Bluff Modified Lip sherds, along with the Middle Woodland sherds, have a greater tendency to occur outside of the pits than other pottery groupings. This distribution probably reflects the earlier temporal position of these ceramic groups and the continuation of the Middle Woodland subsistence system which, at this site, appears to lack pits as a feature of the adaptation. The distribution of the small side- and corner-notched points also tends to be outside of pits when compared with the small triangular points. This would also argue for an early temporal position for these points.

This Late Woodland tradition continues through the latter part of the first millenium, with triangular points probably appearing around A.D. 700-800 and small collared vessels appearing during the eighth century. The Brems site in northwestern Indiana has a strong component of this material associated with a radiocarbon date of A.D. 555. Therefore it is suggested that this early Late Woodland period in northwest Indiana and southwestern Michigan be referred to as the *Brems Phase.*

At about A.D. 1050, marked change is noted in the settlement at the site. During this period, the ceramics are largely of the Moccasin Bluff Impressed Exterior Lip type along with some shell-tempered, cordmarked pottery related to the Fisher-Fifield series of northwestern Indiana and northeastern Illinois. This material marks a period of what may be increased population inferred from the greater density of pottery and a changed subsistence system based upon the marked activity of pit digging. It is during this period that some picture emerges of what the subsistence system of this population might have been. Yarnell notes that it was not until after A.D. 1000 that the full native agricultural complex of corn, beans and squash appears in this area (Yarnell, 1964:118, 149). It is likely and, in fact, most probable, that the marked change seen at the site during this period indicates the increased importance of this group of cultigens in the area. Corn recovered from the site most likely dates from this period or later. The existence of cultigens can also be inferred from the appearance of large numbers of storage pits that appear at this time. Such pits are known historically to have been used for the storage of corn and probably other cultigens. The selection of young, right mandibles of deer mentioned by Cleland is also an indication of the presence of maize agriculture (Cleland, 1966:217-219). These mandibles are well-documented ethnologically as being used for scraping corn from the green cob. The sharp teeth were raked over the kernels to break and cut the hulls and then the hold on the jaw changed and the milk and meat were scraped out with the sharp edge nearest the chin (Parker, 1907:544).

This material strongly implies a transformation of the subsistence pattern during this time based upon the appearance of corn, beans, and squash or perhaps solely upon the introduction of beans, since it is very likely that corn and squash were present at least as early as Middle Woodland times. If maize was present during the Middle Woodland period, its effect does not appear to have been great in this area.

This period from about A.D. 1050 until perhaps A.D. 1300 might be called the *Moccasin Bluff Phase.* It may be possible to distinguish two sub-phases of this period based on the distribution of body sherds in the pits. The first phase begins about A.D. 1050 and is marked by the appearance of Moccasin Bluff Impressed Exterior Lip sherds and some Fisher-Fifield related shell-tempered, cordmarked pottery. The second phase is centered around A.D. 1200, when the amount of shell-tempered cordmarked pottery seems to decrease and the amount of grit-tempered, cordmarked pottery appears to increase, as do the numbers of datable features which, by inference, may indicate a greater population.

The final occupational phase at the site appears to occur around A.D. 1400 and to continue until around A.D. 1600. This period might be named the *Berrien Phase.* The ceramic markers for this phase are the appearance of the Berrien-Huber, shell-tempered, plain surfaced pottery along with the continuation of the earlier grit-tempered pottery. Moccasin Bluff Scalloped pottery also is associated with this period, as is the Moccasin Bluff Notched Applique Strip pottery.

The appearance of these three distinctive types of pottery at this site in what appears to be a similar chronological position may indicate the presence of separate ethnic groups. The Berrien-Huber ware is probably associated with the Miami, the Moccasin Bluff Scalloped Rim pottery most likely reflects the area's indigenous Central Algonkian inhabitants, while the Moccasin Bluff Notched Applique Strip pottery may represent the remnants of groups who were driven from northern Ohio in the early Historic period.

No direct evidence was available from the earlier periods to suggest what base their economies might have had. What little evidence there is appears to be associated with the later occupations and suggests that little difference can be detected in the economy between the Moccasin Bluff period occupations and those of the later Berrien period. Whether or not this conclusion accurately represents the factual situation in these two periods or simply reflects the rather inconclusive nature of the data employed is not, at the moment, completely clear. However, if this problem is put aside, preliminary indications suggest that the economy between these two periods was not very different: a mixed economy representing hunting, gathering, fishing, and horticulture seems to characterize both periods. The role that the agricultural crops played in the economy of these two later periods is unclear, but given the large amount of hunting and fishing that seems to have occupied the people at this site, agriculture may not have played a dominant role. The complex processes that govern the diffusion of agricultural crops, their acceptance by local populations and the integration of the associated activities within the existing cultural framework remains largely unknown or unexplored within anthropology. It may be that in this case the rich and varied natural environment, which seems to have provided so bountifully, retarded a more complete dependence upon a horticultural economy and permitted the continuation of traditional economic pursuits until such times as the return on cultigen production became sufficiently high to encourage greater numbers of people to devote more of their time to that end.

This investigation appears to have raised more questions than it answered, but that is the nature of productive research. The report has defined and outlined a portion of the culture history of one small area of the earth and has traced in part the development of a group of people who became victims of the clash of cultures that still echoes in parts of our land today. More of this culture history remains to be examined and refined; but even more interesting are the underlying processes which determined the outline of that history and the fact that even today they remain only dimly perceived and understood. It is to an understanding of these processes that more of our future efforts should be devoted.

APPENDIX 1

CATALOG OF FEATURES

Pit No.	Type	Trench	Pit No.	Type	Trench
1	pit	A	39B	pit	A
2	pit	A	39C	pit	A
3	hearth	A	40	pit	A
4	pit	A	41	does not exist	
5	does not exist		42	pit	A
6	pit	A	43A	fire pit	A
7	does not exist		43B	fire pit	A
8	pit	A	44	does not exist	
9	pit and hearth	A	45	pit	A
10	pit	A	46	pit	A
11	pit	A	47	hearth	D
11B	pit	A	48	hearth	D
12	pit	A	49	pit	O
13	pit	A	50	fire pit	C
14	pit	A	50A	fire pit	C
15	pit	A	50B	fire pit	C
15A	hearth	A	51	fire pit	C
15B	pit	A	51A	fire pit	C
16	does not exist		51B	fire pit	C
17	pit	A	51C	fire pit	C
18	pit	A	51D	fire pit	C
19	does not exist		52	does not exist	
20	pit	B	53	pit	A
21	fire pit	B	54	hearth	C
22	pit	B	55A	pit	C
23	pit	B	55B	pit	C
24	does not exist		56	does not exist	
25	does not exist		57	pit	A
26A	pit	C	58	pit	A
26B	pit	C	59	pit	A
27	does not exist		60	does not exist	
28	pit	O	61	hearth	C
29	pit	A	62	fire pit	C
29B	hearth	A	63	pit	C
30A	pit	A	64	pit	D
30B	pit	A	65	does not exist	
30C	pit	A	66	fire pit	N
31	does not exist		67	pit	C
32	fire pit	A	68	burial 3	C
32A	fire pit	A	69	hearth	C
33	pit	A	70	not excavated	F
34	pit	A	71	pit	F
34A	pit	A	72	hearth	F
35	does not exist		73	pit	E
36	pit and hearth	A	74	hearth	F
37A	pit	A	75	hearth	F
37B	pit	A	76	hearth	F
37C	pit	A	77	hearth	F
38	does not exist		78	pit and hearth	F
39A	pit	A	79	fire pit	E

APPENDIX 1 (Continued)

CATALOG OF FEATURES

Pit No.	Type	Trench	Pit No.	Type	Trench
80	hearth	E	89	pit	C
81	hearth	F	90	pit	C
82	hearth	F	91	fire pit	C
83	pit	H	92	pit	C
84	pit	C	93	does not exist	
85	pit	C	94	does not exist	
86	fire pit	C	95	pit	C
87	pit	C	96	pit	C
88	pit	C	97	pit	C

APPENDIX 2

PIT MEASUREMENTS

Pit No.	Recognized elevation	-	Base elevation	=	Depth (ft.)	Diameter (ft.)
1	19.25		18.70		0.55	0.75
2	--		18.55		1.00	1.60
4	19.21		17.19		2.02	2.50
6	20.42		20.04		0.38	--
8	19.28		17.26		2.02	--
9	19.03		17.30		1.75	2.50
10	19.31		17.10		2.21	2.5 x 3.5
11	19.64		18.31		1.33	--
11B	18.31		17.98		0.33	--
12	19.08		18.32		0.76	--
13	17.30		16.68		0.62	--
14	19.18		17.52		1.66	--
15	20.10		17.93		2.17	--
15B	18.76		17.26		1.50	--
17	19.96		17.96		2.00	--
18	18.23		--		0.33	--
20	--		16.50		--	*2.50
22	18.10		17.45		0.65	1.83
23	18.69		17.54		1.15	2.50
26A	19.68		18.05		1.63	2.6 x 4.5
26B	19.93		--		1.93	2.2 x 2.65
28	18.82		17.76		1.06	--
29	19.39		17.23		2.16	--
30A	18.50		--		--	2.70
30B	--		--		--	--
30C	--		--		--	--
33	19.68		16.63		3.05	*4.00

*measurement approximate

APPENDIX 2 (Continued)

PIT MEASUREMENTS

Pit No.	Recognized elevation	Base elevation	Depth (ft.)	Diameter (ft.)
34	19.11	16.26	2.85	--
36	19.63	17.20	2.43	3.00
37A	19.25	18.75	0.50	2.50
37B	19.10	17.89	1.21	3.00
37C	19.15	17.82	1.33	2.00
39A	19.04	18.32	0.72	2.50
39B	18.93	17.59	1.34	2.50
39C	18.93	17.78	1.26	2.75
42	18.44	17.89	0.55	2.50
45	17.82	17.02	0.80	2.50
46	18.35	17.00	1.35	2.60
49	16.82	--	--	--
53	18.63	17.12	1.51	--
55A	20.41	19.78	1.63	*1.70
55B	20.41	19.19	1.22	*3.00
57	18.92	18.26	0.66	--
58	19.17	18.84	0.33	--
59	18.56	17.90	0.66	--
63	20.65	18.65	2.00	*3.10
64	--	17.01	--	--
67	19.80	17.27	2.53	--
71	19.30	17.80	1.50	3.2 x 4.0
73	20.87	18.98	1.89	--
78	20.67	19.45	1.22	--
83	16.88	15.68	1.20	--
84	20.22	18.89	1.33	*2.50
85	20.58	18.82	1.76	*2.00
87	20.63	18.86	1.77	--
88	21.67	19.67	2.00	--
89	20.53	19.06	1.47	--
90	21.67	17.62	4.05	*6.00
92	20.65	17.56	3.09	*2.00
95	20.43	18.58	1.85	--
96	20.62	19.49	1.13	1.7
97	20.10	19.06	1.04	--

*measurement approximate

APPENDIX 3

FIRE PIT MEASUREMENTS

Pit No.	Recognized elevation	-	Base elevation	=	Depth (ft.)	Diameter (ft.)
21	17.75		17.12		0.63	3.00
32	19.76		18.01		1.75	3.00
32A	19.66		18.01		1.65	*3.00
43A	18.23		17.08		1.15	3.0 x 2.5
43B	18.23		17.02		1.21	2.5 x 2.0
50	20.52		19.81		0.71	1.25
50A	20.31		16.73		3.58	3.16
50B	20.02		19.00		1.02	2.75
51A	20.86		18.81		2.05	--
51B	20.86		18.55		2.31	--
51C	20.86		18.72		2.14	*3.00
51D	19.27		18.82		0.45	*3.00
62	20.61		19.23		1.38	2.50
66	--		19.94		*2.00	--
79	19.17		18.51		0.66	*2.00
86	20.61		19.90		0.71	2.30
91	20.69		19.36		1.33	--

*measurement approximate

APPENDIX 4

HEARTH MEASUREMENTS

Pit No.	Recognized elevation -	Base elevation =	Depth (ft.)	Diameter (ft.)
3	18.48	17.63	0.85	2.5
9	19.03	17.30	1.73	2.5
15A	20.10	17.93	2.17	--
29B	18.82	18.61	0.21	--
36	--	--	--	--
47	18.70	--	--	--
48	18.50	--	--	--
54	20.41	19.64	0.77	--
61	20.56	20.13	0.43	2.0 x 2.75
69	19.77	19.41	0.36	--
72	18.72	18.31	0.41	3.0
74	20.97	20.51	0.46	--
75	20.28	19.91	0.37	--
76	19.57	19.45	0.12	2.0 x 3.0
77	20.25	19.95	0.30	--
78	20.67	19.45	1.22	*2.0
80	19.42	19.17	0.25	--
81	18.37	18.37	--	--
82	19.00	18.56	0.44	3.0 x 4.0

*measurement approximate

APPENDIX 5

CONTENTS OF PITS*

Pit No.	1	2	4	6	8	9	10	11	11B	12
sherds	2		18	3	8	26	43	17		17
complete bifaces			2		1	2	4	1		1
point fragments			4							
flakes			27		1	9	5	9	4	
drill										
abraded pebble pendant										
abrading stone										
hammerstone										
celt										
anvil stone										
worked stone			1		1					
smooth stone										
flaking tool							1	1		2
elk antler										
bone/antler chisel										
beaming tool										
elk scapula tool										
worked bone										
stone pipe										
clay pipe fragment										

*This listing is only suggestive since it was compiled from a variety of sources, catalogues, notes, photos, and was not directly observed. Some of the items found in the pits according to these sources was not found in the Museum collections while other items found in the Museum collections are not on this list, e.g. some of the bone tools.

13	14	15	15B	17	18	20	22	23	26A	26B	28	29
	31	269		72		84	48	11	399	58		61
		12		1		4	2	1	3	1		1
		1		1				1				
		30		5		10	14	1	20	7	2	13
	1	1										
								2				
		1										
		3		1								
						1			1			
								1				
		4										
		2										1
		1				1						
		1										
										1		

APPENDIX 5 (Continued)

CONTENTS OF PITS

Pit No.	30A	30B	30C	33	34	36	37A	37B	37C	39A
sherds	36	25	2	37	44	25	3	2	21	4
complete bifaces				1						
point fragments										
flakes	7	2		6	7	1				3
drill										
abraded pebble pendant										
abrading stone										
hammerstone										
celt					1					
anvil stone										
worked stone										
smooth stone										
flaking tool										
elk antler										
bone/antler chisel				1						
beaming tool										
elk scapula tool										
worked bone					1					
stone pipe						1				
clay pipe fragment						1				

39B	39C	40	42	45	46	49	53	55A	55B	57	58	59
	37		1		58	129	1	4		11		1
			1									
	7		1			20						
						1						
		1										
1												
1												
						1						

APPENDIX 5 (Continued)

CONTENTS OF PITS

Pit No.	63	64	67	71	73	78	83	84	85	87
sherds	56	27	22	171	68	15	23	35	50	46
complete bifaces	1		1		1			1		3
point fragments						2				
flakes	8	2	1	5	2	36	6		10	
drill										
abraded pebble pendant										
abrading stone										1
hammerstone										1
celt										
anvil stone										
worked stone										
smooth stone										
flaking tool										
elk antler										
bone/antler chisel										
beaming tool			1							
elk scapula tool										
worked bone										
stone pipe										
clay pipe fragment		1								

88	89	90	92	95	96	97
75		50	111	20	15	
		1	16			
1				1		
2		5	4	1	1	
			1			
			2			
				1		
			1			

APPENDIX 5 (Continued)

Pit No.	1	2	4	6	8	9	10	11	11B	12
scattered stones			X			X				
clustered stones										
ash						X		X		
fired perimeter						X				
charcoal		X						X		
Fauna (figures refer to number of bones identified. X means species present but number of bones unknown; XX means species abundant)										
deer			22							
beaver			1							
elk			1							
bear										
coyote			1							
porcupine			1							
rabbit										
raccoon										
dog										
woodchuck										
turkey			6							
duck			X							
turtle			1			X		X		
sturgeon		X	X				X	X		
shell unidentified							X			

Note: Attributes - X = present*
*Absence of X may mean trait absent or it may mean that the observation is missing or unknown.

13	14	15	15B	17	18	20	22	23	26A	26B	28
						X					
		X				X					
	22	X		28		15	8			34	
	5										
	X			1						1	
	2										
	5			2		X					
	1			3			1				
	2					3				X	
						X					
	X	X		2		1	X			1	
	X	X		X		X			X	X	
						X					
X									X		

APPENDIX 5 (Continued)

Pit No.	29	30A	30B	30C	33	34	36	37A	37B	37C
scattered stones										
clustered stones										
ash										
fired perimeter										
charcoal										
Fauna										
(figures refer to number of bones identified. X means species present but number of bones unknown; XX means species abundant)										
deer						3				
beaver										
elk										
bear										
coyote										
porcupine										
rabbit										
raccoon						2				
dog										
woodchuck										
turkey										
duck										
turtle										
sturgeon	X	X			X	X			X	
shell unidentified					X					

39A	39B	39C	45	46	49	53	55A	55B	57	58	59
	10										
	1										
	1				X						

APPENDIX 5 (Continued)

Pit No.	63	64	67	71	73	78	83	84	85	87
scattered stones				X						
clustered stones						X		X		
ash										
fired perimeter										
charcoal										
Fauna										
(figures refer to number of bones identified. X means species present but number of bones unknown; XX means species abundant)										
deer				6				X	18	
beaver		X							4	
elk										
bear										
coyote										
porcupine									1	
rabbit										
raccoon										
dog										
woodchuck										
turkey										
duck										
turtle										
sturgeon	X			X				X	X	X
shell										
unidentified										

88	89	90	92	95	96	97
		X	X			
		X				
32	XX	5	28			
3		1	2			
	X	1				
3			2			
1						
1	X					
1						
2		3	1			
		X				
X		X		X		
				X		

APPENDIX 6

CONTENTS OF FIRE PITS

Pit No.	21	32	32A	42	43A	43B	50	50A
sherds	23	27	3	1	30		55	13
complete bifaces		3					1	
point fragments	1			1				
flakes	1	4	1	1		2	1	
hammerstone								
abraded pebble								
beaming tool		1					1	
flaking tool		1					1	
elk antler bone awl		1						
Attributes X = present*								
scattered stones								
clustered stones								
ash			X				X	
fired perimeter		X	X		X	X	X	
charcoal			X					
Fauna (XX means species abundant)								
deer								
beaver								
dog								
turtle								
fish		X	X					
bone								

*Absence of X may mean trait absent or it may mean that the observation is missing or unknown.

50B	51	62	66	79	86	91
	166	20	4		112	36
	4	1			1	
						1
	8	2		2	1	8
	1					
		1				
		1				
	1					
	1					
			X			
	X		X	X	X	X
	20	3				
	2					
	3					
					X	
		X			XX	
			X		X	

APPENDIX 7

CONTENTS OF HEARTHS

Hearth No.	3	9	15A	29B	36	47	48	54
sherds	3	26		3		8	12	11
complete bifaces	2	2					1	
point fragment								
flakes	8	9					11	1
hammerstone								1
Attributes - X = present*								
scattered stones	X	X	X					
clustered stones						X	X	
ash	X	X						X
fired perimeter		X		X				X
charcoal	X					X	X	X
Fauna								
deer	X							
fish	X							
turtle shell		X						
bone								

*Absence of X may mean trait absent or it may mean that the observation is missing or unknown.

61	69	72	74	75	76	77	78	80	81	82
				2	2	2	15	29		10
			1							
							2	1		1
			5			2	36	2		7
X										
			X				X			over 100
		X								X
										X
X							X			

APPENDIX 8

DISTRIBUTION OF CHIPPED STONE BY PIT

Pit No.	3	4	8	9	10	11	11B
<u>Pit type trench</u>							
Primary flakes		3	1	2		2	1
Block flakes	1	3					
Simple flakes	5	16		3	3	4	2
Utilized and/or retouched flakes		2s		1s		1cc	
Flakes of bifacial retouch	1	1					
Blades							
Scrapers							
Thumb nail							
oval							
hafted							
other							
Points							
small triangular	2	2	1		4		
humped triangles							
small stemmed							
large stemmed							
expanding based							
small side & corner notched							
A							
B							
C							
D						1	
E							
F							
Dustin-like							
large blades or blanks							
ovate blades							
Drills							
Gravers							
Small, thick, steep-edge tools					1	1	
Misc.		core					
Fragments							
tips							
small triangular				1			
other							
base							
small triangular		1		1			
other		1					
misc.							

*shouldered point
**crude biface
***drill
#stemmed
##dustin

12	14	15	17	20	21	22	23	26A	26B	28
		5		3		1		1		2
	2	4	2			3		2	1	
		11	3	2		7	1	7	4	1
								2s		
		3s						1cc	1s	
			1							
		1								
	1	6	1	3		1	1	1		
						1				
		1								
		1								
		2								
		1								
	1							1		
		2						1	1	
1*					1**					
					1					
		1								
		1	2					1		
			1***	1#		1##		1 blade		

APPENDIX 8 (Continued)

DISTRIBUTION OF CHIPPED STONE BY PIT

Pit No.	29	30	32	33	34A	39A	39C
Pit type trench							
Primary flakes	2			2	1		2
Block flakes	5		1	2	2	1	
Simple flakes	6	7	4	1	3	2	3
Utilized and/or retouched flakes							1cc
Flakes of bifacial retouch		1	1				
Blades							
Scrapers							
Thumb nail							
oval							
hafted							
other							
Points							
small triangular			3		1		
humped triangles							
small stemmed							
large stemmed							
expanding based							
small side & corner notched							
A							
B	1						
C							
D							
E							
F							
Dustin-like							
large blades or blanks							
ovate blades							
Drills							
Gravers							
Small, thick, steep-edge tool				1			
Misc.							
Fragments							
tips							
small triangular							
other					1*		
base							
small triangular				1			1
other							
misc.							

*large ovate

40	42	43A	48	49	50A	51	62	63	64	67
1		1	1	2		1				
1		1	1	2	1	2	1	1		
			9			5	1	5	2	
								1		
1			1			1				1
						1				
					1			1		
			1			1				
				1						
								1		
				1		1				
								1		
							1			
	1									

APPENDIX 8 (Continued)

DISTRIBUTION OF CHIPPED STONE BY PIT

Pit No.	71	73	74	77	78	79	80
Pit type trench							
Primary flakes							
Block flakes	2			2	1		
Simple flakes	1	1	1		31	1	2
Utilized and/or retouched flakes					1cv		
Flakes of bifacial retouch					1		
Blades	1	1					
Scrapers							
Thumb nail							
oval							
hafted							
other							
Points							
small triangular					1		
humped triangles							
small stemmed							
large stemmed							
expanding based		1					
small side & corner notched							
A							
B							
C							
D							
E							
F							
Dustin-like							
large blades or blanks							
ovate blades			1				
Drills							
Gravers							
Small, thick, steep-edge tool							
Misc.							
Fragments							
tips							
small triangular							
other						1*	
base							
small triangular					1		
other							
misc.							

*large point
**large blade

82n	84b	85	86	88	90	91	92	96
						1	2	1
1		1				2	10	
5		2	1	1	4	3	11	
						1cc	1s	
		1			2	1		
		1						
	1					2	16	
			1					
							11	
1						1		
				2			2	
						1**	1	

APPENDIX 9

BIRDSELL COLLECTION: CHIPPED STONE

Description	No. of Sherds
Scrapers	
thumb nail/end	37
oval	1
hafted	20
other	10
Points	
small triangular	116
small stemmed	5
large stemmed	4
other stemmed	31
side and corner notched	
A	35
B	8
C	16
D	25
E	1
F	4
other notched	66
bifurcated base points	7
Blades or knives	74
Ovates	10
Drills	
small T-shaped	7
large T-shaped	6
I-shaped	8
other	4
Gravers/perforators	5
Thick bifacial tools	34
Other	1
Large crude bifaces	21
Elongated, narrow bifaces	3
Fragments of bifacial tools	
tips	112
bases	
small triangular	46
stemmed	27
notched	116
blades	46
bifurcated	6
blade fragments	32

APPENDIX 10

BIRDSELL COLLECTION: SUMMARY OF RIM SHERDS

Description	No. of Sherds
Moccasin Bluff Ware	
Moccasin Bluff Cordmarked	
Variety 1a black temper, orange-red color	18
Variety 1b	
Group 1 square and flattened lip with cordmarking on top of lip	43
Group 2 protruding exterior rim	1
Group 3 beveled lip	3
Group 4 lip squared and top plain	49
Group 5 small collar	13
Group 6 smoothed over cordmarking plain lip	11
Moccasin Bluff Collared	33
Moccasin Bluff Modified Lip	
Group 1 cord wrapped stick	12
Group 2 paddle edge	3
Group 3 finger nail	3
Group 4 lunate impressions	1
Group 5 thickened and notched	1
Group 6 punctates	2
Moccasin Bluff Impressed Exterior Lip	
Group 1 impressed exterior lip	103
Group 2 smoothed paste	1
Moccasin Bluff Plain	36
Moccasin Bluff Plain Modified Lip	
Group 1 finger impressed	10
Group 2 narrow notched	46
Group 3 rounded lip and small notches	5
Moccasin Bluff Notched Applique Strip	34
Moccasin Bluff Scalloped Lip	27
Berrien Ware	
Group 1 well developed shoulder, long neck	10
Group 2 well developed shoulder, short neck	5
Group 3	21
Group 4	6
Group 5	12
Miscellaneous	22
Middle Woodland sherds	65
Miniature vessels	2
Fine line and punctate over cordmarking (plate 71)	3
Victory brushed body sherds	12
Shell-tempered bottle	1 vessel

APPENDIX 11

BIRDSELL COLLECTION: MIDDLE WOODLAND RIM AND DECORATED SHERDS

Description	No. of Sherds
Naples dentate-straight dentate on rim	6
Hummel cresent dentate-gradual curve	4
Nettler cresent dentate-sharp curve	
Cord-wrapped stick stamped	11
Havana plain with nodes	1
Havana plain with nodes and impressions on exterior of lip	2
Hopewell plain rocker dentate	1
Hopewell plain	8 = 1 vessel
Bar dentate (shell-tempered)	
Sister Creek punctate	1
Havana cordmarked	6
Cross hatched rim	2
Havana plain	1
Dentate rim—type indeterminant	3
Crescent stamped	1
Notching on interior of rim-exterior plain	1
Sloppy rocker stamping	1
Dentate stamped—cord wrapped stick impressions on top of lip	1
Finger nail punctates on body sherd (Montezuma ?)	1
Fabric impressed body sherds	2
Miscellaneous	11

APPENDIX 12

BIRDSELL COLLECTION: STONE AND MISCELLANEOUS OBJECTS

Description	No. of Objects
Celts or celt fragments (pl. 62)	11
Hammerstones	
small roundish	3
elongated	2
flat oval	1
Small grinding stone	1
Round stones (gaming stones ?)	2
Grinding-anvil stone fragment	1
Unfinished pipe bowls	2
Pendant fragments	5
Knife	1
Pipe fragments (pl. 62)	6
Abrading stones (pl. 62)	7
Flat circular badly battered slate objects	9
Slate piece with cut marks	1
Small flat round stones (pl. 61)	5
Flat ovals of granitic rock-badly battered	3
Banner stones	
Slate with drilled hole (pl. 61)	2
Semi-keeled gorget (pl. 61)	1
Copper celt (pl. 64)	1
Pieces of copper (pl. 64)	2
Long cylindrical stone object (pl. 61)	1
Trade pipe fragments (pl. 64)	3
Trade pipe stem fragments (pl. 64)	2
Piece mica	1

APPENDIX 13

BREMS SITE, (STARKE CO., INDIANA) POTTERY: RIM SHERDS

Marion thick-like	1
Middle Woodland	
Naples Ovoid Stamped	1
Naples Cord-Wrapped Stick Stamped	2
Cross hatched on exterior of cordmarked rim	2
Sister Creeks Punctated	1
Havana Zoned Dentate Stamped	2
Zoned Rocker Dentate	1
Punctates	2
Havana Plain	2
Plain exterior, interior rim impressed with cord-wrapped stick	1
Plain exterior with nodes	5
Moccasin Bluff Cordmarked	
Variety 1a	16
Variety 1b	
Group 1	1
Group 2	2
Moccasin Bluff Collared	8*
Moccasin Bluff Modified Lip	
Group 1-cord wrapped stick	5
Group 2-fingernail	1
Group 5-thickened and notched	1
Group 6-punctates	1
Other-incised	4
" -finger impressed	9+
" -tool impressed	2
Moccasin Bluff Impressed Exterior Lip	
Group 1	1
Moccasin Bluff Plain Modified Lip	
Group 1-finger impressed	3
Berrien Ware	
Group 1	2
Group 5	4
Indeterminate	3

*All from group A. Three have impressions on the top of the lip and four have shallow notching at the bottom of the collar.
+Five from one vessel.

APPENDIX 14

BREMS SITE (STARKE CO., INDIANA) POTTERY: DECORATED BODY SHERDS

Incised lines over cord	6
Zoned dentate	3
Incised on smoothed over cordmarking	3
Zoned	1
Dentate Stamped	1
Punctates on cordmarked	4
Nodes on plain	1
Brushed	2
Other	
Exterior-interior cordmarking	4
Shell tempered	
cordmarked	2
incised on plain	5
plain	5
indeterminate	2
Thick flat bottom base	1

Many, many grit-tempered cordmarked and plain body sherds, mostly cordmarked.

APPENDIX 15

THE MOCCASIN BLUFF CORN HOLES*

Richard I. Ford
Museum of Anthropology
University of Michigan

Late Woodland populations are assumed to have subsisted on corn, and sites of this period are expected to yield corn. Certainly the occurrence of maize on these sites is more frequent than in earlier periods, but its actual role in the diet and economic life requires careful attention. Corn was not abundant at Moccasin Bluff. In fact, it was found only in two shallow circular pits, which were designated by their excavators corn hole A and corn hole B. Unfortunately, the contents were misplaced and unavailable for study until their accidental rediscovery in August 1972.

Corn hole A was part of pit 51 in trench C (Plate 83) which measured 10" in diameter and 2" in depth. In addition to carbonized corn cobs, it contained charcoal and a wild plum pit (see Table 37). The corn cobs were carefully removed in the field by excavating the feature in two levels. Level II was assigned field number B8-273 and level III was labeled field number B8-538. A third collection of corn cobs contained two labels, B8-538 and B8-545. The latter, according to Hale G. Smith's field notes, is the field number for level IV, pit 68, trench C which did not contain any corn. On this basis we have assigned these corn cobs to corn hole A.

Corn hole B was recognized as a second feature containing corn while level III of trench C was being excavated 21" below the surface (Plate 84). It is oval with a diameter ranging from 6" to 8" and a 2-inch depth. All obvious cobs were removed and carefully wrapped in gauze bandages; the remainder of the feature was packaged intact for shipment to Ann Arbor. After years of neglect, when this box was finally opened, the outline of the corn hole was no longer distinguishable. Nonetheless, the cobs were in good condition. The contents were screened to remove all organic items larger than 1.0 mm and the remaining soil and carbonized residue was submitted to water flotation separation technique and microscopic examination.

A standard laboratory procedure was employed for measuring each cob (Tables 38 and 39). One assistant made all the observations which were subsequently checked by the author. The row number was determined at the point at which both maximum and minimum diameters were measured. In cases where a cupule row segment was missing, the single measurement was recorded in the maximum diameter column. No correction for shrinkage was added to these or any other measurements. Length represents the actual length of each archaeological specimen. No complete cobs were found.

The two most subjective observations are the shape of the cob's cross-section and area of the complete cob represented by each specimen. In the first instance, when the floral characters were eroded from the cupules, the outline was usually obvious; but difficulties arose when

*UMMA Ethnobotanical Laboratory Report No. 472.

they were intact. For example, a cob with its glumes might appear circular or quadrilateral, and such cobs were arbitrarily coded as circular. For the second observation it was often difficult to locate the segment along a model corn cob. When this was the case an M, signifying middle or mid-cob, is coded, when the tip is actually present then the segment is recorded T, tip, or T-M, tip to middle, depending upon the length. If the tip was missing but the taper of the cob suggests upper end of the cob, then M-T is recorded. The same procedure applies to the basal end of the cob. If the bottom of the cob segment is starting to flare, then it is assumed that part of the base is present and M-B is recorded. No complete butts with shanks were present in either sample. The last decision concerns general cob morphology or type of cob. If it seemed mature and completely fertilized, it was considered typical or regular and so coded. However, if fertilization is incomplete or if the cob has the general skinny or irregular appearance of tiller cobs or nubbins an N is signified.

Three cupule features are also recorded. The degree of pairing between the cupule rows is the first. When the rows have a narrow groove between them, a + is used, but if the row is quite wide an S, strongly paired, is noted. Sometimes the corners of the cupules overlap slightly and a W, weakly paired, indicates this. When the kernels are not aligned or evenly spaced, they are interpreted as irregular and a "no" is recorded indicating the absence of any pairing. A second observation is the number of cupules at mid-cob in 10 mm of cob length. This observation gives an indication of cupule height and can be transformed into a rough estimate of the number of kernels on a cob. The third recorded cupule measure is the width. This follows the procedure outlined by Nickerson (1953) and used most often by Cutler (see Cutler and Blake, 1969). The cupule width, in this study, is the largest cupule observed as close to the mid-point of the cob as possible. A final measurement, the thickness of the cupule margin, was made for comparative purposes but not systematically recorded.

Each measurement or observation is useful for solving different problems. The significance and utility of each will be discussed separately in the sections which follow. The corn cobs and other associated plant remains from Moccasin Bluff are useful for understanding three problems related to aboriginal corn cultivation in the Great Lakes region. The first concerns the identification of the corn and its age. The second addresses the variability within these populations of corn cobs for understanding prehistoric cultivation practices and the potential dietary significance of this maize. The third problem is the treatment of the corn in preparation for use in smudge pits, as Bettarel interprets these features.

Classification and Relative Age of the Corn

A general outline of the history of corn in the Great Lakes area is now available (Yarnell, 1964 and Jones, 1968) although some specific interpretations still engender debate. The earliest maize to enter the Midwest and probably the Great Lakes was genetically quite variable, with affinities to Chapalote corn grown at higher elevations in Mexico and the preceramic Southwest. The most securely dated early corn comes from the Middle Adena Daines Mound 2 near Athens, Ohio (Murphy, 1971).

Radiocarbon dated at 280 B.C. ± 140, it is small, 10-rowed, and in other characteristics not unlike Chapalote-derived maize.

Other late Early Woodland corn with incipient Eastern Complex characteristics is known from the Hornung site in northern Kentucky (Ford, 1971) and Tom Baker site in Missouri (Cutler and Blake, 1969:133).

These, combined with maize from Hopewell sites in Ohio and Illinois, indicate a range of variability including some traits typical of Late Woodland and Mississippian corn. Yarnell (1964) and Cutler (1965) have discussed the "Easternization" of corn in the Midwest.

Easternization refers to the evolution of Eastern Complex corn as defined by Carter and Anderson (1945) and operationalized for applicability to archaeological remains by Jones (1949 and 1968). Eastern Complex maize cobs are generally large, hard, and 8-rowed with grooves separating the cupules or row pairs. In outline the cob is straight except at the butt which expands to the largest diameter on the cob. The rows of kernels are straight and regular with the exception again of the base where the kernel pattern is often spiral or irregular. Both cupules and kernels are wider than they are high, yielding a crescent shape which is often accentuated by the loss of the endosperm through carbonization. The most extreme form of the Eastern Complex, called North Flint, occurs in the damp, cool northern latitudes of New York, New England, and southern Canada.

Through environmental and cultural selection the genetically variable Middle Woodland maize was selected for qualities of both high yield and environmental tolerance which led to the development of the Eastern Complex. Archaeologically this selectivity leading to Easternization appears best as changing frequencies of percentages of corn with different row numbers. The earliest maize is mainly 12- and 14-rowed with a low percentage of 8- and 10-rowed cobs. In the Great Lakes area 8- and 10-rowed cobs predominate after A.D. 1000 and by the Late Prehistoric period 8-rowed are dominant with 10-rowed corn appearing in low percentages and 12- or more rowed cobs rarely present. Eastern Complex corn cobs also tend to become larger and harder toward the Historic period.

The Moccasin Bluff corn is representative of evolved Eastern Complex as determined by the cob features discussed above (Tables 38, 39, 40). Plates 85 and 86 depict the range of cob forms found in both features. The mean row numbers are 7.9 for corn hole A and 7.6 for B. They are less than eight because nubbins and tiller cobs are included. Of the completely fertilized, mature cobs, only one is 10-rowed (Plate 85); the remainder have eight kernel rows. The cupule widths are 8.3 mm for A and 9.1 mm for B. Although they differ significantly from each other, they still fall within the range of Eastern Complex corn. The margins of most cupules are hard, woody, and exceed 1.0 mm in thickness which is typical of evolved Easternized corn. The cupules are paired with many so strongly separated (Plate 85D) that the cobs are quadrilateral in cross-section. One peculiar aspect of these cobs is that of the 59 cobs examined only portions of three butts are present (Plate 86D). They have the flaring characteristic of this maize. No kernels were present.

These characteristics indicate that the Moccasin Bluff corn is representative of Eastern Complex varieties and its high degree of Easternization indicates it was grown just prior to the contact period. The ceramic analysis of this site independently confirms this conclusion.

Population Variability and Horticultural Techniques

Although this corn fits the general description of the Eastern Complex, the two samples are not from the same population. For each cob at the approximate mid-point of its length the largest cupule was measured. While their variances are not significantly different (F = 1.23), the difference between the means of each sample is (t = 2.48 or P<.01). The differences indicate that the corn may have been grown in separate fields or more likely at different times. Despite this difference, in other regards the corn is identical in size, shape, type of cob, and yield (Table 40).

The corn from both corn holes was a combination of mature and nubbin cobs, a most fortunate mixture since it indicates that tiller ears or cobs borne on suckers, as well as diminutive and partially fertilized cobs which grow above or below the main cobs on a stalk, were permitted to mature and their kernels were used as food. The ratio of three or four regular cobs for each nubbin is not particularly unusual, but it does indicate that sucker stalks probably were not removed as they sometimes were by aboriginal American farmers.

Undeveloped and nubbin cobs with reduced row numbers may also result from climatic stress. We do not know if this was a factor at Moccasin Bluff. The charcoal from the corn holes indicates a floristic composition of oak-hickory forest probably in the uplands above the river and a more humid, mixed forest along the river terraces consisting of maple, hackberry, plum, willow, and probably many other mesic trees not represented in the meager charcoal samples found in these features and in others identified by Fel Brunett (see p. 124). These forest elements reveal nothing about short-run environmental calamities for a locality which has a growing season exceeding 180 frost-free days.

The importance of plants in the diet of the Late Woodland inhabitants at Moccasin Bluff remains unanswered. Unlike some bone, floral remains are not readily visible and considering the techniques current in 1948, many probably were undetected. On the other hand, with a great reliance on meat from large fish and ungulates the Moccasin Bluff population while encamped at this site may have to an appreciable extent ignored acorn and hickory nuts (Yarnell [1964:196] reported a butternut from the site but reexamination demonstrates it is fresh and rodent gnawed; Brunett identified one hickory nut fragment). The fruits, grape and plum, were the only non-cultivated edible plant remains found. One specimen of each is not very helpful for reconstructing a diet.

The restricted inventory of plants in contrast with the faunal remains directs our interest to the idea that in its final phase of occupation Moccasin Bluff was an important fishing-hunting camp and that agricultural and other plant processing activities occurred elsewhere. The corn in the cornholes may have been brought to the site for a specific purpose unrelated to its subsistence value. Unless the plums and grapes were stored through the winter, their presence suggests these corn holes were used at some time between September and October.

Smudge Pit Hypothesis

Bettarel accepts Binford's hypothesis that corn holes such as these may have functioned to smoke cure hides. However, Munson (1969:83-84) has identified another ethnographically recorded function of these features, the interior smoking of pottery vessels, which should also be tested. We must not miss sight of Binford's original argument that ethnographic analogies are appropriate for archaeological interpretations only after they are tested *independently* with prehistoric data. If these pits were smudges, then we would expect to find features with small diametered orafices for controlling oxygen, carbonized remains with little or no ash, and materials, such as corn cobs, damp oak wood, and bark, which produce a thick smoke when burned in a reducing environment.

Both corn holes correspond to the minimum diameters of archaeological and ethnographically recorded smudge pits (Binford, 1967; Munson, 1969:83). However, unless compaction or erosion has taken its toll, the two inch depth is certainly much less than the 6" minimum noted in the same sources. Such a shallow pit would not provide a smudge for a very long period of time and it is questionable if, without renewing the contents, a deer hide, could have been completely smoked.

The contents of these interesting pits, on the other hand, do indicate that they were burnt in an oxygen-starved environment. Very little ash is present and the wood and corn cobs are totally carbonized. The wood content is not extensive (Table 37) with oak predominant which we would expect especially if it were damp. The other twigs, bark, and corn stalk/ shank fragments may have served as a starter fire for the more important corn cobs. Corn cobs without kernels are typically used in smudge pits as they were at Moccasin Bluff.

A mimimum amount of preparation preceded the ignition of the corn cobs. The cobs were broken beforehand into almost identical lengths ($\overline{X}_A$ = 20.2 mm; $\overline{X}_B$ = 20.3 mm), although both have rather large standard deviations. In both features the complete butt and attached shanks are absent and a total of only three obviously basal end fragments were recovered. Why the butts and shanks were excluded is unknown. Of the cob types both mature and nubbins were used in about the same proportion in both features (Table 40). The mean diameters (Table 40) also indicate that the cobs were generally the same size.

The Moccasin Bluff smudge pits contrast with one slightly younger from the Johnson Site in Missouri. There Cutler and Blake (1969:126) discovered that the cobs were broken like at Moccasin Bluff and large cobs were selected while small ones were excluded. At Moccasin Bluff the whole range of cob sizes was used.

The contents of the pit and their method of preparation support the proposition that both features were used for similar purposes. The fact that the corn cobs were preserved as a result of combustion in a reducing atmosphere indicates that a smudge had been made.

Conclusions

By all measures the corn from Moccasin Bluff is developed Eastern Complex and is compatible with an archaeological date after A.D. 1400. This corn was fully mature indicating that some care was taken in its cultivation although tiller ears and nubbins were permitted to grow and mature for use along with the other grain. The two corn holes were most likely used to produce a smoke smudge with the contents of both prepared in similar fashion including the unexplained rejection of butts and shanks as fuel.

The contribution of maize to the diet of these people cannot be assessed. No complete cobs were found nor were any kernels. The other combustible items did include wood from nut and fruit trees, a grape seed, and a plum pit, but although such a meager inventory of possible food stuffs is tantalizing, it is nutritionally-speaking uninformative.

TABLE 37

SUMMARY OF CONTENTS FROM CORN HOLES A AND B

	Corn Hole A				Corn Hole B			
Class and Name	No.	%	Weight (gm)	%	No.	%	Weight (gm)	%
Charcoal	26	13.40	5.6	16.76	51	14.40	7.7	11.25
Quercus sp. (white oak group)	24	12.37	5.3	15.86	36	10.17		
Quercus sp. (oak)					3	.85		
Celtis occidentalis (hackberry)					5	1.41		
Acer sp (maple)					2	.56		
Carya sp. (hickory)	2	1.03	.3	.90				
Salix sp. (willow)					1	.28		
Unidentified diffuse porous					4	1.13		
Bark								
Quercus sp. (oak)					2	.56	2.4	3.50
Seeds								
Prunus americana (plum)	1	.52	.1	.30				
Vitis sp. (grape)					1	.28	.1	.15
* *Chenopodium album* (lambs quarters)					3	.85	.1	.15
Rhizome — grass					2	.56	.5	.74
Corn	167	86.08	27.7	82.93	295	83.33	57.6	84.21
Cobs	26	13.40	26.7	79.94	33	9.32	56.5	82.75
Cupules and fragments	133	68.56			254	71.75		
Shanks/stalks	8	4.12	1.0	2.99	8	2.26	1.0	1.46
Carbonized Charcoal and cupule fragments (< .1mm)	not collected				--		(39.3)	
TOTAL	194	100.00	33.4	99.99	354	99.98	68.4	100.00

*non-carbonized contamination.

TABLE 38

ATTRIBUTES OF CORN COBS, CORN HOLE A
(all measurements in mm; not corrected for shrinkage)

Feature Level	Row No.	Diameter Max.	Diameter Min.	Cross-Section	Length	Area Measured	Cupule Features Pairing	Cupule Features No/10mm	Cupule Features Width	Cob Type
B8-273	8	12.6	--	--	18.3	M-T	S	3	9.5	R
Level II	8	11.4	--	--	18.2	M	+	3	6.8	R
	8	13.0	--	Q	22.8	M-T	S	3	8.8	R
	8	13.7	11.1	Q	9.7	M	S	4	8.7	R
	8	13.9	12.4	C	19.6	M	+	2.5	8.8	R
	8	9.2	8.1	C	19.8	M-T	+	2.5	7.6	R
	8	17.8	--	--	20.8	M-T	+	3	10.2	R
	8	8.8	--	Q	11.4	M	+	3	6.9	N
	8	12.8	--	Q	11.8	M	+	3	10.7	R
	4	9.4	8.2	Q	16.6	M	S	3	9.0	N
B8-538	10	16.7	16.0	C	37.8	M-T	+	2	9.3	R
Level III	8	16.5	13.0	E	59.7	M-T	+	2.5	9.7	R
	8	13.5	13.6	Q	20.5	M	S	3	9.1	R
	8	11.1	10.7	C	19.2	T-M	S	3.5	7.7	R
	8	12.8	11.7	E	19.5	M-T	S	2	8.0	R
	8	13.8	11.2	E	14.0	M-T	S	2.5	9.4	R
	8	12.5	10.3	E	14.7	M-B	S	2	8.2	R
	8	8.1	7.5	C	19.9	M-T	S	3	6.0	N
	8	12.0	10.8	E	12.4	M	S	2	8.0	R
	8	12.8	11.9	C	19.9	M	S	2.5	8.3	R
	8	10.3	9.4	C	16.6	M	+	3	7.0	R
	8	8.8	--	C	28.4	M-B	+	3	6.8	N
	8	8.2	7.9	Q	10.2	M	+	2.5	6.8	N
	8	15.0	--	--	22.8	M	S	2.5	9.4	R
Probably	8	16.5	12.7	Q	16.2	M	S	1.5	7.2	R
B8-538	8	8.8	--	E	24.6	M-T	+	3.5	6.9	R
Level III										

Key:
-- = insufficient data
Q = quadrangular
C = circular
E = elliptical
M = middle
T = tip
B = butt

\+ = paired
S = strongly paired
W = weakly paired
R = regular cob
N = nubbin or tiller
I = irregular

TABLE 39

ATTRIBUTES OF CORN COBS, CORN HOLE B
(all measurements in mm; not corrected for shrinkage)

Row No.	Diameter Max.	Min.	Cross-Section	Length	Area Measured	Cupule Features Pairing	No/10mm	Width	Cob Type
8	10.7	10.4	Q	20.8	M	+	4	7.7	R
8	11.0	10.9	Q	37.4	T-M	+	3	7.4	R
8	17.1	15.4	E	29.2	M	+	3	11.6	R
8	16.0	14.3	E	28.6	M	W	3	9.2	R
8	13.9	13.0	Q	22.0	M-B	+	3	8.9	R
8	14.0	13.9	Q	28.3	M	+	2.5	9.8	R
8	13.7	--	--	24.9	T-M	+	3	8.9	R
8	15.1	9.2	Q	15.4	T-M	+	3	8.4	R
8	13.6	10.5	Q	12.6	M	S	3	10.1	R
8	10.9	9.6	Q	18.6	T-M	+	2.5	9.2	R
8	9.5	8.4	C	13.9	M	+	3	6.8	N
8	13.3	12.8	Q	12.4	M	+	3	9.1	R
8	12.0	11.6	Q	23.2	M-T	+	3	8.8	R
8	8.9	--	--	19.4	M	S	2	11.3	R
8	11.8	--	--	14.9	M	S	3	12.6	R
8	12.2	--	Q	29.9	T-M	S	2.5	9.5	R
6	10.2	8.2	E	24.8	M	+	2.5	8.4	N
8	13.7	12.5	C	9.6	T	W	3	8.4	R
8	15.0	--	C	20.0	M	+	3	11.4	R
I	11.6	10.0	C	17.5	T-M	No	3	7.8	N
8	12.6	--	C	18.9	T-M	+	2	10.7	N
8	9.8	9.0	C	19.4	M	+	3	6.9	N
8	10.7	8.4	Q	11.3	M	+	2.5	7.7	R
8	12.1	--	--	17.2	T-M	S	3	9.8	R
4	10.9	8.2	E	20.0	M	S	3	8.6	N
8	17.4	15.8	E	41.7	M-T	+	2.5	10.7	R
5	12.0	10.0	Q	33.4	M	+	3	7.7	N
5	12.7	11.9	Q	18.7	M	+	3	9.1	N
8	11.8	--	C	8.4	M	+	3	8.8	R
8	12.7	12.5	C	17.1	M	+	3	8.7	R
8	11.7	8.9	Q	15.9	M	+	3	8.4	R
8	13.3	--	C	9.6	M	+	3	11.1	R
8	11.6	--	Q	14.7	M	+	4	8.2	R

Key: See Table 38.

TABLE 40

SUMMARY OF CORN COB ATTRIBUTES, CORN HOLES A AND B
(Corn hole A N=26; corn hole B N=33)

Corn Hole	$\overline{X}$	Row Number					
		4	5	6	8	10	I
		Percent					
A	7.9	4	0	0	92	4	0
B	7.6 (N=32)	3	6	3	84.8	0	3

	Cob Cross-Section			
	C	E	Q	Insuf.
	Percent			
A	30.8	23	30.8	15.4
B	27.3	15.2	45.4	12.1

	Area Represented (measured)				
	T	T-M	M	M-B	B
	Percent				
A	0	42.3	50	7.7	0
B	3.0	30.3	63.3	3.0	0

	Pairing			
	S	+	W	Absent
A	53.8	46.2	0	0
B	18.2	72.7	6.0	3.0

	Cob Type	
	R	N
	Percent	
A	80.8	19.2
B	75.7	24.3

	Maximum Diameter (mm)	Length	No. cupules/10mm	Cupule Width (mm)
A	$\overline{X}$ = 12.3	$\overline{X}$ = 20.2	$\overline{X}$ = 2.7	$\overline{X}$ = 8.3
B	$\overline{X}$ = 12.5	$\overline{X}$ = 20.3	$\overline{X}$ = 2.9	$\overline{X}$ = 9.1

BIBLIOGRAPHY

Anderson, Melville B. (ed.)
1901 Relation of the discoveries and voyages of Cavelier de La Salle from 1679 to 1681. Chicago: The Caxton Club.

Baerreis, David A. and Reid A. Bryson
1965 Climatic episodes and the dating of Mississippian cultures. The Wisconsin Archaeologist, 46(4):203-20.

Baerreis, David A. and Joan E. Freeman
1958 Late Woodland pottery in Wisconsin as seen from Aztalan. Wisconsin Archaeologist, 39(1):35-61. Lake Mills.

Baker, George A.
1899 The St. Joseph-Kankakee Portage. Northern Indiana Historical Society. Publication no. 1. South Bend, Indiana.

Bareis, Charles J.
1965 Excavation of two burials at the Material Service Quarry site, La Salle County, Illinois. Wisconsin Archaeologist, 46(2):140-143. Lake Mills.

Barrett, Samuel Alfred
1911 The dream dance of the Chippewa and Menominee Indians of northern Wisconsin. Milwaukee Public Museum Bulletin Vol. 1, Art. IV, pp. 251-406. Milwaukee.

Bigger, H. P.
1925 The works of Samuel De Champlain. Toronto: The Champlain Society.

Binford, Lewis R.
1963 Red ocher caches from the Michigan area: a possible case of cultural drift. Southwestern Journal of Anthropology, 19(1):89-108.

1967 Smudge pits and hide smoking: the use of analogy in archaeological reasoning. American Antiquity, 32(1):1-12. Salt Lake City.

Binford, Lewis R. and Sally R. Binford, Robert C. Whallon, and Margaret Ann Hardin
1966 Archaeology at Hatchery West, Carlyle, Illinois. Southern Illinois University Museums Archaeological Salvage Report No. 25, Carbondale.

Binford, Lewis, R. and Mark L. Papworth
1963 The Eastport site, Antrim County, Michigan. *In* Miscellaneous studies in typology and classification. Anthropological Papers No. 19, Museum of Anthropology, The University of Michigan, Ann Arbor, Michigan.

Binford, Lewis R. and George I. Quimby
1963 Indian sites and chipped stone materials in the northern Lake Michigan area. Fieldiana-Anthropology 36(12):277-307.

Blair, Emma Helen
1911 The Indian tribes of the Upper Mississippi Valley and region of the Great Lakes. Arthur H. Clark Co. Cleveland, Ohio.

Blasingham, Emily
1961 Indians of the Chicago area. *In* Chicago area archaeology, Elaine A. Bluhm (ed.) Illinois Archaeological Survey, Inc., Bulletin No. 3, University of Illinois, Urbana.

Bluhm, Elaine A. and Gloria J. Fenner
1961 The Oak Forest site. *In* Chicago area archaeology, Elaine A. Bluhm (ed.), Illinois Archaeological Survey, Bulletin No. 3, pp. 138-161. Carbondale.

Bluhm, Elaine A. and Alen Liss
1961 The Anker site. *In* Chicago area archaeology, Elaine A. Bluhm (ed.), Illinois Archaeological Survey, Bulletin No. 3, pp. 89-137. Carbondale.

Bordes, Francois
1961 Typologie du Paleolithique Ancien et Moyen. Publications de L'Institut de L'Universite de Bordeaux, Memoire, No. 1. Bordeaux.

Brose, David S.
1970a The archaeology of Summer Island: changing settlement systems in northern Lake Michigan. Anthropological Papers, No. 41, Museum of Anthropology, University of Michigan. Ann Arbor.
1970b Summer Island III: An early historic site in the Upper Great Lakes. Historical Archaeology 6:3-33.

Brown, James A.
1964 The northeastern extension of the Havana tradition. *In* Hopewellian studies, Joseph R. Caldwell and Robert L. Hall (eds.), Illinois State Museum Scientific Papers, Vol. 12. Springfield.
1965 The prairie peninsula: an interaction area in the eastern United States. Ph.D. thesis. University of Chicago.

Brown, James A. (ed.)
1961 The Zimmerman site. A report on excavations at the Grand Village of the Kaskaskia, La Salle County, Illinois. Illinois State Museum, Report of Investigations, No. 9. Springfield.

Brown, James A., Roger W. William, Mary A. Barth, and George K. Neuman
1967 The Gentleman Farm site, La Salle County, Illinois. Illinois State Museum, Report of Investigations, No. 12. Springfield.

Broyles, Bettye J.
1966 Preliminary report: the St. Albans site (46Ka 27), Kanawha County, West Virginia. West Virginia. West Virginia Archaeologist, No. 19, pp. 1-13. Moundsville.

Callender, Charles
1962 Social organization of the Central Algonkian Indian. Milwaukee Public Museum, Publications in Anthropology, No. 7. Milwaukee.

Clark, David L.
1968 Analytical archaeology. Methuen, London.

Cleland, Charles E.
1966 The prehistoric animal ecology and ethnozoology of the Upper Great Lakes region. Anthropological Papers, No. 29, Museum of Anthropology, University of Michigan. Ann Arbor.

Cole, Fay-Cooper and Thorne Deuel
1937 Rediscovering Illinois. University of Chicago Press. Chicago.

Crabtree, Don E. and E. L. Davis
1968 Experimental manufacture of wooden implements with tools of flaked stone. Science 159:426-428.

Crane, H. R. and J. B. Griffin
1958 University of Michigan radiocarbon dates II. Science 127: 1098-1105.
1961 University of Michigan radiocarbon dates VI, Radiocarbon 3:105-125.
1966 University of Michigan radiocarbon dates XI, Radiocarbon 8:256-285.
1968 University of Michigan radiocarbon dates XII, Radiocarbon 10:61-114.
1970 University of Michigan radiocarbon dates XIII, Radiocarbon Vol. 12, No. 1.

Cutler, Hugh C.
1965 Cultivated Plants. *In* Olaf H. Prufer, The McGraw Site, A Study in Hopewellian Dynamics. Scientific Publications of the Cleveland Museum of Natural History, New Series 4(1):107-109. Cleveland.

Cutler, Hugh C. and Leonard W. Blake
1969 Corn from Cahokia Sites. *In* Melvin L. Fowler, ed., Explorations in Cahokia Archaeology. Illinois Archaeological Survey Bulletin No. 7:123-136. Urbana.

Deevey, Edward S., L. J. Gralenski, and Vance Hoffren
1959 Yale natural radiocarbon measurements IV. American Journal of Science Radiocarbon Supplement, Vol. 1, pp. 144-172. New Haven.

Densmore, Frances
1929 Chippewa customs. Bureau of American Ethnology, Bulletin 86. United States Government Printing Office. Washington, D.C.

Dillingham, Betty
1963 Oklahoma Kickapoo. Ph.D. thesis. University of Michigan.

Dragoo, Don W.
1959 Archaic hunters of the Upper Ohio Valley. Carnegie Museum Anthropological Series, No. 3, pp. 139-246. Pittsburgh, Pennsylvania.

Duncan, Otis D.
1954 Human ecology and population studies. *In* The study of population, an inventory and appraisal. Philip M. Hauser and Otis D. Duncan (eds.). University of Chicago Press, Chicago.

Faulkner, Charles H.
N.D. Archaeological reconnaissance in the Kankakee Valley: a summary. Manuscript in the Museum of Anthropology, University of Michigan.
1964a The Morrow site: a red ocher workshop site in the Kankakee Valley, Indiana. Wisconsin Archaeologist, 45(4):151-157.
1964b The Rader site. Central States Archaeological Journal, 11(3): 90-98. East St. Louis.
1970 The late prehistoric occupation of northwestern Indiana. A study of the Upper Mississippi cultures of the Kankakee Valley. Ph.D. thesis, Indiana University.

Fenner, Gloria
1961 The Bowmanville site. *In* Chicago area archaeology, Elaine A. Bluhm (ed.). Illinois Archaeological Survey, Bulletin No. 3. Illinois Archaeological Survey, Carbondale.
1963 The Plum Island site, La Salle County, Illinois. *In* Reports on Illinois prehistory, Elaine A. Bluhm (ed.). Illinois Archaeological Survey, Bulletin No. 4, pp. 1-105.

Fitting, James E.
1964a Bifurcate-stemmed projectile points in the Eastern United States. American Antiquity 30(1):92-94.
1964b Ceramic relationships of four Late Woodland sites in northern Ohio. Wisconsin Archaeologist, 45(4):160-175.
1965 Late Woodland cultures of southeastern Michigan. Anthropological Papers, No. 24, Museum of Anthropology, University of Michigan. Ann Arbor.
1966 Radiocarbon dating the Younge tradition. American Antiquity, 31(5):738. Salt Lake City.
1967 The camp of the careful Indian: an Upper Great Lakes chipping station. Papers of the Michigan Academy of Science, Arts, and Letters, Vol. LII, pp. 237-242. Ann Arbor.

Fitting, James E., Jerry De Visscher, and Edward Wahla
1966 The Paleo-Indian occupation of the Holcombe Beach. Anthropological Papers No. 27, Museum of Anthropology, University of Michigan. Ann Arbor.

Fitting, James E., John R. Halsey, and H. Martin Wobst
1968 Contributions to Michigan Archaeology. Museum of Anthropology, University of Michigan. Anthropological Paper No. 32. Ann Arbor.

Flanders, Richard E.
1965 A comparison of some Middle Woodland material in Michigan and Illinois. Ph.D. thesis, University of Michigan.

Ford, Richard I.
1969 Nuts for Hopewellians. Paper presented at Society for American Archaeology meeting, Milwaukee, Wisconsin.

1971 Corn from the Hornung Site, Jefferson County, Kentucky. University of Michigan, Museum of Anthropology, Ethnobotanical Laboratory Report No. 459.

Fowler, Melvin L.
1952 The Robinson Reserve Site. Journal of the Illinois State Archaeological Society, 2(2-3):50-82. Springfield.
1959 Summary report of Modoc Rock Shelter. 1952, 1953, 1955, 1956. Report of Investigations No. 8, Illinois State Museums.

Frison, George C.
1967 Archaeological evidence of the Crow Indians in northern Wyoming: A study of the Late Prehistoric Period buffalo economy. Ph.D. thesis, University of Michigan.

Greenman, Emerson F.
1935 Excavations of the Reeve Village Site, Lake County, Ohio. The Ohio State Archaeological and Historical Quarterly, 44(1): 3-64.
1937 Two prehistoric villages near Cleveland, Ohio. The Ohio State Archaeological and Historical Quarterly, 46(4):305-366. Columbus.

Griffin, James B.
1943 The Fort Ancient aspect. Its cultural and chronological position in Mississippi Valley archaeology. University of Michigan Press, Ann Arbor.
1946 Cultural change and continuity in Eastern United States Archaeology. *In* Man in Northeastern North America, Frederick Johnson, ed., Papers of the Robert S. Peabody Foundation for Archaeology, Vol. 3, pp. 37-95.
1949 The Cahokia ceramic complexes. Proceedings of the fifth plains archaeological conference, Laboratory of Anthropology, Notebook 1:44-58. University of Nebraska Press.
1952 Some Early and Middle Woodland pottery types in Illinois. *In* Hopewellian communities in Illinois, Thorne Deuel (ed.). Scientific Papers, Vol. V, Illinois State Museum, Springfield.
1960 A hypothesis for the prehistory of the Winnebago. *In* Culture in history: essays in honor of Paul Radin, Stanley Diamond (ed.); pp. 809-865. Columbia University Press, New York.
1965 Hopewell and the dark black glass. Michigan Archaeologist, 11(3-4):115-155.

__________, R. E. Flanders and P. F. Titterington
1970 The burial complexes of the Knight and Norton mounds in Illinois and Michigan. Memoir Number 2, Museum of Anthropology, University of Michigan, Ann Arbor, Michigan.

Griffin, John W.
1946 The Upper Mississippi occupation at the Fisher site, Will County, Illinois. Unpublished M.A. thesis, University of Chicago.

Hall, Robert L.
1962*a* The archaeology of Carcajou Point: with an interpretation of the development of Oneota culture in Wisconsin. University of Wisconsin Press, Madison.

1962*b* A newly designated pottery type from northern Illinois. Mimeographed for distribution at the Midwest Archaeological Conference, Springfield, Illinois.

Harkness, W. J. K. and J. R. Dymond
1961 The lake sturgeon. Field and Wildlife branch, The Ontario Department of Lands and Forests, Ontario, Canada.

Herrick, Ruth
1958 A report on the Ada site, Kent County, Michigan. Michigan Archaeologist 4(1):1-27.

Hinsdale, W. B.
1927 Indian corn culture in Michigan. Papers of the Michigan Academy of Science, Arts, and Letters, Vol. VIII, pp. 31-49. Ann Arbor.
1929 Reports of archaeological field work in the summer of 1928 in Montmorency, Newaygo, and Lake Counties, Michigan. Papers of the Michigan Academy of Science, Arts, and Letters, Vol. XII, pp. 127-135. Ann Arbor.
1931 Archaeological Atlas of Michigan. University of Michigan Press. Ann Arbor.
1932 Distribution of the aboriginal population of Michigan. Occasional contributions from the Museum of Anthropology of the University of Michigan, No. 2. Ann Arbor.

Hooton, Ernest A. and Charles C. Willoughby
1920 Indian village site and cemetery near Madisonville, Ohio. Papers of the Peabody Museum of America Archaeology and Ethnology, Harvard University, Vol. VIII, No. 1. Cambridge, Massachusetts.

Jones, Volney H.
1949 Maize from the Davis Site: Its Nature and Interpretation. *In* H. Perry Newell and Alex D. Krieger, The George C. Davis Site, Cherokee County, Texas. Memoirs of the Society for American Archaeology, No. 15. Menasha.
1968 Corn from the McKees Rocks Village Site. Pennsylvania Archaeologist 38(1-4):81-86. Ann Arbor.

Kenoyer, Leslie A.
1934 Forest distribution in southwestern Michigan as interpreted from the original land survey (1826-32). Papers of the Michigan Academy of Science, Arts and Letters. Vol. XIX, pp. 107-111. Ann Arbor.

Kinietz, W. Vernon
1940 The Indians of the western Great Lakes, 1615-1760. Occasional Contributions from the Museum of Anthropology of the University of Michigan, No. 10, Ann Arbor.

Kroeber, A. L.
1939 Cultural and natural areas of native North America, University of California Publications in American Archaeology and Ethnology, Vol. 38, 242 pp.

Langford, George
1927 The Fisher Mound group, successive aboriginal occupations near the mouth of the Illinois River. American Anthropologist, 29(3):153-206. Menasha, Wisconsin.

Lee, Thomas E.
1958 The Parker Earthwork, Coranna, Ontario. Pennsylvania Archaeologist, 28(1):3-20. Honesdale, Pennsylvania.

McAllister, J. Gilbert
1932 The archaeology of Porter County. Indiana History Bulletin, Vol. X, No. 1. Indianapolis.

McCullough, Dale E.
1969 The Tule elk, its history, behavior, and ecology. University of California Publications in Zoology, Vol. 88. University of California Press, Berkeley.

McKenzie, Douglas H.
1967 The Graham Village site, a Fort Ancient settlement in the Hocking Valley, Ohio. *In* Studies in Ohio archaeology, by Olaf A. Prufer and Douglas H. McKenzie (eds.). The Press of Western Reserve University, Cleveland.

McKern, William C.
1945 Preliminary report on the Upper Mississippi phase in Wisconsin. Bulletin of the Public Museum of the City of Milwaukee, 16(3):109-285. Milwaukee.

McPherron, Alan
1967 The Juntunen Site and the Late Woodland prehistory of the Upper Great Lakes area. Anthropological Papers No. 30, Museum of Anthropology, University of Michigan. Ann Arbor.

Margry, Pierre
1878-1888 Decouvertes et etablissements des Francais dans l'ouest et dans le sud de l'Amerique Septentrionale, 1614-1754. Six Vols., Maison-neuve et Co. Paris.

Mason, Otis T.
1896 The influence of environment upon human industries or arts. Smithsonian Institution, Annual report for 1895, pp. 639-665.

Mason, Ronald J.
1966 Two stratified sites on the Door Peninsula of Wisconsin, Anthropological Papers, No. 26, Museum of Anthropology, University of Michigan. Ann Arbor.

Mills, William C.
1926 Certain mounds and village sites in Ohio. Vol. IV, Columbus, Ohio.

Mooney, James and Cyrus Thomas
1907 Mascoutens. In Handbook of the American Indians, Fredrick Hodge (ed.), Bulletin No. 30, Bureau of American Ethnology, Smithsonian Institution. United States Government Printing Office, Washington, D.C.

Morgan, Richard G. and H. Holmes Ellis

1943 The Fairport Harbor Village site. The Ohio State Archaeological and Historical Quarterly, 52(1):1-62, Columbus.

Munson, Cheryle A. and Patrick J. Munson'

1969 Preliminary report on an early historic site, Cook County, Illinois. Wisconsin Archaeologist, 50(3):184-188. Lake Mills, Wisconsin.

Munson, Patrick J.

1966 The Sheets site: a Late Archaic-Early Woodland occupation in west-central Illinois. Michigan Archaeologist, 12(3):111-120.

1969 Comments on Binford's "Smudge Pits and Hide Smoking: The Use of Analogy in Archaeological Reasoning." American Antiquity 34(1):83-84. Salt Lake City.

Munson, Patrick J. and N. L. Downs

1966 A surface collection of truncated barb and bifurcated base projectile points from central Illinois. Wisconsin Archaeologist 47(4):203-207.

Murie, Olaus J.

1951 The elk of North America, Wildlife Management Institute, Washington, D.C.

Murphy, James L.

1971 Maize from an Adena Mound in Athens County, Ohio. Science 171(3974):897-898. Washington.

Neumann, Georg K. and Melvin L. Fowler

1952 Hopewellian sites in the lower Wabash Valley. *In* Hopewellian communities in Illinois, Thorne Deuel (ed.), Scientific Papers, Vol. V, Illinois State Museum.

Nickerson, N. H.

1953 Variation in Cob Morphology Among Certain Archaeological and Ethnological Races of Maize. Annals of the Missouri Botanical Garden 40(2):79-111. St. Louis.

Parker, A. C.

1907 Excavation in the Erie Indian Village and Burial Site at Ripley, Chautaugua Co., N.Y. Albany, N.Y. State Mus. Bull. 117. Arch. 14.

Prahl, Earl J.

1970 The Middle Woodland period of the Lower Muskegon Valley and the northern Hopewellian frontier, Ph.D. thesis, University of Michigan.

Prator, Clifford H.

1941 La Salle's trip across southern Michigan in 1680. Michigan Alumnus Quarterly Review, Feb. 22, 1941, Vol. XLVII, No. 11. Ann Arbor, Michigan.

Probst, R. and E. L. Cooper

1955 Age, growth, and production of the lake sturgeon (*Acipenser fulvescens*) in the Lake Winnebago region, Wisconsin. Trans-American Fish Society, 84:207-227.

Quimby, George I.
1937 Discovery of a non-Iroquoian Upper Mississippi site in Kent County, Michigan. Manuscript on file in the Museum of Anthropology of the University of Michigan. Ann Arbor.
1941 The Goodall Focus. Vol. II, No. 2, Prehistoric Research Series, Indiana Historical Society, Indianapolis.
1952 The archaeology of the Upper Great Lakes area. *In* Archaeology of the Eastern United States, James B. Griffin (ed.), University of Chicago Press, Chicago.
1960 Indian life in the Upper Great Lakes, University of Chicago Press, Chicago.
1966a The Dumaw Creek site, a seventeenth century prehistoric Indian village and cemetery in Oceana County, Michigan. Chicago Natural History Museum, Fieldiana: Anthropology, 56(1):1-91. Chicago.
1966b Indian Culture and European Trade Goods. The University of Wisconsin Press. Madison.

Renfrew, C., J. E. Dixon, and J. R. Cann
1968 Patterns of trade: further analyses of Near Eastern obsidians. Proceedings of the Prehistoric Society 34:319-331.

Shelford, Victor E.
1963 The ecology of North America. University of Illinois Press, Urbana, Illinois.

Silverberg, James
1957 The Kickapoo Indians: first one hundred years of white contact in Wisconsin. Wisconsin Archaeology 38(3):61-181.

Skinner, Robert R.
1951 The Fifield Site (Porter V 37), Upper Mississippi manifestations in Porter County, Indiana. Proceedings of the Indiana Academy of Science, Vol. 60, pp. 38-44. Indianapolis.
1953 The Oakwood Mound, an Upper Mississippi component. Journal of the Illinois Archaeological Society, 3(1):2-14. Springfield.

Special Bulletin
1955 W. L. Coffinbury Chapter, Michigan Archaeological Society.

Taylor, Walter P. (ed.)
1956 The deer of North America. The Wildlife Management Institute, Washington, D.C.

Temple, Wayne C.
1958 Indian villages of the Illinois county. Illinois State Museum, Scientific Papers, Vol. II, Part 2. Springfield.

Thwaites, Reuben G. (ed.)
1896-1901 The Jesuit relations and allied documents. 73 vols. Burrows, Cleveland, Ohio.

Trigger, Bruce G.
1968 Beyond history: the methods of prehistory. Holt, Rinehart, and Winston, New York.
1969 The strategy of Iroquoian prehistory. In Ontario Archaeology No. 14.

Trowbridge, C. C.
1938 Meearmeear traditions. Vernon Kinietz (ed.). Occasional Contributions from the Museum of Anthropology of the University of Michigan, No. 7, Ann Arbor.

Veatch, J. O. and N. L. Partridge
1934 Utilization of land types for fruit production, Berrien County, Michigan. Agricultural Experiment Station, Michigan State College Special Bulletin 257, December.

Wahla, Edward
1966 A rare map of southeastern Michigan and southwestern Ontario and notes on the Fire People. The Totem Pole, 49(8): 48-51.

Wakefield, Francis
1966 The elusive Mascoutens. Michigan History 50(3):228-234. Lansing, Michigan.

West, George A.
1934 Tobacco, pipes, and smoking customs of the American Indians. Bulletin of the Public Museum of the City of Milwaukee, Vol. XVII.

White, A. M., Lewis R. Binford, and Mark L. Papworth
1963 Miscellaneous studies in typology and classification. Anthropological Papers No. 19, Museum of Anthropology, University of Michigan. Ann Arbor.

White, Theodore
1953 A method of calculating the dietary percentage of various food animals utilized by aboriginal peoples. American Antiquity, 18(4):396-398. Salt Lake City.

Williams, Gary R.
1970 Investigations in the white waterlilies (Nymphaea) of Michigan. The Michigan Botanist 9(2):72-86.

Winters, Howard D.
1961 The Adler Mound group, Will County, Illinois. *In* Chicago area archaeology, Elaine A. Bluhm (ed.), Bulletin No. 3, Illinois Archaeological Survey.
1967 An archaeological survey of the Wabash Valley in Illinois. Report of Investigations No. 10, Illinois State Museum, Springfield.

Wissler, Clark
1917 The American Indian. Douglas C. McMurtrie (ed.), New York.

Wittry, Warren L.
1959 Archaeological studies of four Wisconsin rockshelters, Wisconsin Archaeologist 40(4):137-267.
1963 The Bell site, Wm 9, an early historic Fox village. The Wisconsin Archaeologist 44(1):1-57.

Wray, Donald E.
1952 Archaeology of the Illinois Valley: 1950. *In* Archaeology of Eastern United States, James B. Griffin (ed.), pp. 152-164. University of Chicago Press, Chicago.

Wray, Donald E. and Richard S. MacNeish
1961 The Hopewellian and Weaver occupations of the Weaver site, Fulton County, Illinois. Scientific Papers, Vol. VII, No. 2. Illinois State Museum, Springfield.

Yarnell, Richard A.
1964 Aboriginal relationships between culture and plant life in the Upper Great Lakes region. Anthropological Papers No. 23, Museum of Anthropology, University of Michigan. Ann Arbor.

Plate 1. View of the location of the site from a northwestern section of the bluff overlooking the terrace where Moccasin Bluff is located.

Plate 2. Moccasin Bluff prior to excavation. Red Bud Trail Highway is to the left.

Plate 3. Excavations at Moccasin Bluff.

Plate 4. Excavations at Moccasin Bluff. Trench A is in the background; trench C is on the right.

Plate 5. Excavations at Moccasin Bluff. General view of trench A (35' x 40') showing top of level IV. Control areas are still in place.

Plate 6. Hale Smith (l.) and John Birdsell (r.) at pit 21 of trench B.

Plate 7. Trench A, pit 23 (circular pit at level V).

Plate 8. Trench F, pit 71, level III, showing sherds, bone, and fire-cracked rock.

Plate 9. Pit 82, level II, showing hearth with fire pit beneath.

Plate 10. Trench D, pit 48, level II, a hearth.

Plate 11. Trench C, burial 1, level III. Burial intrusive into refuse pit 54 (below knees). The refuse pit 55a lies just outside of the grave (r.). Pit 55b (r. of 55a) is adjacent to the west wall of trench C.

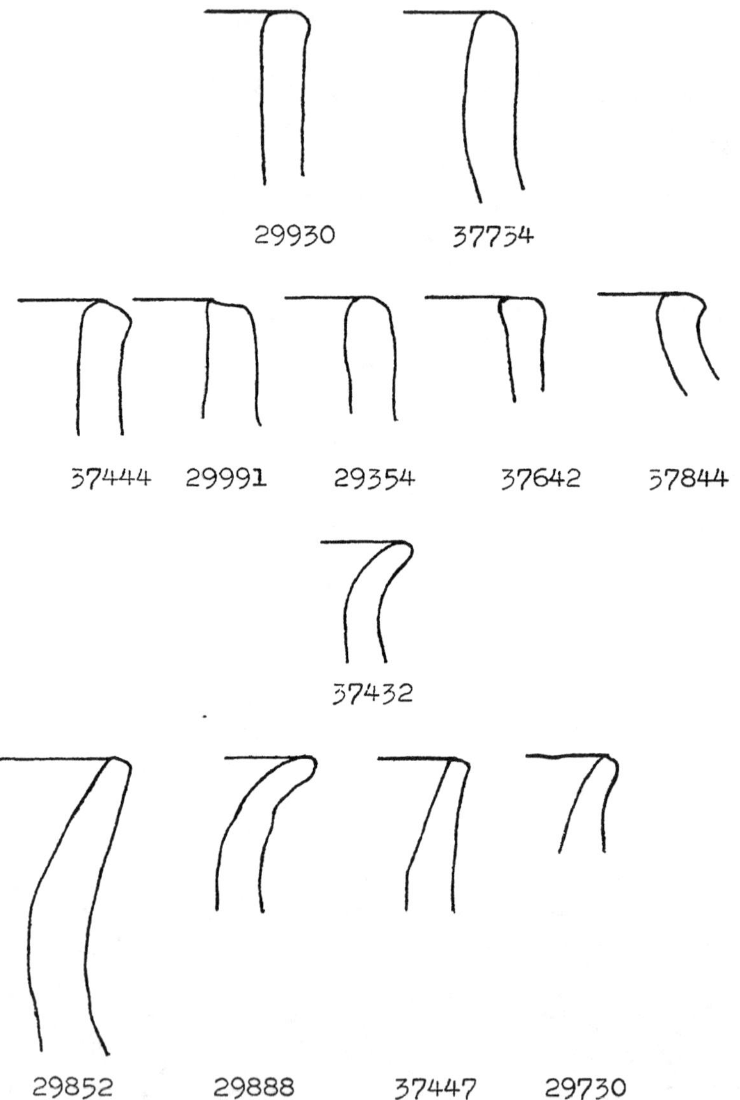

Rim profiles for plate 12 (numbers refer to Museum catalogue)

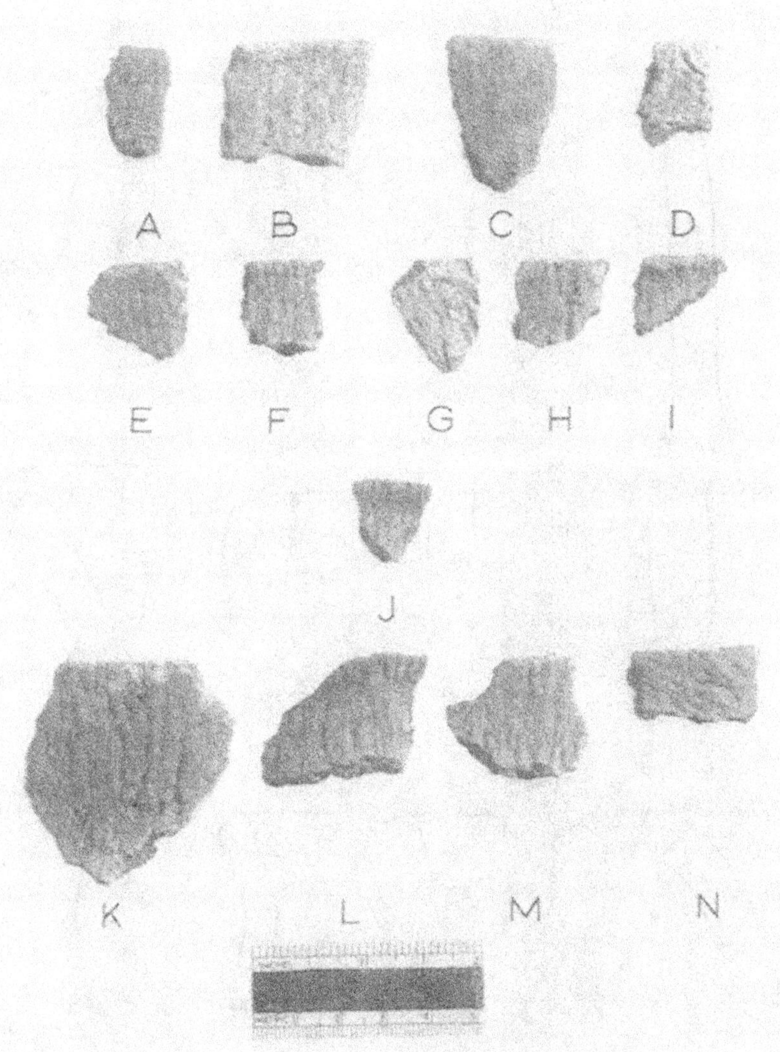

Plate 12. Moccasin Bluff Cordmarked sherds, variety 1a.

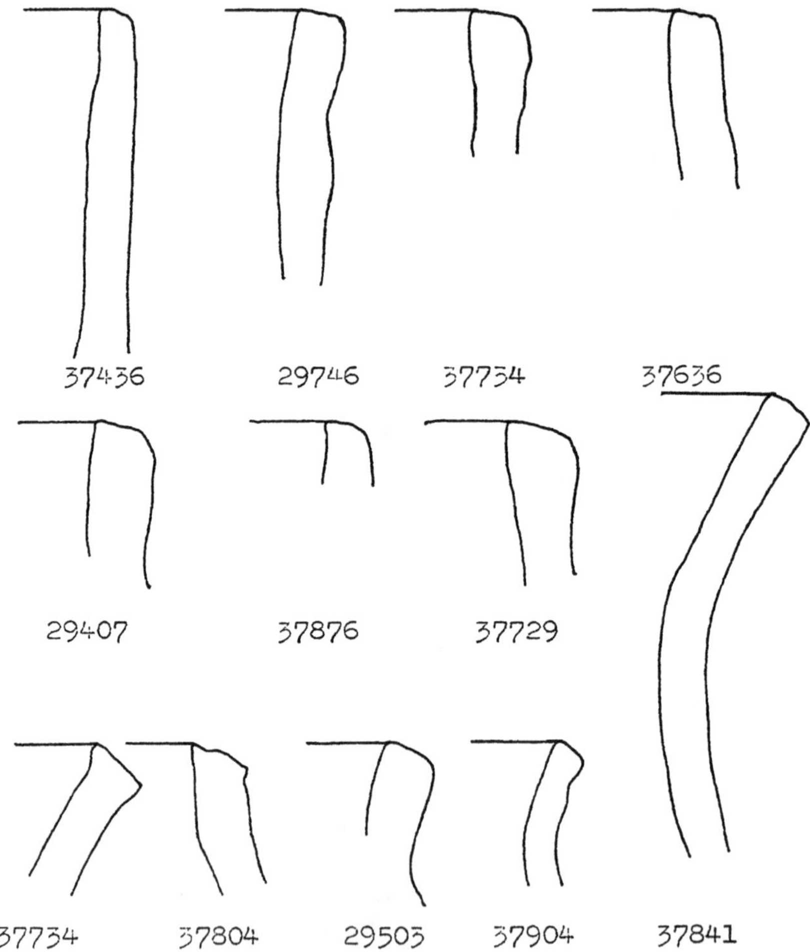

Rim profiles for plate 13.

Plate 13. Moccasin Bluff Cordmarked sherds, variety 1b. A-D, group 1; E-G, group 2; H-L, group 3.

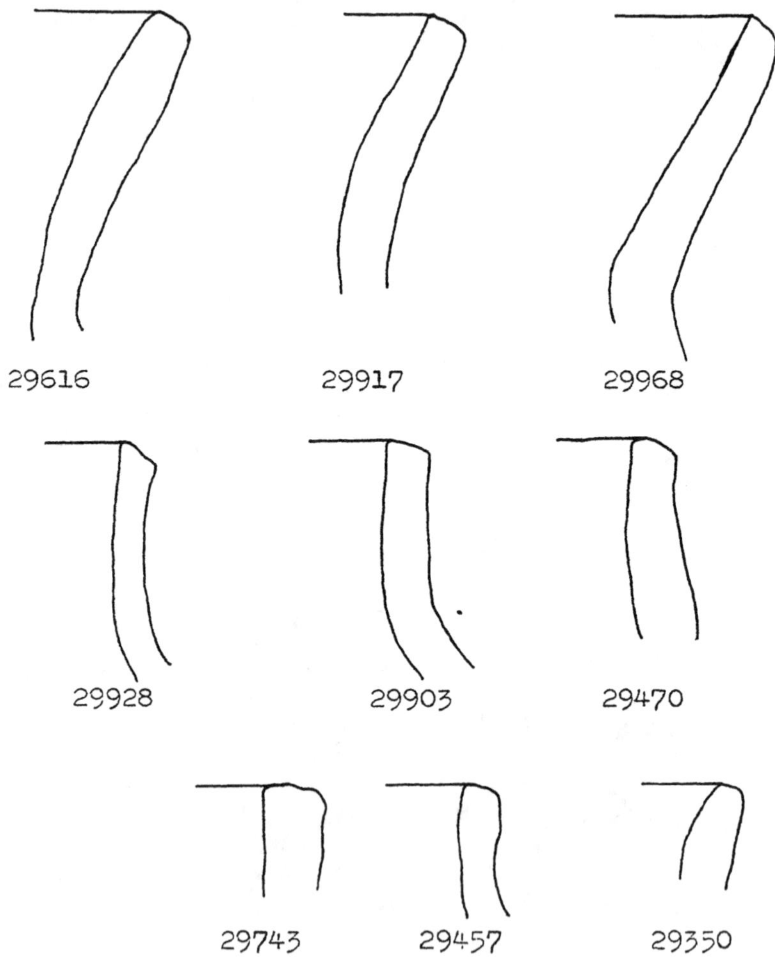

Rim profiles for plate 14.

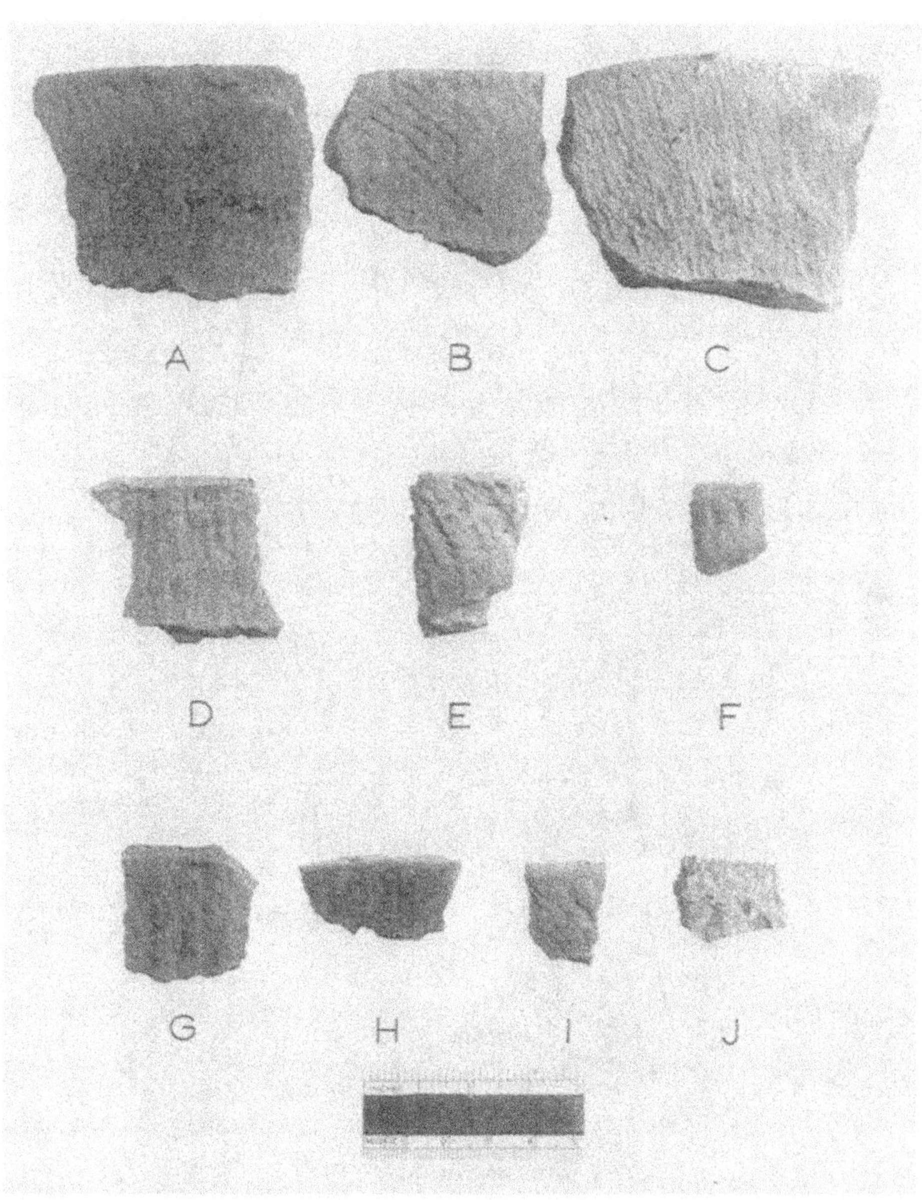

Plate 14. Moccasin Bluff Cordmarked sherds, variety 1b, group 4.

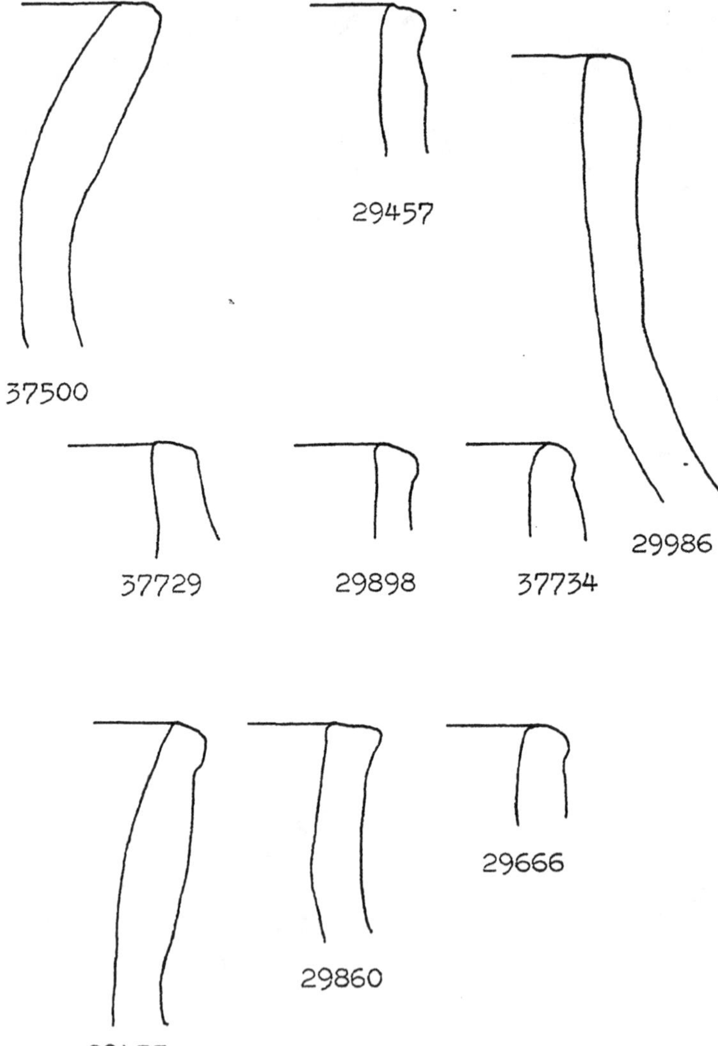

Rim profiles for plate 15.

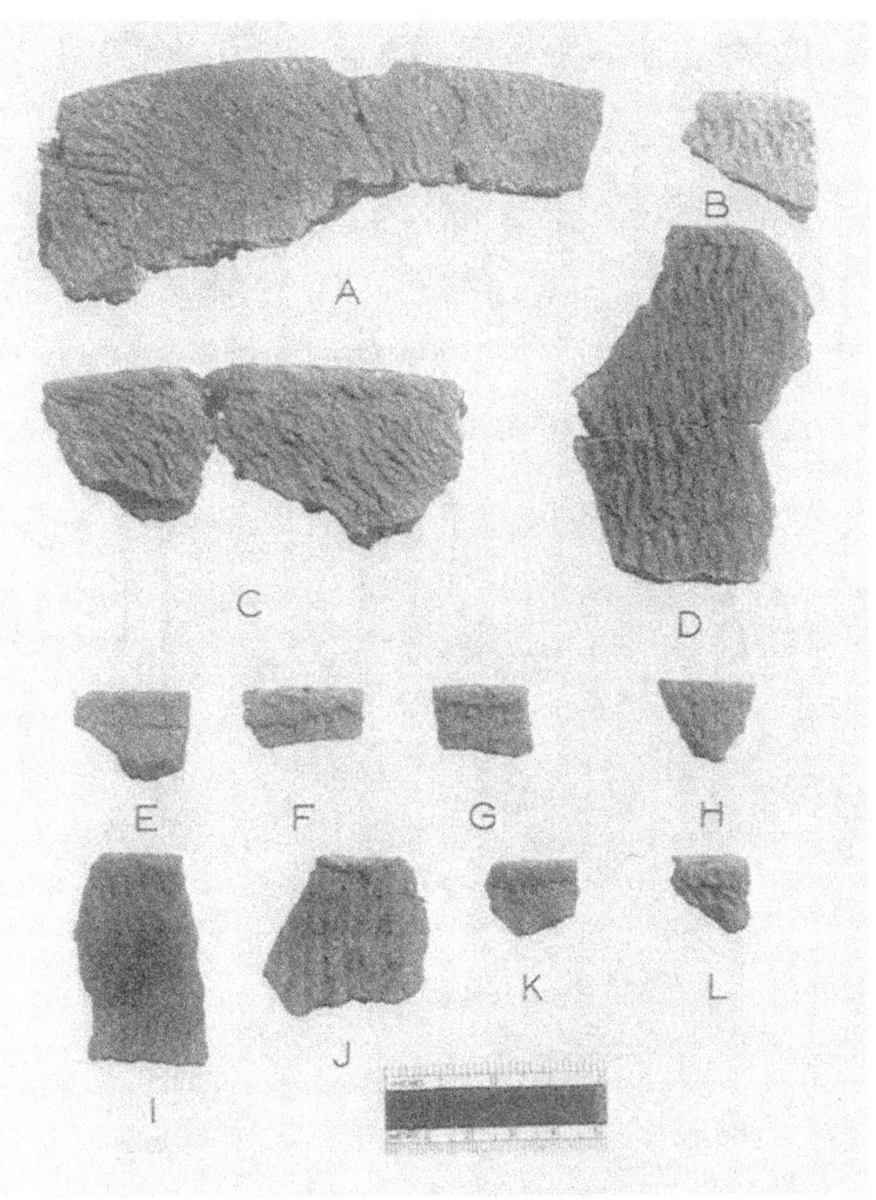

Plate 15. Moccasin Bluff Cordmarked sherds, variety 1b, group 5.

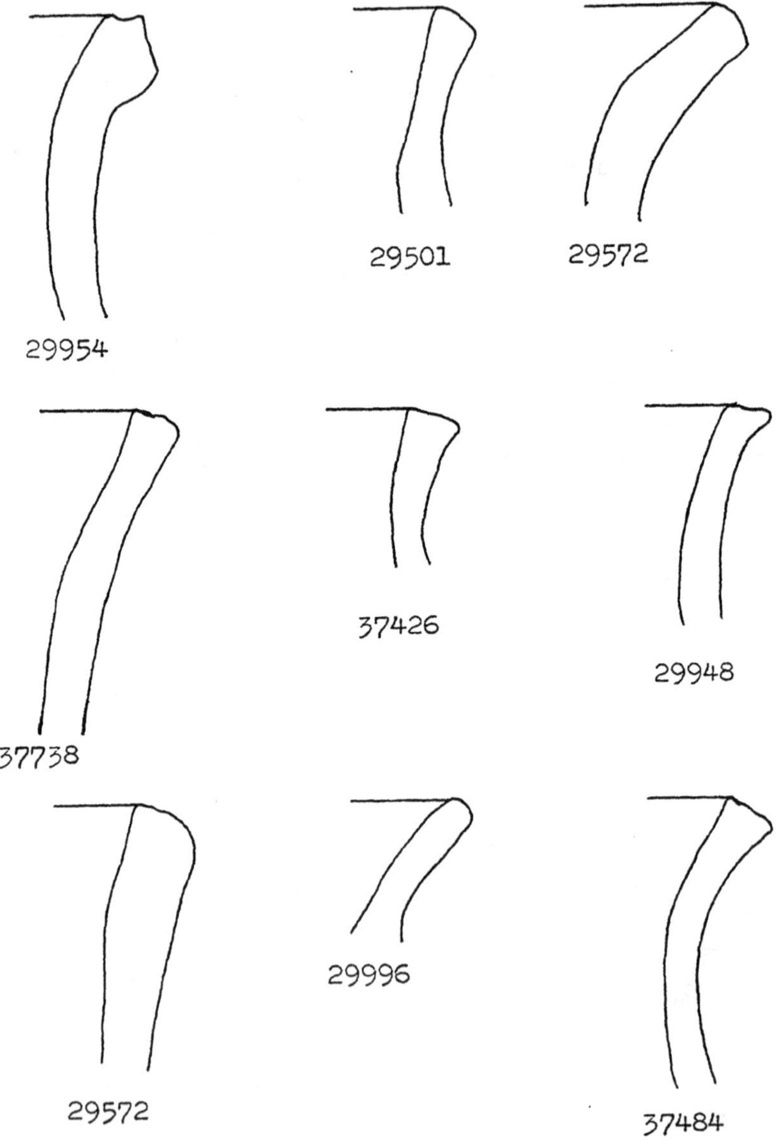

Rim profiles for plate 16.

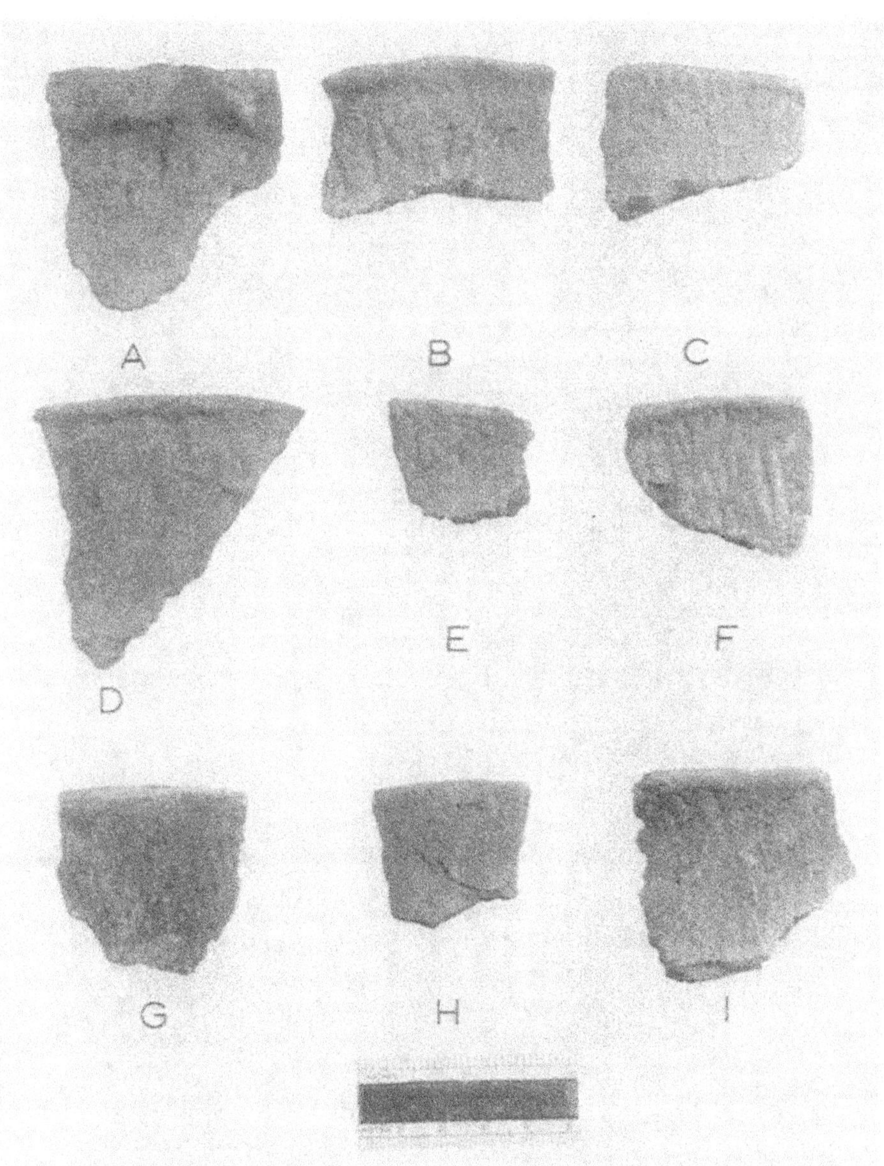

Plate 16. Moccasin Bluff Cordmarked sherds, variety 1b, group 6.

Plate 17. Moccasin Bluff Cordmarked sherd, variety 1b, group 1.

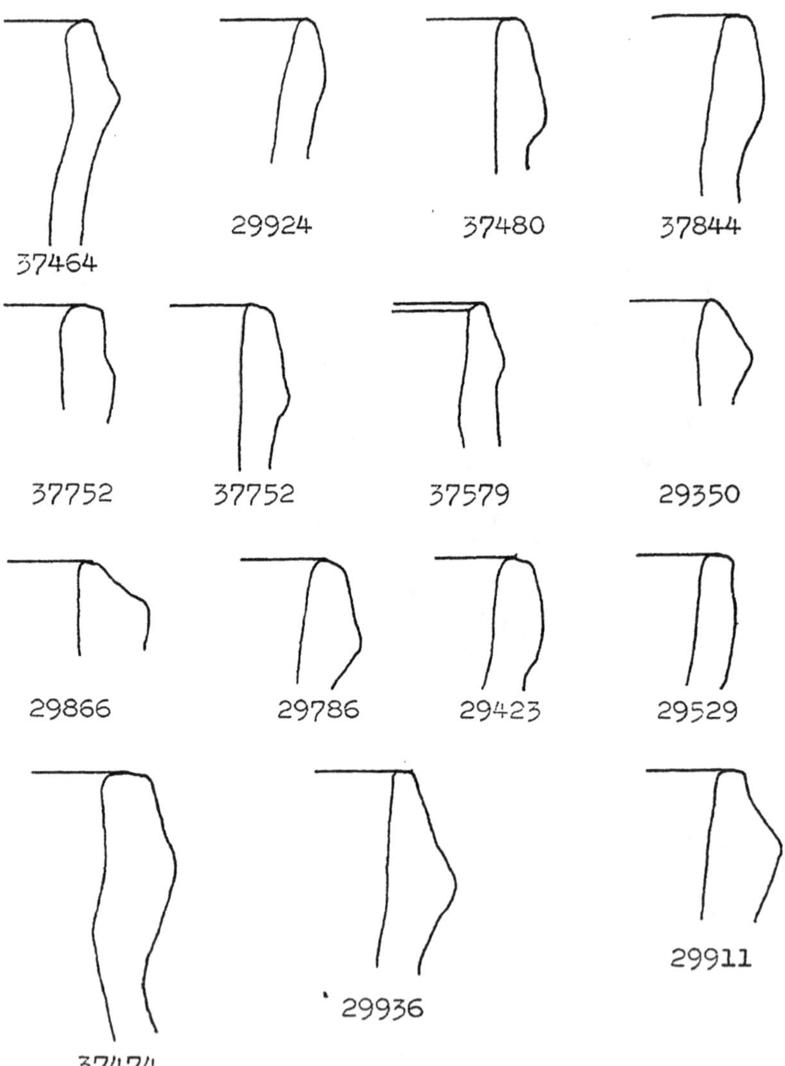

.Rim profiles for plate 18.

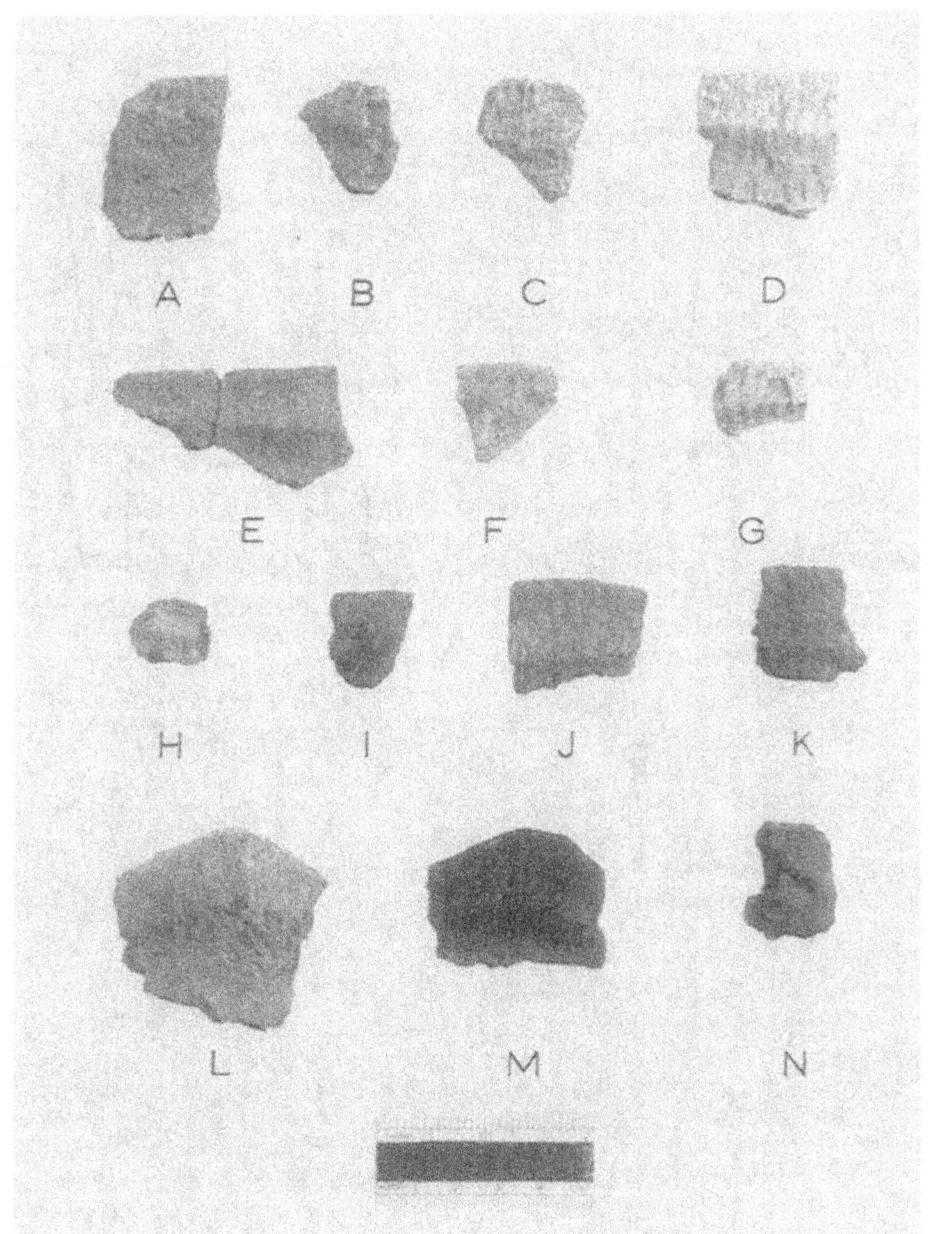

Plate 18. Moccasin Bluff Collared sherds. A-G, group A; H-N, group B.

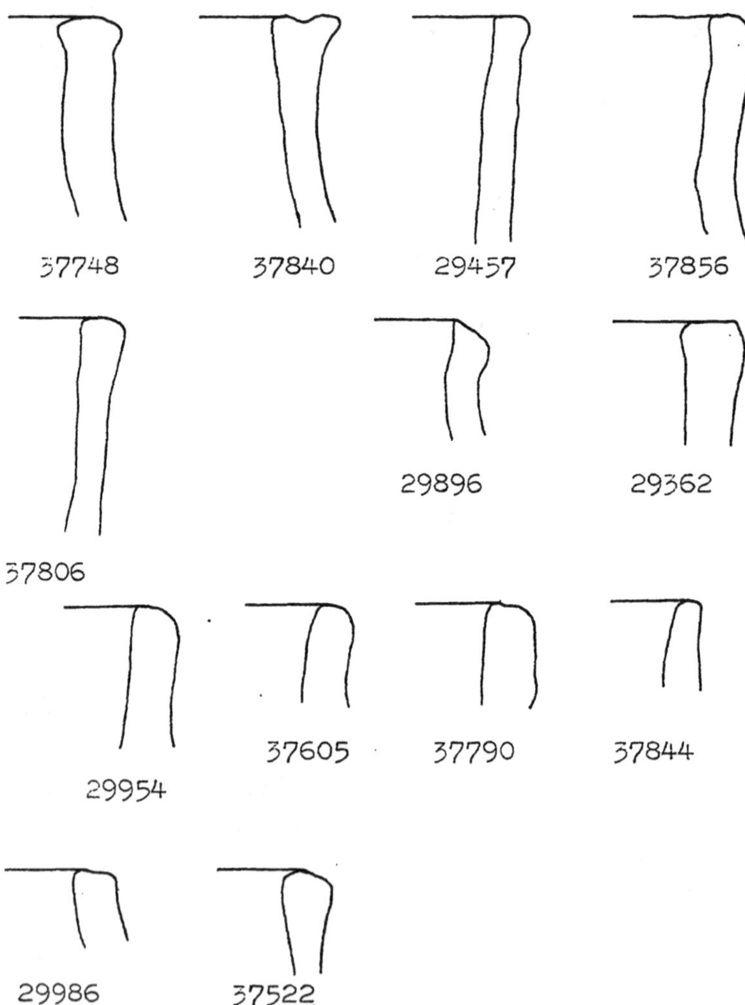

Rim profiles for plate 19.

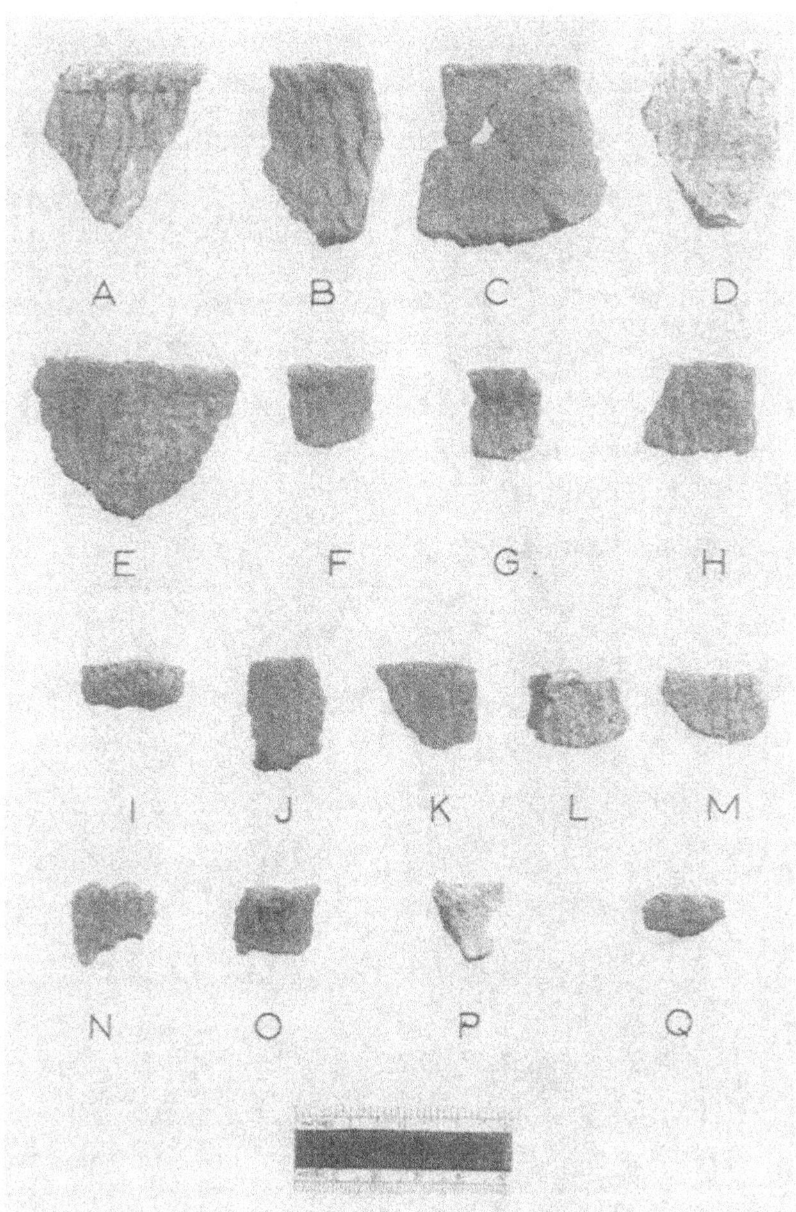

Plate 19. Moccasin Bluff Modified Lip sherds, group 1.

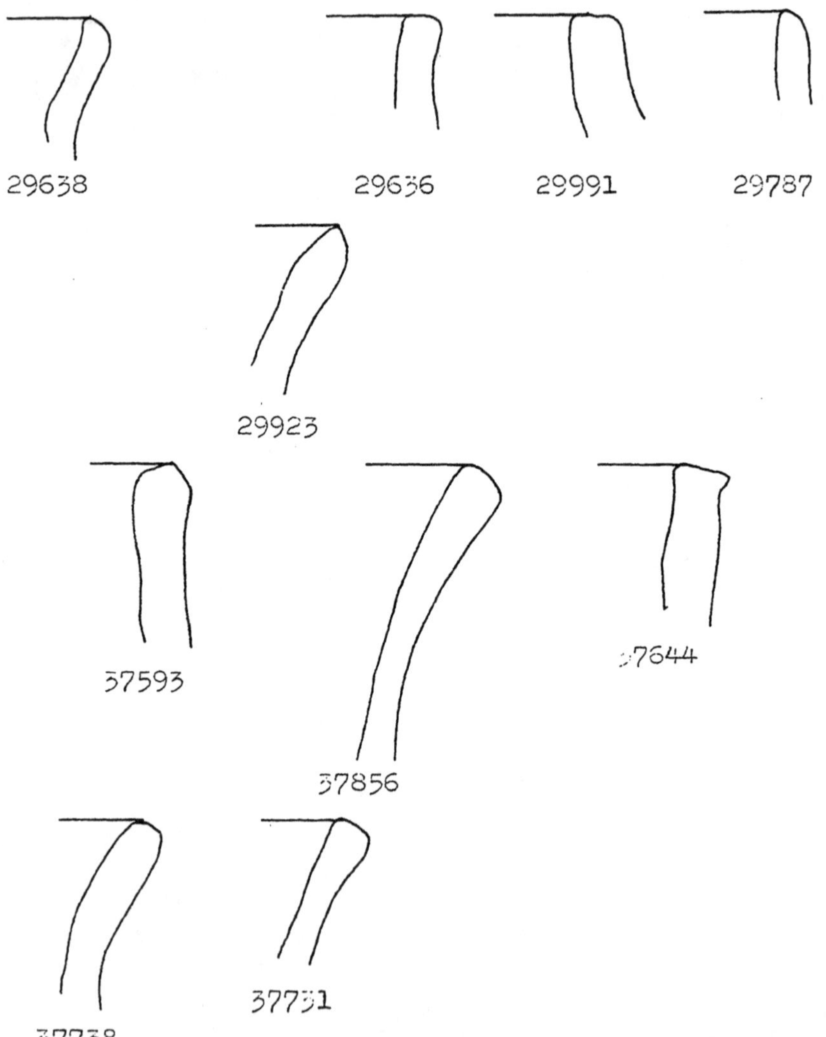

Rim profiles for plate 20.

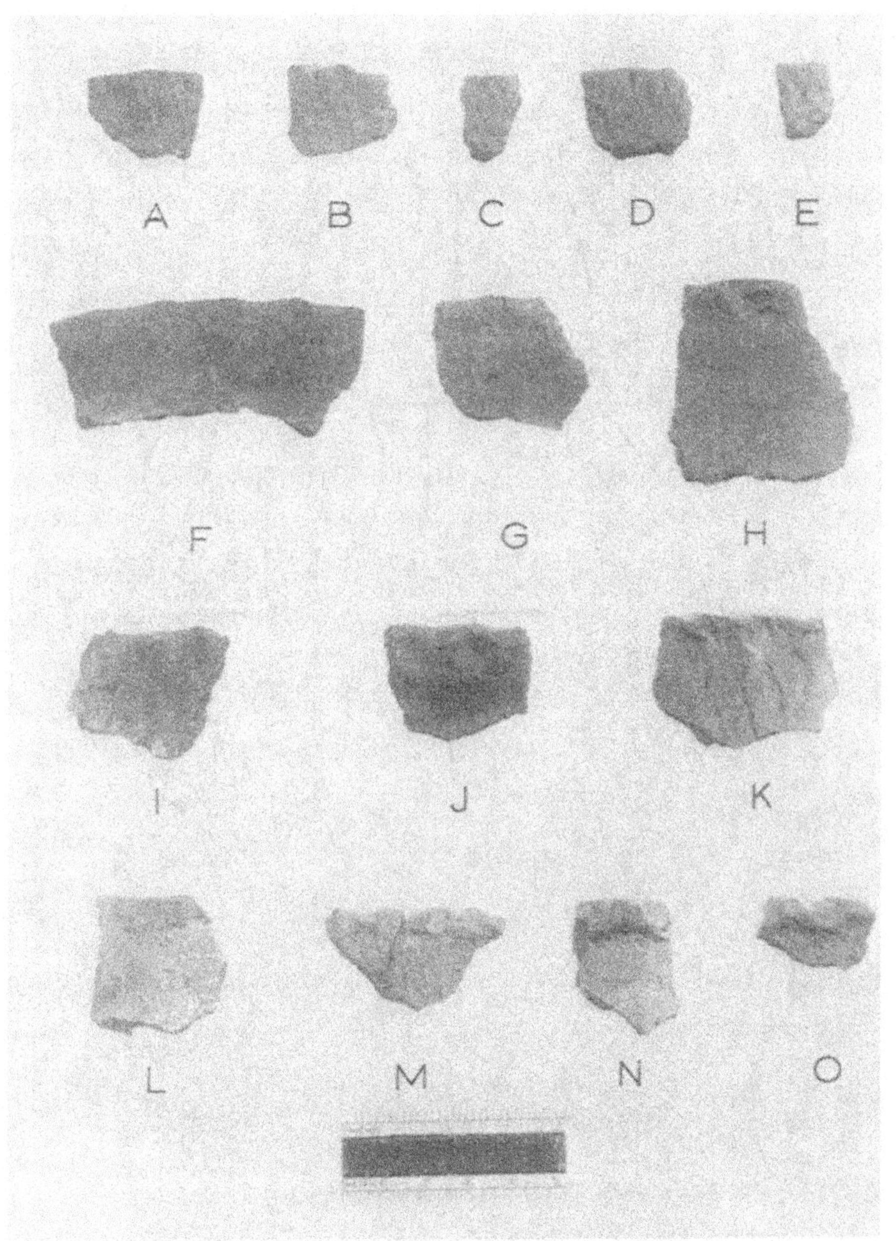

Plate 20. Moccasin Bluff Modified Lip sherds. A-E, group 2; F-K, group 3; L-O, group 4.

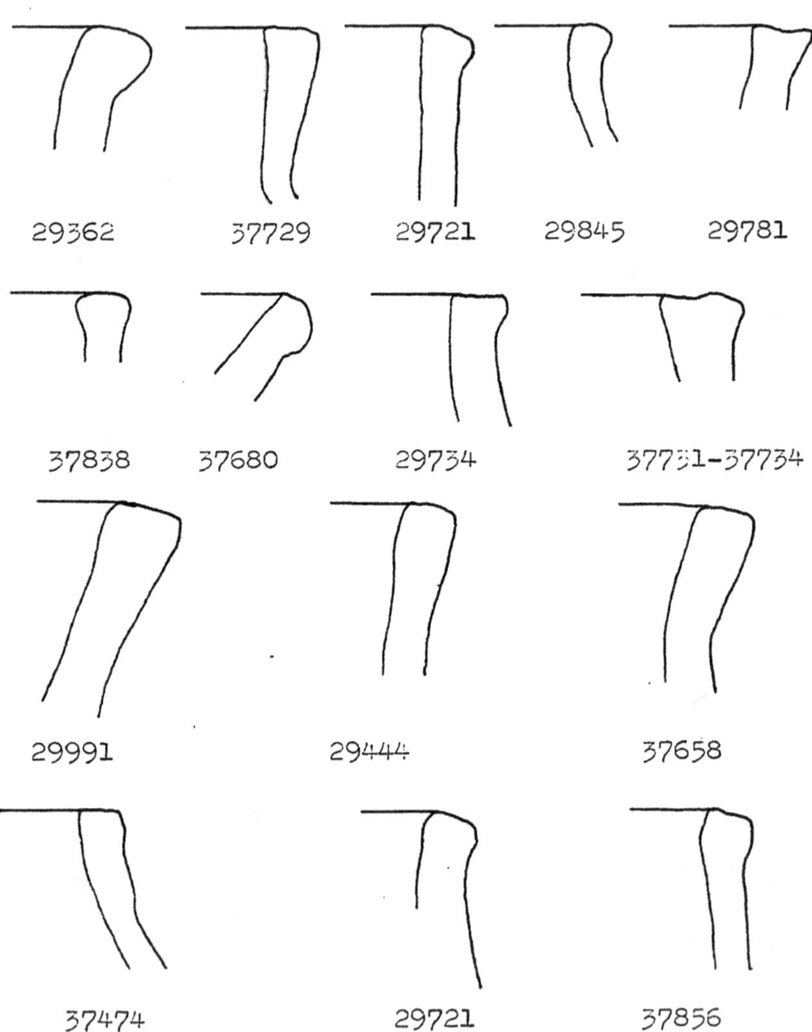

Rim profiles for plate 21.

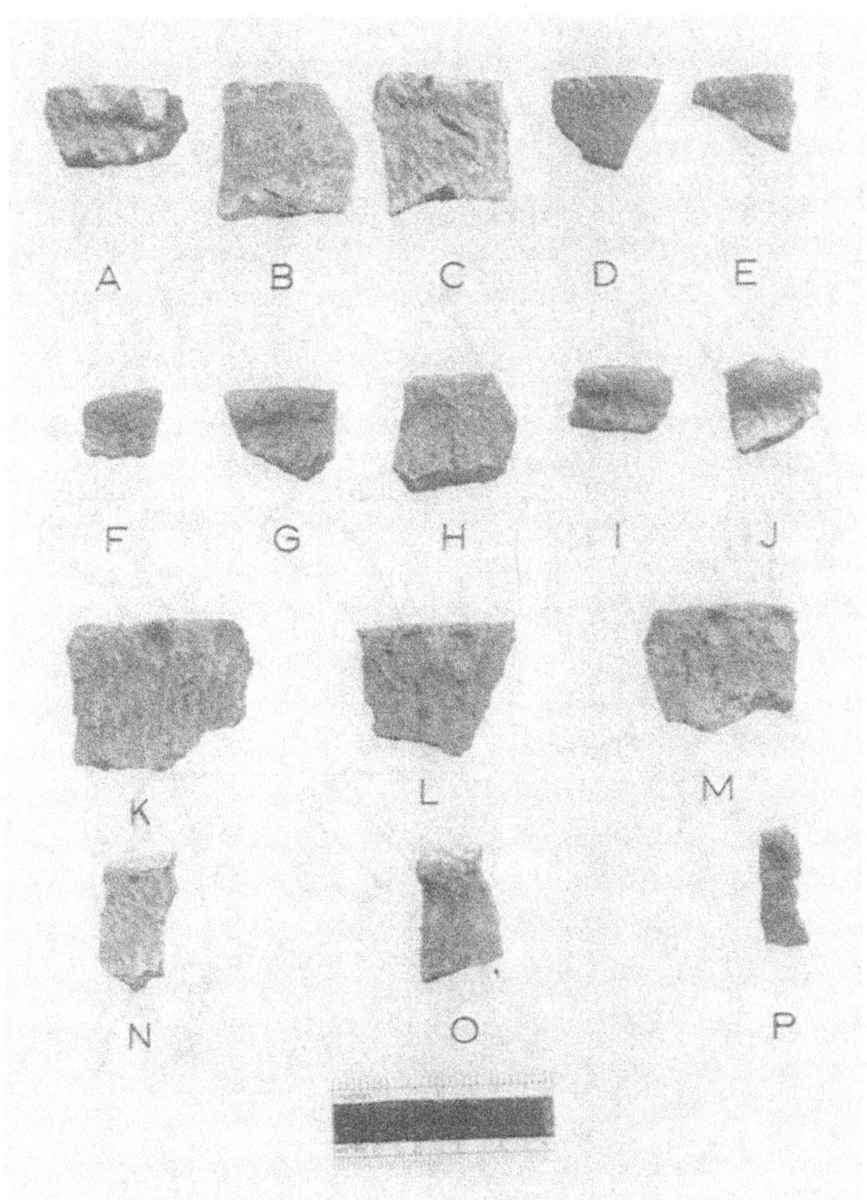

Plate 21. Moccasin Bluff Modified Lip sherds. A-J, group 5; K-P, group 6.

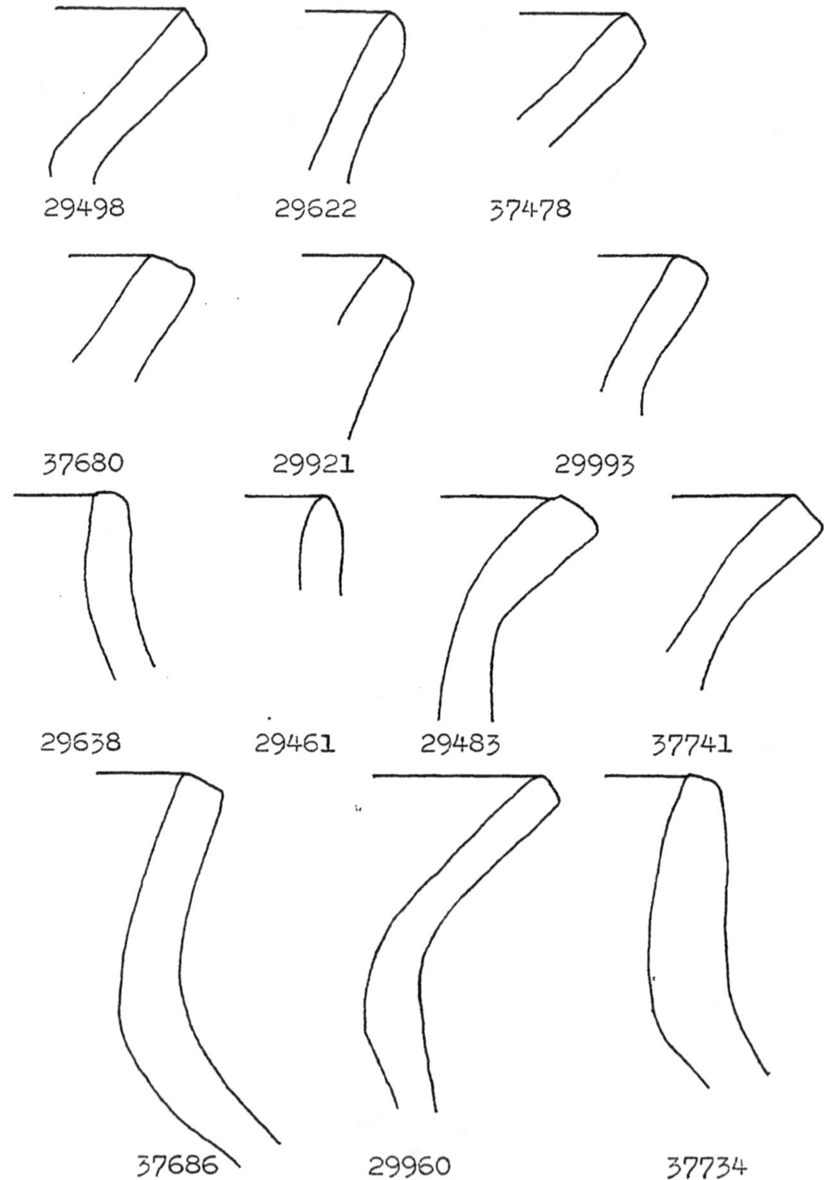

Rim profiles for plate 22.

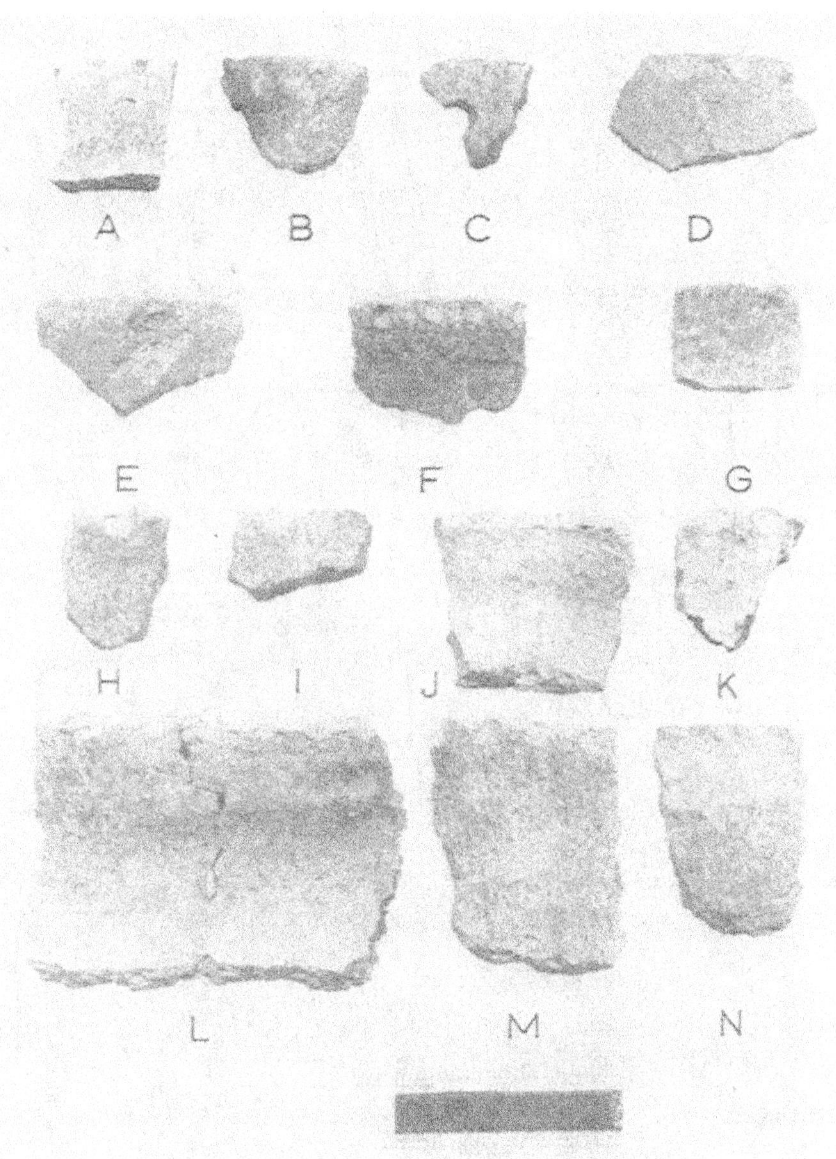

Plate 22. Moccasin Bluff Impressed Exterior Lip sherds, group 1.

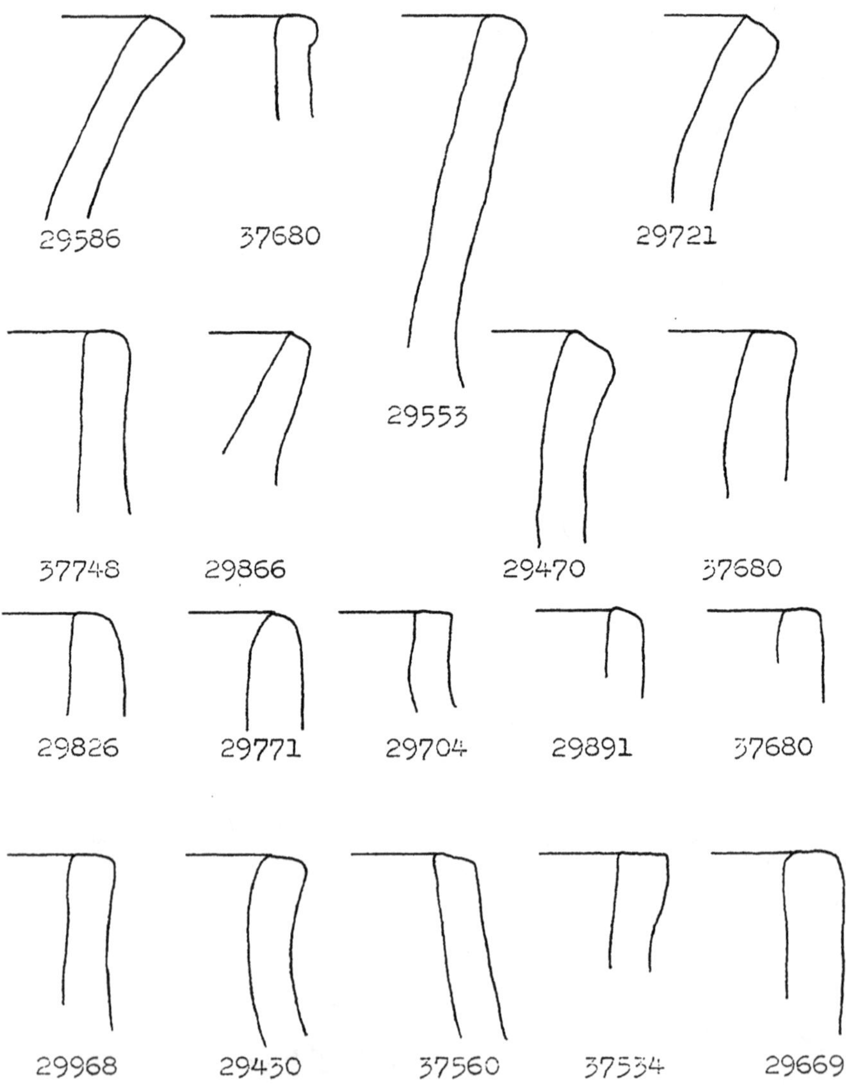

Rim profiles for plate 23.

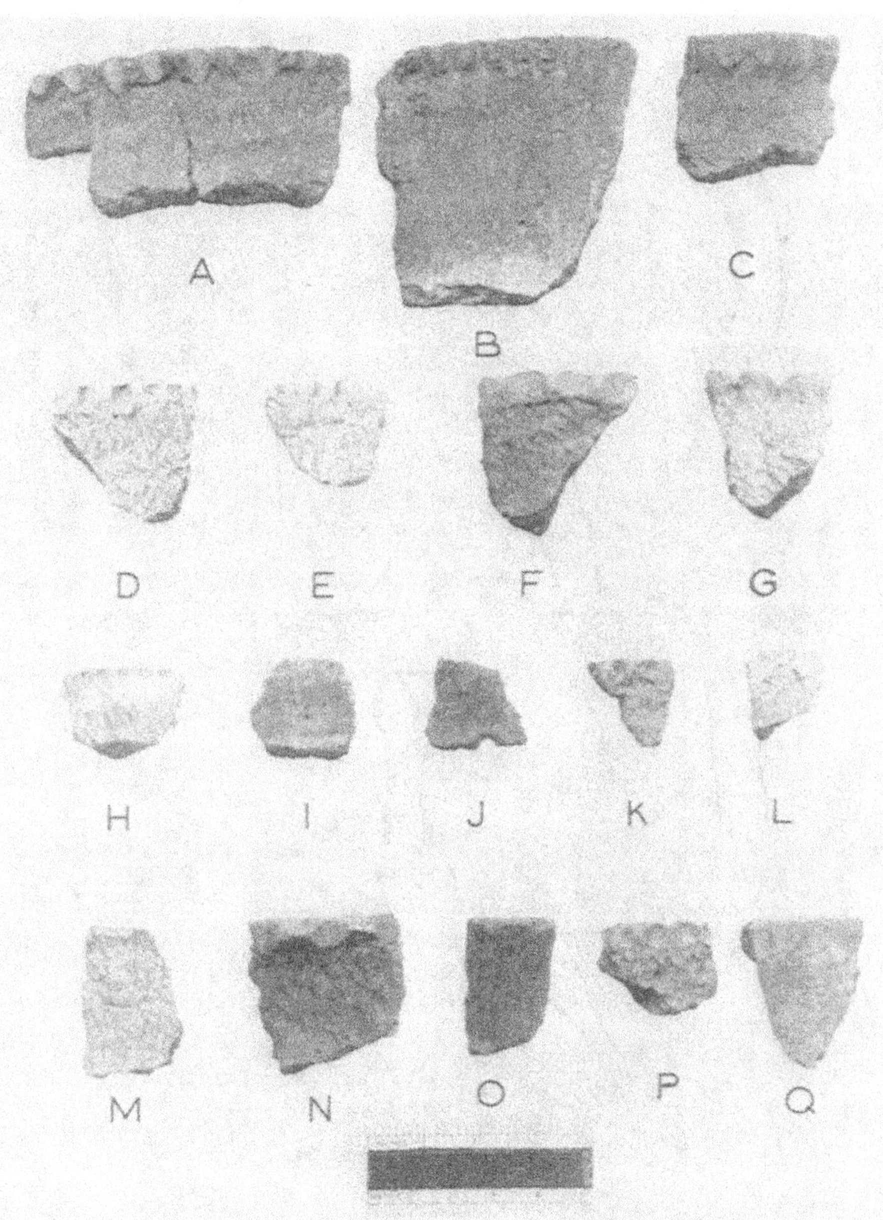

Plate 23. Moccasin Bluff Impressed Exterior Lip sherds, group 1.

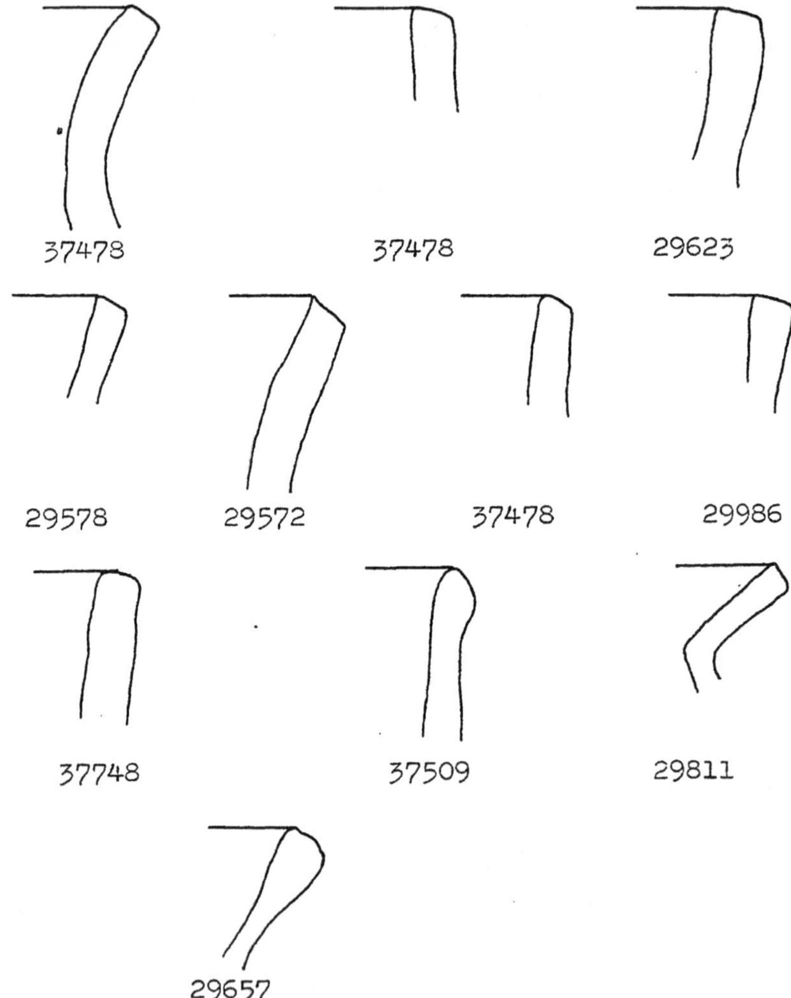

Rim profiles for plate 24.

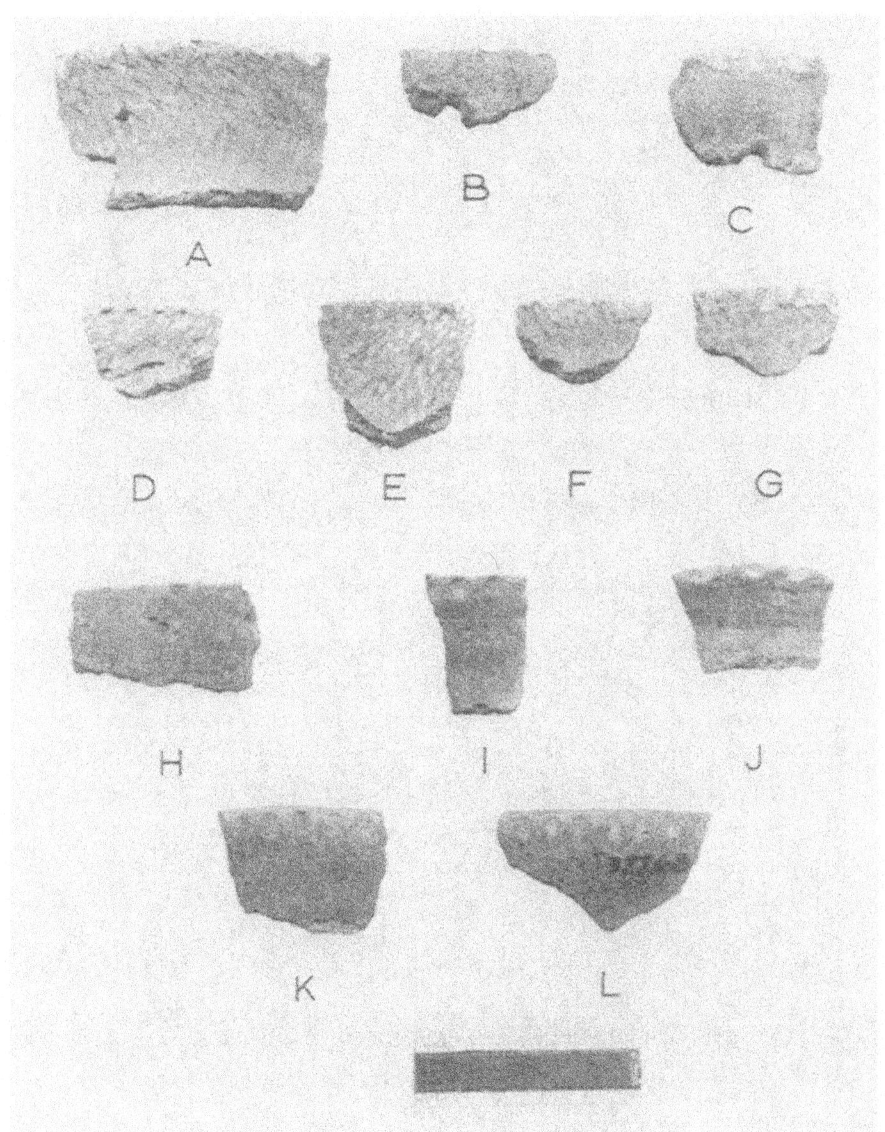

Plate 24. Moccasin Bluff Impressed Exterior Lip sherds. A-G, group 1; H-L, group 2.

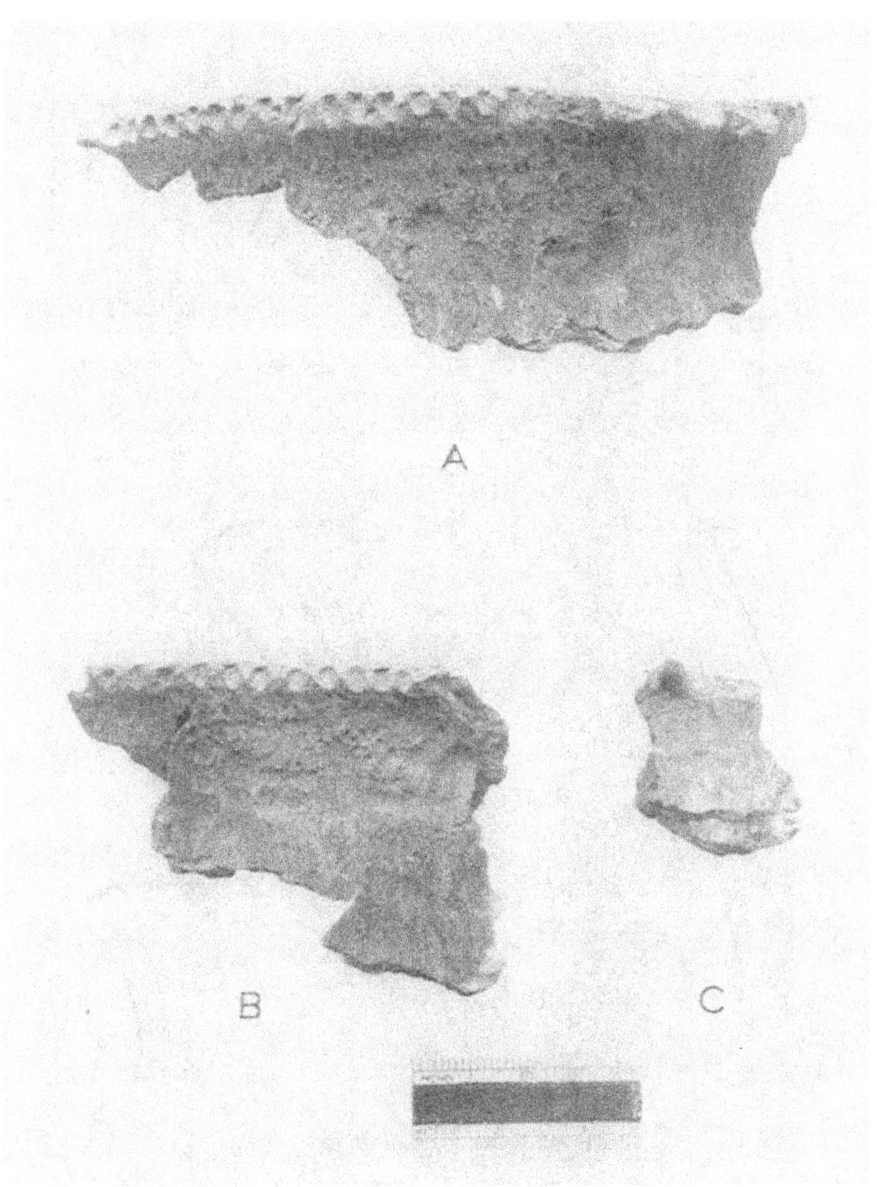

Plate 25. Moccasin Bluff Impressed Exterior Lip sherds, group 1.

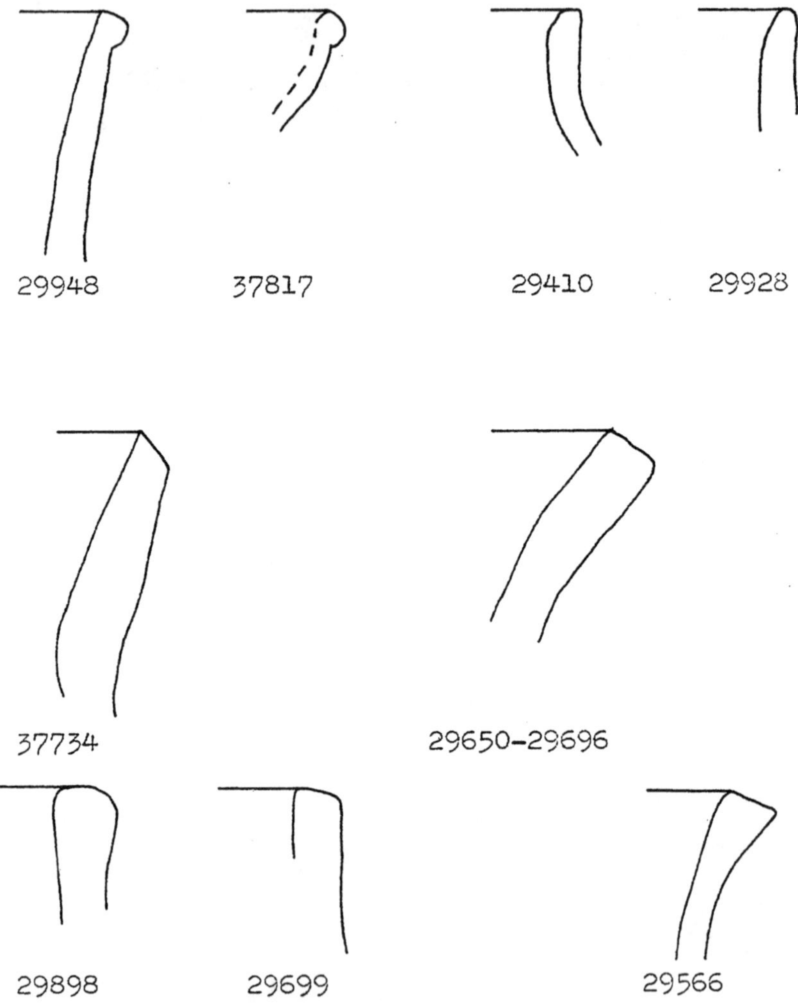

Rim profiles for plate 26.

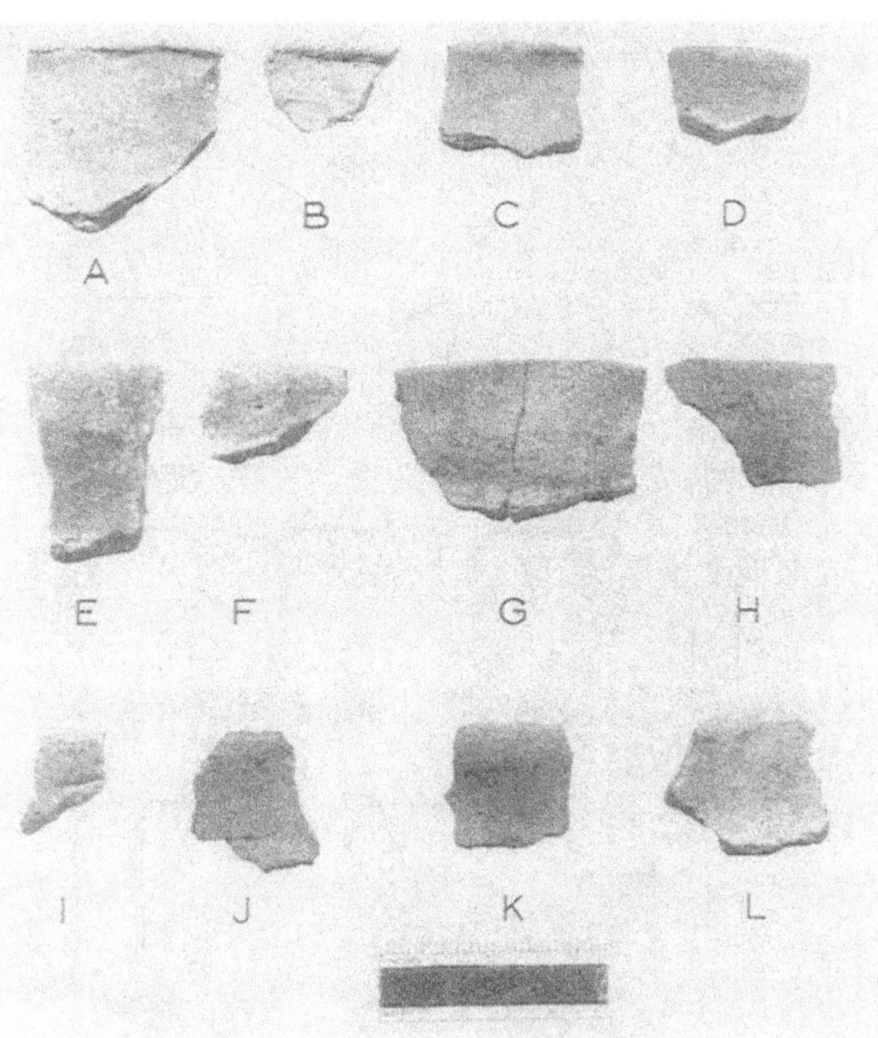

Plate 26. Moccasin Bluff Plain sherds.

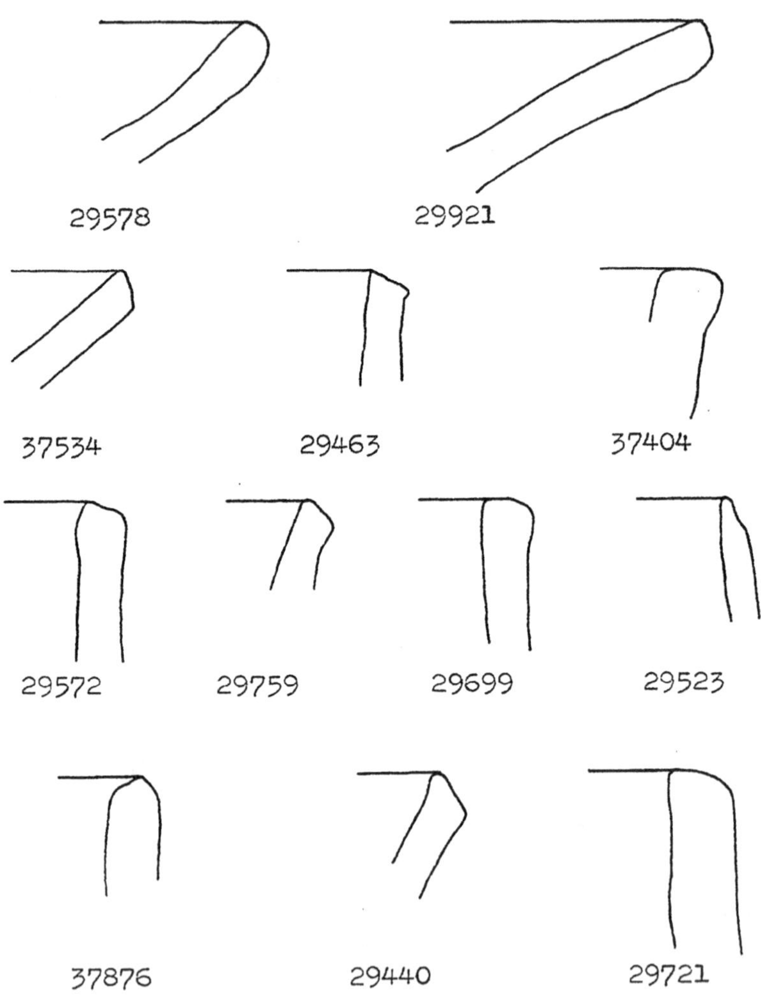

Rim profiles for plate 27.

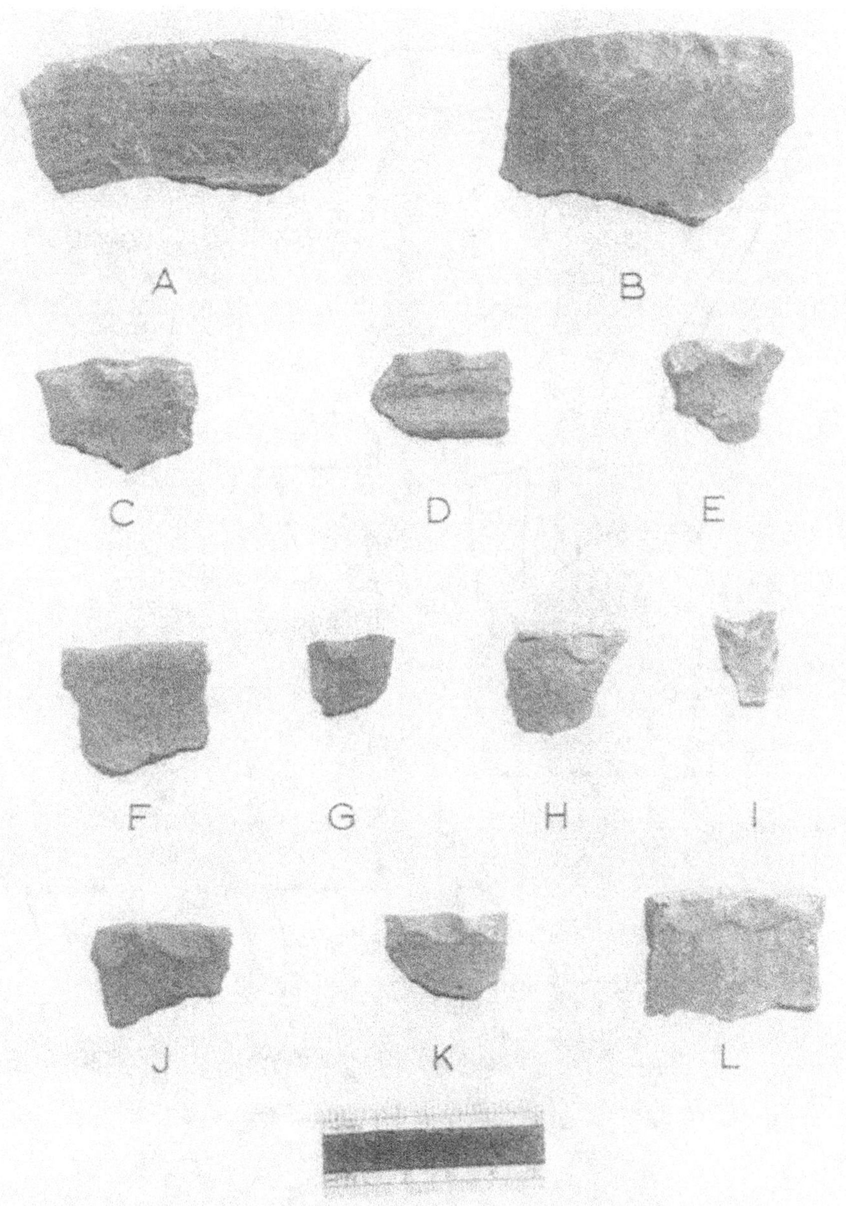

Plate 27. Moccasin Bluff Plain Modified Lip sherds, group 1.

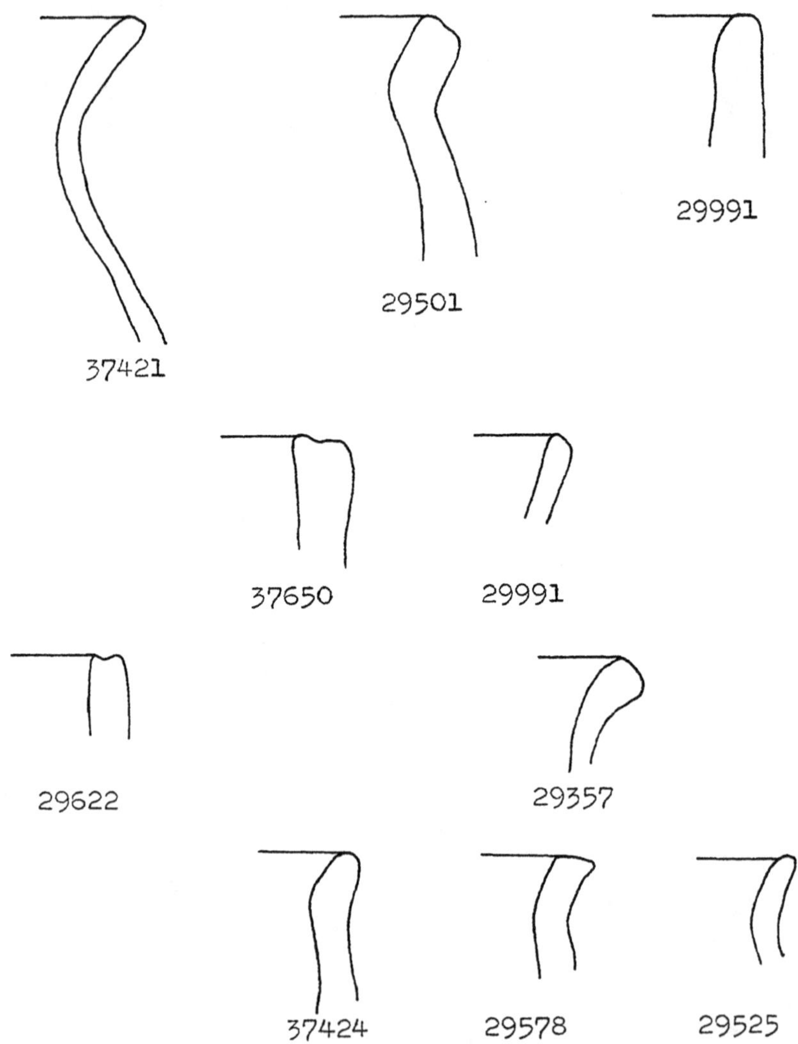

Rim profiles for plate 28.

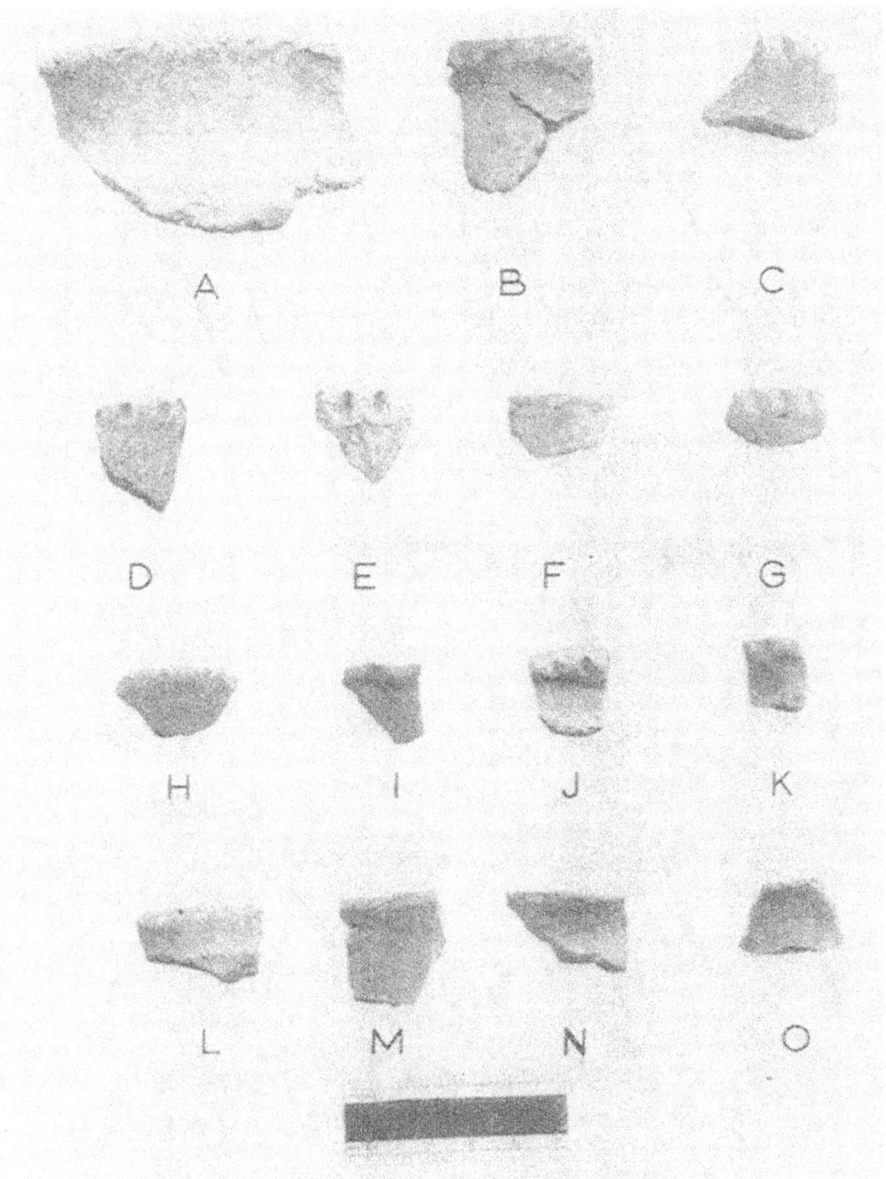

Plate 28. Moccasin Bluff Plain Modified Lip sherds. A-C, group 1; D-K, group 2; L-O, group 3.

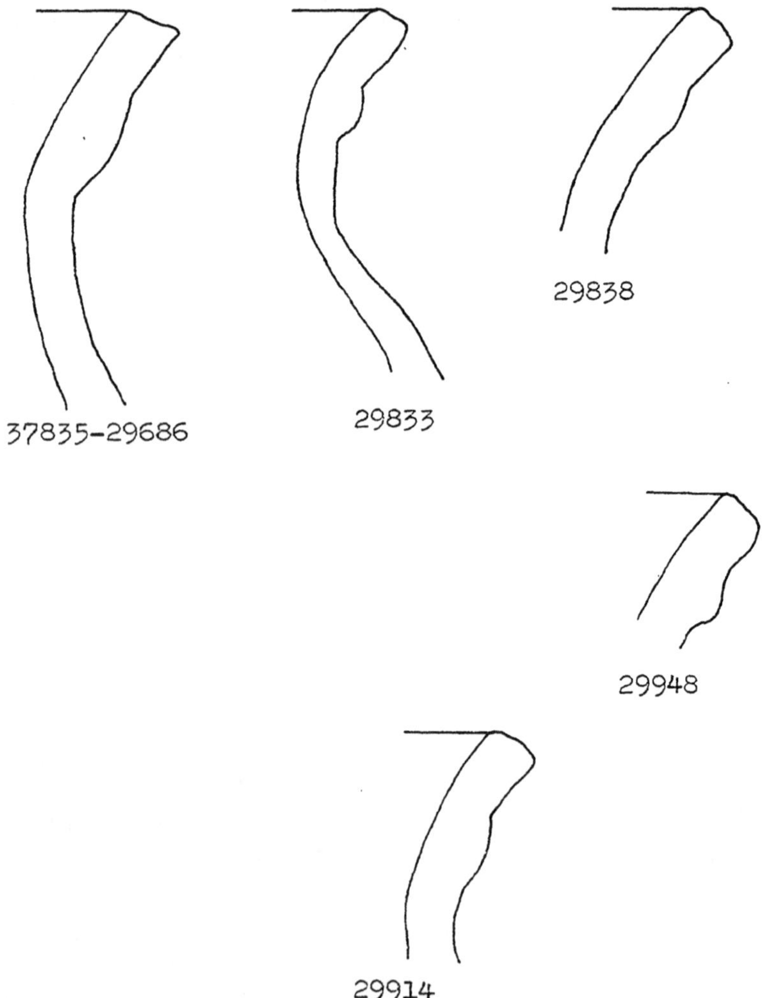

Rim profiles for plate 29.

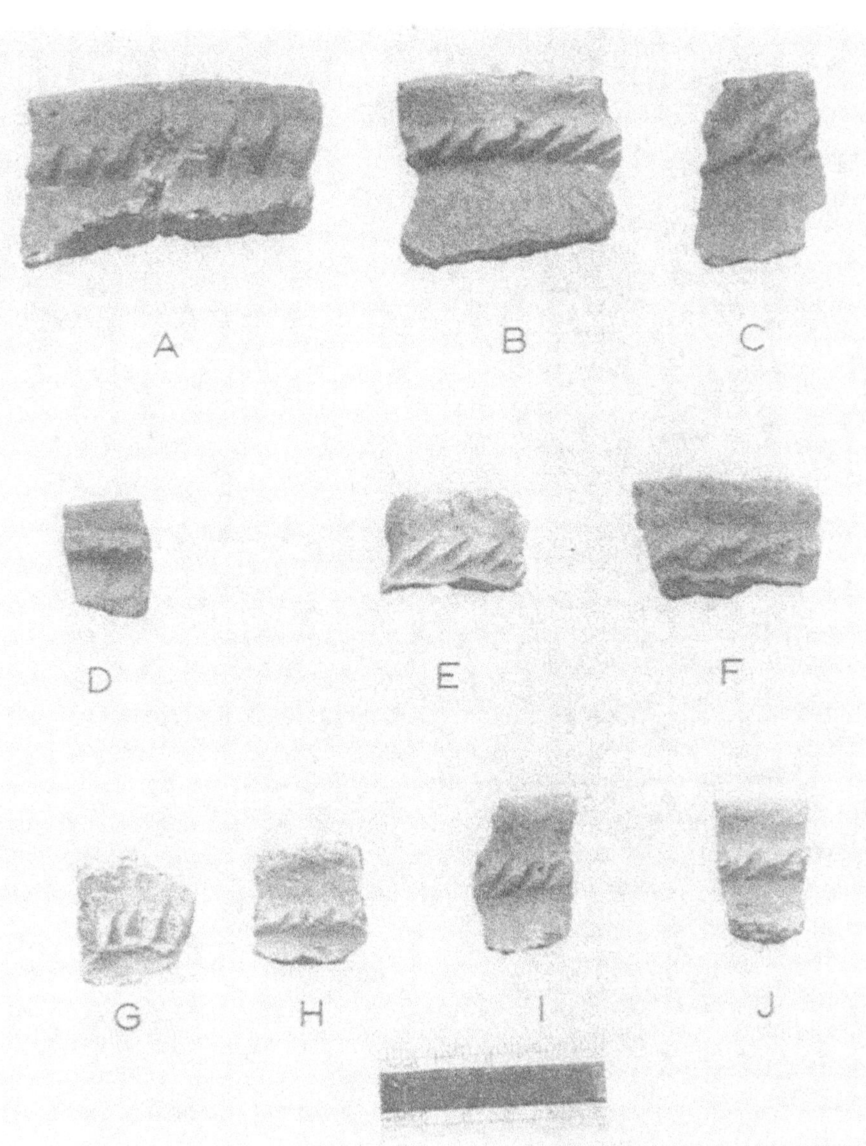

Plate 29. Moccasin Bluff Notched Applique Strip sherds.

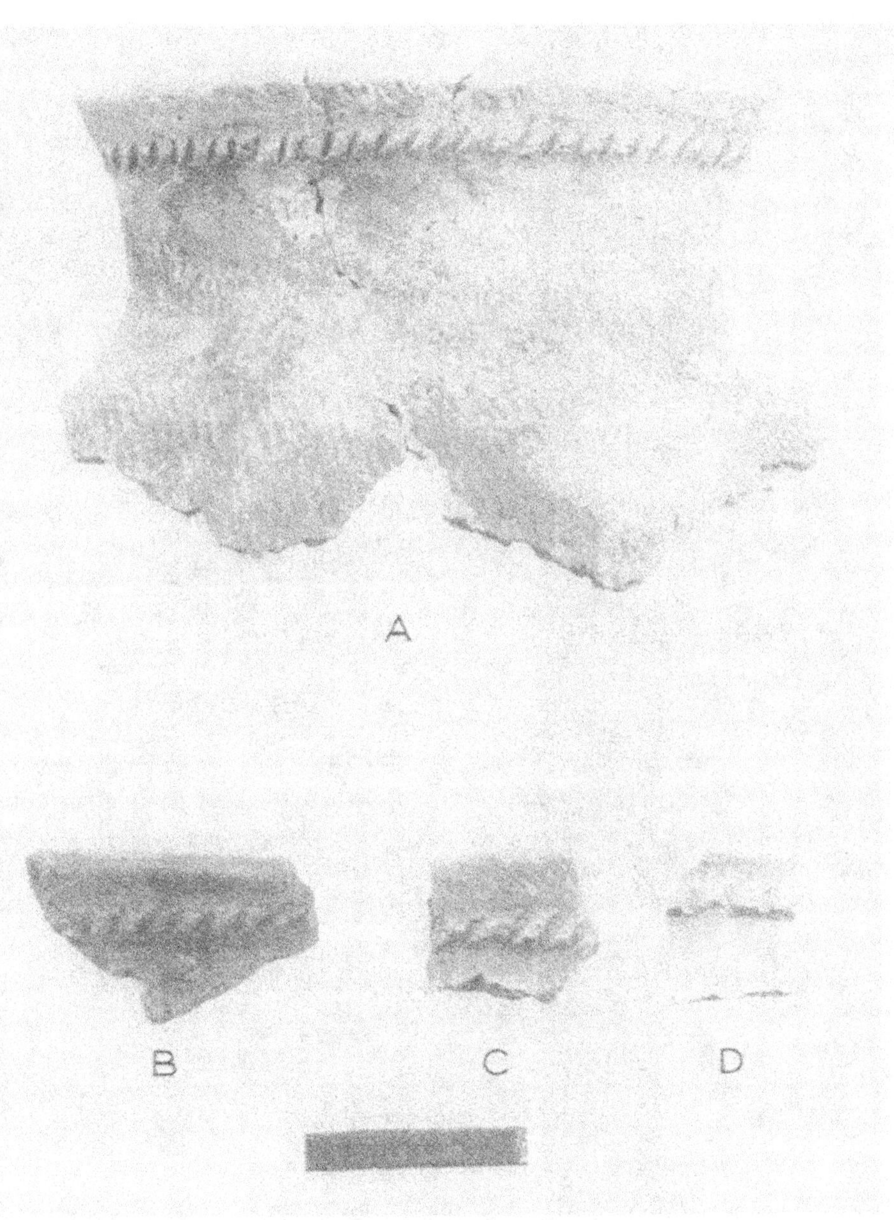

Plate 30. Moccasin Bluff Notched Applique Strip sherds.

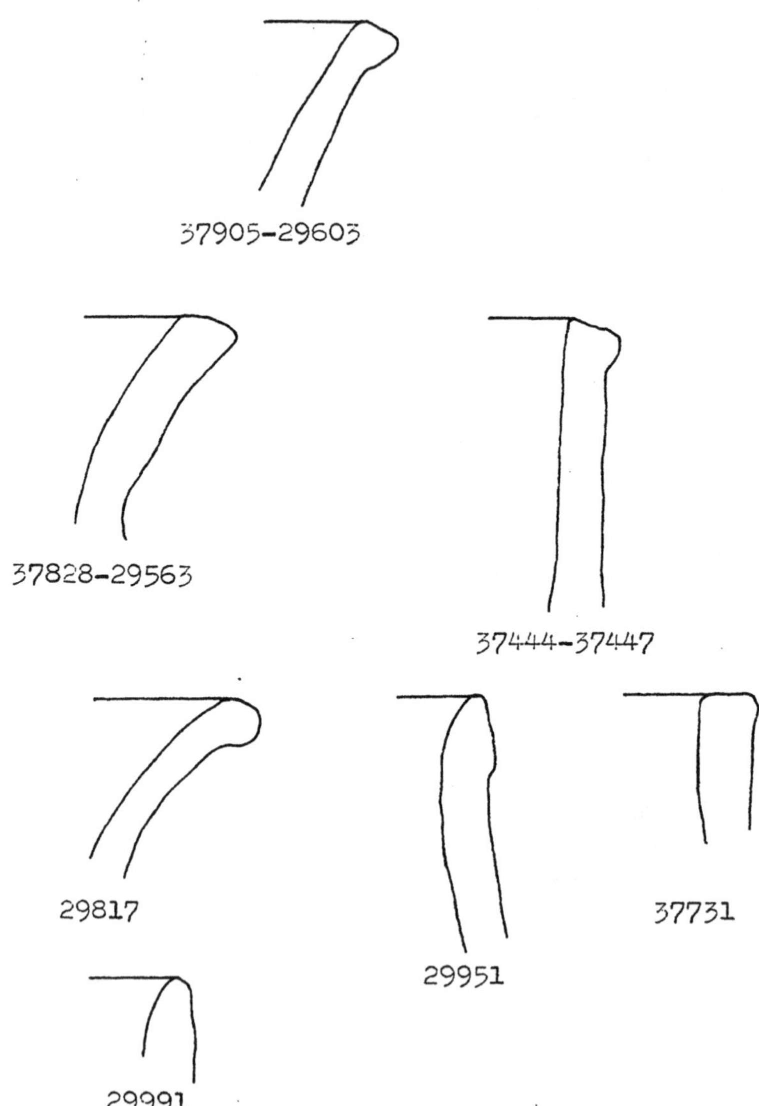

Rim profiles for plate 31.

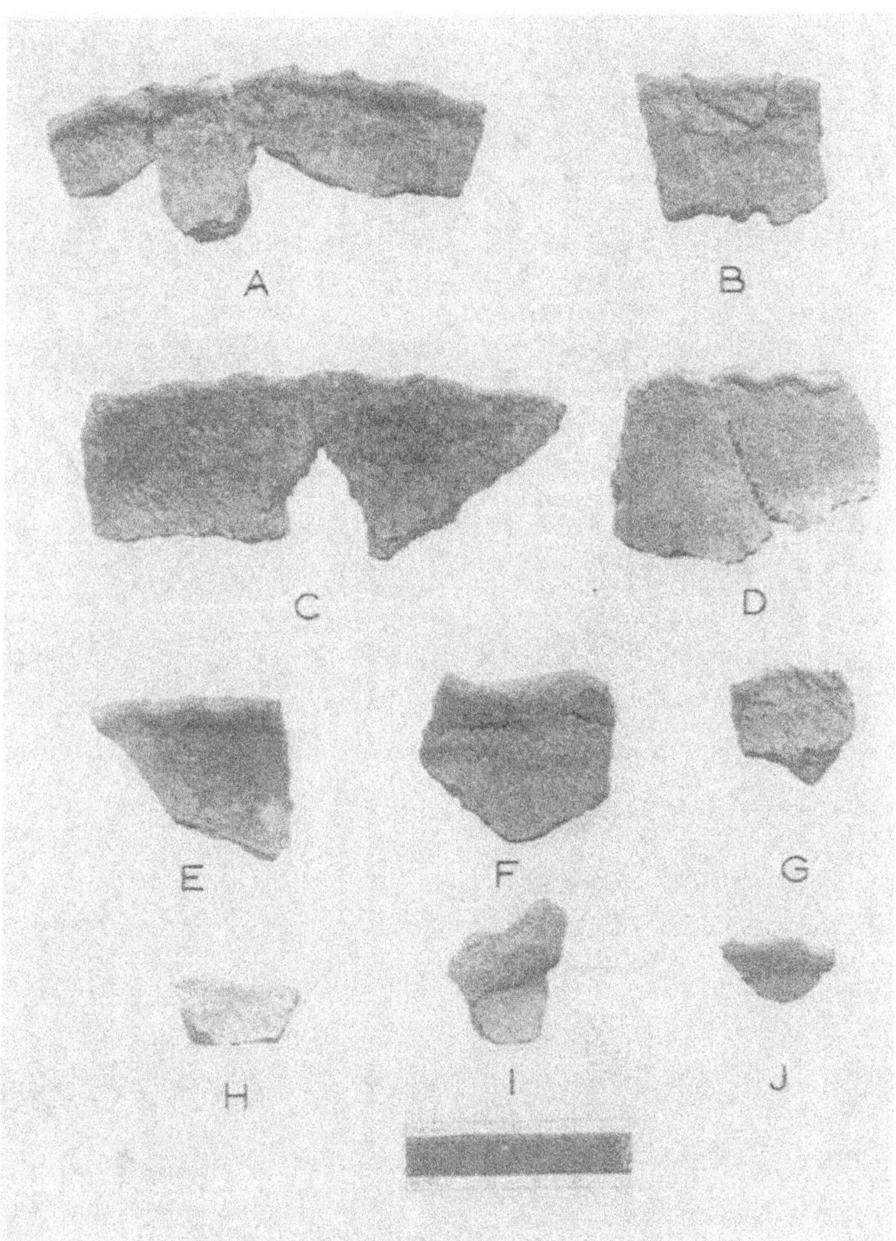

Plate 31. Moccasin Bluff Scalloped sherds.

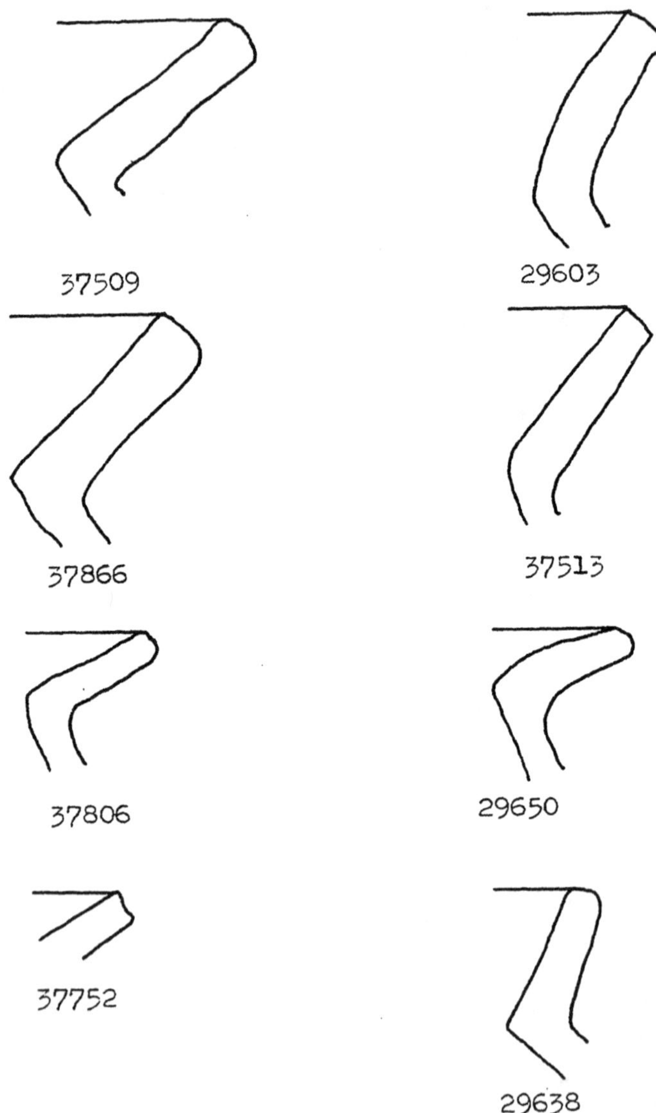

Rim profiles for plate 32.

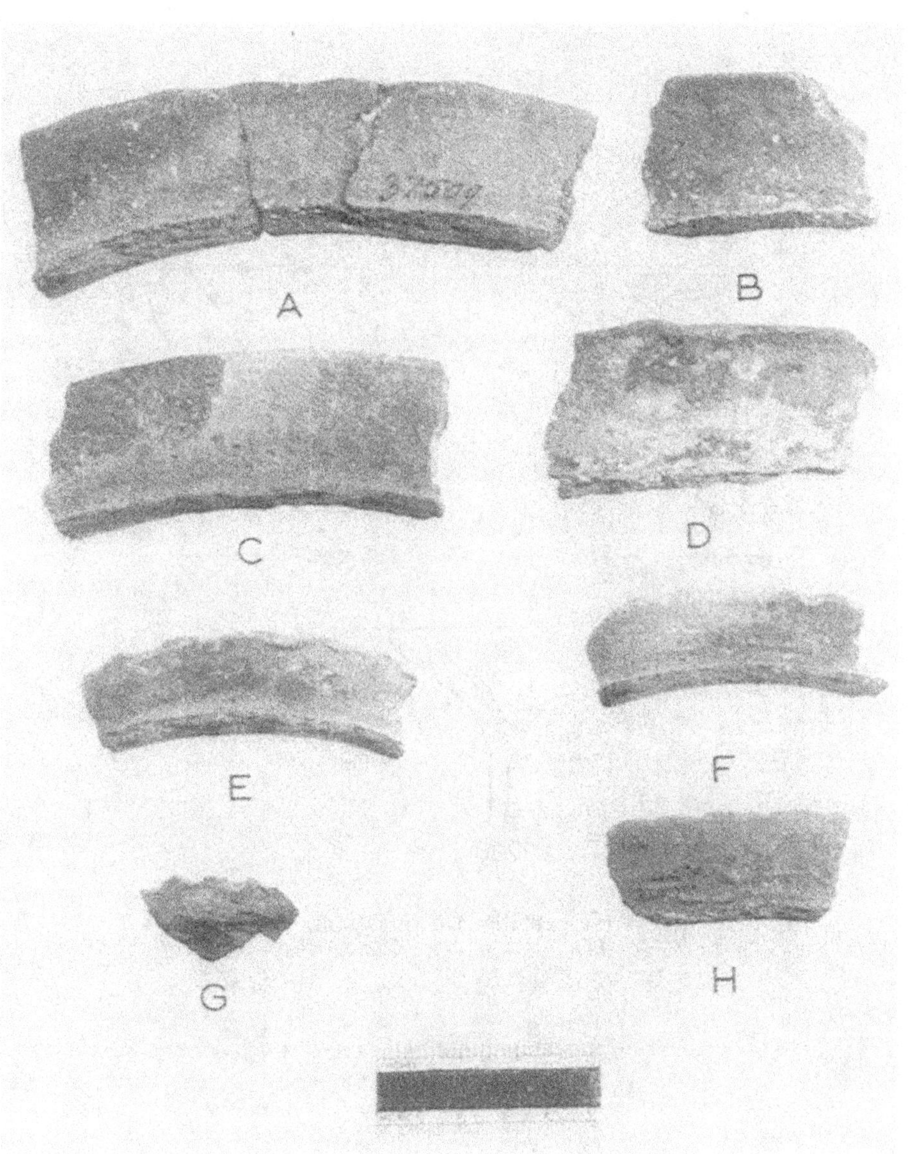

Plate 32. Berrien Ware sherds. A-D, group 1; E-H, group 2.

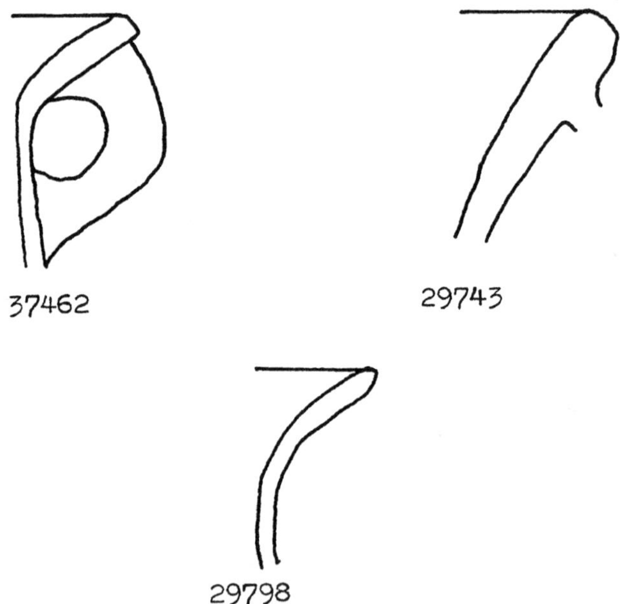

Rim profiles for plate 33.

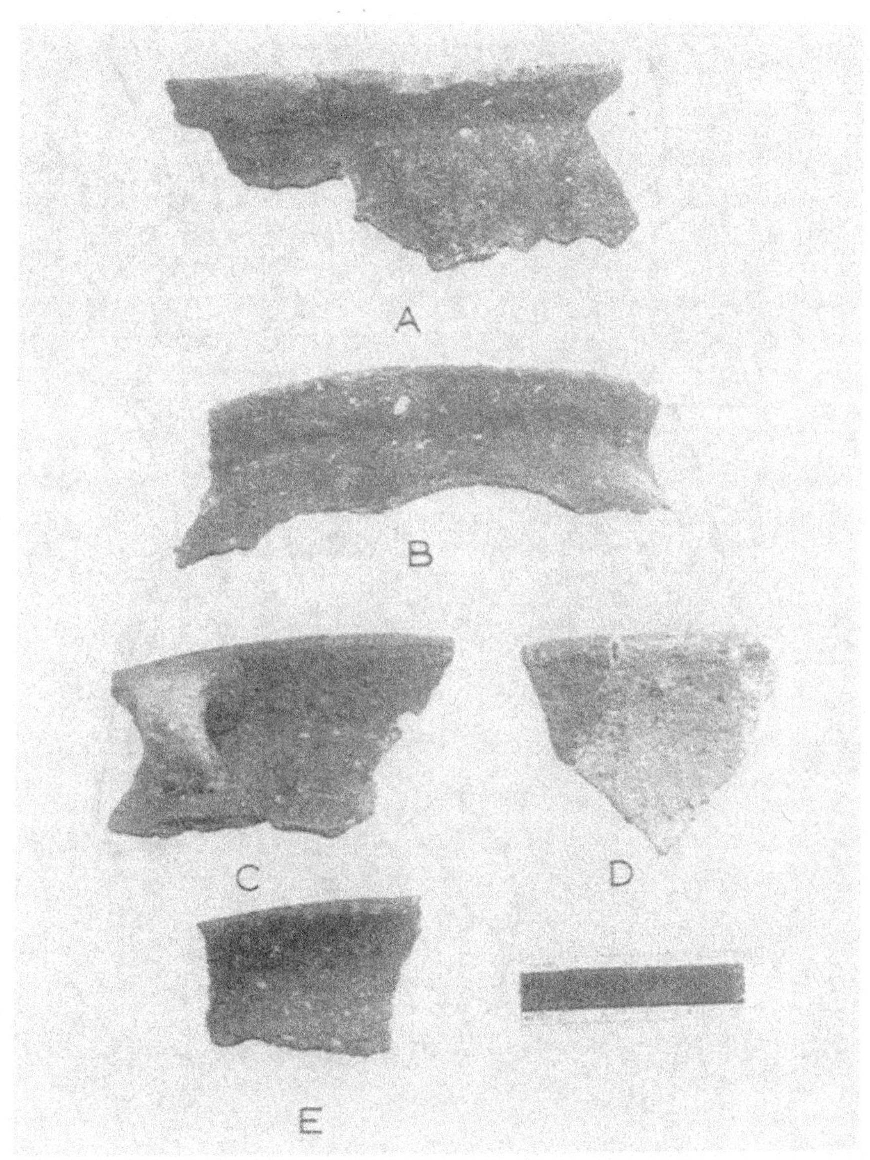

Plate 33. Berrien Ware sherds. A-B, group 2 (parts of the same vessel); C-E, group 3.

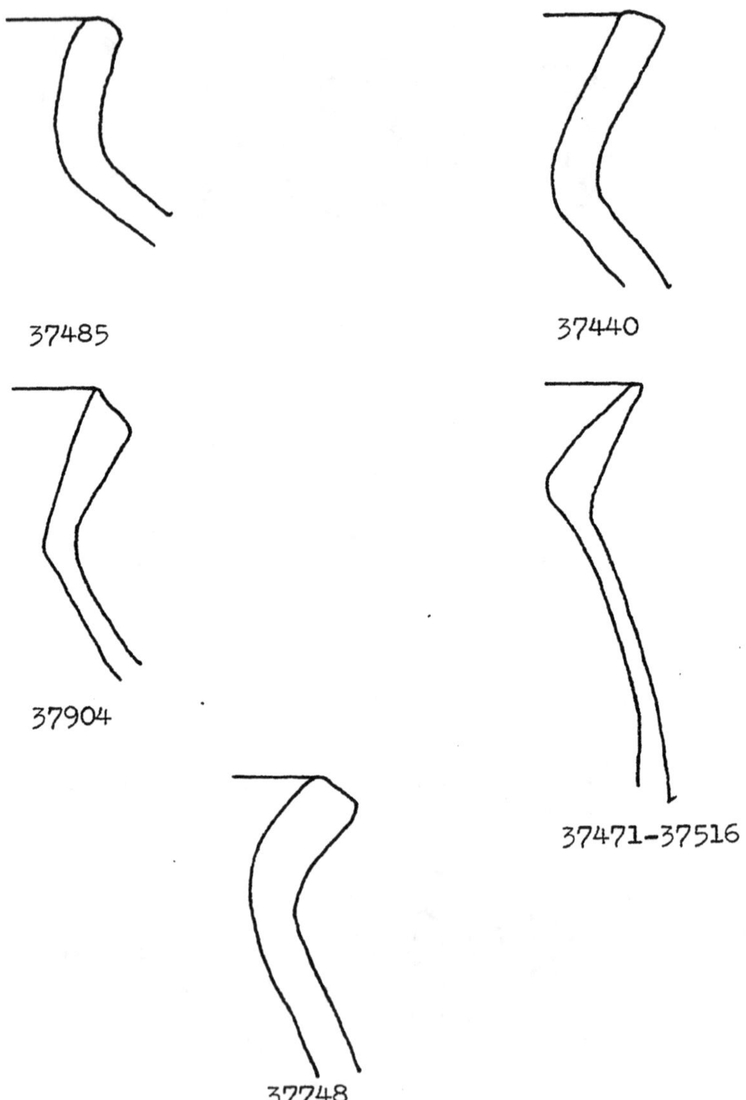

Rim profiles for plate 34.

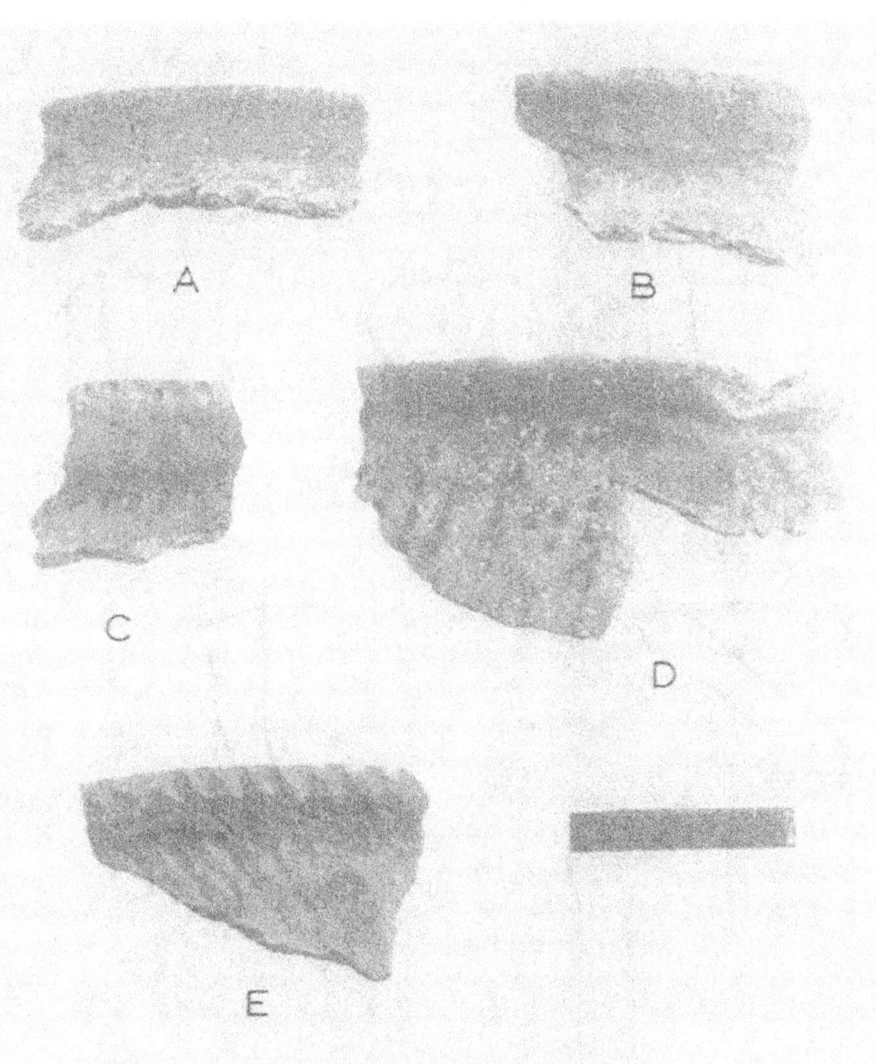

Plate 34. Berrien Ware sherds, group 4.

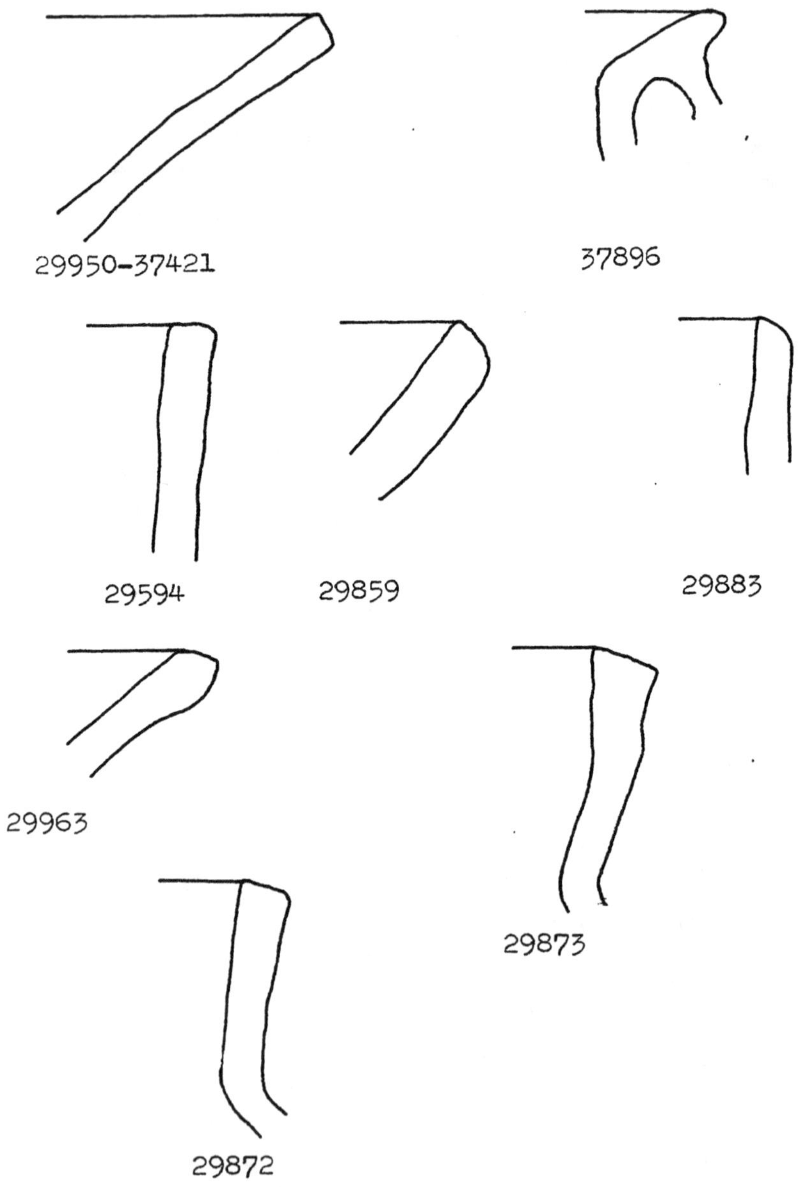

Rim profiles for plate 35.

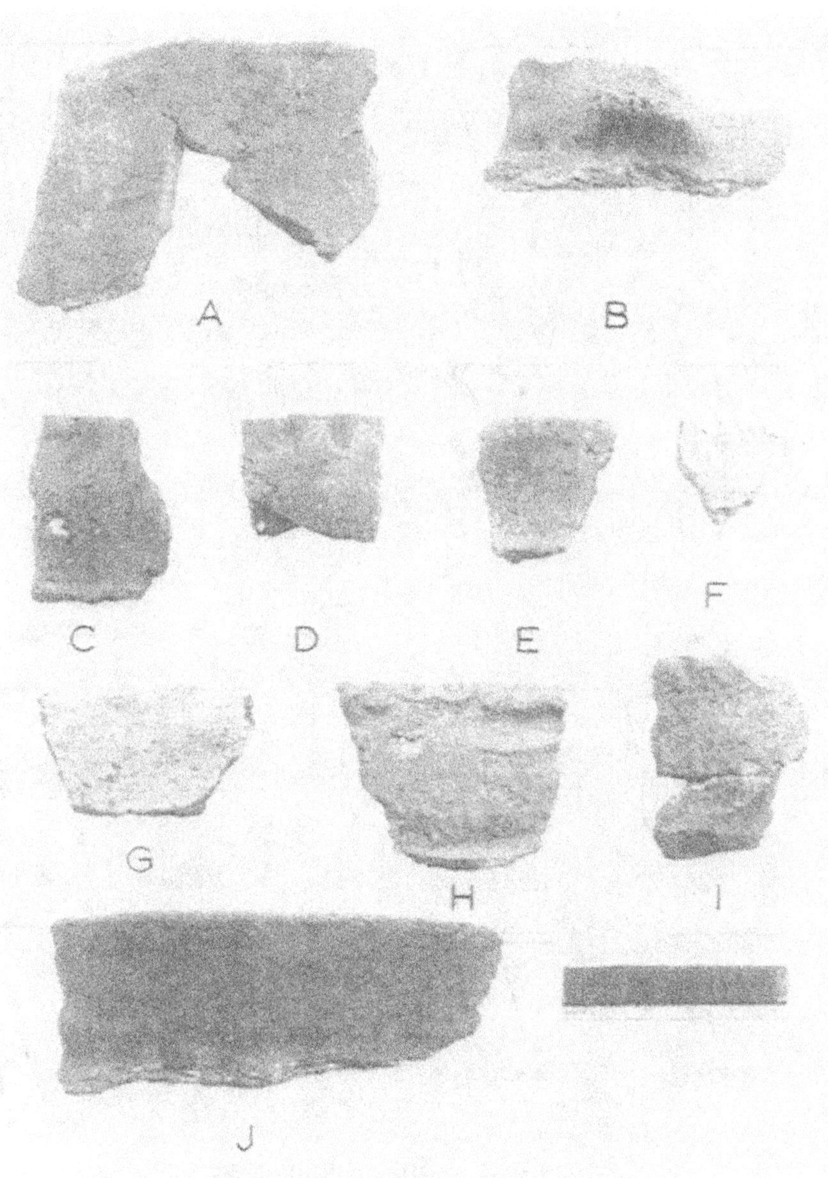

Plate 35. Berrien Ware sherds, group 5.

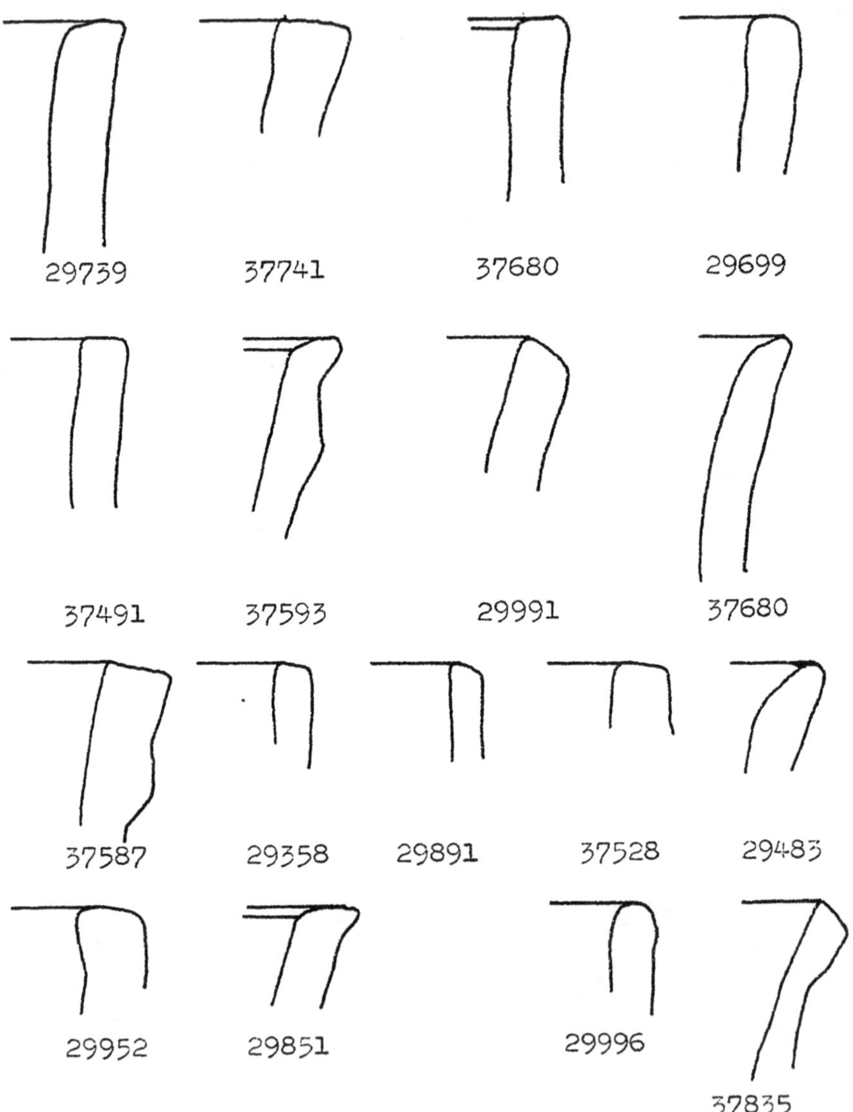

Rim profiles for plate 36.

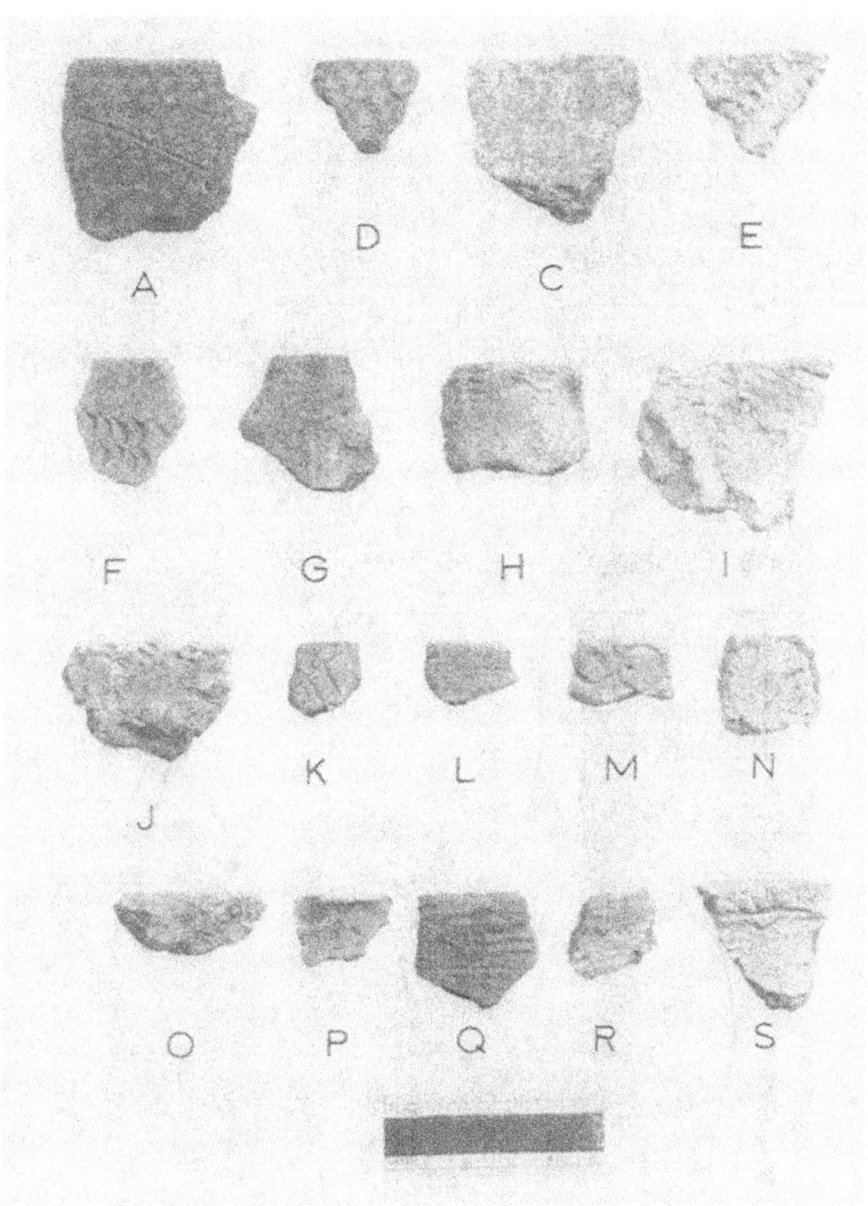

Plate 36. Middle Woodland rim sherds: C (interior of rim notched), H (interior cordmarked), M (interior punctates).

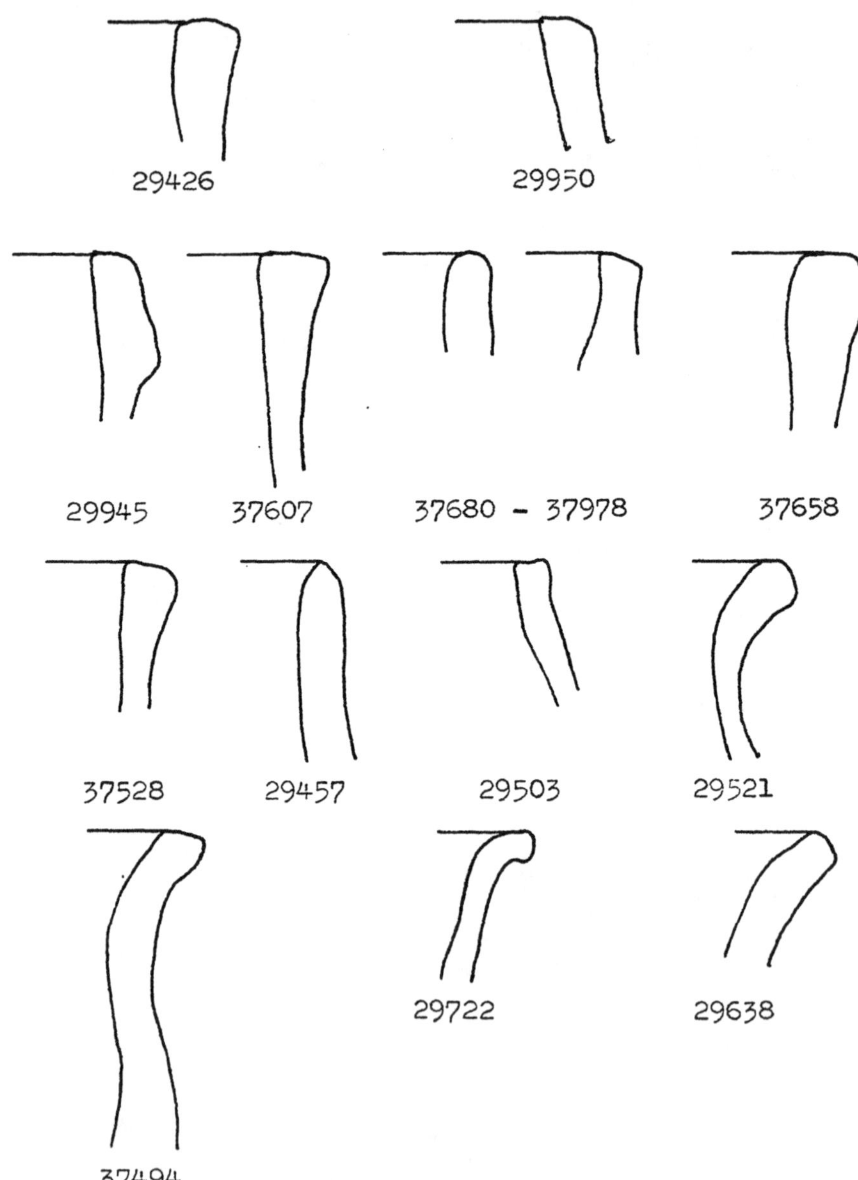

Rim profiles for plate 37.

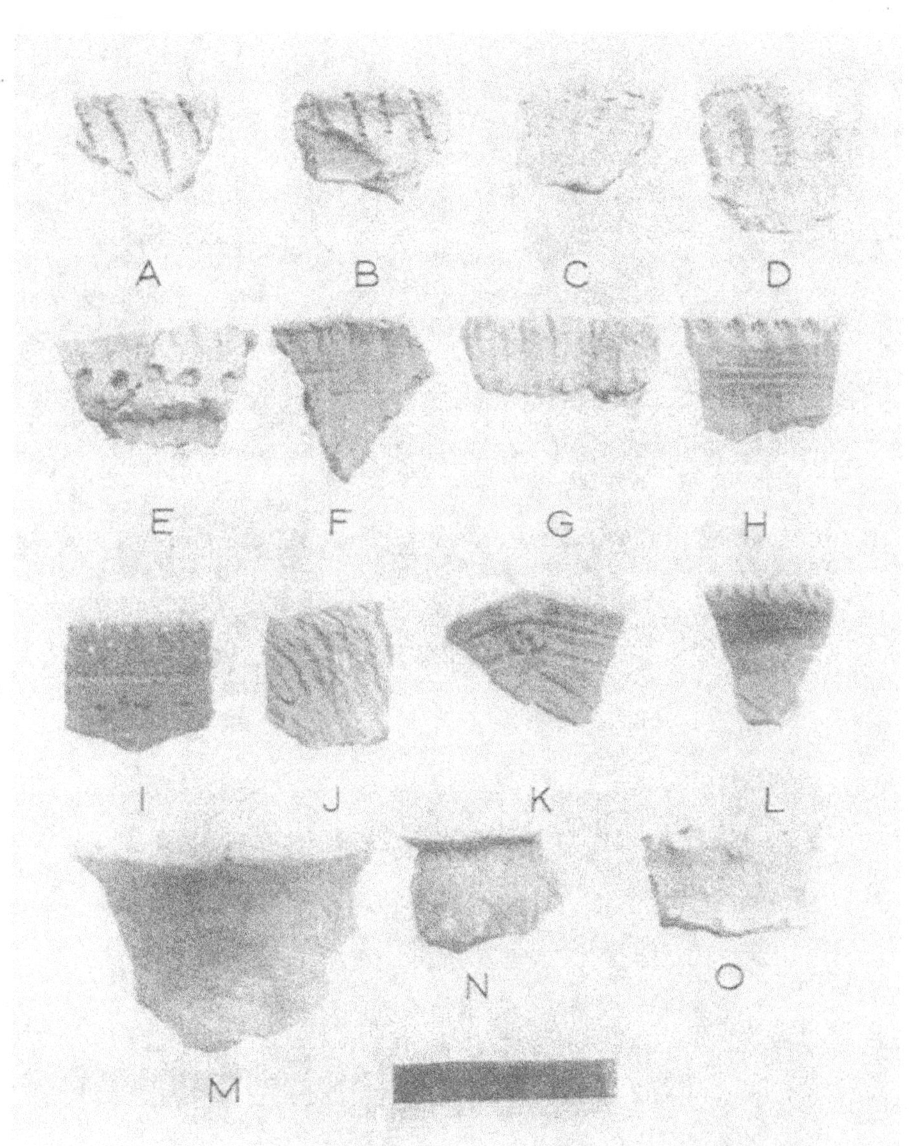

Plate 37. Miscellaneous rim sherds: C, D, and I are shell tempered; all others are grip tempered.

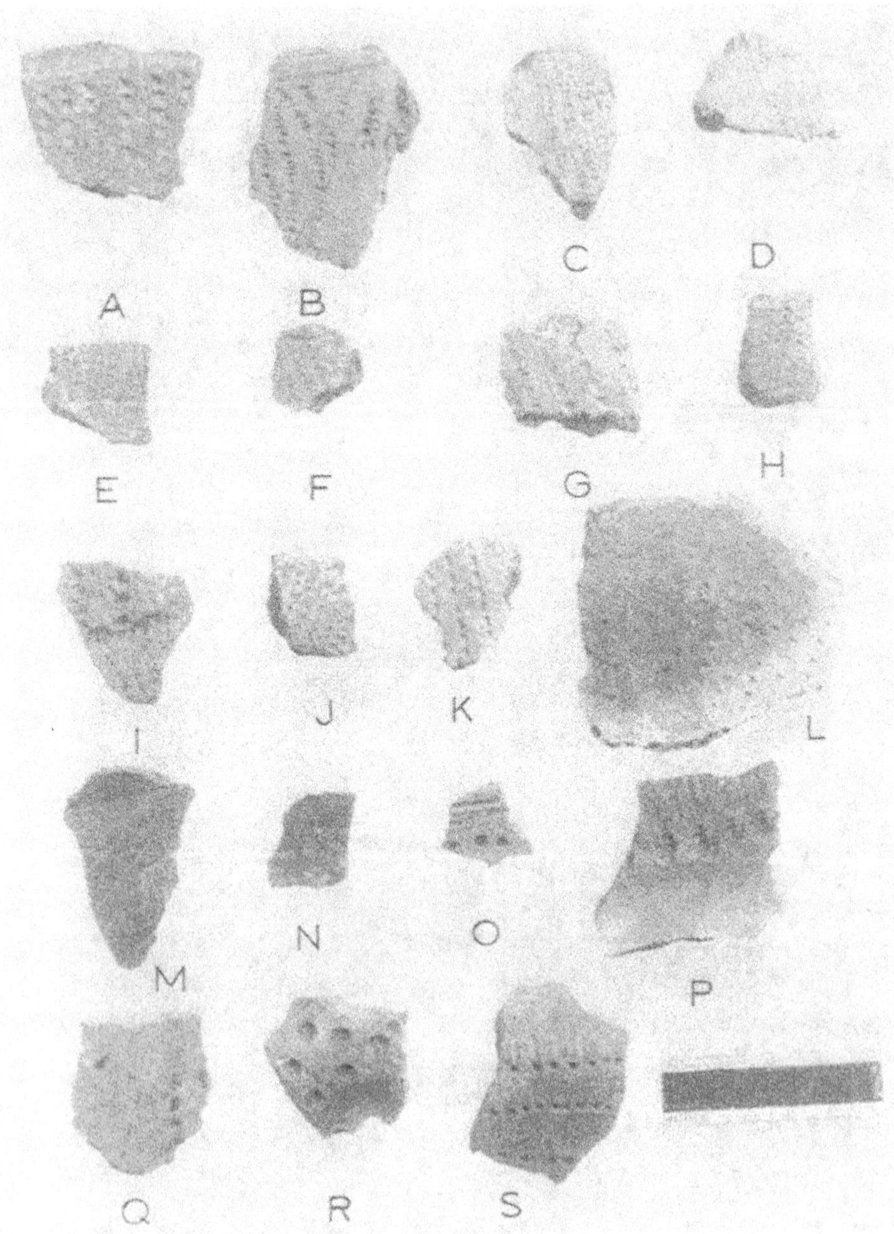

Plate 38. Miscellaneous body sherds.

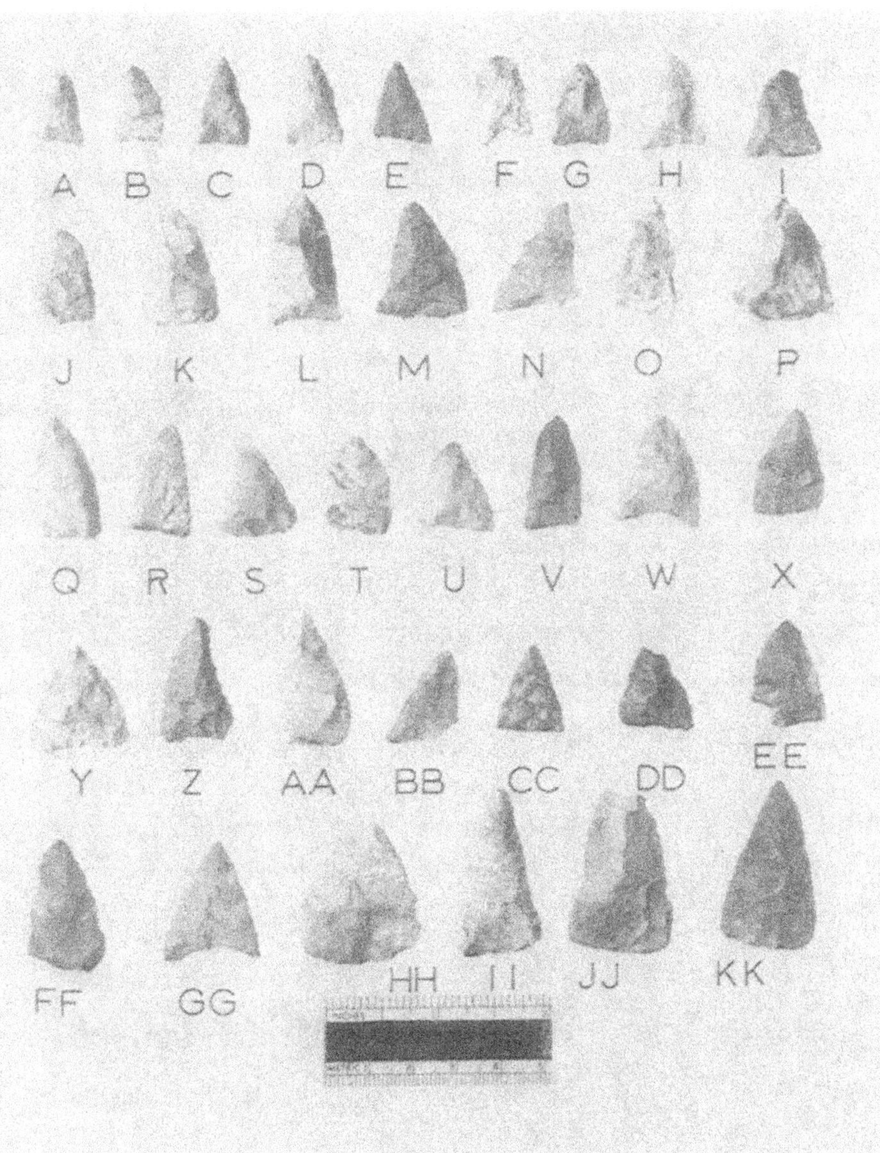

Plate 39. Triangular points.

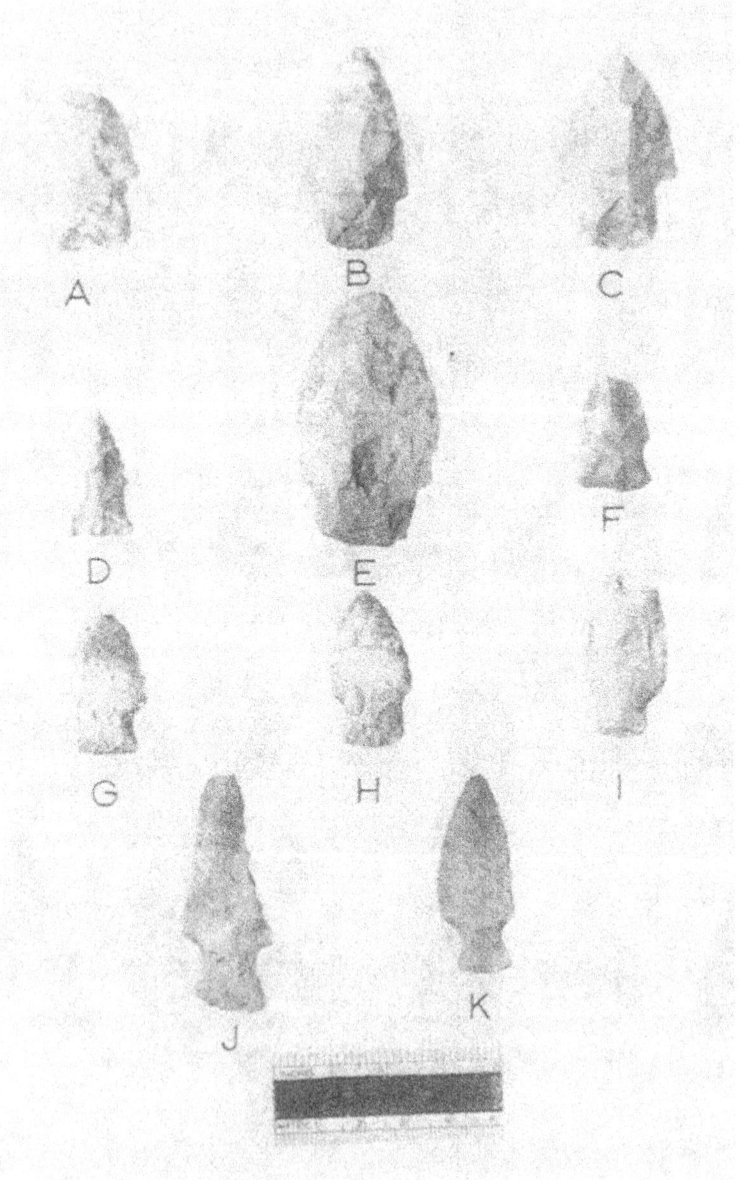

Plate 40. Stemmed points: A-C and E, large stemmed; D and F, expanding stemmed; G-I, small stemmed; J and K, Dustin-like points.

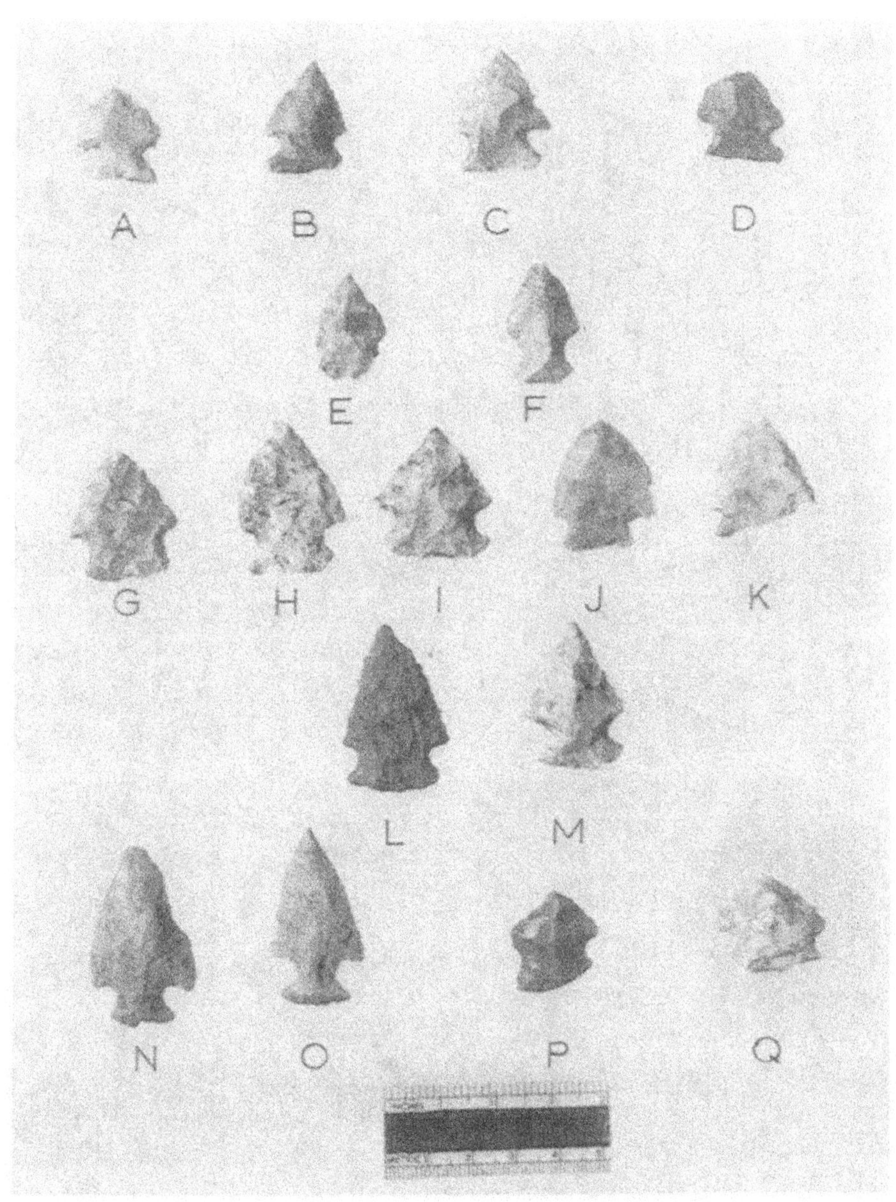

Plate 41. Notched points: A-C, group A; E-F, group B; G-K, group C; L-M, group D; N-O, group E; P-Q, group F.

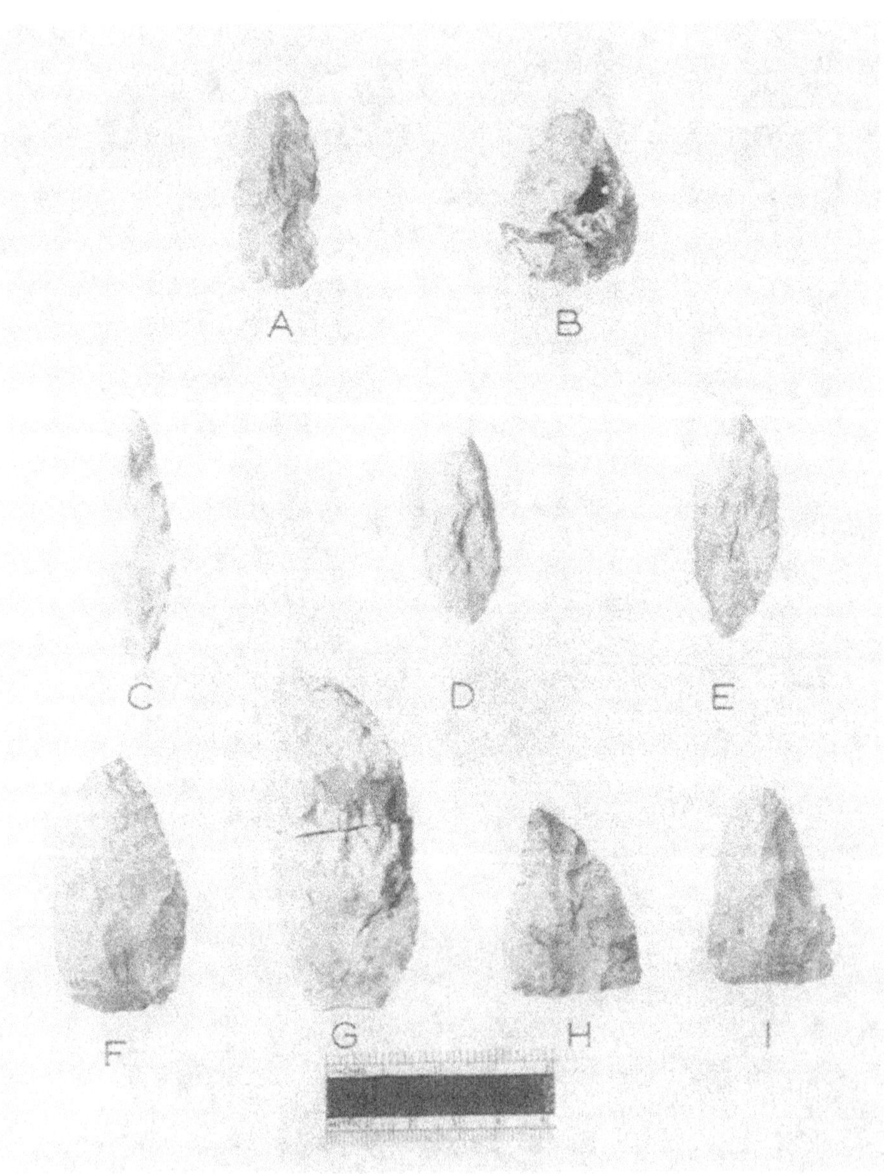

Plate 42. Bifaces: A-B, F-I bifaces (knives?); C-E, ovate bifaces.

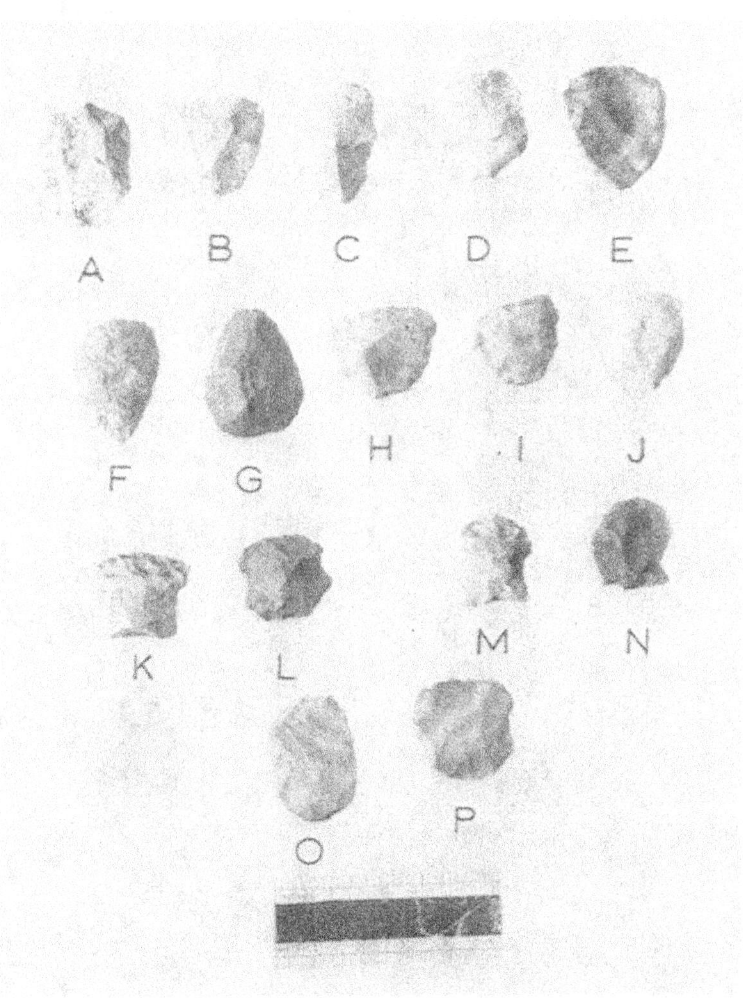

Plate 43. Scrapers: A-J, end scrapers; K-N, hafted scrapers; O-P, miscellaneous.

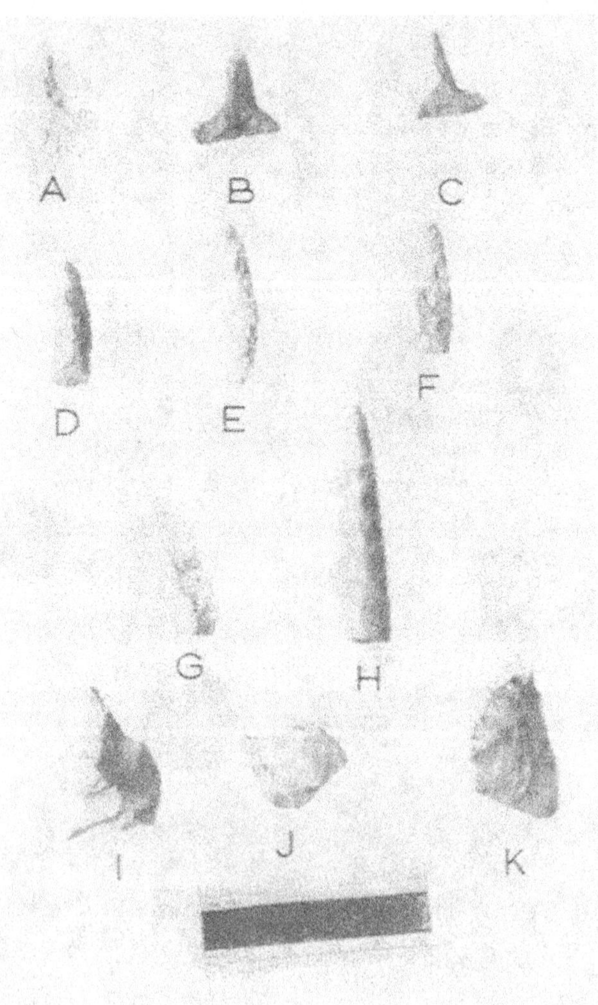

Plate 44. Drills and gravers: A-C, small T-shaped drills; D-E, ovate drills; G-H, fragments of large T-shaped drills; I-K, gravers.

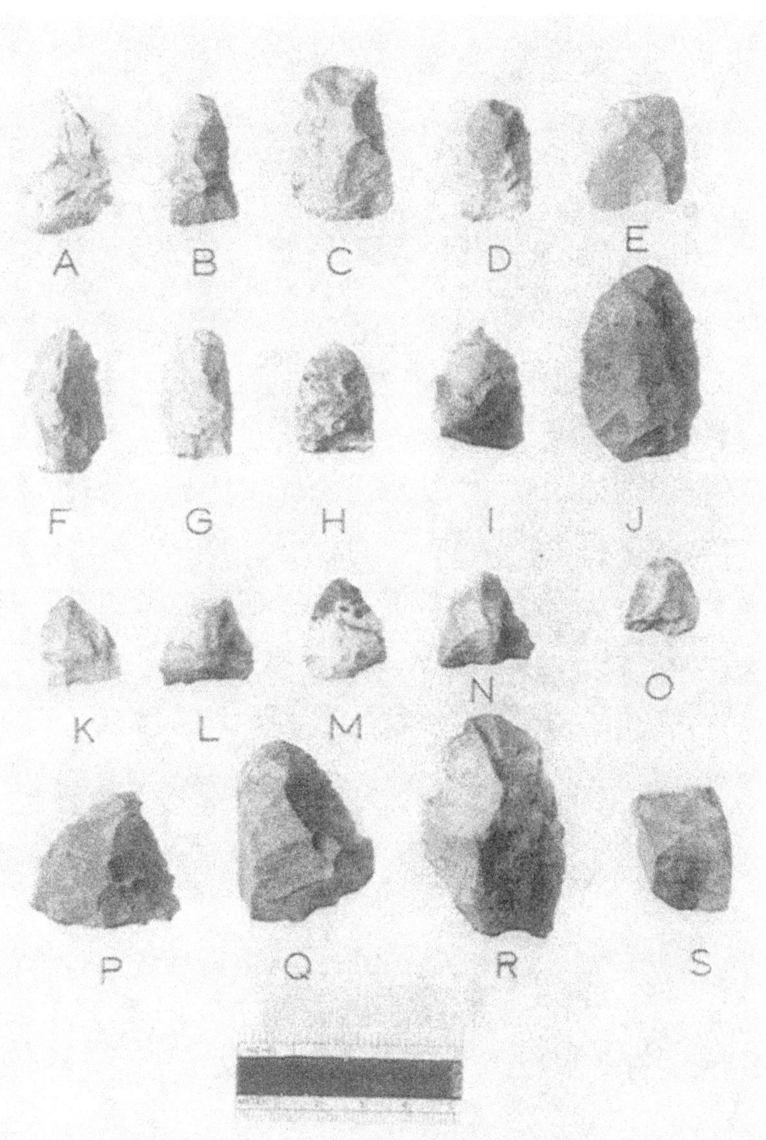

Plate 45. Small, thick, steep-edge pieces: A-O, small, thick, steep-edge pieces; P-S, heavy tools.

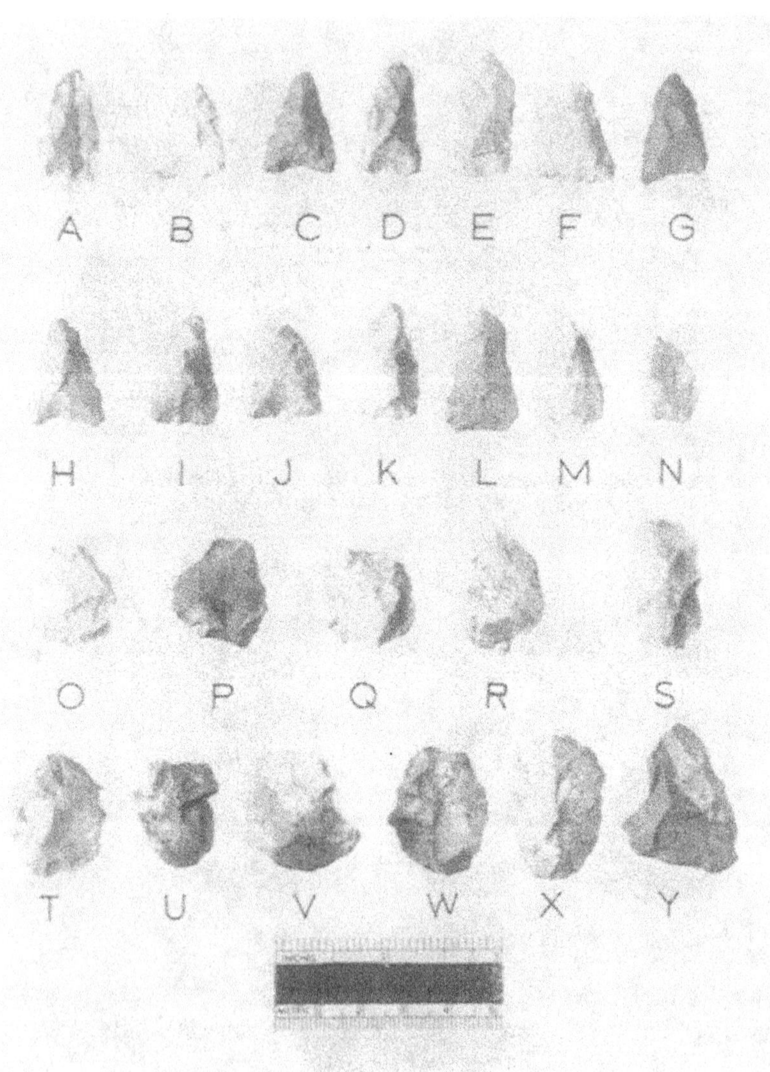

Plate 46. Group of points and small, thick, steep-edge pieces from pit 92: A-N, small, triangular points; O-Y, small, thick, steep-edge pieces.

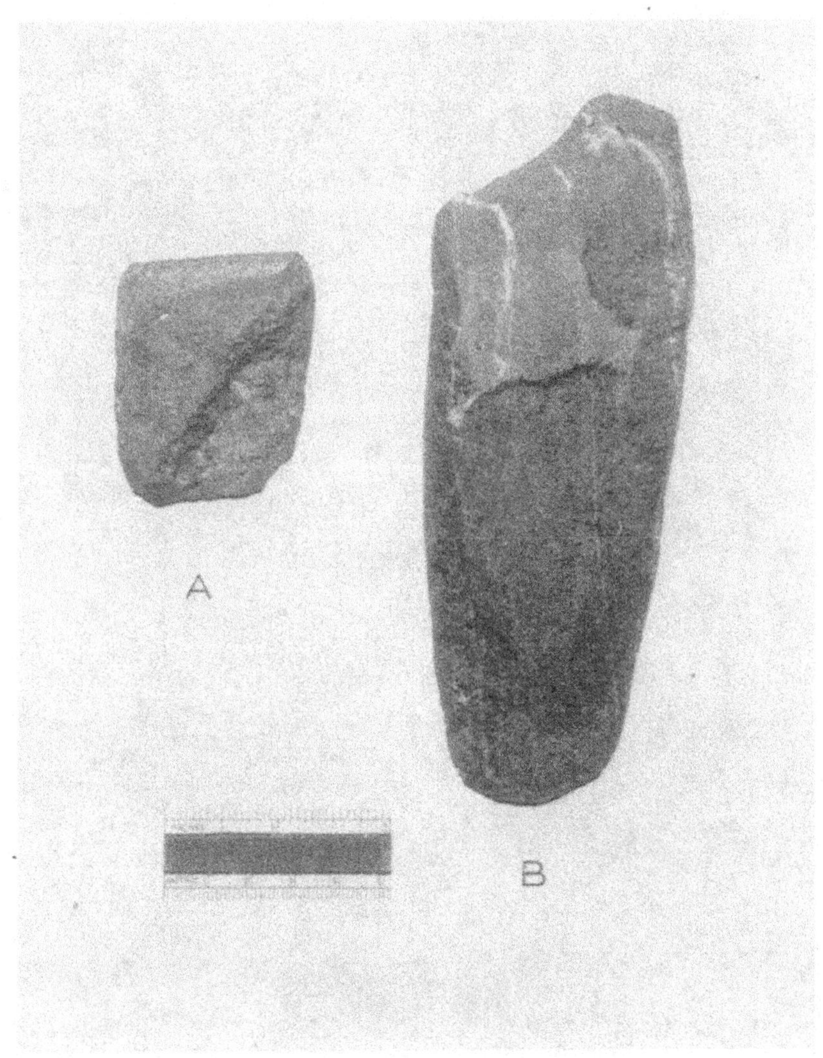

Plate 47. Stone celts.

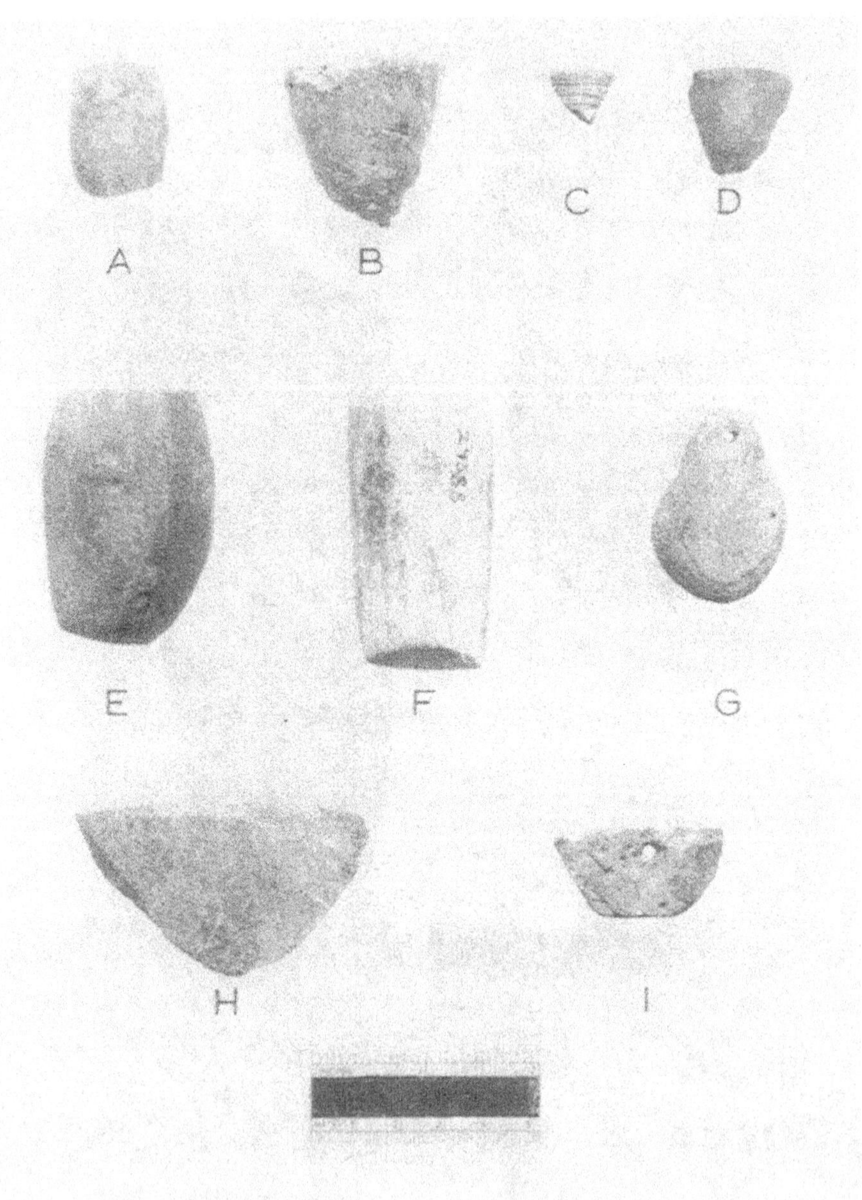

Plate 48. Pipes and ground stone: A-D, pipes; E-F, unfinished block pipes; G-I, pendants; H, argillite.

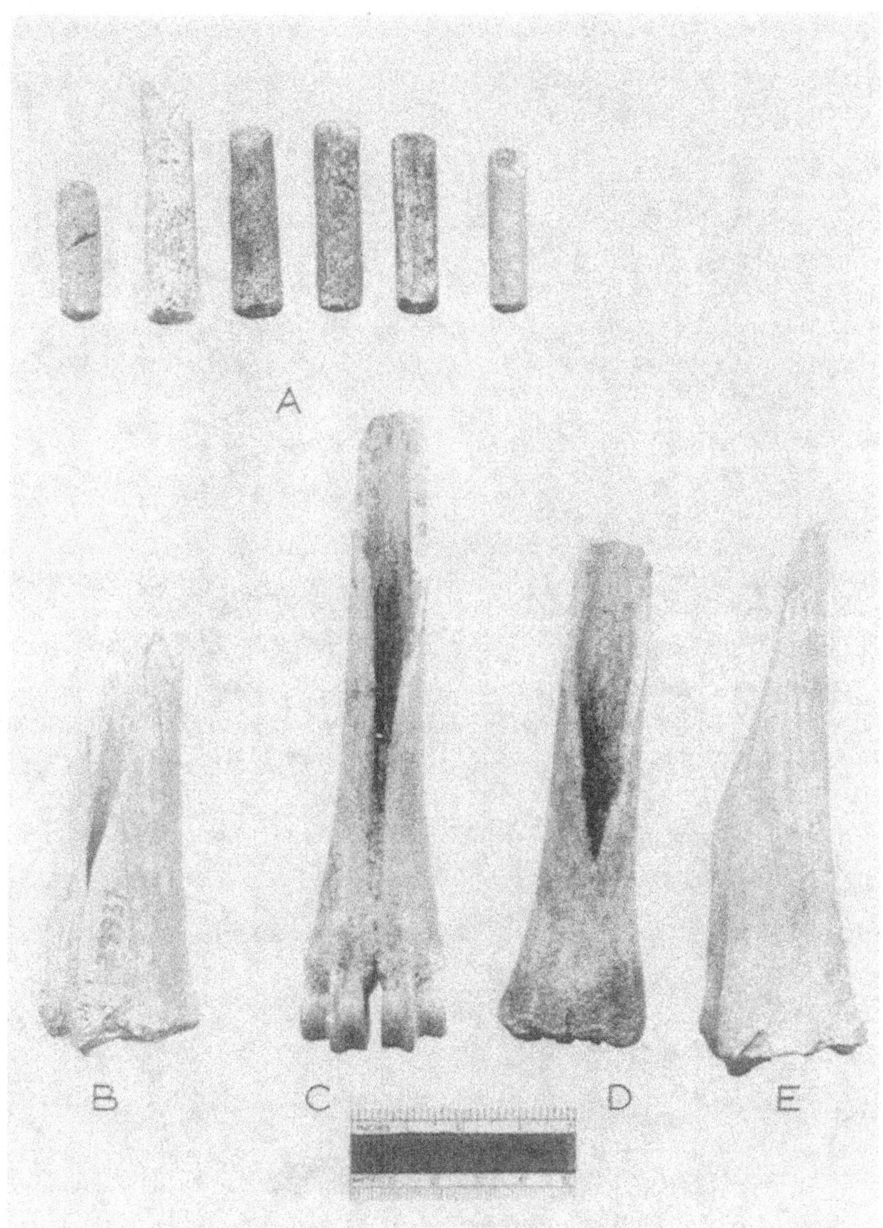

Plate 49. Bone pins and beamers: A, bone pins; B-E, bone beamers.

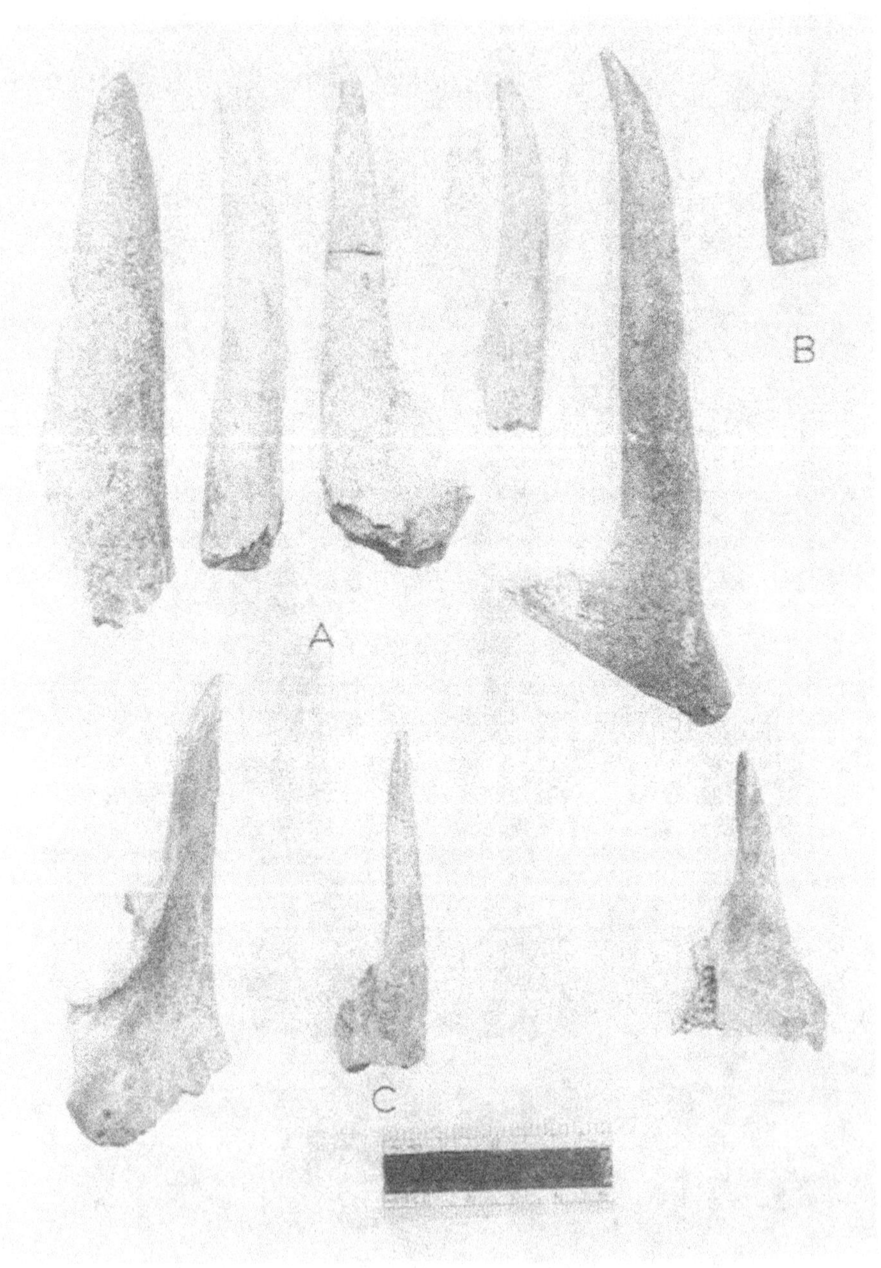

Plate 50. Bone tools: A, antler flaking tools; B, point; C, awls.

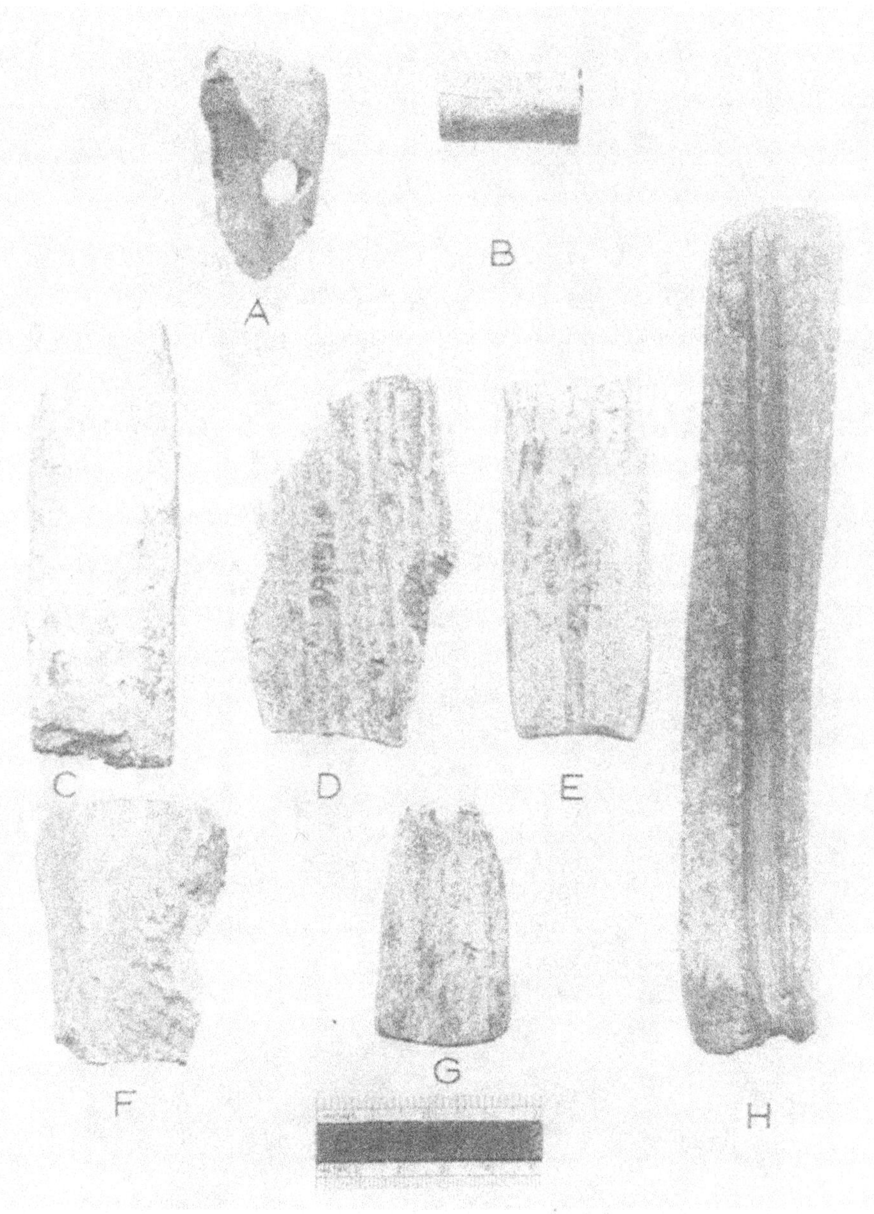

Plate 51. Bone pieces: A, bone with drilled hole; B, bead; C-G, bone spatulates; H, grooved bone.

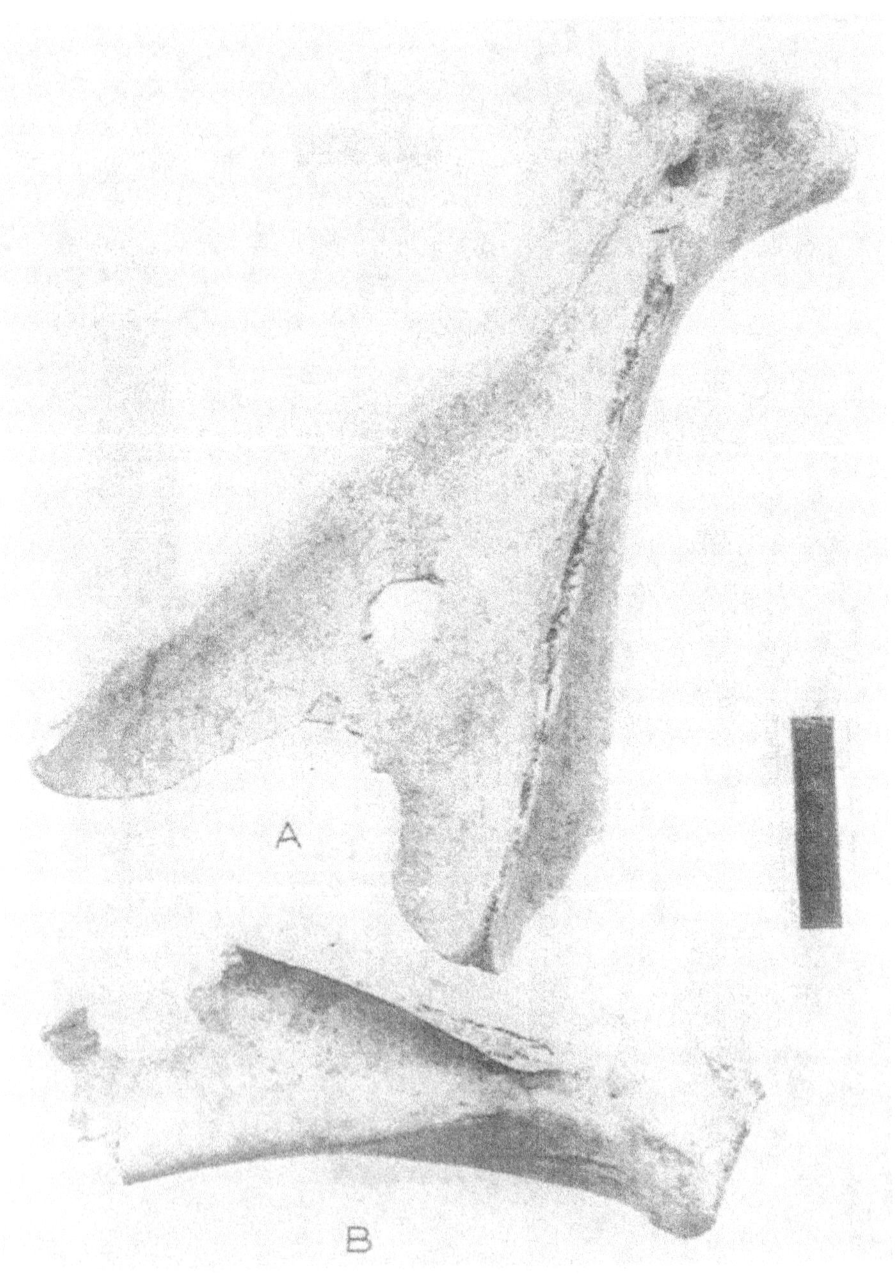

Plate 52. Elk scapula tools.

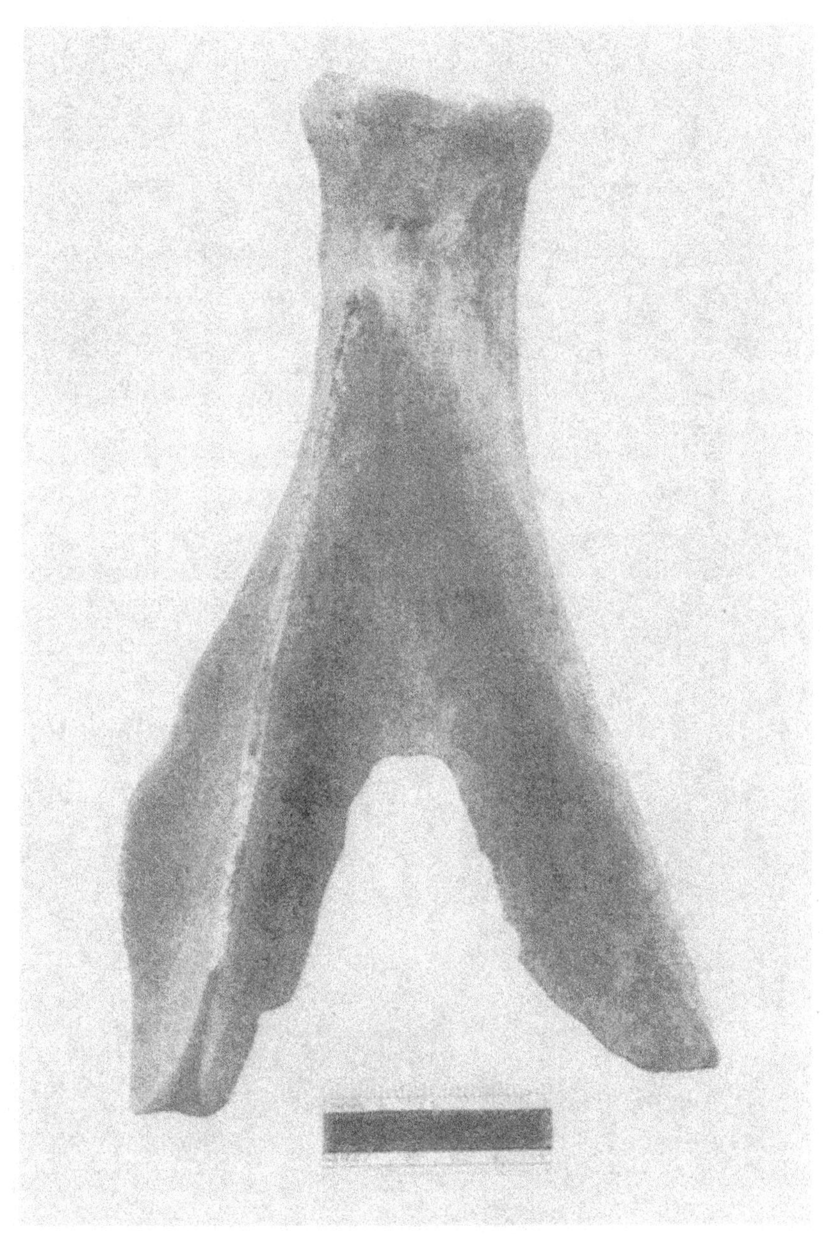

Plate 53. Elk scapula tool.

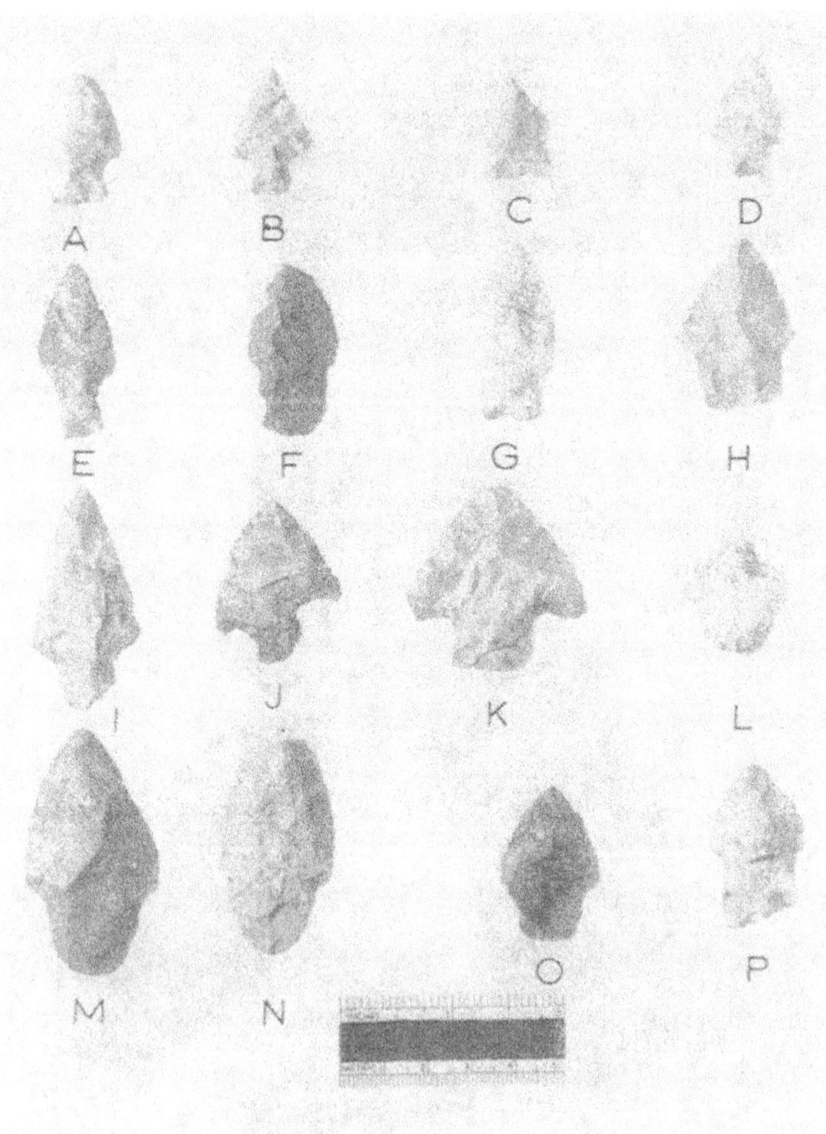

Plate 54. Birdsell Collection: stemmed points.

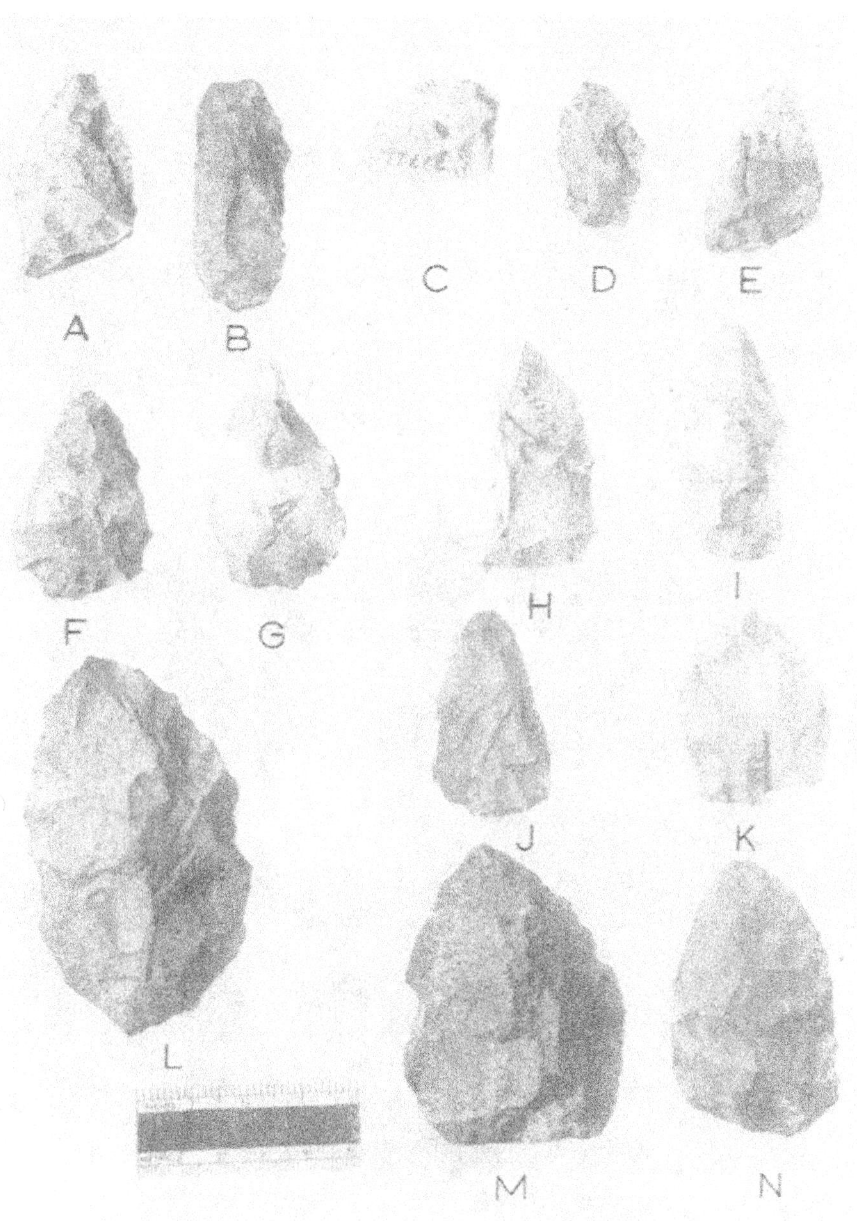

Plate 55. Birdsell Collection: bifacial tools.

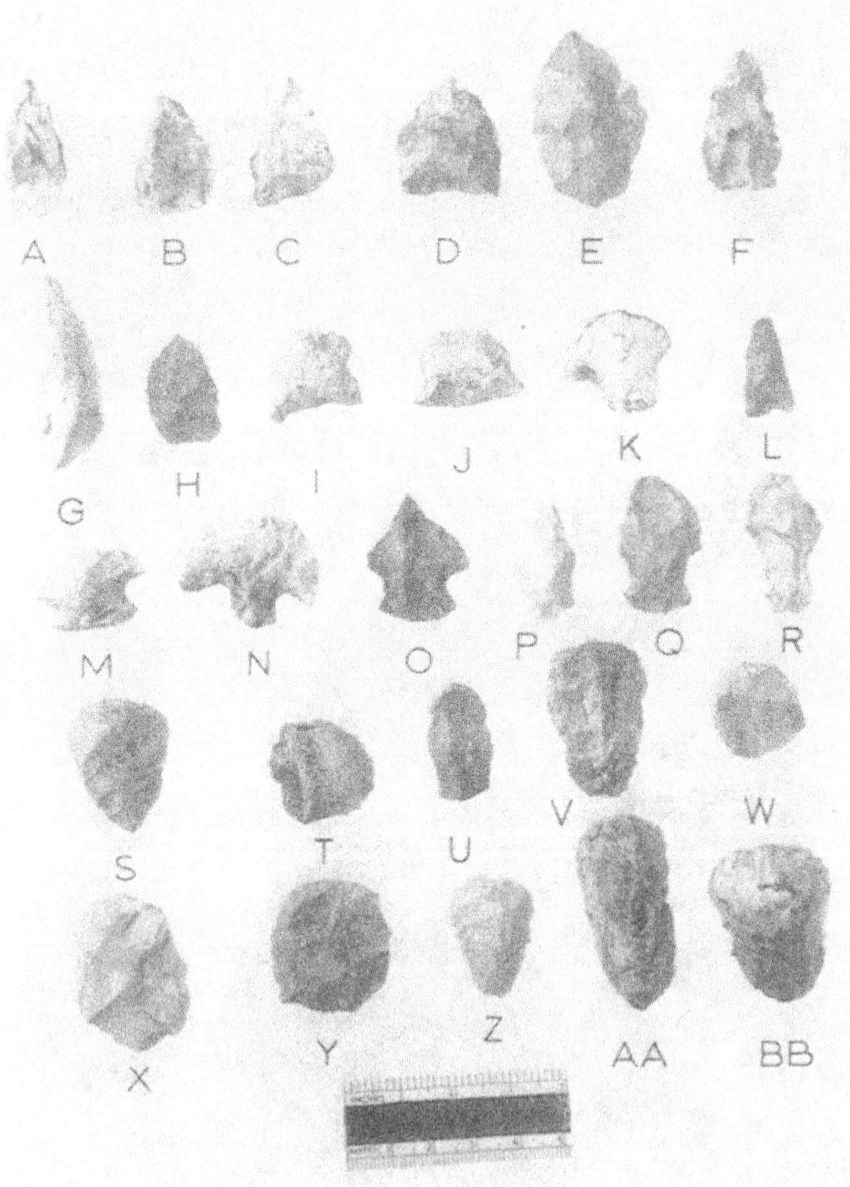

Plate 56. Birdsell Collection: miscellaneous stone tools. A-H, small, thick, steep-edge tools; I-K, M-N, hafted scrapers; L, drill fragment; O-P, perforators; Q-R, battered points; S-BB, scrapers.

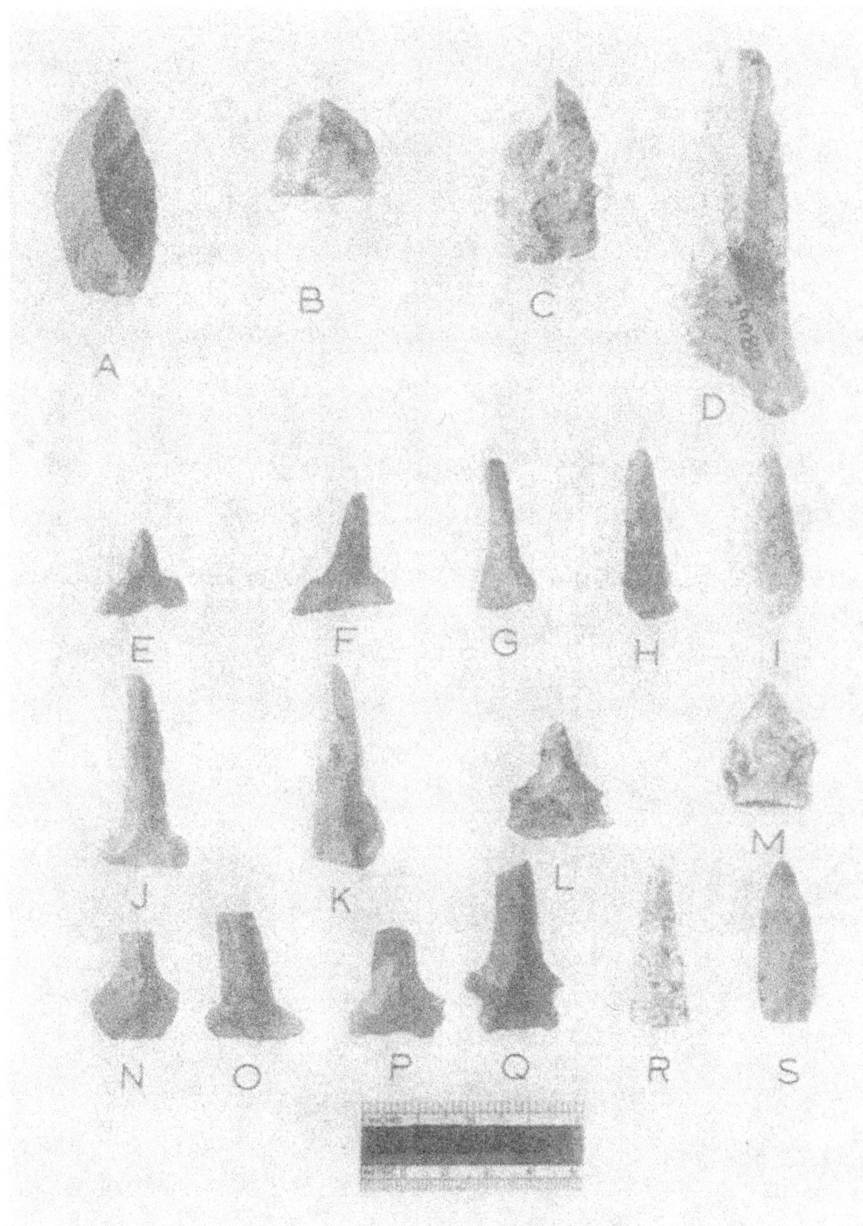

Plate 57. Birdsell Collection: perforators and drills. A-D, perforators; E-S, drills.

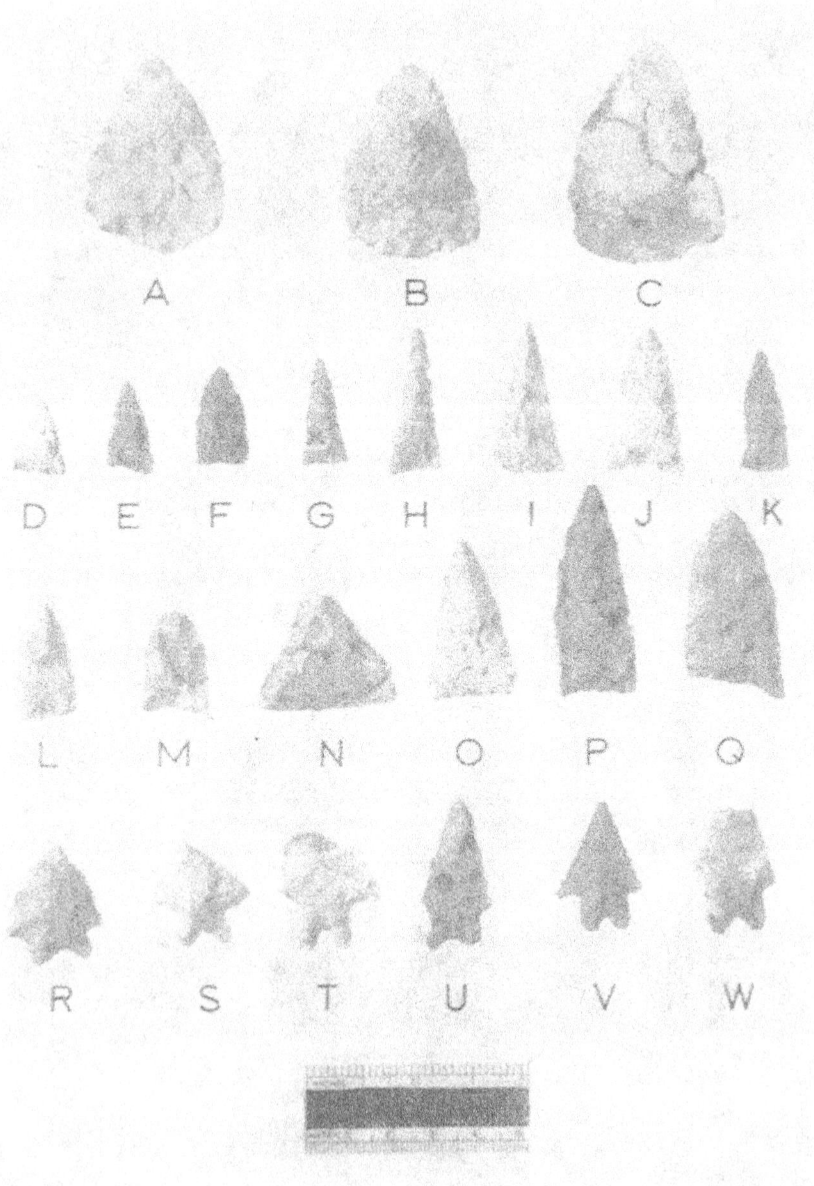

Plate 58. Birdsell Collection: blades, triangular points, and bifurcate base points. A-C, bifaces (knives?); D-Q, triangular points; R-W, bifurcated base points.

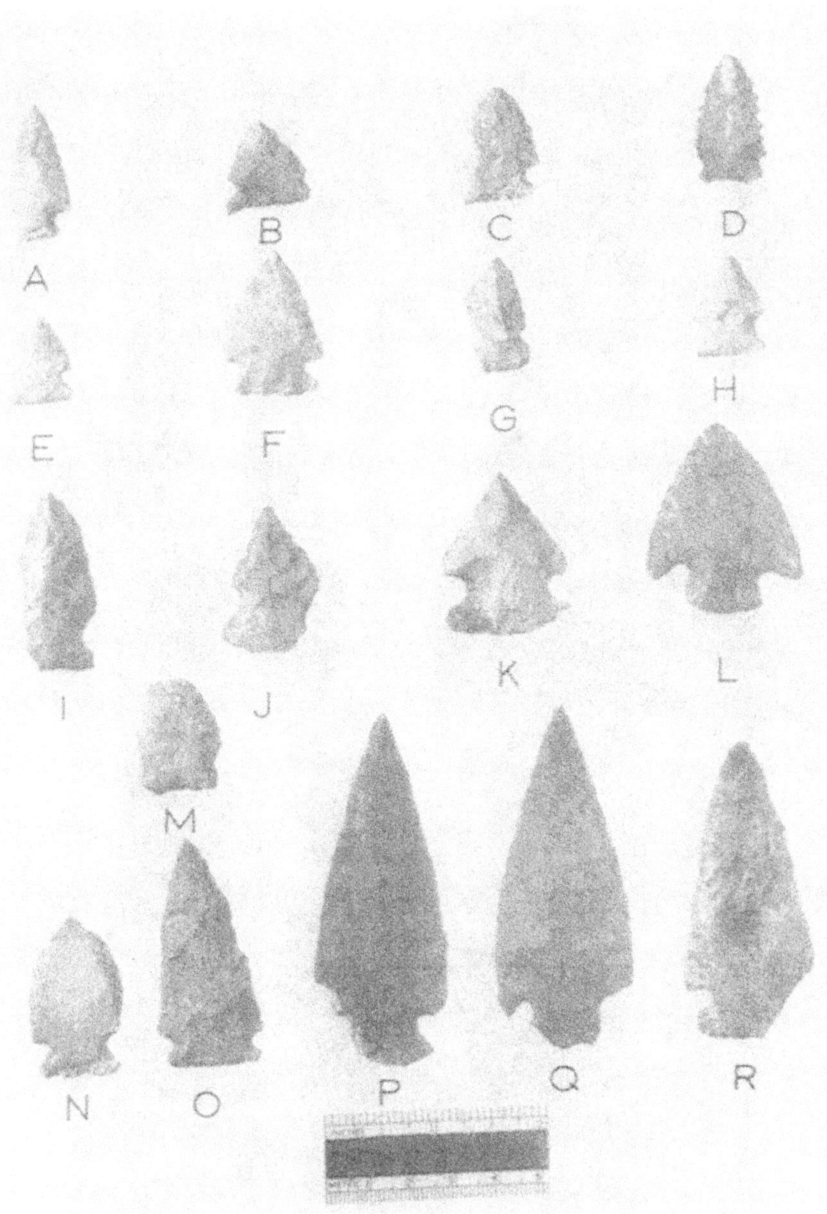

Plate 59. Birdsell Collection: notched points.

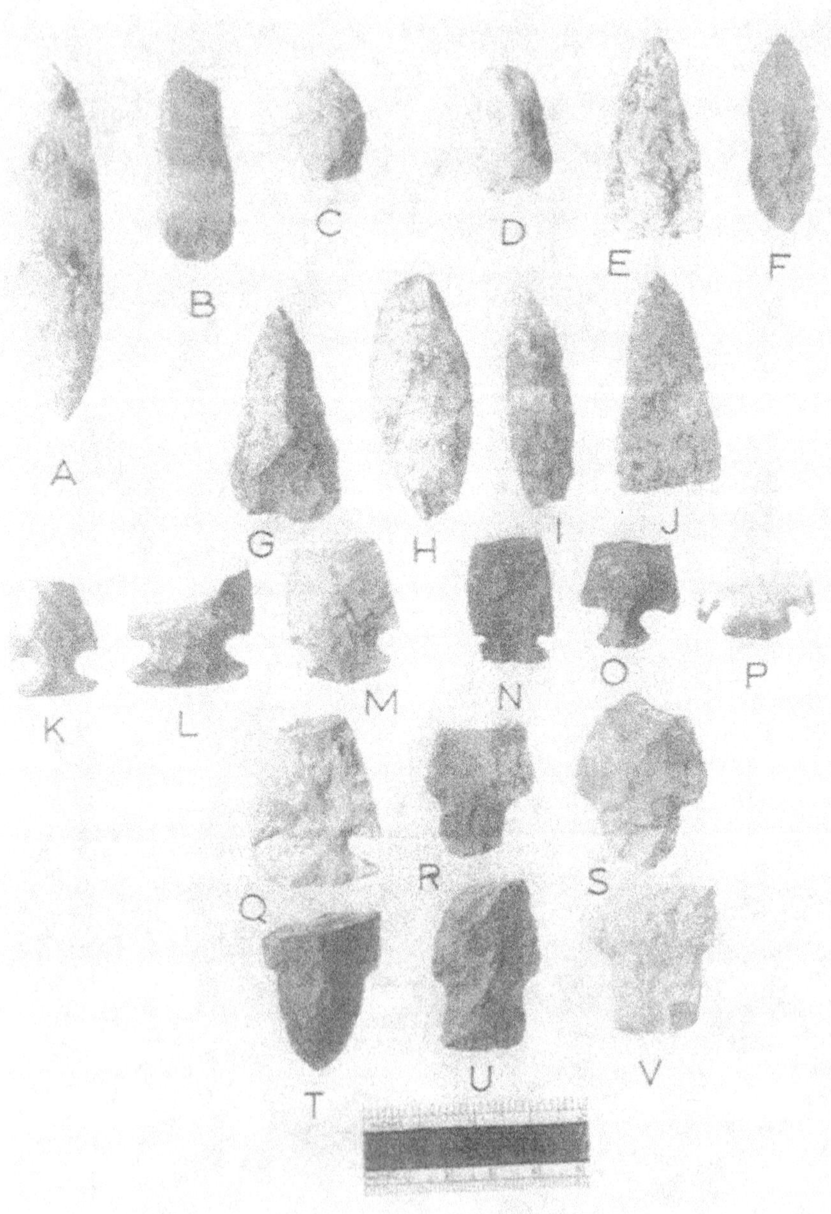

Plate 60. Birdsell Collection: miscellaneous points and blades.

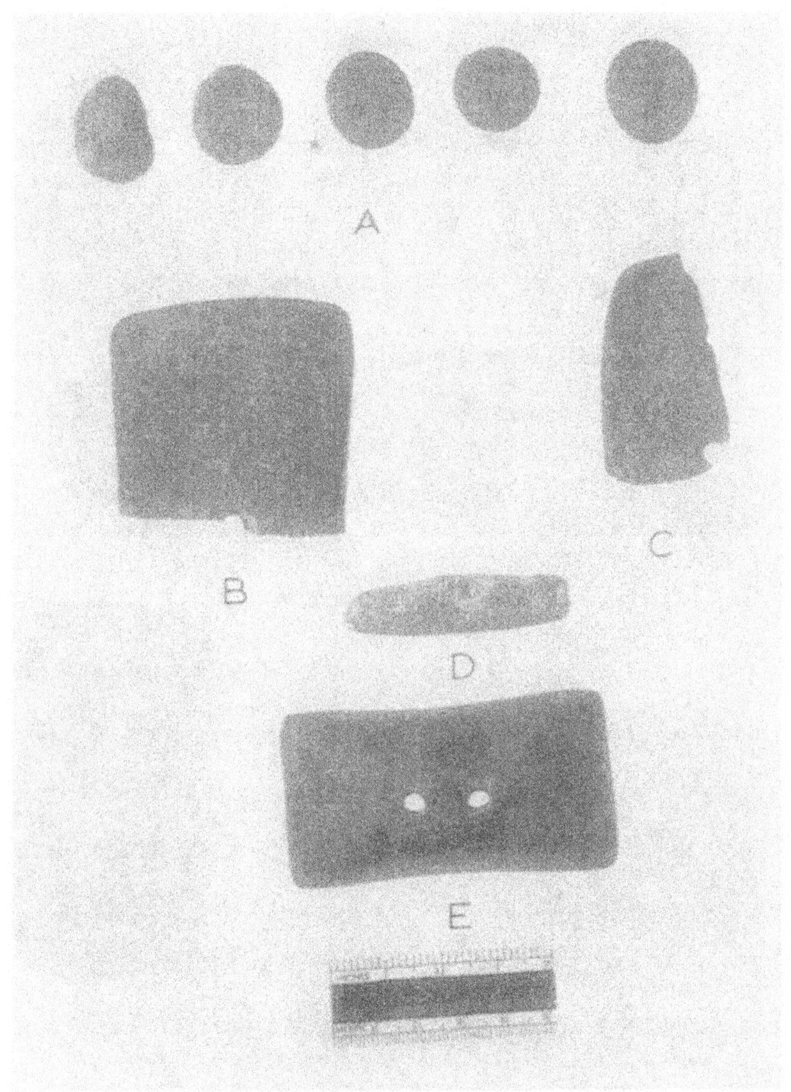

Plate 61. Birdsell Collection: stone and slate objects. A, stones; B-C, slate gorget; D, stone cylinder; E, plano-convex gorget.

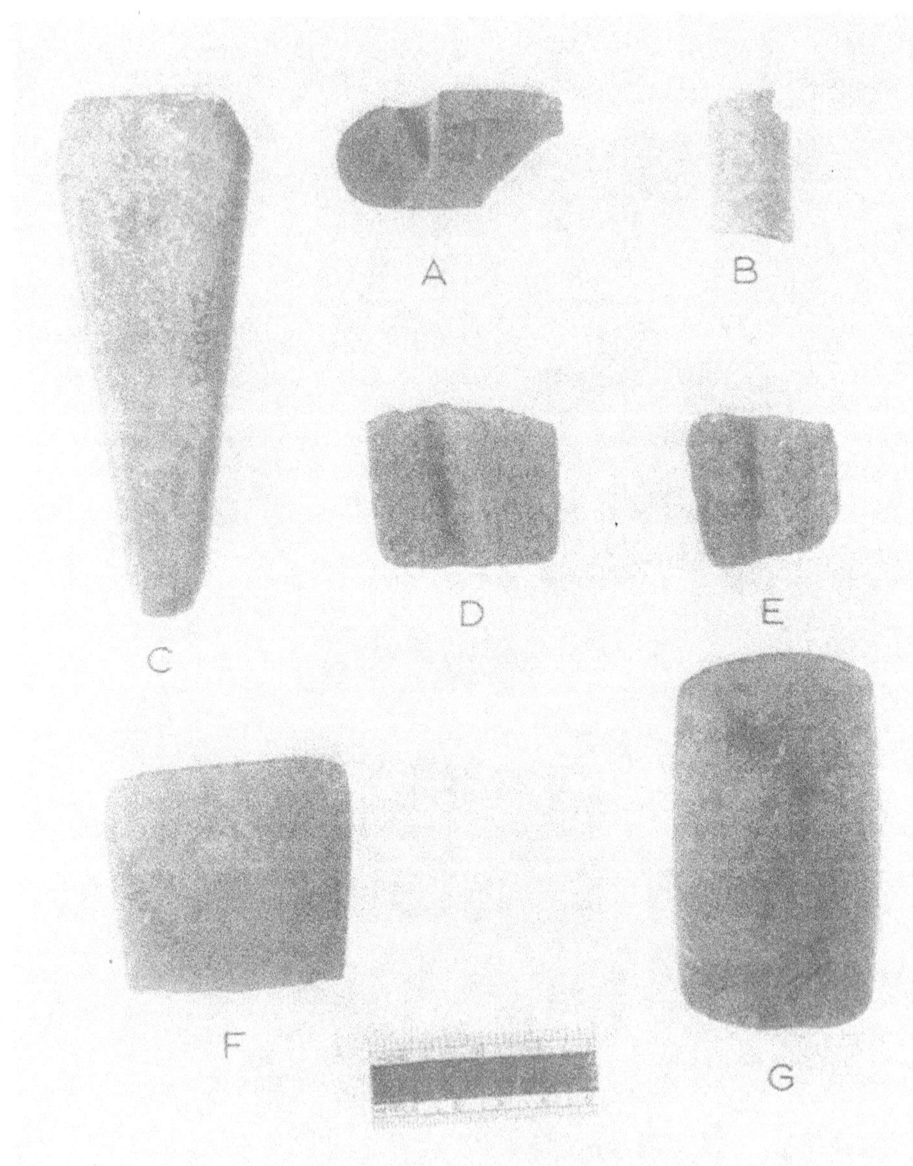

Plate 62. Birdsell Collection: miscellaneous stone objects. A, pipe; B, pipe stem; C, shaped stone; D-E, abrading stones; F-G, celts.

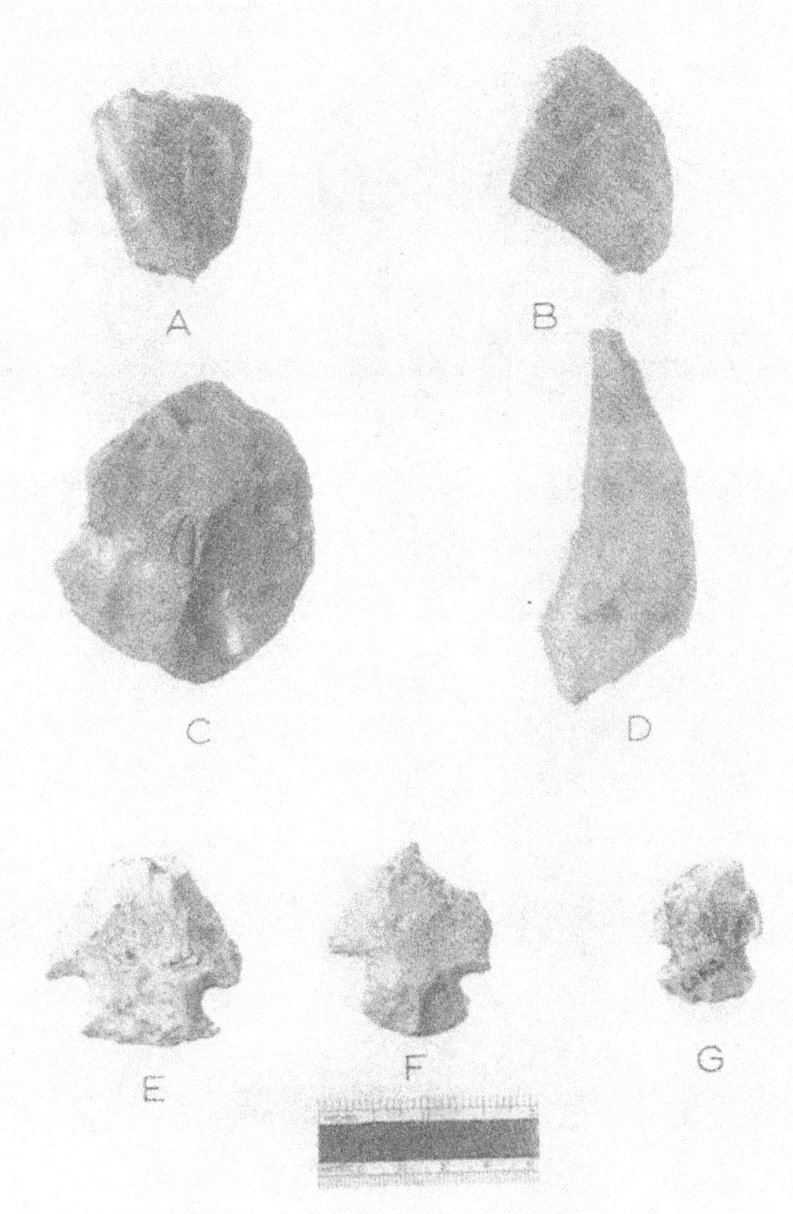

Plate 63. Birdsell Collection: miscellaneous stone tools. A-C, scrapers; B-D, knives(?); E-G, battered points.

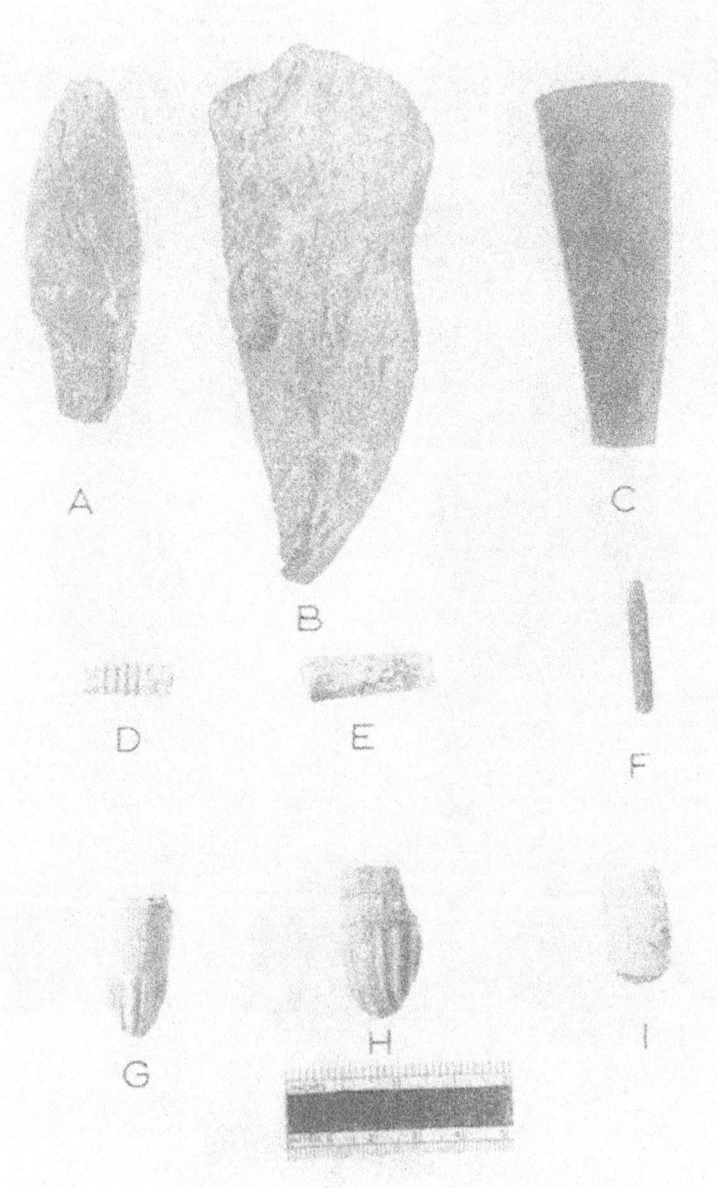

Plate 64. Birdsell Collection: copper and pipes. A-B, copper; C, celt; D-E, kaolin pipe stems; G-I, kaolin pipe bowls.

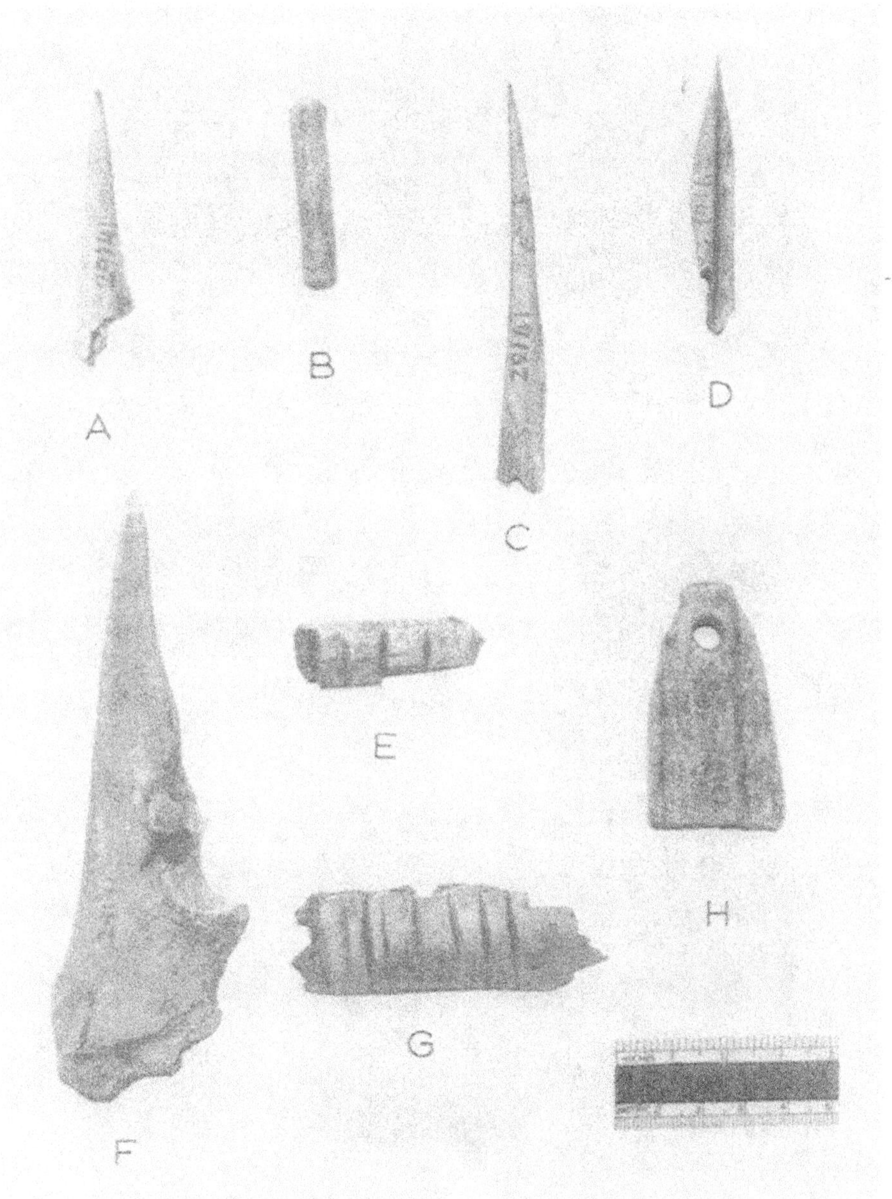

Plate 65. Birdsell Collection: miscellaneous bone artifacts. A, C-D, F, awls; B, pin; E, G, rasp; H, spatulate.

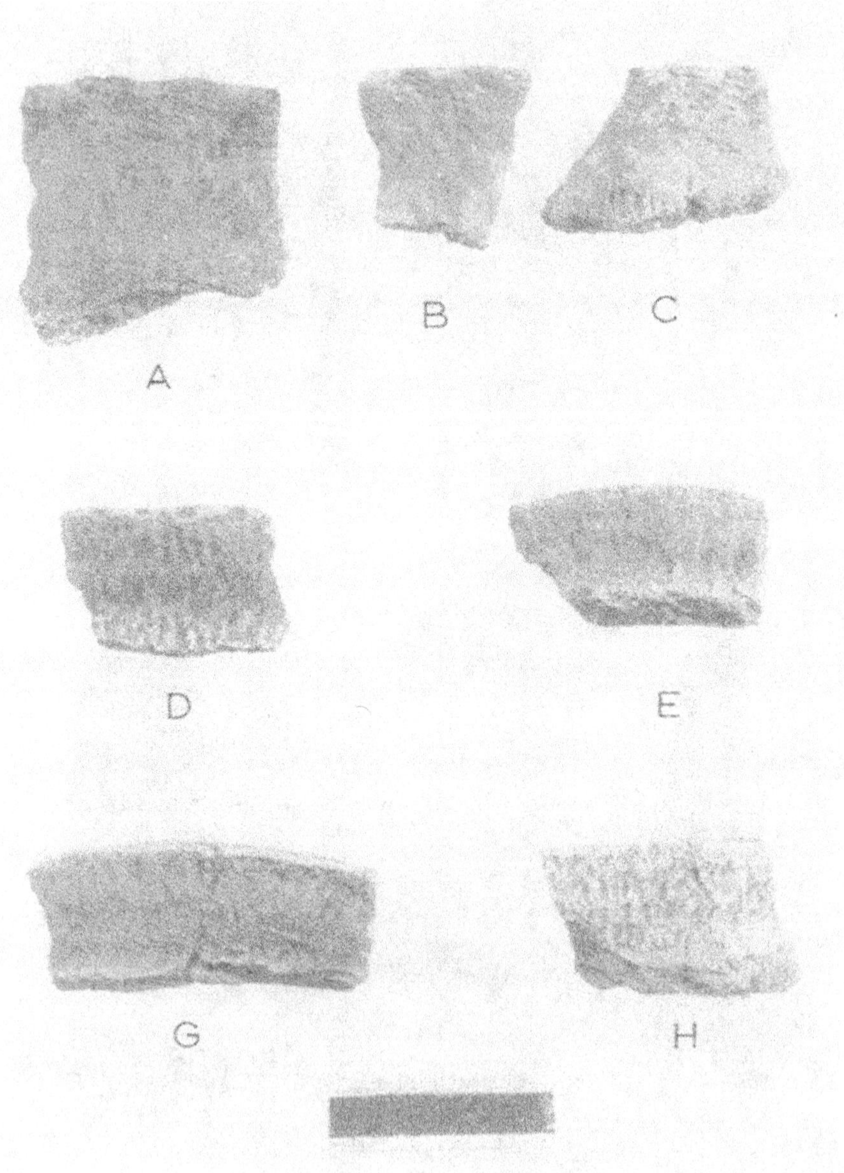

Plate 66. Birdsell Collection: miscellaneous pottery sherds. A-D, Moccasin Bluff Modified Lip, group 3; E-G, Moccasin Bluff Cordmarked, group 5 Langford-like sherds.

Plate 67. Birdsell Collection: decorated body sherds. A-K, shell tempered; F-G, tempered with fine grit.

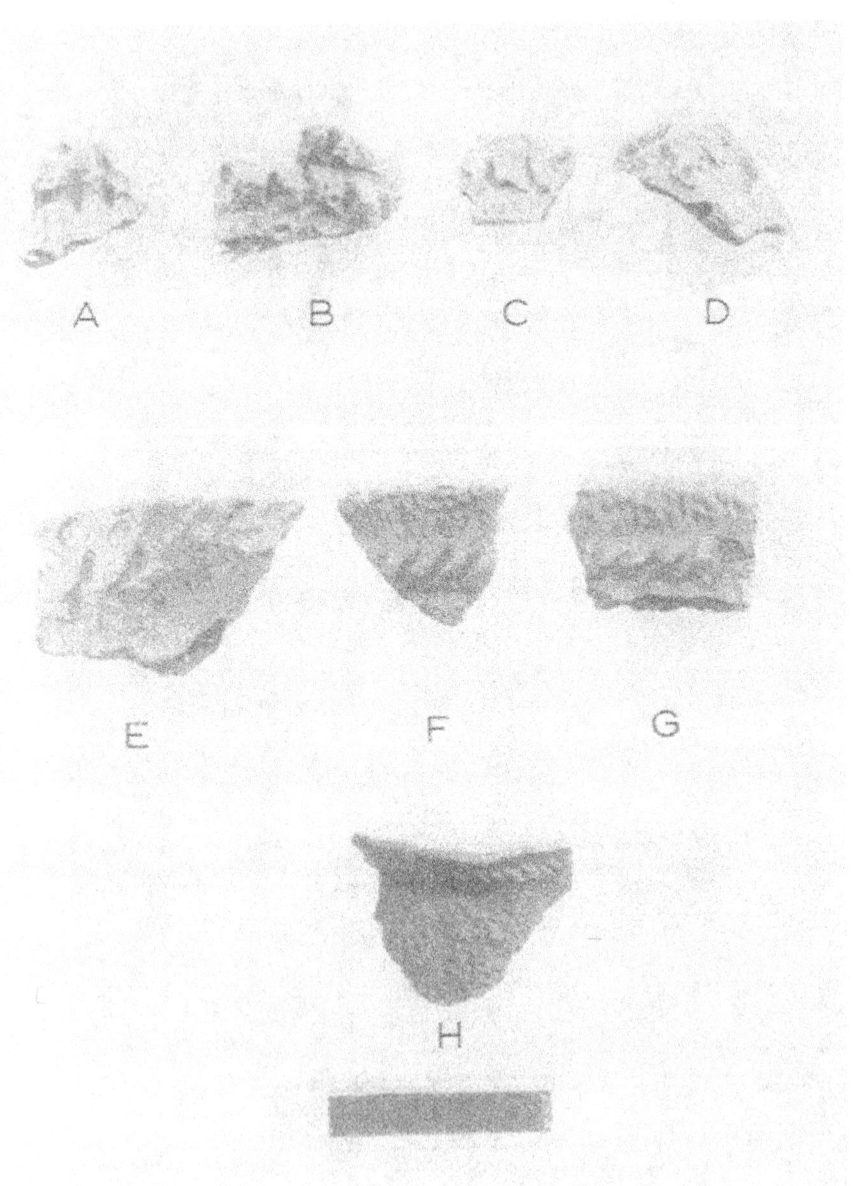

Plate 68. Birdsell Collection: sherds with embossed notched ridge encircling neck. A-D, shell tempered; F-H, grit tempered.

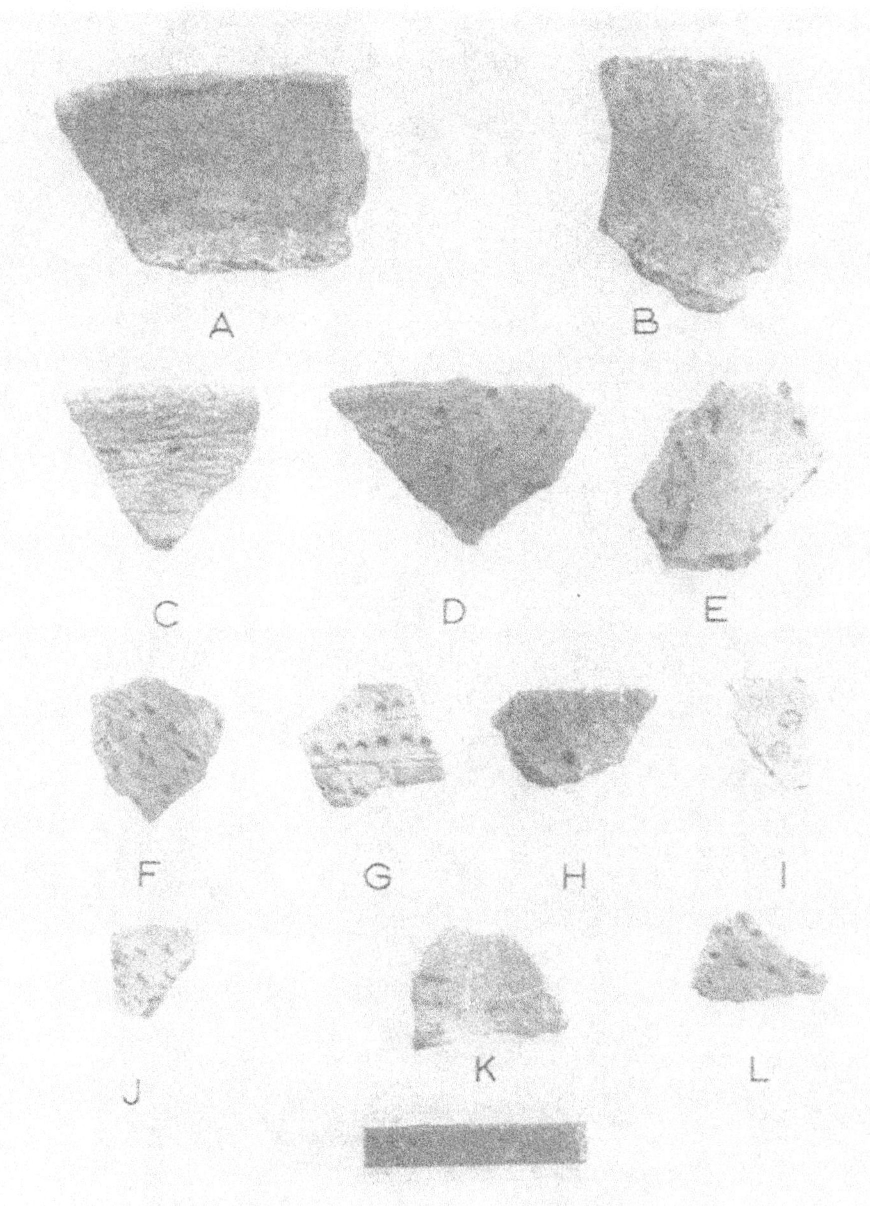

Plate 69. Birdsell Collection: miscellaneous sherds (C has cord impressions on the top of the lip).

UMMA Catalogue Numbers
29131 29116
29116 (shell)
29116 (shell) 39773 39772

Plate 70. Birdsell Collection: miscellaneous sherds.

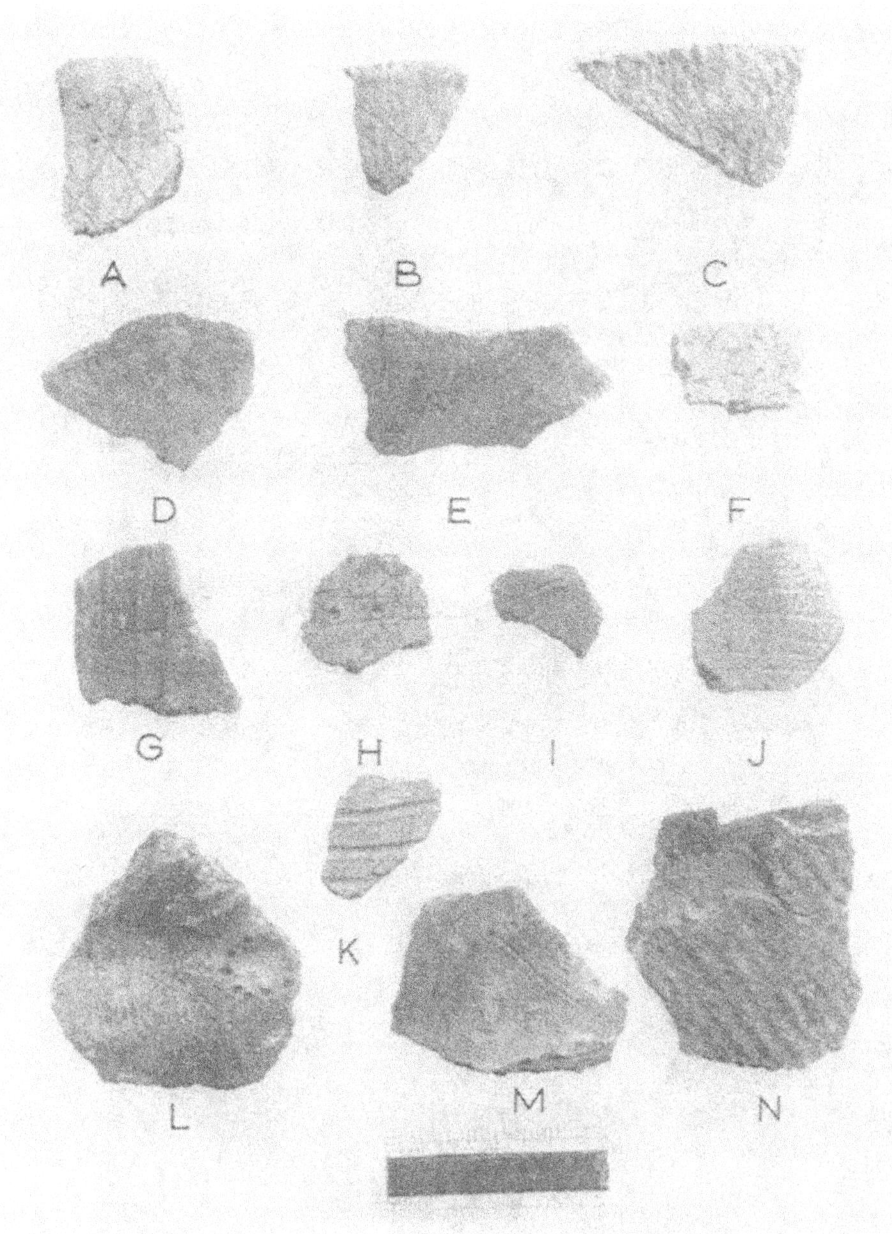

Plate 71. Birdsell Collection: miscellaneous sherds. A-I, L-N, grit tempered; J, shell tempered.

Plate 72. Birdsell Collection: Middle Woodland sherds.

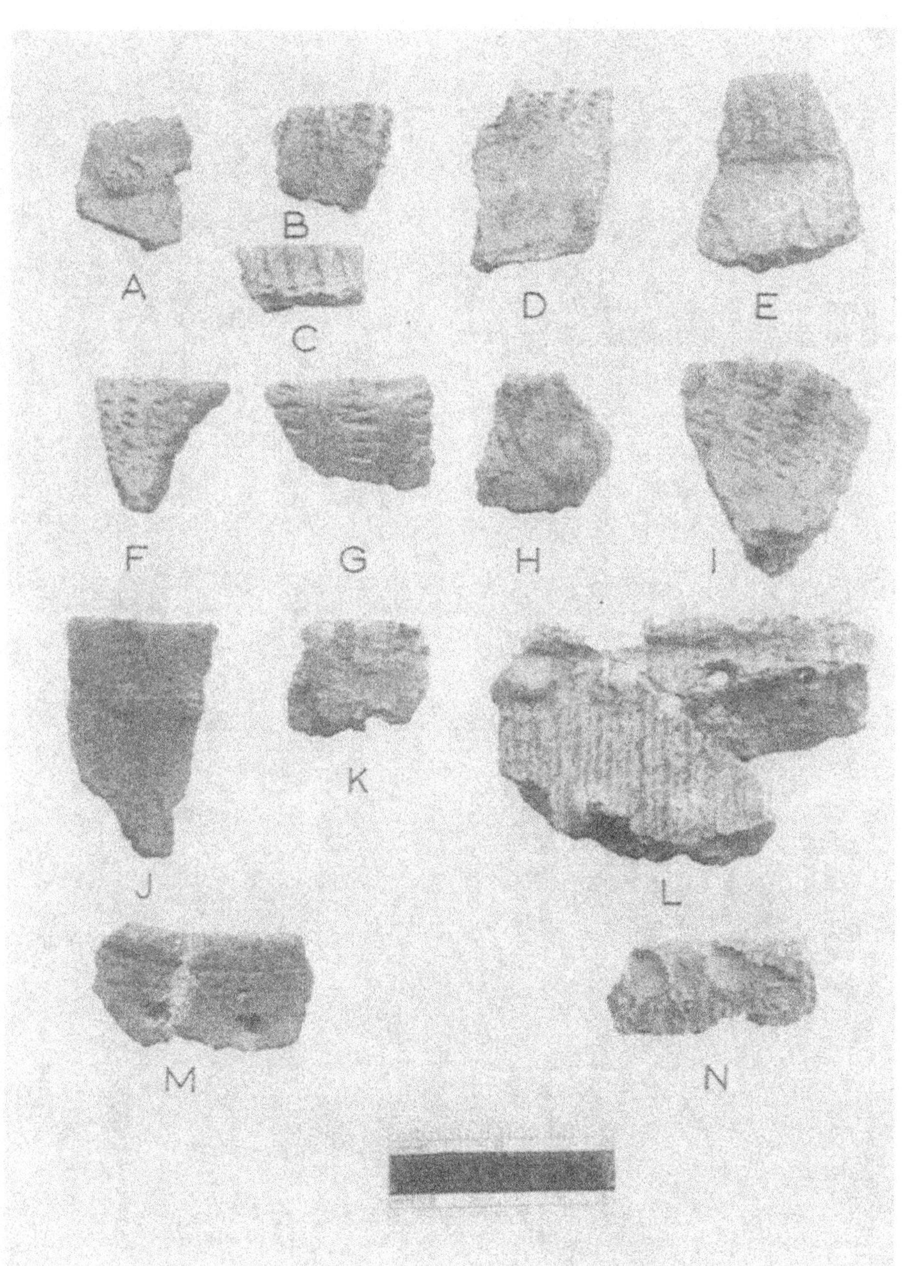

Plate 73. Birdsell Collection: Middle Woodland sherds.

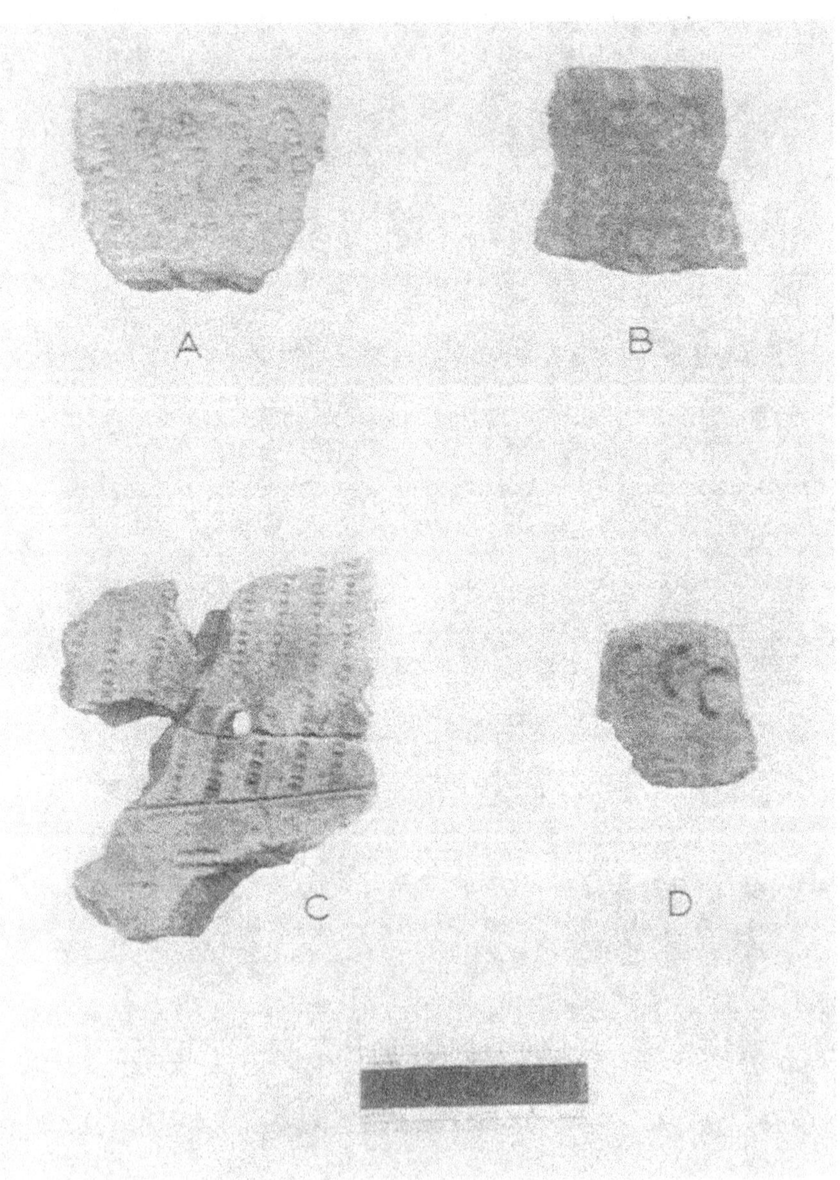

Plate 74. Birdsell Collection: Middle Woodland sherds.

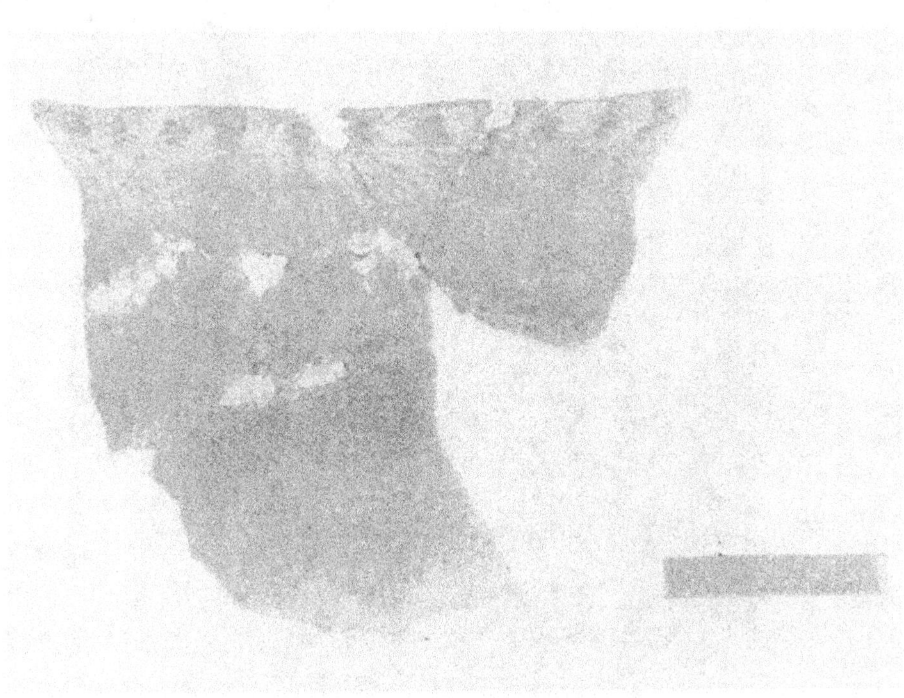

Plate 75. Birdsell Collection: Moccasin Bluff Modified Lip, group 3.

Plate 76. Birdsell Collection: Middle Woodland vessel.

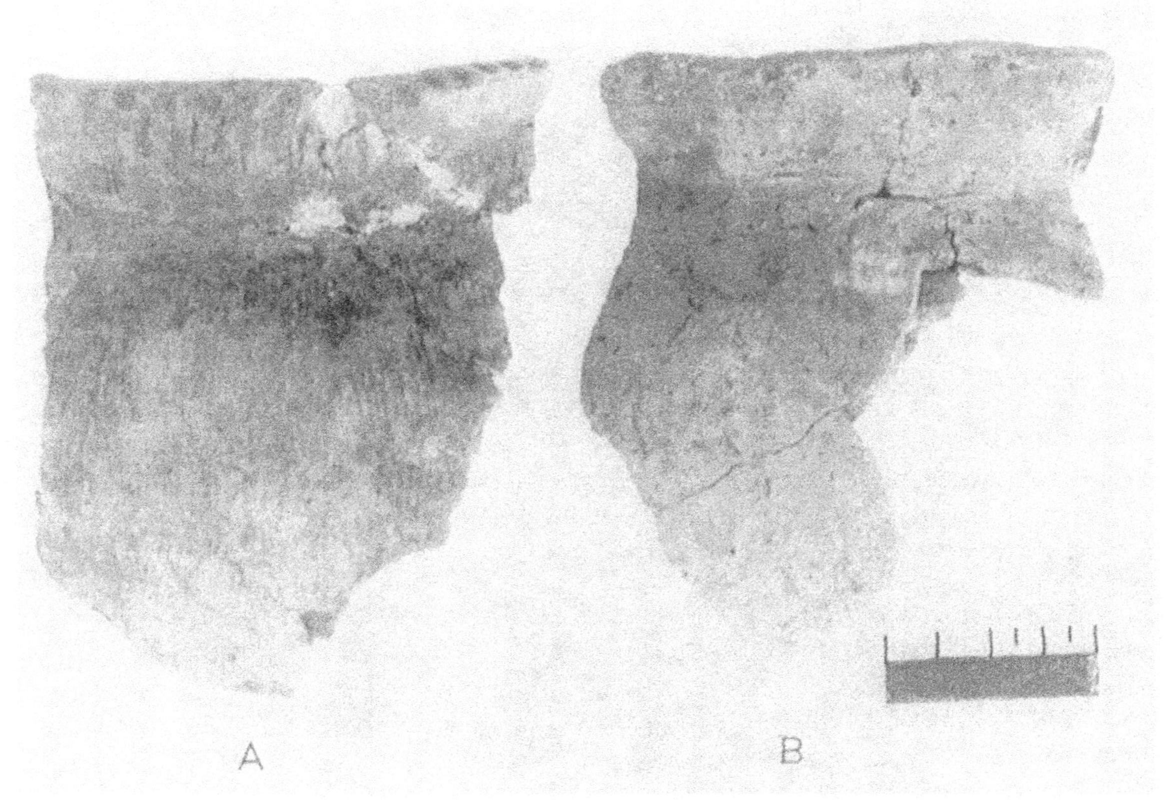

Plate 77. Birdsell Collection: A, Moccasin Bluff Impressed Exterior Lip; B, Moccasin Bluff Plain Modified Lip.

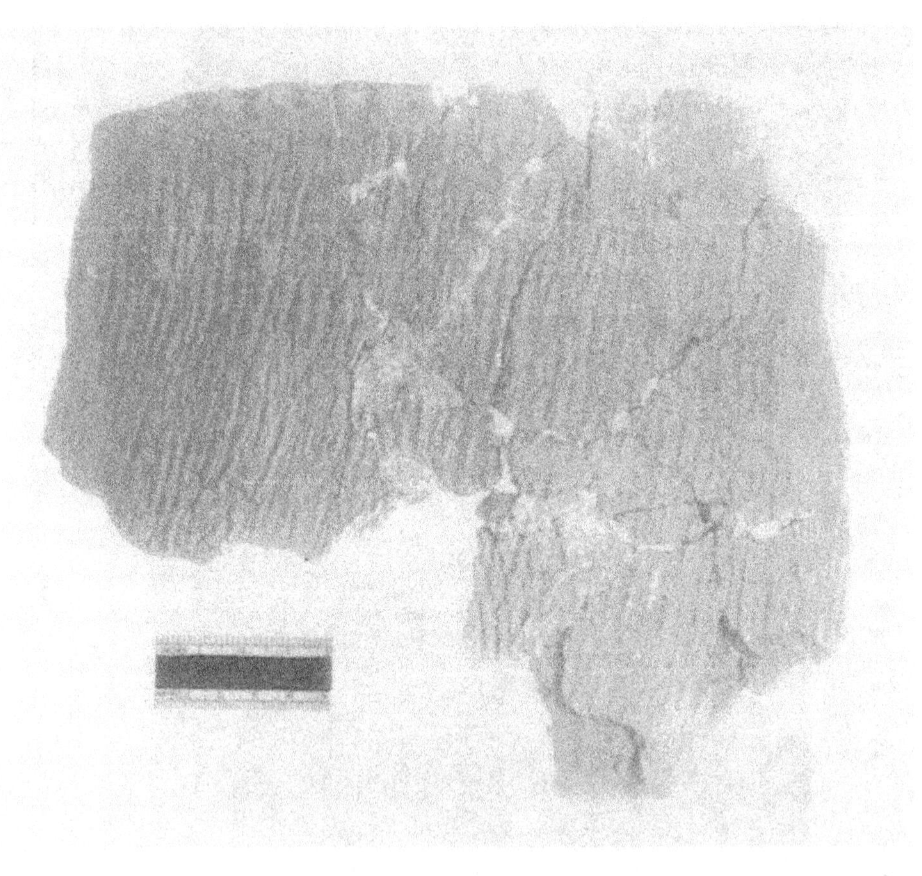

UMMA Catalogue Number
29127

Plate 78. Birdsell Collection: Havana Cordmarked sherd.

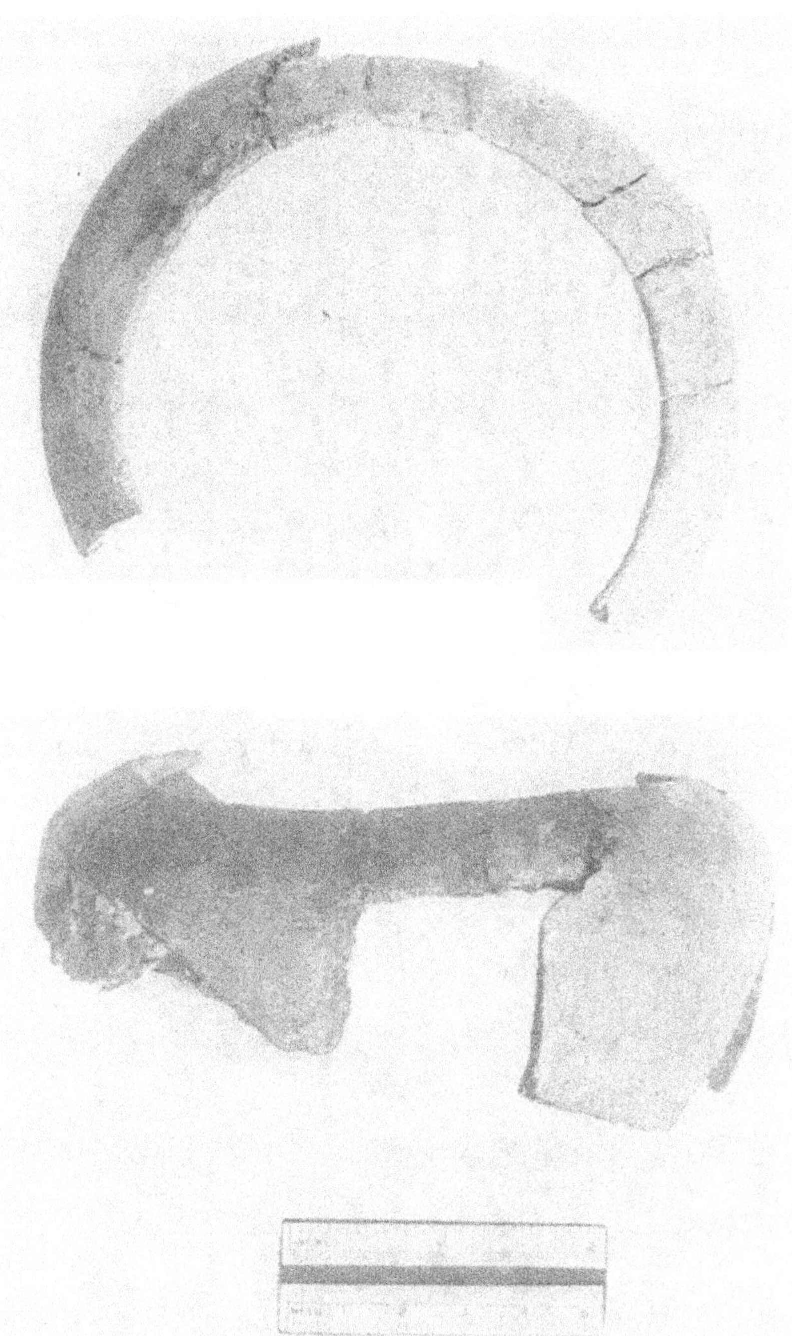

Plate 79. Birdsell Collection: Hopewell Plain bowl.

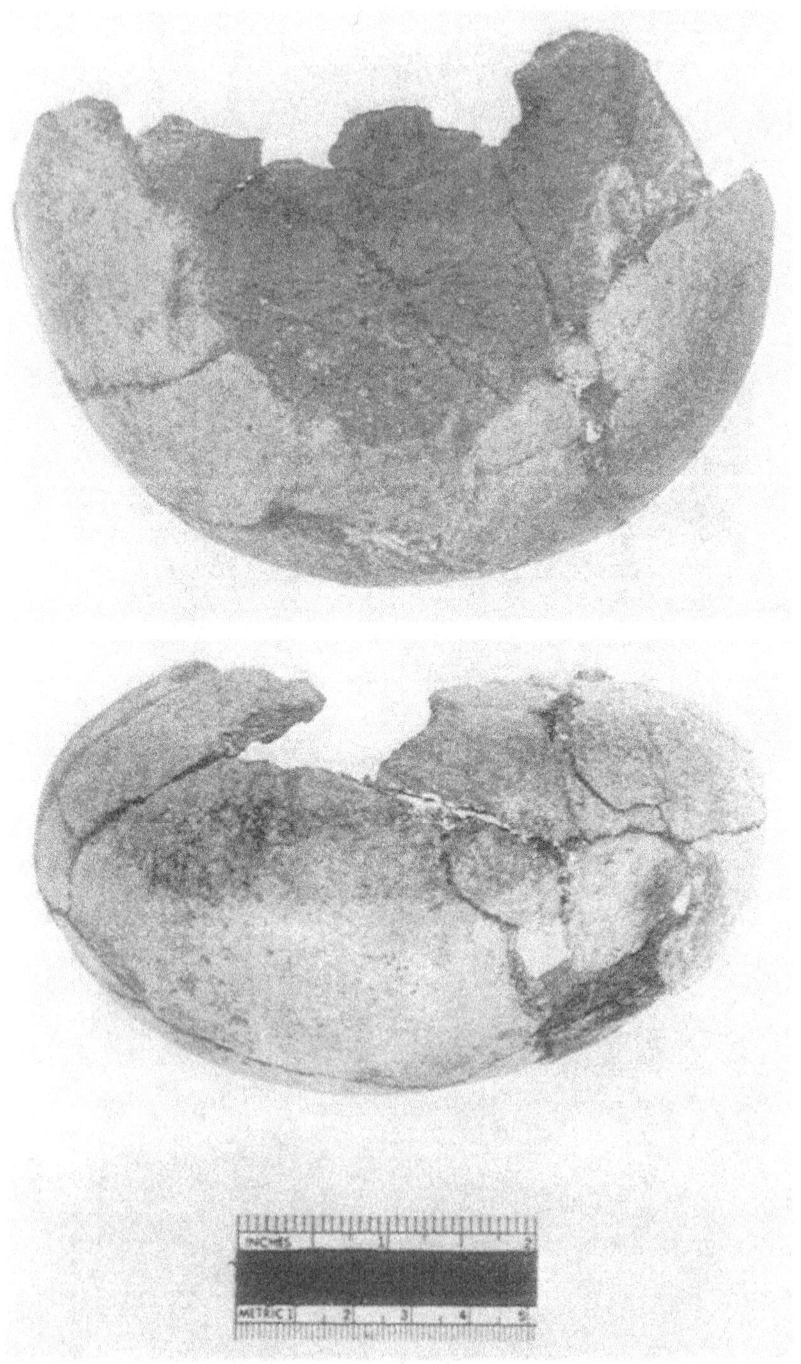

Plate 80. Birdsell Collection: base of shell-tempered, Middle Mississippi bottle.

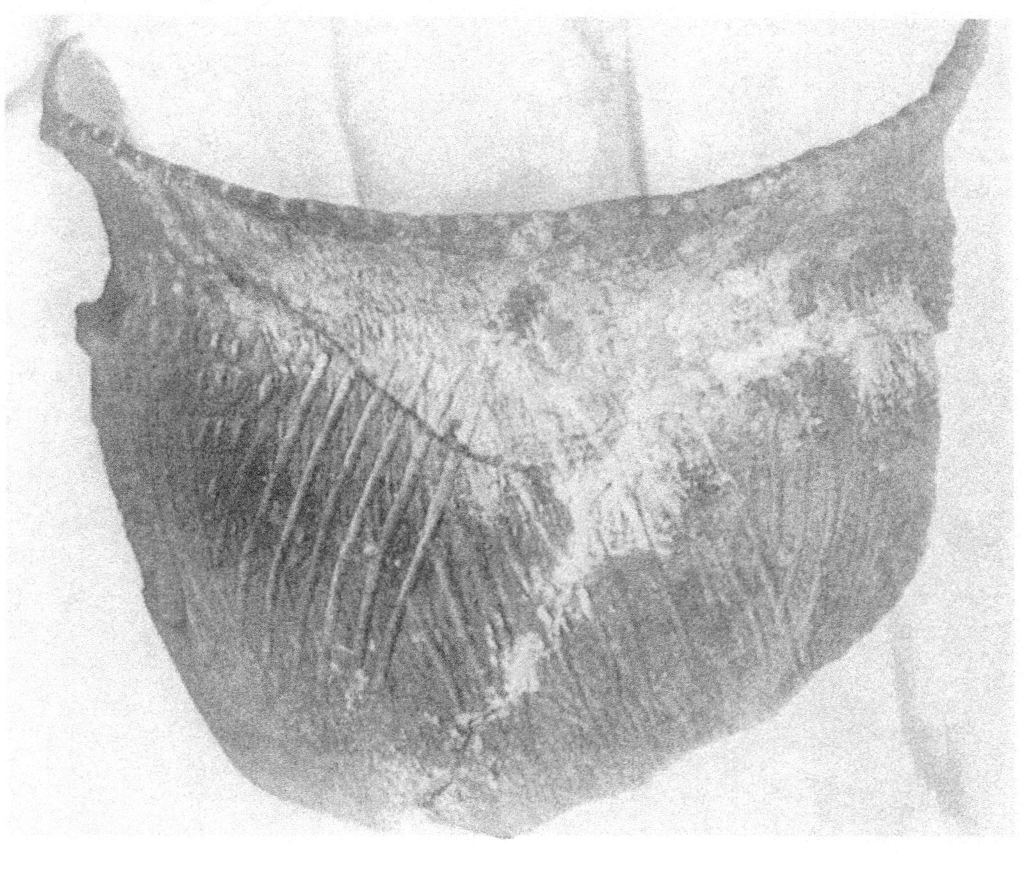

Plate 81. Ada site: Moccasin Bluff Modified Lip vessel.

Plate 82. Shell mask from a burial near Lansing, Michigan.

Plate 83. Corn Hole A prior to excavation.

Plate 84. Corn Hole B during excavation.

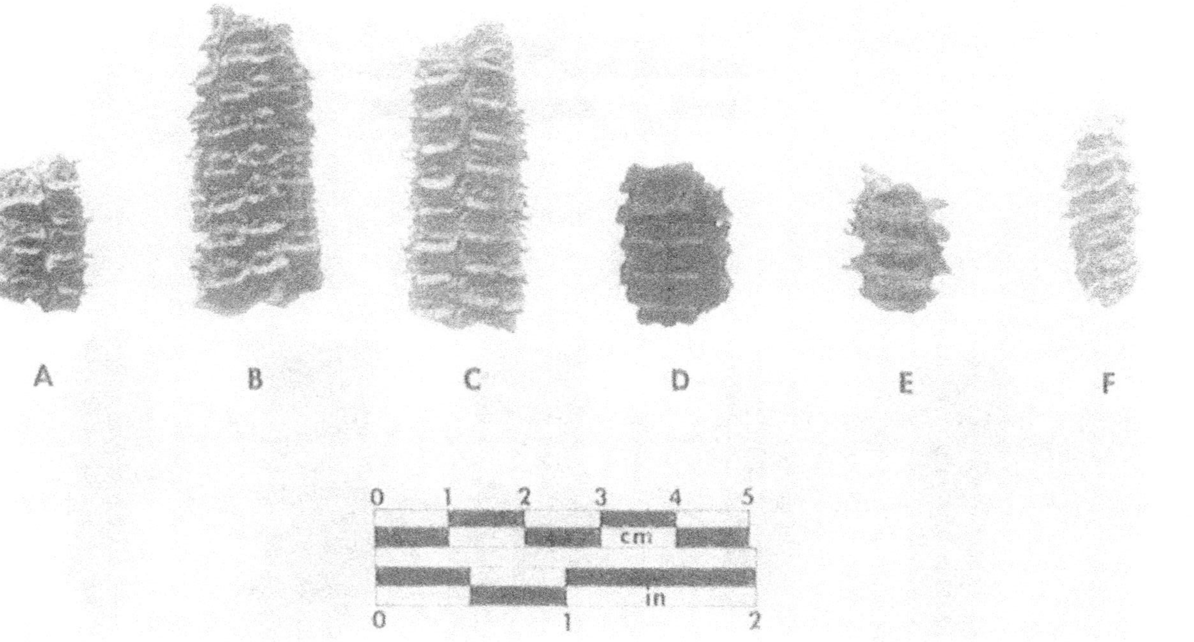

Plate 85. Examples of Charred Corn Cobs from Corn Hole A. A, 8-rowed B8-273, level II; B, 10-rowed B8-538, level III. C, 8-rowed B8-538, level III; D, 8-rowed strongly paired. E, 8-rowed probably B8-538, level III. F, 8-rowed tiller, probably B8-538, level III.

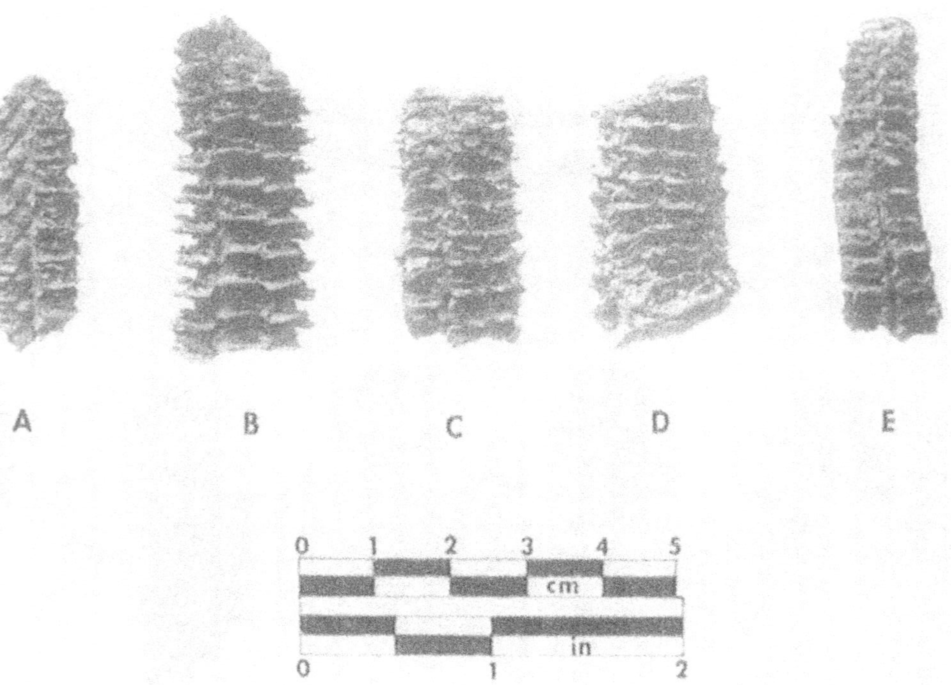

Plate 86. Examples of charred corn cobs from corn hole B: A, 5-rowed nubbin; B, 8-rowed; C, 8-rowed; D, 8-rowed butt end; E, 8-rowed tip end.

www.ingramcontent.com/pod-product-compliance
Lightning Source LLC
Jackson TN
JSHW072058170726
105095JS00009B/59

* 9 7 8 0 9 3 2 2 0 6 4 7 3 *